Introducing Linguistic Morphology

Introducing Linguistic Morphology

Second Edition

Laurie Bauer

Georgetown University Press
Washington, D.C.

First edition © Laurie Bauer, 1988
This edition © Laurie Bauer, 2003

Georgetown University Press
Washington, D.C.

First published in the United Kingdom
by Edinburgh University Press.

Library of Congress Cataloging-in-Publication Data

Bauer, Laurie, 1949–
   Introducing linguistic morphology / Laurie Bauer. -- 2nd ed.
      p. cm.
Includes bibliographical references and index.
   ISBN 0-87840-343-4 (pbk. : alk. paper)
   1. Grammar, Comparative and general--Morphology. I. Title.
   P241.B38 2003
   415--dc21

                              2003007222

Typeset in 10/12 Palatino
by Wyvern 21 Ltd., and
printed and bound in Great Britain.

Contents

Preface

The aim of this book is to provide an introduction to linguistic morphology. The study of morphology has been influenced by all major groups of linguists: by the philologists of the nineteenth century, by the structuralists in the twentieth century, by the transformational grammarians in the second half of the twentieth century and by linguists with other theoretical orientations as well. Part of the function of this book is thus to provide a coherent approach to the study of morphology, without gross distortion of the ideas that have come down to us from so many different sources.

In this book, Part One provides an introduction to the fundamental notions involved in the study of morphology. This Part provides a background in the morphological notions of the philologists and structuralists. Part Two provides an elaboration of this, going into considerably greater detail in a few areas of major importance and specifically raising questions which are glossed over in Part One. Part Three provides an introduction to some of the major issues in morphology today, in the transformational or post-transformational era. In a course on General Linguistics, it is assumed that each Part will be studied as part of the course work for a different year. But in some Universities there may be a specialised course in Morphology, which will consider all three Parts or sections of them. It is hoped that students who have worked their way through this book will have sufficient background to understand the current controversies in morphological theory and to be able to approach the original articles and books in which the developments are taking place at the moment.

To support the theoretical exposition of this book students should ideally, especially in the early stages, carry out exercises in morphological analysis, using data from a variety of languages, to see how the theoretical constructs apply in practice. Only a few such exercises are provided in this book, alongside questions which involve more discussion of the notions which have been expounded in the chapters. Individual teachers may choose problems from the many available in specialised workbooks or invent their own.

In Appendix C there is a glossary of the technical terms of morphology, with definitions and, where appropriate, examples.

Technical terms from other areas of Linguistics such as 'phoneme' or 'direct object' are not listed, only those relevant to the study of morphology. Thus this appendix may be used as a quick reference source for the specialist terms in this book or as a means of revision. For technical terms from Linguistics that are not listed in the glossary, consult Crystal (1980) (or a later edition).

A brief note is also needed on my mode of glossing languages other than English. Morphs are separated out in the data by the symbol '·'. This symbol is also used in the English glosses to show which part of the English gloss corresponds to each morph in the original. Where a single morph in the original is glossed by more than one English word, the English glosses are hyphenated. Where necessary, a translation is also given between inverted commas. A simple example from French will illustrate this:

arriv·ons
arrive·1st-person-plural
'we are arriving'

In general I have tried to avoid abbreviations in the glosses, but *1st*, *2nd* and *3rd* are consistently used, and *sing*, *pl* are occasionally used for 'singular' and 'plural'. Other abbreviations are explained in the text or should be clear from the context.

Transcriptions of data from other languages are dependent on the system used by my sources; in many cases an orthographic form is given rather than a transcription. Where possible, phonetic symbols of the International Phonetic Association have been used. Transcriptions of English employ the system used by Gimson in the *English Pronouncing Dictionary* (Jones, 1977).

I should like to thank all those who have provided me with help, advice and suggestions during the writing of this book. In particular, the following people have commented on parts of various drafts and their aid has been invaluable: Winifred Bauer, Andrew Carstairs-McCarthy, Janet Holmes, Kate Kearns, Paul Warren. They are not to blame if I have not always followed all of their advice and they do not, needless to say, necessarily agree with what I have written. I should also like to thank reviewers of the first edition who pointed out errors and infelicities.

PART ONE: Fundamentals

CHAPTER 1

Introduction

How many words are there in this book? Can we always tell precisely what a word is? Do *motet, motion* and *motive* have anything to do with each other? What ways do we have of making new words in English? Are the same ways of forming new words found in all languages? Is it just coincidence that although you can have a word like *people* which means much the same as 'a lot of persons' and a word *peoples* which means, more or less, 'a lot of lots of persons', you cannot have a word *personss* meaning the same thing? Is it just coincidence that the ablative plural of the Latin word *re:x* 'king', *re:gibus*, meaning 'by/from/with the kings' is so much longer than the nominative singular *re:x*? (I use the phonetic length mark rather than the traditional macron to show long vowels in Latin.) All of these questions relate to **morphology**, the study of words and their structure.

It is a well-established observation that words occur in different forms. It is quite clear to anyone who has studied almost any of the Indo-European languages. Students of these languages learn **paradigms** like those below as models so that they can control the form-changes that are required. As illustrations, consider a verb paradigm from Latin and a noun paradigm from Icelandic. (The word 'paradigm' means 'pattern' or 'example'.)

(1)   amo: 'I love'
        ama:s   'you (singular) love'
        amat   'he/she/it loves'
        ama:mus   'we love'
        ama:tis   'you (plural) love'
        amant   'they love'

(2)   *Singular*
        nominative   hestur 'horse'
        accusative   hest
        dative   hesti
        genitive   hests

        Plural
        nominative   hestar
        accusative   hesta
        dative   hestum
        genitive   hesta

In the nineteenth century, the term 'morphology' was given to the study of this change in the forms of words. The term is taken from the biological sciences and refers to the study of shapes. In linguistics this means the study of the shapes of words; not the phonological shape (which can be assumed to be fairly arbitrary) but rather the systematic changes in shape related to changes in meaning, such as those illustrated in the paradigms above or such as that relating the pairs of words below:

(3)   desert   deserter
        design   designer
        fight   fighter
        kill   killer
        paint   painter
        twist   twister

By extension, the term 'morphology' is used not only for the study of the shapes of words but also for the collection of units which are used in changing the forms of words. In this sense, we might say that Latin has a more complex morphology than English. Again by extension, 'morphology' is also used for the sequence of rules which are postulated by the linguist to account for the changes in the shapes of words. In this sense we might contrast the morphology of language L with the syntax of language L (where the syntax is the sequence of rules postulated by the linguist to account for the ways in which words are strung together). In this sense we might also say that something is part of the job of 'the morphology of language L' or, more generally, of 'morphology', implying that this is true for all languages. We shall see later how all these senses fit together; such extensions of meaning are common within linguistics and do not usually cause problems of interpretation.

Many traditional 'grammars' (in the sense 'grammar books') deal largely with such morphology as can be laid out in paradigms, like those presented above, and have little to say about syntax. This has led to the situation where many lay people today still believe that languages like Chinese or English do not have much grammar because they do not have extensive morphological paradigms. That is, for many people the term 'grammar' is equated with morphology. For most linguists today, however, 'grammar' includes both morphology and syntax (and, for most, phonology as well), and most of the linguistic study of 'grammar' in this sense has, since the middle of the last century, not been of morphology but of syntax. This is understandable. Syntax, especially from 1957 onwards, was a relatively new field of study, while morphology was considered well researched and well understood. It did not seem at that time as if there was a great deal that was new to say about morphology. Morphological descriptions of hundreds of languages were available but all the languages differed in what appeared to be essentially random ways. There did not seem to be any cross-linguistic generalisations to be made in morphology. Syntax, in the middle of the last century, was a far richer ground for linguistic discoveries. It was the excitement of the progress being made in the study of syntax which gave Linguistics such a boost in the 1960s. It was also progress in the study of syntax which eventually led to the realisation that there were still questions to be answered in morphology. As a result, there has, in recent years, been a resurgence of interest in morphology.

Since the 1970s the study of morphology has flourished in ways which could not have been imagined earlier in the twentieth century. This has come about partly through consideration of new data from a range of languages, partly through a consideration of the patterning of morphological data across languages, partly through innovations in the treatment of syntax and phonology (which have held implications for morphology), partly through a renewed interest in how the brain processes words and partly through the detailed study of morphological systems themselves. These various impulses have not led to a unified treatment of morphology but they have led to an increased sense of excitement among people who study morphology as it appears that morphology may provide a window on to wider linguistic behaviour.

This book provides an introduction to the study of morphology, covering the input from these various sources and attempting some kind of synthesis in the light of the most recent research. It discusses both the general background to all morphological study and also some of the detail of recent theories of morphology.

REFERENCES AND FURTHER READING

At the end of each chapter there is a section of references and further reading. The book can be read without these sections although, in some later chapters, there are discussions of a few matters of import which are tangential to the main text. The references in these sections (and in the text of the chapters in Part Three) are given in terms of the surname of the author and the date of publication, and full details can be found in the list of references at the back of the book. It is sensible to get into the habit of reading some of the works referred to. No textbook gives an unbiased presentation of the facts and this one is certainly no exception. Only by reading other works can you make some attempt to counteract the in-built bias of the text. In other cases, it is probably just as well to assure yourself that I have not given an unfair account of other people's research. Sources of data can be consulted either for extra data for analysis or to see many of the extra complications which I have ignored for the sake of the example.

The data from Latin in this chapter, and in many other places in the book, is taken from Kennedy (1962). The data from Icelandic is from Einarsson (1945). Where references are not provided for language data, it is frequently because I am familiar with the language concerned. Much of the complex English data is gleaned from dictionaries and other reference books, only some of which are listed in the list of references at the end of the book.

Exercise

1. Consider the sentences (a)–(e):

(a) I bought a grammar of Maori.
(b) The grammar of English does not permit the ordering subject-object-verb.
(c) I tried to learn Icelandic but the grammar was too hard.
(d) The grammar of a language includes its phonology, its morphology and its syntax.
(e) I always hated grammar lessons in school.

How many different meanings of 'grammar' are there in these sentences and what precisely does 'grammar' mean in each sentence?

CHAPTER 2

The Basic Units

2.1 A CLOSE LOOK AT WORDS

How many words are there in (1)?

(1) The cook was a good cook as cooks go and, as cooks go, she
went.

It probably didn't take you very long to come up with the answer '15'.
Now think about how you arrived at that answer. What you did, in
effect, was to count the items which appeared between spaces on the
page. We could say that a word is a unit which, in print, is bounded
by spaces on both sides. We will call this an **orthographic word**
because it is linked to the spelling (orthography). In practice, we may
not always feel certain just where words begin and end in the written
language but strict application of the definition above will provide us
with consistent answers. Consider the next example:

(2) I've been in hot water so often I feel like a tea-bag.

There are two places in (2) where we might raise questions about how
many words are involved. *I've*, we know, has two parts and could
have been written as *I have*. But an apostrophe is not a space and so,
by applying the definition we formulated earlier, we can say that *I've*
is one orthographic word. The same is true with *tea-bag* in (2). A
hyphen is not a space and we are, thus, able to say that *tea-bag* is a
single orthographic word, even though it is made up of two parts.
Just what those parts are is a question to which we will return.

Now let us turn to a different question with respect to (1). How
many different words does (1) contain? This question is more difficult
to answer because the answer you give will depend on whether you

think *cook* and *cooks*, *go* and *went* are 'the same word' or not. They are clearly different orthographic words: they have different **forms** or shapes. So we might say that there are 11 different **word-forms** (or orthographic words) in (1): *the, cook, was, a, good, as, cooks, go, and, she, went*. On the other hand, there is another sense in which *cook* and *cooks* are forms 'of the same word'. Let us use the term **lexeme** for this sense and say that *cook* and *cooks* are different **word-forms** which belong to, or **realise**, the same **lexeme**. Similarly, *go* and *went* are different word-forms which realise a single lexeme. There are two fewer different lexemes in (1) than there are word-forms, so there are nine different lexemes in (1). The name by which we choose to refer to the lexeme is arbitrary and depends on the classification required in the general theory within which we are working. We could call the lexeme realised by *cook* and *cooks* '762' or '85/a/17-U5' or 'Samantha' but, to make things easier, we'll agree to call it COOK, using capital letters when we write it. We can now say, more succinctly than was possible before, that *cooks* is one of the word-forms which can realise the lexeme COOK. Similarly, we can say that *went* is one of the word-forms that can realise GO. The lexemes in (1) are THE, COOK, BE, A, GOOD, AS, GO, AND, SHE.

We can look at the same facts and the same terminology from a different angle. Suppose you were reading a book and you suddenly came across the following sentence, which you didn't understand.

(3) The posset was disembogued from the rehoboams.

Suppose you didn't understand the fourth orthographic word in (3). You might want to consult your dictionary to find out what it means. But you would not look up *disembogued* with a final *d* in your dictionary because your knowledge of English is sufficient to tell you that *disembogued* is just a form of the lexeme DISEMBOGUE. Similarly you wouldn't look up *rehoboams* but REHOBOAM, which is the name of the lexeme. Lexemes are dictionary words (not necessarily in the sense that they will be given a separate entry and act as a headword in the particular dictionary you happen to have on your shelf, but in the sense that you might expect their separate identity to be acknowledged in an ideal dictionary or the ideal dictionary that a speaker might have in their head). A lexeme comprises all the word-forms which can realise that lexeme. Thus the lexeme REHOBOAM is sometimes realised by the word-form *rehoboam* and sometimes by the word-form *rehoboams*.

The units which actually occur, which have a shape (whether that is an orthographic shape or a sound shape), are word-forms. Word-forms realise (represent, belong to) lexemes. Lexemes, correspondingly, do not actually occur but are abstract dictionary words: abstract in that each lexeme may comprise a number of possible forms. The lexeme is, in a sense, what all the word-forms associated with it have in common.

For the time being, we shall assume that the word-forms of the spoken language are identical with the word-forms of the written language (that is, with orthographic words). This is actually an extremely awkward point and it will be taken up again in greater detail in Chapter 4.

We are now in a position to distinguish between the lexemes and the word-forms in a sentence like (1) but this will not always be sufficient for all purposes. Consider the next four sentences.

(4) (a)   Lee walked home.
    (b)   Lee went home.
(5) (a)   Lee has walked home.
    (b)   Lee has gone home.

The word-form *walked* occurs in both (4a) and in (5a) and, in both cases, it realises the lexeme WALK. Yet *walked* in these two sentences is not precisely the same element, as we can see when we compare with (4b) and (5b), which contain equivalent forms of the lexeme GO. In (4a) *walked* realises WALK + past tense, while in (5a) it realises WALK + past participle. We might want to say that *walked* in (4a) and (5a) are different words, even though they are homophonous word-forms and realise the same lexeme. We will say that they are different **grammatical words**. Grammatical words are defined in terms of their place in the paradigm and named by descriptions such as 'the past participle of WALK', which spell out that place.

We now have three different kinds of 'words': word-forms (including orthographic words), lexemes and grammatical words. The word 'word' might seem to be rather a liability under these circumstances. However, it turns out that the amount of specificity in the three other terms is not always needed and it is useful to have a superordinate term for word-form, lexeme and grammatical word. This allows us to avoid, when appropriate, the precision implicit in these other terms. In this book, **word** will be used with this less specific meaning.

In the printed text, word-forms are already separated out for us. But, even if they were not, we would still be able to discover the beginnings and ends of words fairly simply. Indeed, Ancient Greek was frequently written without gaps between the words and this corresponds to the way in which we talk. There are no gaps between the words in normal conversation. If there were, schoolboy jokes such as asking someone to say 'I chased the bug around the tree' or 'I'll have his blood, he knows I will' would not work, and neither would elaborate jokes like the following French couplet:

(6) Gal, amant de la reine, alla, tour magnanime,
Galamment de l'arène à la Tour Magne, à Nîmes.

'Gal, the queen's lover, went (which was generous of him) gallantly from the arena to the Magne Tower at Nimes.'

The two lines in this couplet are (or can be) absolutely homophonous, even though they mean different things because the word-breaks come in different places. So there are no gaps between words in speech and what we hear could be represented by running all the words together in print, as in

(7) Menbecomeoldbuttheyneverbecomegood.

Even here it is a relatively straightforward task for a speaker of English to sort out where the word-forms begin and end. We do this because we can recognise patterns and carry out substitutions. Firstly, we recognise certain strings of letters (or strings of sounds in the spoken language) which we know are found in other sentences with a meaning which would also make sense here. So we can recognise the sequence *men* in (7) because it also comes up in sentences like:

(8) Menareconservativeafterdinner.

(9) Menlosetheirtempersindefendingtheirtaste.

(10) Afterfortymenhavemarriedtheirhabits.

In a similar way we could isolate each of the word-forms in (7). Notice that we might try to isolate the first two letters of (7) and we would find *me* in other places, but then we would be unable to find a word beginning *nb*. So firstly we can recognise recurrent sequences. But, even if we found a sequence which we did not recognise, we could substitute other things which we know are word-forms in the place of these strings. So for *men* in (7) we could substitute *people, lecturers, sopranos* and so on, in place of *become* we could have *get, are, turn,* and so on, but we could not replace the *m* in *men* or *menb* in (7) with a word-form like *weeds* and still end up with a sentence. So substitution allows us to determine word-forms.

Before we leave words, we need to consider constructions like *kick the bucket* 'die' or *red herring* 'irrelevant distraction'. These look like ordinary syntactic constructions but their meanings are not derivable from the meanings of the component elements, as would be the case with *kick the ball* or *red paint*. Such phrases are called **idioms** and we would expect to find them listed in a dictionary (whether an actual book or an ideal mental facility). Idioms thus share with lexemes the quality of having dictionary entries. At the same time, an idiom like *red herring* seems to be made up of two lexemes, each of which has its own dictionary entry. So, while lexemes are, roughly defined, dictionary words, they are not the only things that are found in dictionaries. This means we need a different label for things listed in dictionaries. Several such labels are found in the literature, including **lexical item** and **listeme**. Lexical items in this sense include lexemes, idioms, phrasal verbs in English (*root out*, equivalent to *eradicate*), proverbs such as *a stitch in time saves nine* and possibly quotations such as *to be or not to be, that is the question*.

2.2 ELEMENTS SMALLER THAN THE WORD

Now consider the following sentence:

(11) He was born stupid and greatly increased his birthright.

We could isolate all the word-forms in this sentence in the ways outlined above, but we can also look within the word-forms and isolate recurrent forms within the word-form. For instance, if we consider the word-form *birthright*, we can divide that into two parts. For the first part, *birth*, we could substitute within the word-form things like *copy* and *water*, for the second part, *right*, we could substitute things like *day*, *place* and *rate*. In a similar way, we could divide the word-form *greatly* up into two parts. For the first part, *great*, we could substitute other forms like *vast* and *incredible* and, within the word-form (though not within this particular sentence), we could substitute items like *-ness*, *-er*, *-est* for *-ly*. Again, in a similar way, we can divide *increased* in (11) into two portions: *increase* and *-d*. For the first, we could substitute items like *enlarge* and *minimise*, for the second, items like *-s* and *-ing*. In other words, the same techniques that allow us to segment sentences into word-forms also allow us to segment word-forms. The units which we arrive at within the word-form we will call **morphs**. A word-form may contain only one morph (*stupid*, *and*) or it may contain several (*great·ly*, *increase·d*, *birth·right*). In this book, the decimal point will be used to separate morphs. A morph, then, is a unit which is a segment of a word-form. It has a constant form and realises or is related to a constant meaning.

Some morphs have the potential of being word-forms on their own. In

(12) Every·one live·s by sell·ing some·thing.

this applies to the morphs *every, one, live, by, sell, some* and *thing*. Such morphs are called **potentially free morphs**. Notice that the potentiality is not actually exploited for all of these morphs in (12). Indeed, only *by* is actually free in (12) but the others listed are potentially free. Morphs which cannot be word-forms by themselves but which need to be attached to other morphs are termed **obligatorily bound morphs**. In (12) only the morphs -*s* and -*ing* are obligatorily bound. Notice that there are words in English (and far more in many other languages) which are made up entirely of obligatorily bound morphs. Examples from English include: *Euro·crat, octo·pus, phil·anthrop·y, phonet·ic, quadra·phon·ic, wis·dom* and so on. In (12), it so happens that all of the potentially free morphs realise lexemes and none of the obligatorily bound morphs do. This is typically the case in English but not invariably the case, as the examples above show. In other languages, such as Latin, for example, it is typically the case that the morphs realising lexemes are also obligatorily bound.

In most cases in English (and, indeed, in all languages) and in all of the cases in (12) – though there are exceptions which will be dealt with below – the morph which realises the lexeme does not also realise anything else. Any morph which can realise a lexeme and which is not further analysable (except in terms of phonemes) is termed a **root**. Obligatorily bound morphs which do not realise lexemes and which are attached to roots to produce word-forms are called **affixes**. In a word like *dealings, deal* is the root and -*ing* and -*s* are affixes In *something* in sentence (12) there are two roots. Note that this implies that *some* and *thing* in *something* realise the lexemes SOME and THING, respectively, even though SOMETHING is also a lexeme in its own right. Affixes can be added directly to a root, as in *fool·ish*, or they can be added to a root and some already attached affix, as is the case with -*ness* in *fool·ish·ness*. We can call anything we attach affixes to, whether it is just a root or something bigger than a root, a **base**. So in the formation of *dealings* the root is *deal* but the base to which the -*s* is added is *dealing*. Note that in this case the final -*s* was not added to a root.

If an affix is attached before a base, it is called a **prefix**, if it is attached after a base it is called a **suffix** and, if it is attached in the middle of a base, it is called an **infix**. In the word *prepacked*, there is a root *pack*, a prefix *pre-* and a suffix *-ed*. All of the affixes that have been illustrated in (11) and (12) have been suffixes, which are more common in English than prefixes are. There are no infixes in English: the closest we have is the use of expletives in the middle of words like *absobloominglutely* and *kangabloodyroo*.

2.3 INFLECTION AND DERIVATION

Affixes can be of two kinds, inflectional or derivational. An **inflectional affix** is one which produces a new word-form of a lexeme from a base. A **derivational affix** is one which produces a new lexeme from a base. Take a word-form like *recreates*. This can be analysed into a prefix *re-*, a root *create*, and a suffix *-s*. The prefix makes a new lexeme RECREATE from the base *create*. But the suffix *-s* just provides another word-form of the lexeme RECREATE. The prefix *re-* is derivational but the suffix *-s* is inflectional. In English (though not in every language) prefixes are always derivational. Suffixes in English, though, may be either derivational or inflectional. In the word-form *formalises* the root is *form* and there are three suffixes: *-al, -ise* and *-s*. *Formal* belongs to a different lexeme from *form*, so *-al* is a derivational suffix; *formalise* belongs to a different lexeme from *formal*, so *-ise* is a derivational suffix; but *formalises* belongs to the same lexeme as *formalise*, so *-s* is an inflectional affix.

There are a number of ways of telling whether a suffix is inflectional or derivational if you are not sure whether or not it produces a new lexeme.

(a) If an affix changes the part of speech of the base, it is derivational. Affixes which do not change the part of speech of the base are usually (though not invariably) inflectional. So, because *form* is a noun and *formal* is an adjective, *-al* has changed the part of speech; it is, thus, a derivational affix. *Formal* is an adjective and *formalise* is a verb; *-ise* has changed the part of speech; it is a derivational suffix. *Formalise* is a verb *formalises* is still a verb; *-s* has not changed the part of speech so *-s* is likely to be an inflectional affix. Note, however, that, while all prefixes in English are derivational, very few of them change the part of speech of the base.

(b) Inflectional affixes always have a regular meaning. Derivational affixes may have an irregular meaning. If we consider an inflectional affix like the plural *-s* in word-forms like *bicycles, dogs, shoes, tins, trees* and so on, the difference in meaning between the base and the affixed form is always the same: 'more than one'. If, however, we consider the change in meaning caused by a derivational affix like *-age* in words like *bandage, cleavage, coinage, dotage, drainage, haulage, herbage, mileage, orphanage, peerage, shortage, spillage* and so on, it is difficult to sort out any fixed change in meaning or even a small set of meaning changes.

(c) As a general rule, if you can add an inflectional affix to one member of a class, you can add it to all members of the class, while, with a derivational affix, it is not generally possible to add it to all members. That is, inflectional affixes are fully **productive** while derivational affixes are not. For example, you can add *-s* to any non-modal verb in English to make the 'third person singular of the present indicative' but you cannot add *-ation* to any non-modal verb to make a noun: *nationalis·ation* is a perfectly good word, so it works some of the time, but none of **com(e)·ation, *inflect·ation, *produc(e)·ation* or **walk·ation* are words of English. We can summarise this criterion in the following way: affixes which show limited productivity with large numbers of gaps are derivational; affixes which are fully productive (can be used with all members of a class) may be either inflectional or derivational.

In fact, the distinction between inflectional and derivational affixes is more complex than this suggests and the matter will be taken up again in Chapter 6. The criteria provided here, though, will cover most of the straightforward cases.

2.4 ALLOMORPHS AND MORPHEMES

Sometimes two or more morphs which have the same meaning are in complementary distribution. That is, the two can never occur in precisely the same environment or context, and between them they exhaust the possible contexts in which the morpheme can appear. For example, there are two morphs in English which can be glossed as 'indefinite article': *a* and *an*. Some examples of their distribution can be seen below.

(13) (a) a man   (b) an oak
        a horse   an elephant
        a kettle   an uncle
        a university   an apple
        a green apple an old man

From the examples in (13) and from your knowledge of the rest of the language, you can see that *a* occurs when the next word begins with a phonetic consonant and that *an* occurs when the next word begins with a phonetic vowel. The word 'phonetic' is important, since *university* begins orthographically with a *u* but phonetically with a consonant, /j/. (In some rather conservative varieties of English this rule is not quite true, since it is possible to say *an hotel* and *an historical novel*. Not all such speakers pronounce these words without an /h/, which would make them conform to the general rule. We shall, provisionally, ignore these varieties.)

In this case, the choice between the two morphs *a* and *an* is determined or conditioned by the following phonetic sound. We can say that their distribution is **phonetically** (or **phonologically**) **conditioned**. In other cases, the distribution of morphs may be determined by other factors. For example, consider the way we make adjectives from nouns describing people which end in *-or*. While there are words with no corresponding adjective (like *juror, vendor*), most such words make an adjective by adding *-ial*, as in *editor·ial* and *professor·ial*. In a very few cases, though, we simply add *-al*: *doctor·al* is the clearest example. From the examples cited, it might seem that this is a phonologically conditioned difference but a pair such as *doctoral* versus *censorial* suggests that the difference has nothing to do with the phonology of the bases concerned. It is simply a fact about DOCTOR that its corresponding adjective is DOCTORAL; the choice between *-ial* and *-al* in such cases is **lexically conditioned**. Morphs can also be **grammatically conditioned**. In a language like German, adjectives change their form depending on the gender of the noun they modify. Thus, in the nominative singular, we find the following pattern:

(14)   ein gross·er Wagen   'a big car (masculine)'
        ein gross·er Fisch   'a big fish (masculine)'
        ein gross·es Haus   'a big house (neuter)'
        ein gross·es Tier   'a big animal (neuter)'
        eine gross·e Feder   'a big feather (feminine)'
        eine gross·e Schlange   'a big snake (feminine)'

The suffix on the adjective is not determined by the phonetic shape of the base or of the next word, nor is it determined by the particular lexeme following, but by the grammatical gender class that lexeme belongs to. The conditioning is thus neither phonetic nor lexical but grammatical.

But, if English *a* and *an*, or *-al* and *-ial*, or German *-er*, *-es*, and *-e* are clearly separate morphs because of their different shapes, they, nevertheless, have things in common. They have their meaning in common: 'indefinite article', 'adjective' or 'nominative singular'. Between them, they divide up a single distribution: always before a singular countable noun, always on the end of a noun ending in *-or*, or always on the end of an attributive adjective following an indefinite determiner. They even have a similarity in form. There is a sense, therefore, in which *a* and *an* (and the other sets) are 'the same thing'. We will say that these various sets of morphs realise the same **morpheme**.

As with lexemes, the name we use to refer to the morphemes is arbitrary. We could call the morpheme realised by *a* and *an* '9,673' or '99/0/7245-T2' or 'Zoë' – whatever made sense in our classification. But, to simplify matters, we will agree to call a morpheme either by a label describing its meaning (in this case 'indefinite article') or by one of its morphs, say 'a'. If we make the latter choice, we will usually use the morph that occurs most widely in the language. To show we are talking about a morpheme we will enclose this name in braces when we write it: {indefinite article} or {a}.

Notice that the morpheme, like the lexeme and the phoneme, is realised by something else. You cannot hear a morpheme or say a morpheme (just as you cannot say or hear a lexeme or a phoneme): you can only say or hear something which realises a morpheme (or a lexeme or a phoneme). You can hear or say a morph (or a word-form or a phone) but not what it realises. Morphemes (like lexemes and phonemes) are abstract units. The morpheme {a} is whatever all the morphs which can realise {a} have in common.

Morphs which realise a particular morpheme and which are conditioned (whether phonetically or lexically or grammatically) are called the **allomorphs** of that morpheme. (If we consider the written form of the language, it is also possible to talk about orthographically conditioned allomorphs of a morpheme, as in *come* and *com-*, the latter of which occurs in *coming*.) *A* and *an* are the two phonetically conditioned allomorphs of the morpheme {a}. Notice that every allomorph is a morph. The term allomorph is simply more informative than is morph on its own because it says that the morph is one of several realisations of the same morpheme.

It should be noted that the terms 'morpheme' and 'allomorph' are frequently used by other linguists in rather different senses from the ones they have been given here. We will consider this in more detail in Chapter 7. The implication of this is that you will have to take care, when you meet these terms in other works, that you know precisely what is intended.

This abstractness of morphemes frequently causes problems of understanding for students who are new to morphology.

A parallel might be helpful. Consider the various symbols presented below:

(15) R r *ᴕ*

What do these symbols have in common? The answer, fairly simply, is that they are all kinds of 'R'. What is it about them that shows, then, that they are all kinds of 'R'? How can you tell that they are 'R's? The answer lies not in their particular shape, which varies depending on the kind of script they happen to occur in. The answer lies in their function; they all function as 'R', they all have the same value in the system, they all, for instance, can be used at the beginning of the word *rat*. But this is an abstract quality. The 'R-ness' of the symbols presented in (15) is something abstract. The 'R-ness' corresponds, in the analogy, to the morpheme. The different forms for these 'R's which have the same function in the system correspond to morphs. The symbol 'r' is just one of the morphs that can realise the morpheme, the abstract notion of what 'R' is.

2.5 RECAPITULATION

Armed with all this terminology, consider the word-form *was* in the sentence

(16) While he was not dumber than an ox, he was not any smarter.

Was is a word-form which is probably not further analysable into morphs. This word-form realises, among other things, the lexeme BE, as we can see if we change the syntactic environment of (16), but not its meaning:

(17) Being not dumber than an ox, but being no smarter, he was not a brilliant conversationalist.

(18) I hope, at least, to be not dumber than an ox.

But there are also other morphemes realised by the word-form *was*. Firstly, *was* is singular, because if it had a plural subject it would be replaced by *were*:

(19) While they were not dumber than oxen, they were not any smarter.

You cannot say in standard English

(20) While they was not dumber than an ox, they was not any smarter.

Secondly, *was* also marks past tense. You cannot say:

(21) While he was not any dumber than an ox, he was not any smarter at the moment.

You have to say:

(22) While he is not any dumber than an ox, he is not any smarter at the moment.

In other verbs, pastness is shown by a separate morph (as, for example, in the difference between *compliment* and *compliment·ed*) but, here, this difference is included in the single word-form. So *was* is a single morph that realises not only the lexeme BE (which is made up of a single morpheme {be}) but also the morphemes {singular} and {past tense}. A morph which realises more than one morpheme in this way is called a **portmanteau morph**.

To summarise, we can say that an actual speech event can be analysed into a series of word-forms, some of which will be made up of a single morph, others of which will be made up of more than one morph. The morphs realise (though not necessarily in a one-to-one manner) morphemes. Morphemes are abstract units of grammatical and semantic analysis. One or more morphemes may form a lexeme, an abstract vocabulary item. This is presented in tabular form (with a certain amount of simplification) in Figure 2.1.

LEXEMES	made up of one or more	MORPHEMES
realised by	.	realised by
WORD-FORMS	made up of one or more	MORPHS

Figure 2.1: Summary of basic terms

REFERENCES AND FURTHER READING

Most introductory linguistics textbooks cover the kind of material that has been covered in this chapter. It should be noted, however, that the terminology used here derives from a British tradition, which is, in this area, distinct from the American tradition. In particular, many

American sources do not distinguish between 'morph' and 'morpheme' in the way that has been done here. For a discussion of the various ways in which the term 'morpheme' has been used in Linguistics, see Mugdan (1986). It is clear from that article just how careful you have to be when reading works which discuss morphemes.

Among the best books to consult for consolidation of the discussion here are Brown & Miller (1980), Lyons (1968) and Matthews (1991). Of these, I would particularly recommend Brown & Miller (1980) for beginners. Note that Matthews's use of the term 'word' is different from the one in this book.

The discussion of abstractness in terms of letter-shapes is loosely based on Lass (1984).

Not all authorities agree that allomorphs can be lexically conditioned. Lyons (1968), for example, is in a tradition of excluding the use of the term 'allomorph' in such circumstances. It is true that it is far less clear that there is 'conditioning' involved in lexical conditioning, which is far more random than other kinds of conditioning. There are, therefore, advantages to this kind of restriction. But there are also advantages (albeit less obvious ones) to the wider usage of the term adopted in this book.

The sentences used as examples are, of course, not my own. Many of them can be found in Bentley & Esar (1951). The data from Yingkarta in the exercises comes from Dench (1998).

EXERCISES

1. Which of the following are lexemes of English: *superstition*, CAT, BEFORE, {neat}.

2. For each of (a), (b) and (c):
   - i.   How many orthographic words does the sentence contain?
   - ii.   How many different word-forms does the sentence contain?
   - iii.   How many different lexemes does the sentence contain?
   - iv.   How many different grammatical words does the sentence contain?
   - a.   I walked to town yesterday, she has walked there this morning.
   - b.   Not many banks have branches on the banks of the Avon.
   - c.   She stoops to refill the stoops of wine and, having refilled them, wishes the wine-waiter refilled them himself.

3. In the example sentence (b) in (2) above, is *banks* the same word-form occurring twice or two different word-forms?

4. Consider the following data from English, presented in transcription.

Infinitive	Past tense	Infinitive	Past tense
kɪl	kɪld	kɒf	kɒft
fɪz	fɪzd	wɒʃ	wɒʃt
əlaʊ	əlaʊd	pjuːk	pjuːkt
græb	græbd	pɑːs	pɑːst
hʌm	hʌmd	slaʊʧ	slaʊʧt

What determines whether the past tense is marked by a /d/ or a /t/? What kind of conditioning is that? /d/ and /t/ both mean 'past tense' and are both alveolar plosives (and so share form). What does that imply about these two forms? Consider the past tense of the verbs WANT and PRETEND. How do they fit into the pattern? Using appropriate notation and terminology, write a statement of what is going on here. Confirm the predictions made in your statement by considering what happens with the verbs PRODUCE, INSULT and CONTAIN.

5. In Yingkarta, an aboriginal language of Western Australia, nouns and adjectives are marked for a case which has a number of functions and which is, therefore, called the genitive/dative case. On pronouns, the marker for this case is *-ngu*. On nouns and adjectives, the markers are as shown in the table below (which is presented in orthography).

Base	Genitive/Dative	Gloss
mantu	mantuwu	'meat'
papa	papawu	'water'
pika	pikawu	'sick'
pipi	pipiwu	'mother'
thuthu	thuthuwu	'dog'
kurtan	kurtanku	'bag'
majun	majunku	'turtle'
mangkurr	mangkurrku	'three'
nginthirn	nginthirnku	'cold'
nyanyjil	nyanyjilku	'woman'

What are the allomorphs of the morpheme {genitive/dative}? How is each allomorph conditioned? Given the base forms *purlijiman* 'policeman' and *kartu* 'man', what would you expect the genitive/dative forms to be?

6. Affixes are usually defined as obligatorily bound morphs. Choose one of the sets of data provided below (preferably from a language with which you have some familiarity) and decide whether this must always be the case.

(a) English
   absobloodylutely
   confronbloodytation
   guaranbloodytee
   imbloodypossible
   inbloodyfallible
   incanbloodydescent
   kangabloodyroo
   unbebloodylievable
   unibloodyversity

(b) French

sous-entendre	surchauffer	suspendre
sous-exposer	surclasser	
sous-louer	suréquiper	
sous-tendre	surestimer	
soustraire	surfaire	
sous-traiter	surmonter	

(c) German

auf·drucken	aus·drucken	be·drucken
auf·fallen	aus·fallen	be·fallen
auf·geben	aus·geben	be·geben
auf·halten	aus·halten	be·halten
auf·nehmen	aus·nehmen	be·nehmen
auf·schreiben	aus·schreiben	be·schreiben
auf·stehen	aus·stehen	be·stehen
auf·steigen	aus·steigen	be·steigen
auf·stellen	aus·stellen	be·stellen
auf·tragen	aus·tragen	be·tragen

(d) Latin

ac·curro:	re·curro:
ac·ce:do:	re·ce:do:
ad·du:co:	re·du:co:
ad·fero:	re·fero:
ad·ficio:	re·ficio:
ad·lego:	re·lego:
ad·mitto:	re·mitto:

ap·po:no: re·po:no:
ap·porto: re·porto:

7. Are derivational affixes such as *-al* and *-ise* lexemes?

CHAPTER 3

The Morphological Structure of Words

In this chapter, we shall consider the various processes by which words can be built. I shall illustrate these processes from a number of languages, some of which will be familiar to you and others of which will not be familiar to you. It is the wide range of ways in which it is possible to build words which is the central focus of this chapter. In passing, attention will also be drawn to some of the difficulties that arise in morphological description, to show why linguists find morphology interesting. One reviewer said about morphology recently that 'we do not understand all that we know'. This is part of the interest and the challenge provided by morphology.

3.1 WORD-BUILDING PROCESSES USING AFFIXES

By far the most common way of building new words in the languages of the world is by using affixes. The commonest type of affix by far is the suffix. There are several languages in the world which use suffixes to the exclusion of any other type of affix (Basque, Finnish and Quechua are examples) but only very few which use prefixes to the exclusion of other types of affix (Thai is frequently cited as an example) and none which use any other type of affix exclusively. Thus, the obligatorily bound morph *par excellence* in the languages of the world is the suffix.

3.1.1 Suffixes

Suffixes are used for all purposes in morphology. They are used derivationally as in:

(1)   *English:*   constitut·ion·al·ity
      Finnish: asu·nno·ttom·uus
                   live·noun·without·abstract-noun
                   'houselessness'
      Mam: txik·eenj
                   cook·patient
                   'something cooked'

and inflectionally as in:

(2)   *Finnish:*   talo·i·ssa·an
                   house·plural·in·3rd-person-possessive
                   'in their houses'
      Turkish: gel·é·miy·eceğ·im
                   come·be-able·negative·future·1st-person
                   'I will not be able to come.'

Notice that all of the suffixes in (2) are inflectional, even though some of them are translated into English by separate lexemes. The meaning of an affix is not sufficient to tell you whether that affix is inflectional or derivational. This will be taken up again in Chapter 6. Neither is it the case that a given type of meaning is always realised in the same kind of way across languages. Even plurality may not always be an inflectional category. In Diyari, an aboriginal language of South Australia, plurality is marked optionally by a derivational suffix.

As is clear from the examples given above, suffixes can occur in sequences although there is no expectation that they will. When both inflectional and derivational suffixes co-occur in the same word-form, the general rule (although it is by no means exceptionless, see below section 6.5) is that the derivational suffixes precede the inflectional ones, so that the cases in (3) are typical.

(3)   *Diyari:*   jiŋki·mali·ji
                  give·reciprocal (deriv)·present (infl)
                  'give one another'
      Finnish: kirja·sto·sta·mme
                  book·collective (deriv)·out-of (infl)·our (infl)
                  'out of our library'
      French: égal·is·a
                  equal·verb (deriv)·3rd-person-singular-past

(infl)
'[he/she/it] equalised'

Portmanteau morphs are very common as suffixes in highly inflecting languages. This is illustrated by the case and number marking on the nouns in many Indo-European languages. The paradigm for the Latin noun ANNUS 'year', given below, will provide an example.

(4)

	Singular	Plural
Nominative	ann·us	ann·i:
Vocative	ann·e	ann·i:
Accusative	ann·um	ann·o:s
Genitive	ann·i:	ann·o:rum
Dative	ann·o:	ann·i:s
Ablative	ann·o:	ann·i:s

In this paradigm, it can be seen that there is neither a consistent realisation of singularity, nor one of plurality. Neither is there a single realisation of any one of the cases (and if the other genders were taken into consideration, this would be even more striking). Rather, the final morph analysed in the word-forms in (4) has to be seen as a portmanteau morph, realising simultaneously the category of number and that of case. The alternative position, where a single morpheme is realised in more than one morph, can also be illustrated from Latin. Consider the realisation relations shown by the arrows in the Latin word-form *re:ksisti:* 'you (sing) ruled'.

(5)   RULE perfective 2nd singular

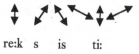

re:k   s   is   ti:

Each of the morphs analysed in (5) can be motivated by comparison with other forms of Latin and the realisation relations can be justified since, if any of the morphemes were changed, the morphs realising those morphemes would also change. Compare, for example, the form for 'I ruled':

(6)   RULE perfective 1st singular

re:k   s   i:

3.1.2 Prefixes

Although they are rarer than suffixes, prefixes work in very much the same way. They can be derivational, as in:

(7)	*English*:	dis·en·tangle
	Mam:	aj·b'iitz
		agent·song
		'singer'
	Tagalog:	pan·ulat
		instrument·write
		'pen'

or inflectional as in:

(8)	*Mam*:	t·kamb'
		3rd-singular-possessive·prize
		'his prize'
	Swahili:	a·si·nga·li·jua
		he·negative·concessive·past·know
		'if he had not known'
	Tagalog:	i·sulat
		modal·write
		'writing (participle)'

These examples show that, like suffixes, prefixes can occur in sequences. The norm is for derivational prefixes to occur to the right of inflectional prefixes within the same word-form, as is shown below in the data from Achenese, a language of Sumatra.

(9) (a) jih ji·langŭ
        he 3rd-person-(younger) (infl)·swim
        'he swims (transitive, e.g. swims the river)'
     (b) jih ji·mi·langŭ
        he 3rd-person-(younger) (infl)·intransitive (deriv)·swim
        'he swims (intransitive)'
     (c) jih ji·pi·langŭ
        he 3rd-person-(younger) (infl)·causative (deriv)·swim
        'he makes [someone] swim'

Prefixes can, of course, co-occur in the same word with suffixes and all possible combinations of derivational and inflectional are found in such cases.

(10) *English*: un·thank·ful
               (deriv) (deriv)

English:	re·think·s
	(deriv) (infl)
Mam:	ky·xoo·ʔkj
	3rd-person-plural-ergative (infl)·
	throw·processive (deriv)
	'they went and threw'
Turkana:	è·ràm·i
	3rd-person (infl)·beat·aspect (infl)
	'he is beating'

3.1.3 Circumfixes

In some cases, a prefix and a suffix act together to surround a base. If neither of these affixes is used on its own and the two seem to realise a single morpheme, they are sometimes classed together as a **circumfix**. This can be illustrated from German, where the past participle of weak verbs is made by adding a prefix *ge-* and, simultaneously, a suffix *-t*. That is, the base is enclosed in affixes, neither of which can occur on its own in the forms in question. This is illustrated below.

(11)   film·en   'to film'   ge·film·t   'filmed'
       frag·en   'to ask'   ge·frag·t   'asked'
       lob·en   'to praise' ge·lob·t   'praised'
       zeig·en   'to show'   ge·zeig·t   'shown'
       Ge·film, etc. do not occur.
       Film·t, etc. do not occur in this meaning but only as 3rd person singular present tense forms.

If the circumfix *ge...t* is taken to be a single affix, it is a **discontinuous morph**. Discontinuous morphs are considerably rarer than continuous morphs. Circumfixes are a special case of a more general phenomenon whereby two or more affixes act together to provide a meaning which neither can have in isolation. Although many such cases are found, circumfixes are the only cases which are common enough to have a special term applied to them.

3.1.4 Infixes

Since infixes create discontinuous bases, the rarity of discontinuous morphs also accounts for the relative rarity of infixation (the use of infixes) in the languages of the world. Consider the following examples. (12) from Chrau, a language of Vietnam, and (13) from Tagalog, a language of the Philippines.

(12)   vŏh   'know'   v·an·ŏh   'wise'

           căh   'remember' c·an·ăh   'left over'

(13)   sulat   'write'

           s·um·ulat 'wrote'

           s·in·ulat 'was written'

[handwritten annotation: drama to dramatic → stem extension]

Note that, to count as an infix, a morph must actually interrupt another morph, not merely occur between two morphs. The morph meaning 'negative' in the Swahili example in (8) is a prefix, not an infix. In (12) and (13) the infix is inserted after the initial consonant of the base, interrupting the base at a defined point. Note that in (12) the infix is used derivationally, while in (13) it is used inflectionally. Infixes can co-occur in the word-form with prefixes and suffixes. This is illustrated below from Tagalog. Verbs like *sulat* in Tagalog have three different passive themes. The first was illustrated above in (13), the second involves prefixation as well and the third suffixation, as can be seen in (14a) and (14b) respectively.

(14) (a) i·s·in·ulat   second passive theme (preterite)

       (b) s·in·ulat·an   third passive theme (preterite)

3.1.5 Interfixes

A rather special kind of affix can be found, for example, in many of the Germanic languages, where there is a linking element which appears between the two elements of a compound. This can be illustrated from German.

(15)	Element 1	Element 2	Compound	Gloss
(a)	Auge	Arzt	Auge·n·arzt	'eye doctor'
	Schwester	Paar	Schwester·n·paar	'pair of sisters'
	Tag	Reise	Tag·e·reise	'day's journey'
	Uhr	Kasten	Uhr·en·kasten	'clock case'
(b)	Bauer	Frau	Bauer·s·frau	'farmer's wife'
	Jahr	Zeit	Jahr·es·zeit	'season' (*lit.* year time)
	Tag	Licht	Tag·es·licht	'day light'
	Wirt	Haus	Wirt·s·haus	'inn' (*lit.* host house)
(c)	Stern	Banner	Stern·en·banner	'stars and stripes'
	Strauss	Ei	Strauss·en·ei	'ostrich egg'

(d) Arbeit	Anzug	Arbeit·s·anzug	'work clothes'
Geburt	Jahr	Geburt·s·jahr	'year of birth'
Liebe	Brief	Liebe·s·brief	'love letter'
Verbindung	Tür	Verbindung·s·tür	'connecting door '

The linking element in the compound is an affix which only comes between two other forms. It is, therefore, sometimes termed an **interfix**. The -o- that occurs in neo classical compounds such as *electrolyte* in English (see below, section 3.6) might also be seen as an interfix.

The German interfixes in (15) raise a small problem for morphological description. In (15a) the interfix has the same form as the appropriate morph of the morpheme {plural}. In (15b) the interfix has the same form as the appropriate morph of the morpheme {possessive}. In (15c) the interfix has the same form as the appropriate realisation of the dative plural. But in (15d), the interfix does not share the form of any morph which otherwise could be attached to the first element. Words like these suggest that these interfixes, whatever they are derived from etymologically, probably do not synchronically represent the morphemes {plural}, {possessive} or {dative}. That being the case, though, there does not seem to be any morpheme which these interfixes do realise. They seem to be morphs that do not realise morphemes, morphs which have no meaning attached to them. They are **empty morphs**. It is sometimes useful to have a label which can be used to refer to all kinds of morphs, whether or not they realise morphemes. The term 'morph' itself usually implies a realisation of a morpheme. We can use the label **formal element** to refer to morphs and empty morphs or to be deliberately vague as to whether a particular recurrent form is a realisation of a morpheme or not.

3.1.6 Transfixes

Another special kind of affix involves not only discontinuous affixes but also discontinuous bases. These are affixes which occur throughout the base and they are, thus, termed **transfixes**. Transfixes appear only in the Semitic languages. In these languages, roots are made up of a number of consonants and can never occur in isolation. Transfixes are then added to these roots, sometimes also with prefixes or suffixes. The transfixes are made up of a number of vowels and may also involve operations on consonants (for example, consonants may be doubled). The position of the transfix varies from transfix to transfix: some of them allow clusters of the consonants in the root, others do not. Each transfix occurs in a fixed position in the root. This very complex state of affairs is illustrated for the roots *ktb* 'write' and *drs* 'study' below, using data from Egyptian Arabic.

(16)
ˈkatab	'he wrote'	ˈdaras	'he studied'
ˈjiktib	'he will write'	ˈjidris	'he will study'
makˈtuub	'written'	madˈruus	'studied'
makˈtaba	'bookshop'	madˈrasa	'school'
maˈkaatib	'bookshops'	maˈdaaris	'schools'
		dars	'lesson'
kiˈtaab	'book'		
ˈkaatib	'clerk'		
		muˈdaris	'teacher'

Since they involve two sets of discontinuous morphs, transfixes are the most complex type of affix. Accordingly, they have received quite a lot of attention in recent times from linguists as test cases for various morphological theories. They raise very important problems for morphological description but these need not concern us further here.

3.2 REDUPLICATION

Reduplication, or using some part of the base (which may be the entire base) more than once in the word, is far more common across languages than the rarer types of affixation illustrated above. If the entire base is reduplicated, reduplication resembles compounding (see below, section 3.6). Reduplication can also form types of affix. That is, the part of the word which is repeated may be added to the end or the beginning of the base. All these types will be illustrated below. The examples in (17) are from Afrikaans and show whole words being reduplicated. The examples in (18) are from Motu, a language of Papua New Guinea, and illustrate the use of reduplicated prefixes as well as whole word reduplication. In the Maori data in (19) the reduplicated part is used as a suffix.

(17)
amper	'nearly'	amper·amper	'very nearly'
dik	'thick'	dik·dik	'very thick'
drie	'three'	drie·drie	'three at a time'

(18)
tau	'man'	ta·tau	'men'
mero	'boy'	me·mero	'boys'
		meromero	'little boy'
		memeromemero	'little boys'

(19)   aahua   'appearance'   aahua·hua   'resemble'
      hiikei   'step'   hiikei·kei   'hop'
      maakuu   'moisture'   maakuu·kuu   'rather moist'

Reduplication is frequently used iconically. By this, I mean that the form of the word in some way reflects its meaning. So reduplication is frequently used to indicate plurality, intensity and repetition, which are some of the meanings illustrated in examples (17) to (19). However, reduplication is also found in less iconic uses. For example, compare the data in (13) with that below:

(20)   sumulat   'to write'   su·sulat   'will write'
      bumasa   'to read'   ba·basa   'will read'
      ʔumaral   'to teach'   ʔa·ʔaral   'will teach'

In (20), it can be seen that the future tense in Tagalog is formed by reduplicating the first consonant and vowel of the base to form a prefix. The marking of futurity with reduplication is far less iconic than marking, say, plurality with reduplication. Note also that here reduplication has been used to mark inflection, while in most of the other cases illustrated here it has been used derivationally.

Reduplication, then, is, in effect, a special way of making affixes or a way of creating a special kind of compound. These affixes or compounds may, however, act differently from other affixes or compounds in the language concerned. This is, for instance, clearly the case with the Afrikaans examples cited above, which are formally distinct from other compounds in that language. Reduplication is usually determined in phonological terms so that a reduplication rule will state how much of the base is to be reduplicated in terms of consonants, vowels, syllables and word-forms.

3.3 WORD-BUILDING BY MODIFICATION OF THE BASE

Where affixes are not used for creating new words, the most common method is to make some kind of phonological change to the base. The change may be segmental or suprasegmental and, if segmental, it may affect consonants or vowels and one or more segments. The terminology surrounding the various types of change is complex and, unfortunately, not always illuminating, as will be seen below.

Consider first modifications to the segmental make-up of the base. In the examples below, a change from a voiceless fricative to a voiced fricative causes a change from noun to verb in English:

(21) mouth   mouth
      sheath   sheathe
      strife   strive
      thief   thieve
      wreath   wreathe

There is no special name for this type of internal modification. It is found along with affixation in the following irregular English plurals:

(22) house   house·s
      mouth   mouth·s
      path   path·s
      self   selve·s
      shelf   shelve·s
      wharf   wharve·s
      wife   wive·s
      youth   youth·s

More common is modification to a vowel sound. Such modification has a different name depending on its historical source. Where it is the result of assimilation to a following vowel (even if that later vowel has subsequently disappeared) it is called **Umlaut**. Otherwise it is called **Ablaut**. Either can be referred to as **vowel mutation**. The following are examples of Umlaut from some of the Germanic languages:

(23) *Danish*
      gås   'goose'   gæs   'geese'
      mand   'man'   mænd   'men'

      English
      mouse   mice
      foot   feet
      tooth   teeth
      louse   lice

      Icelandic
      stór   'big'   stærri   'bigger'
      mús   'mouse'   mýs   'mice'
      son·ur   'son'   syn·ir   'sons'
      full·ur   'full'   fyll·ri   'fuller'

Note that, in some of the Icelandic examples, Umlaut co-occurs with a suffix while, in other examples, there is no affix. Co-occurrence of modification of the base and affixation is, in fact, a very common phenomenon.

Examples of Ablaut from irregular past tenses in some of the Germanic languages are listed in (24):

(24)   *Dutch*

bijten	'bite'	beet	'bit'
doen	'do'	dee	'did'
dragen	'carry'	droeg	'carried'
stelen	'steal'	stal	'stole'

Frisian

bliede	'bleed'	blette	'bled'
drage	'carry'	droech	'carried'
gean	'go'	gong	'went'
glimme	'glimmer'	glom	'glimmered'
helpe	'help'	holp	'helped'

Icelandic

ber	'I carry'	bar	'I carried'
gef	'I give'	gaf	'I gave'
kýs	'I choose'	kaus	'I chose'
tek	'I take'	tók	'I took'

That Ablaut is also found along with affixation can be illustrated from the past participle forms of the same verbs:

(25)   *Dutch*

gebeten	'bitten'
gedaan	'done'
gedragen	'carried'
gestolen	'stolen'

Frisian

blet	'bled'
droegen	'carried'
gongen	'gone'
glommen	'glimmered'
holpen	'helped'

Icelandic

bor·inn	'carried'
gef·inn	'given'
kos·inn	'chosen'
tek·inn	'taken'

Although these examples have all come from the Germanic languages and the very names Umlaut and Ablaut are German loan words, vowel mutation is not restricted to these languages by any means, as can be seen from the examples in (26).

(26)   *Dinka*

dom	'field'	dum	'fields'
kat	'frame'	kɛt	'frames'
met	'child'	miit	'children'

Welsh

singular	plural	gloss
bychan	bychain	'little'
byddar	byddair	'deaf'
garw	geirw	'rough'
caled	celyd	'hard'

Transfixes (see above, section 3.1.6) are viewed by some linguists as types of internal modification.

Turning now to internal modification in suprasegmental structure, consider the following data from Kanuri, a language of Nigeria. The example shows the differences between the 3rd person singular conjunctive ('s/he VERBS and ...') and optative ('s/he is to VERB') tenses in Kanuri

(27)

conjunctive	optative	gloss
lezê	lezé	'go'
tussê	tussé	'rest'
kərazê	kərazé	'study'
´ = high tone,	^ = falling tone	

Such processes are relatively common in the tone languages of Africa. Since these morphs are suprasegmental in their realisation, they are sometimes treated as suprasegmental affixes and called suprafixes or **superfixes**. It has been pointed out that such affixes are no more on top of the other morphs than they are underneath them and that simulfix would probably be a better term, but this suggestion has not been generally adopted. Stress differences such as those that distinguish the following English noun-verb pairs (at least in some varieties) are also superfixes, in this sense, or cases of suprasegmental internal modification.

(28)

ˈdiscount (*n*)	disˈcount (*v*)
ˈimport (*n*)	imˈport (*v*)
ˈinsult (*n*)	inˈsult (*v*)

Some authorities view cases of this kind as **replacive morphs**. They would claim that the replacement of one phonological sequence by another is a morph realising the appropriate morpheme in all the cases that have been discussed in this section. For example, they would say that the distinction between *mouse* and *mice* is marked by a replacive morph of the form '/aʊ/ → /aɪ/'. The replacive morph is everything between inverted commas in the last sentence. This analysis is controversial. The most usual understanding of morphs is that they are forms, while replacive morphs would be not so much forms as processes. This is clearly an extension of the term 'morph' although whether such an extension goes beyond what is justified, particularly within a generative framework, is less clear. Other analysts might see cases of infixation in these examples. The main argument against this position is that, in most of these cases, the form of the modification is lexically determined and there is no constant form. There is also a typological argument, in that the languages which use modification most freely (for example, the Germanic languages) do not generally have any other infixes. It is partly for this reason and partly in order to give some kind of formal statement of internal modification that the term 'replacive morph' is used.

3.4 RELATIONSHIPS WITH NO CHANGE OF FORM

There are many instances to be found where, although there appears to be an inflectional or derivational relationship between two words, they have precisely the same form. Some examples are given below:

(29) *English*

singular	*plural*		
deer	deer		
fish	fish		
sheep	sheep		

English

better (*adj*)	to better	a better
empty (*adj*)	to empty	an empty
round (*adj*)	to round	a round
clean (*adj*)	to clean	
	to farm	a farm
nasty (*adj*)		a nasty

French

devoir	'to have to'	le devoir	'duty'
pouvoir	'to be able to'	le pouvoir	'power'
savoir	'to know'	le savoir	'knowledge'

Yoruba

gígùn	'long'	'length'
dídùn	'sweet'	'sweetness'

The examples in (29) have to be distinguished in principle from the cases where there is no change of form but, equally, no reason to hypothesise the existence of an extra morpheme. For instance, the English plural forms in (29) do not work in the same way as the Maori plural forms in (30).

(30)

korou	'channel'	korou	'channels'
kurii	'dog'	kurii	'dogs'
kuumara	'kumara'	kuumara	'kumaras'

In English it is normal for plurals to be overtly marked on nouns, while in Maori it is the exception for plural nouns to carry any morphological mark. Plurality in Maori is marked by determiners. Since morphemes have to do with both form and meaning, every morpheme must have both a form (or series of forms) and a constant meaning. If there is never any form, we cannot set up a morpheme. Thus we cannot postulate a morpheme {singular} for English nouns because singularity is never marked by an affix on nouns.

Some linguists postulate a **zero morph** to account for the difference in function between homophonous forms such as those in (29). The argument runs as follows. In most instances where there is a change in the part of speech, there is an affix to mark that change. In *legal·ise*, for example, the fact that an adjective has been turned into a verb is marked by the suffix. In *to empty*, on the other hand, there is no overt affix. In order to treat both of these the same way, a zero morph is postulated on the end of *empty·Ø*, marking its status as a verb.

Zero morphs, however, are controversial. They are most generally accepted in inflectional cases, where parallelism with other forms in a paradigm appears to demand an affix. Consider the following example from Russian, where the word for 'drinking glass' is a masculine noun and the word for 'school' is a feminine noun.

(31)

	'school'		'drinking glass'	
	Singular	*Plural*	*Singular*	*Plural*
Nominative	ʃkol·a	ʃkol·i	stakan	stakan·i

Accusative	ʃkol·u	ʃkol·ɨ	stakan	stakan·ɨ
Genitive	ʃkol·ɨ	ʃkol	stakan·a	stakan·ov

Here all cases and numbers are typically marked with a suffix (there are more cases than are illustrated here and also a third gender), and the nominative and accusative singular of the masculine and the genitive plural of the feminine are the exceptions. The case of each individual noun can be worked out when its gender is known. A zero might, thus, be seen in such instances as a kind of place-holder. Note that, if it were true that the nominative, say, was never marked in Russian, then we would not be able to talk in terms of zero morphs for that case.

In derivation, however, the case for a zero morph is less compelling. Consider the English data in (32) below.

(32)   He walked *round* the car.
She was looking *round*.
They sat at the *round* table.
As soon as I *round* the corner, I want you to start running.
I always enjoy theatre in the *round*.

Let us assume that we can work out which *round* is the basic form of all of these (this is feasible but not immediately obvious). That basic type of *round* presumably has no zero morph on the end of it. The others, though, would have a zero morph. So a zero is contrasting with nothing at all, a lack of even a zero. What is more, all the other *rounds* must have different zero morphs, so that different zeros contrast with each other. Even if this state of affairs is possible within a generative theory of morphology, it does not have much plausibility as an account of the way in which real speakers process language. For that reason, the term **conversion** will be used here for the derivational cases illustrated in (29), rather than **zero-derivation**, a term which is also current. A third term is **functional shift**. Some authorities differentiate between some or all of these terms but, for most, they are synonymous.

3.5 CASES INVOLVING SHORTENING BASES

In rather rare cases, the base may actually be longer than the form created from it. Consider the following data from spoken French:

(33)

masculine	*feminine*	*gloss*
movɛ	movɛz	'bad'

œʁø	œʁøz	'happy'
gʁã	gʁãd	'big'
lɔ̃	lɔ̃g	'long'
ʃo	ʃod	'hot'
vɛʁ	vɛʁt	'green'
fʁwa	fʁwad	'cold'
pəti	pətit	'little'
blã	blãʃ	'white'
fʁɛ	fʁɛʃ	'fresh'
fo	fos	'false'

It is clear that the feminine form of these adjectives is the same as the masculine form but with an extra consonant. However, there is no way to predict from the form of the masculine adjective which consonant will be added to make the feminine form. We can only make predictions if we start with the feminine form. Then it is quite simple: if we subtract the final consonant from the feminine form we have the masculine form. Some authorities term this final consonant a **subtractive morph**, a morph which is removed by a morphological process.   → Historical process

In cases where the element subtracted is (or looks like) a morph with an independent existence elsewhere in the language, and especially where the process is a derivational one, we talk of **backformation**. For instance, when P. G. Wodehouse writes: → creation of a shorter word based Principle of transition

(34) I could see that, if not actually disgruntled, he was far from being gruntled.

he forms the word *gruntled* by the deletion of the prefix *dis-*. The lexeme GRUNTLE actually existed at the time that *disgruntled* first appeared in the English language but now a sentence like (34) strikes us as funny because we do not expect to find a lexeme GRUNTLE; we are not familiar with it. *Gruntle* is thus a backformation for a modern speaker. In the line

(35) Little spider, spiding sadly ....

the *-er* that has been deleted is not a real suffix, there is no familiar lexeme to SPIDE. It has, however, the same form as the familiar suffix in words such as *pointer*, *retriever* and *warbler*, and this is sufficient to allow it to be deleted in backformation.

There is one very important point about backformation: in retrospect, it is invisible. It is only noticeable when the backformed (this is an example of backformation!) word is unfamiliar. Unless the difference is pointed out by someone with an understanding of etymology, you could not tell that EDIT comes from EDITOR but that EXHIBITOR comes from EXHIBIT. This has led some linguists to deny that backformation has any synchronic status as a morphological process. But it must be remembered that backformation continues to be synchronically used to produce new lexemes and, thus, must be included in any synchronic grammar.

Another type of shortening is **clipping**. Clipping is the process of shortening a word without changing its meaning or part of speech. As will be clear from the examples given below, clipping frequently does change the stylistic value of the word. As far as is known, there is no way to predict how much of a word will be clipped off in clipping, nor even which end of the word will be clipped off. Neither is it possible to say that any given syllable will definitely be retained in clipping. Some examples from English are given below:

(36)   binoc(ular)s
        deli(catessen)
        (de)tec(tive)
        (head-)shrink(er)
        op(tical) art
        sci(ence) fi(ction)

Since the parts that are deleted in clipping are not clearly morphs in any sense, it is not necessarily the case that clipping is a part of morphology, although it is a way of forming new lexemes.

3.6 PROCESSES INVOLVING SEVERAL LEXEMES

The formation of a new lexeme by adjoining two or more lexemes is called **compounding** or **composition**. Nearly all languages have compounds and, in many languages, compounds are the main type of new lexeme. Some random examples are given in (37).

(37)   *Finnish*   *Maori*
        kirje·kuori   puku·aroha
        letter cover   belly·love
        'envelope'   'sympathetic'
        maa·talous·tuotanto   whare ruuna·nga
        land·economy·production   house draw-together·
                                     nominalisation

'agricultural production'
huone·kalu·tehdas
room·article·factory
'furniture factory'

'meeting house'
mate·wai
lack·water
'(be) thirsty'

French
oiseau·mouche
bird·fly (*n*)
'humming bird'
ouvre·boîte
open·box
'tin opener'
année lumière
year light
'light year'

Vietnamese
bàn·ghê´
table·chair
'furniture'
hỏa·xa
fire·vehicle
'train'
biên chép
jot-down·copy
'transcribe'

Kanuri
súro·zàu
stomach·pain
'stomach ache'
kam·cejí
man·he-killed
'murderer'
nóŋgù·ba
shame·no
'shameless'

Yoruba
í·gbà·lé
noun·sweep·ground
'broom'
ì·bọ·wọ̀
noun·insert·hand
'glove'
oní·ṣ·òwò
having·to-do·trade
'trader'

In the most typical cases, compounds do not contain internal inflections but there are instances where internal inflections (or what appear to be internal inflections) are found:

(38)   *Danish*
        byg·ning·s·fejl
        build·nominalisation·genitive·error
        'astigmatism'
        ny·t·år
        new·neuter·year
        'new year'

        Finnish
        hallit·ukse·ssa·olo·aika
        rule·nominal·in·be·time
        'period in government'
        kansa·n·taju·inen

people·genitive·grasp·adjective
'easily comprehensible'

Icelandic
barn·s·skó·r
child·genitive-singular·shoe·plural
'the shoes of a child'
barn·a·skól·i
child·genitive-plural·school·nominative-singular
'school for children'

Turkish
din·i·bütün
religion·possessive·whole
'devout'
el·i·açık
hand·possessive·open
'generous'

Most of the compounds that have been illustrated so far (though not all) are **endocentric** compounds, that is they denote a sub-class of the items denoted by one of their elements. A *sea-bird* is a kind of *bird*, in Finnish a *huone·kalu·tehdas* is a kind of *tehdas* 'factory', in French a *oiseau-mouche* is a kind of *oiseau* 'bird' and so on. Similarly, if you *type·write* you *write* in a certain way; if something is *grass-green* it is *green* in a certain way. In each of these cases, the compound as a whole is a hyponym of its main or **head** element.

Exocentric compounds, in contrast, denote something which is not a sub-class of either of the elements in the compound, that is they are not hyponyms of either of their elements. An *egg-head*, for example, is neither an *egg* nor a *head*. In French, an *ouvre-boîte* is neither an *ouvre* nor a *boîte*. Names of people, animals and plants are often exocentric compounds, where the compound states some feature of the entity it names:

(39)   *Danish*
grå·ben
grey·leg
'stem canker'
lang·øre
long·ear
'long-eared bat'

English
high·brow

red·skin
yellow·tail

Turkana
ɓ·karì·mɔjɔŋ
plural·thin·old
'the Karimojong tribe'
ɓ·surù·lac
at·mosquito·louse
'type of tree used as medicine against vermin'

Exocentric compounds are sometimes called **bahuvrihi** compounds, 'bahuvrihi' being a Sanskrit exocentric compound meaning 'having much rice'.

Many languages also have compounds which denote an entity made up of the two elements mentioned in the compound together. These compounds are given the Sanskrit name of **dvandva** compounds or are sometimes termed **copulative** compounds. Some examples are given in (40).

(40) *French*
bleu-blanc-rouge
blue·white·red
'the French flag'

Tamil
appaa·v·amma
father·empty-morph·mother
'parents'
aṇṇan·tampi
elder-brother·younger-brother
'brothers' (e.g. 'Do you have any brothers?')

Vietnamese
bàn·ghế
table·chair
'furniture'
sốt·rét
be-hot·be-cold
'malaria'

There are various similar compounds which are often not distinguished from dvandvas but whose status is slightly different. For example, *maid-servant* and *man-servant* might look as though they fit the category above, but *maid* and *man* are really only gender-markers here. A *fighter-bomber* might be a fighter and a bomber but, unlike the real dvandvas, it is not both machines put together but a single machine which has both functions. The same point applies to *actor-director* or *singer-songwriter*. In *a French-English dictionary* or *the Wellington-Auckland flight*, while the two languages or cities might appear on an equal footing, it is the movement between them which is crucial and the order is obviously meaningful, which it is not with clear dvandvas. In that these are sometimes described as dvandvas and sometimes not, their precise status is controversial but they provide a number of categories which should be distinguished from true dvandvas on a careful analysis.

Compounds, such as those that have been illustrated in this section, are sometimes termed **root compounds** (or **primary compounds**). These are contrasted with **synthetic compounds** (or **verbal (nexus) compounds**) where the head element contains a verb as its base and the modifying element contains an element which, in a sentence, could function as an argument of that verb. For example, an English synthetic compound is *dish-washer*. The verb is WASH and the noun DISH could act as the direct object of that verb in a sentence like *We are washing the dishes*. When the compound created in this way is itself a verb, it is normal to speak in terms of **incorporation**. In the most typical cases of incorporation, the noun in the modifying element of the compound has the same semantic function as the direct object of the verb involved. Some typical cases are illustrated in (41).

(41)   *Lahu*
      jĭ thà' dɔ   jĭ dɔ
      liquor accusative drink   liquor drink
      'to drink (the) liquor'   'to drink liquor'

      Tupinambá
      s·oβá a·jos·éj   a·s·oβá·éj
      his·face I·it·wash   I·him·face·wash
      'I washed his face'   'I face-washed him'

In the example from Lahu (which is spoken in China, Myanmar and Thailand) the form in the first column indicates that liquor is drunk, as opposed to tea or water, and we may be dealing with a known type or containerful of liquor. The form in the second column indicates something about drinking liquor in general. In the example from Tupinambá (a language once spoken in Brazil), the face involved is pragmatically the same in either case but, while the form in the first column puts some stress on the fact that it was the face and not the hands or feet which were washed, the form in the second column presents washing faces as a typical unitary action. Note that the verb with an incorporated object in the Lahu example is intransitive, whereas that in the Tupinambá example is transitive.

While, as was stated earlier, the most frequent type of incorporation involves the direct object of the verb, other patterns are also found. Firstly, sometimes a subject noun is incorporated, particularly with an intransitive verb. The first example is from Paiute:

(42)   paːyɨnːaˑxːqaɽɯˈpʊɣa
        fog·begin-to-sit·remote-past
        'It got foggy' (*lit.* fog began to sit)

The next example is from Takelma, a language of Oregon:

(43)   moth·woːkh
        son-in-law·arrived
        'he visited his wife's parents'

Nouns which are in other relationships to the verbs are also found. In (44) there are two examples from the Mexican language, Nahuatl, in the first of which an instrument noun is incorporated and, in the second of which an object of comparison is incorporated. In (45) there is an example from Paiute with an instrument incorporated; and in (46) there is an example from Dasenech (spoken in Kenya and Ethiopia) with a locative incorporated.

(44)   niˑkˑtleˑwatsa in nakatl
        I·it·fire·roast the meat
        'I roast the meat'

        ʃoːtʃiˑkwepoːni in noˑkwik
        flower·blossom it my·song
        'my song blossoms like a flower'

(45)   wiiˑtːonːoˑpːʊɣa
        knife·stab·remote-past
        'he stabbed with a knife'

(46)   ʔanj tikkid' eˑg'orˑhiði
        goat one verbfocus-perfective-3rd-sing·tree·tie-perfective-
        3rd-sing
        'one goat he tied to the tree'

Compounds formed by reduplication were discussed in section 3.2 above.

In English and some other European languages there are also some words which are compounds in one sense, although of a rather unusual variety. The two lexemes involved in their make up are not English lexemes (or lexemes of the other European languages involved) but lexemes of the Classical languages, Greek and Latin. These are words such as:

(47)   biometry
       biology
       geology
       geometry

Their status and the rules governing their formation are not clear at the moment and they are something of a linguistic oddity. Because they are new words coined in modern languages but from Greek and Latin elements, these words are called **neo-classical compounds**.

3.7 ALPHABET-BASED FORMATIONS

Some ways of creating new lexemes (but not ways of creating new word-forms of lexemes) depend upon the existence of a writing system. They are thus not universal since not all languages are written. Neither do they clearly belong under the heading of morphology although they are included here for the sake of completeness. In particular, two types are relevant here, **blends** and **acronyms**.

Blends are also called **portmanteau words** because, as Humpty Dumpty explained to Alice, they are 'like a portmanteau – there are two meanings packed up into one word'. In some cases two words are simply merged where they overlap, so that no information is lost, but repetition of letter combinations is avoided:

(48)   glass + asphalt → glasphalt
       war + orgasm → wargasm
       slang + language → slanguage
       guess + estimate → guestimate
       swell + elegant → swelegant

In many of these cases, the overlap is phonetic as well as orthographic but not in all, as can be seen from *glasphalt* in British Received Pronunciation. In most cases, however, there is no overlap and the new word is created from parts of two other words, with no apparent principles guiding the way in which the two original words are mutilated. Some examples of this type are given below.

(49)   miserable + flimsy → mimsy
        parachute + balloon → paraloon
        dove + hawk → dawk

Here it does not seem to be possible to predict that the words would not be *fliserable* or *balachute* instead of what actually occurs, although there have been some attempts at predicting both the order of the elements in such blends and the final phonetic form for any two given words being blended. It is also extremely doubtful whether such words can be analysed into morphs and, thus, we can question whether they form a real part of morphology. The answer to this may depend on theoretical assumptions about how morphology works (see further below, section 12.5).

Acronyms are words coined from the initial letters of the words in a name, title or phrase. They are more than just abbreviations because they are actually pronounced as new words. In many cases the acronym may be selected before the title which it purports to abbreviate or, at least, the title may be manipulated in order to give an acronym which is considered suitable for the group concerned. This is particularly the case with pressure groups which are in the public eye. Some examples are:

(50)   *AIDS* < Acquired Immunity Deficiency Syndrome
        BASIC < Beginners' All-purpose Symbolic Instruction Code
        SALT < Strategic Arms Limitation Talks
        WASP < White Anglo-Saxon Protestant

Acronyms tend to merge into blends and clipped compounds when more than one letter is taken from each of the words of the title, as in the German *Ge(heime) Sta(ats) Po(lizei)*, 'secret state police' or Gestapo. Other even more complex forms of similar types are found. Consider the following examples from Indonesian, which illustrate both final and medial letters or letter combinations being used to form new lexemes.

(51)   danyon   ← komandan bataliyon   'battalion commandant'
        Ekubang   ← Ekonomi, Keuangan,   'Economics, Finance
                      dan Pembangunan   and Development'
        hansip   ← pertahanan sipil   'civil defence'
        Irjen   ← Inspektur Jendral   'Inspector General'
        zipur   ← zeni tempur   'combat troop'

It will be clear the blends share with compounds the fact that they involve two lexemes in the base. Clippings (see above section 3.5) may also, at least in some cases, be orthographically based.

3.8 UNIQUE MORPHS

Unique morphs are morphs that occur in only one fixed expression in the language under discussion. Occasionally unique morphs can look like potentially free morphs, as English *kith* in *kith and kin* or (at least in the days before scouring powders) *vim* in *vim and vigour*. Even here, though, the morphs are bound to this particular collocation. More frequently there are unique morphs which look like obligatorily bound morphs. Examples are *-ter* in *laughter*, *-ert* in *inert*, *luke* in *lukewarm* and *cran* in *cranberry*. Because of this last example, such items are sometimes called **cranberry morphs**.

The status of unique morphs is determined by parallelism with other morphs which are not unique. The *-ter* in *laughter* is seen to be a suffix because of parallels with things like *arriv·al, marri·age, inject·ion* which also have a verb in first position, where the meanings are relatable and where there are clearly repeated suffixes in parallel constructions. *Cran* is considered to be some kind of root because of parallels with *blackberry, blueberry, cloudberry, snowberry, waxberry* and the like. We must demand parallels of a general type before we analyse a unique morph in order to avoid analysing a unique morph *h-* in *hear*.

The meaning associated with a unique morph is determined by subtracting the meanings associated with the known morphs in the construction from the meaning of the construction as a whole. So the meaning associated with *cran* is precisely what makes cranberries a subset of all berries.

3.9 SUPPLETION

Although morphologists are continually seeking regularities in the patterns of language, there comes a time when they have to admit defeat, when word-forms of what appear to be the same lexeme are so different from each other that they cannot be derived by general rules at all. In such cases, we talk of **suppletion**. Consider, for example, regular verbs in French. The patterns in the present, future and imperfect can be illustrated with the regular verb DONNER 'to give':

(52)   je donn·e   je donn·er·ai   je donn·ais

In this verb, the root *donn-* can be seen in all three forms. However, when we look at the verb ALLER 'to go', the pattern is completely different:

(53)   je vais   j'ir·ai   j'all·ais

Although some of the endings can still be recognised, the roots are so completely different that we talk of them as being **suppletive forms**. Historically this is explained by the fact that they are derived from different verbs. Suppletion is shown in English in the lexeme GOOD with the two forms *good* and *better*, and in the lexeme GO with the two forms *go* and *went*. In the examples cited, it is not controversial to claim that suppletion is involved. We shall see later, though, that the boundaries of suppletion are not clear and that different people draw them in different places.

3.10 CONCLUSION

It can be seen that there are a large number of ways of building words in the languages of the world. Compounding is an extremely common method of forming new lexemes, otherwise affixation and, in particular, suffixation is clearly the most common way of building words. Other processes can, to a certain extent, be seen as deviations from this expected norm. In most languages which have morphological structure they are minority formations. They are the processes which cause problems of description. Some explanation of why this should be will be given in Chapter 14.

REFERENCES AND FURTHER READING

The quotation on page 24 is from an anonymous review of Bauer (1983) published in the periodical *Choice*, for November, 1983.

Example (5) is taken from Matthews (1972: 132), and (6) is from the same work, page 94. Many similar examples can be found in that book.

The terms interfix, circumfix and transfix, while not widespread in morphological discussions, can be found in, for example, Bergenholtz & Mugdan (1979). The term empty morph is from Hockett (1947). The suggestion about simulfix is from Hockett (1954).

Although Lukas (1937) calls the forms in (27) 'tenses', 'moods' might be a better label.

For a discussion of how to determine which part of speech is basic in cases of conversion such as those in (32), see Marchand (1964).

Although it was stated on page 40 that nearly all languages have compounds, there are some languages which have relatively few compounds and in which compounding may not be productive. Dimmendaal (1983: 292) says that the Nilotic language Turkana is one such but his suggestion that this is typical of verb-initial languages does not seem to hold up, as can be seen from the Polynesian languages. For some discussion of this point and compounds in general, see Bauer (2001a).

Brandt (1984) points out that 'cranberry morph' is in fact a misnomer since *cran* is, etymologically speaking, a regularly derived version of *crane* (the bird) and could, thus, simply be an allomorph of {crane}. There is plenty of comparative Germanic evidence to support this. He suggests a Danish replacement, *brombær* 'blackberry', where *bær* means 'berry' and *brom* has no independent existence. *Bilberry* might be a more coherent English example. Despite the etymological inaccuracy, the label 'cranberry morph' is widely recognised.

For more details on acronyms, backformation, clipping, blends, conversion and neoclassical compounding with specific reference to English, see the appropriate sections of Bauer (1983). For more detail on prefixation, suffixation, infixation, reduplication, replacive and subtractive morphs, see Chapter 7 of Matthews (1991). For incorporation see Gerdts (1998). For circumfixes, transfixes and modification of the base, see Spencer (1998).

Data from various languages (including those in the exercises) has been gleaned from the following sources: Achenese from Lawler (1977), Afrikaans from Botha (1984a), Chrau from Thomas (1971), Dasenech from Sasse (1984), Dinka from Gleason (1955), Dutch from de Haas & Trommelen (1993), Egyptian Arabic from Mitchell (1956, 1962), Finnish from Karlsson (1983), Frisian from Tiersma (1985), Hua from Haiman (1998), Icelandic from Einarsson (1945), Indonesian from Dardjowidjojo (1979), Kanuri from Lukas (1937), Khmer from Jacob (1968) and Ehrman (1972), Lahu from Mithun (1984), Mam from England (1983), Maori from W. Bauer (1981a, b, personal communication), Moroccan Arabic from Harrell (1962), Motu from Taylor (1970), Nahuatl from Sapir (1911), Paiute from Sapir (1911), Sesotho from Doke & Mofokeng (1957), Swahili from Ashton (1944), Tagalog from Blake (1925) and Gleason (1955), Takelma from Sapir (1911), Tamil from Asher (1982), Tupinambá from Mithun (1984), Turkana from Dimmendaal (1983), Turkish from Lewis (1967), Tyvan from Anderson & Harrison (1999), Welsh from Williams (1980), Vietnamese from Thompson (1965), Yoruba from Rowlands (1969).

EXERCISES

1. Turkish
The data below is presented in orthography: <ö> = [œ], <y> = [j], <c>
= [ʤ], <ş> = [ʃ], <ü> = [y]

el	'hand'	eller	'hands'
köy	'village'	köyler	'villages'
diş	'tooth'	dişler	'teeth'
gün	'day'	günler	'days'
gece	'night'	geceler	'nights'
civciv	'chick'	civciver	
soför		şoförler	'drivers'

What would you predict the Turkish word for 'chicks' and for 'driver'
would be? What kind of affix is used and what does it mean? What
is the root in the word meaning 'nights'?

2. (Southern) Sotho or Sesotho
The data below is presented in transcription.

marabɛ	'puff-adder'	bomarabɛ	'puff adders'
matsale	'mother-in-law'	bomatsale	'mothers-in-law'
ɱampʊli	'chief herd boy'	boɱampʊli	'chief herd boys'
rakhali	'maternal uncle'	borakhali	'maternal uncles'
raŋoanı	'paternal uncle'	boraŋʊanı	
		bomaŋkhanı	'bats'

What would you predict the Sesotho word for 'paternal uncles' and
that for 'bat' to be? What is likely to be the difference between /maŋ/
and /bomaŋ/ both of which can be glossed as 'who'? What kind of
affix is illustrated in this data? What is the base for the affixation in
the word meaning 'maternal uncles'?

3. Moroccan Arabic
The data below is presented in transcription.

ʁɛtta	'cover'	tʁɛtta	'be covered'
ʃaf	'see'	tʃaf	'be seen'
ƭuwweƭ	'lengthen'	ƫƫuwweƭ	'be lengthened'

What kind of affix is illustrated in the data here? What is the form of
the affix? What is the meaning of the affix? What is the base of the
word meaning 'be covered'? From what you have learned about
Arabic in the chapter, is this base likely to be a root?

4. Cambodian or Khmer

The data below is presented in transcription.

de:k	'to sleep'	dɔmne:k	'sleep'
kat	'to cut'	kɔmnat	'piece cut off'
suo	'to ask'	sɔmnuo	'question'

Identify the affix illustrated in the data set above. What kind of affix is it? What is its form? What is its meaning?

5. Dutch

The data below is presented in orthography: <g> = [x], <v> = [f], <e> = [ə] when unstressed (the first syllable of each root is stressed), double vowel letters indicate long vowels.

been	'bone'	gebeente	'skeleton'
berg	'mountain'	gebergte	'mountain range'
raam	'frame'	geraamte	'framework'
stern	'star'	gesternte	'stars'
vogel	'bird'	gevogelte	'poultry'

NB: There is no Dutch word *gebeen nor *beente (and similarly for the other examples).

What kind of affix is illustrated here? What is the form of the affix? What is its meaning? What is the root in the word meaning 'framework'?

6. Tyvan

The data below is presented in orthography: <ɪ> = [ɯ], <ü> = [y], <č> = [ʧ]

qɪzɪl	'red'	qɪpqɪzɪl	'completely red'
uzun	'long'	upuzun	'very long'
türgen	'quickly'	tüptürgen	'very quickly'
činge	'thin'	čipčinge	'very thin'

What kind of affix is illustrated in this data? How is the affix formed? What does the affix mean (approximately)? Is there an infix involved here?

7. Hua

The data below is presented in orthography.

dogue	'I will eat'
dogane	'you will eat'

dogie	's/he will eat'
dogue	'we two will eat'
dega'e	'you two will eat'
dega'e	'they two will eat'
dogune	'we all will eat'
degae	'you all will eat'
degae	'they all will eat'

What do you think is the root in the above forms? How many allomorphs does the root have? What are they? Can you tell how they are conditioned? What do you think is the future morpheme in this data? What are the allomorphs of the future marker? The person markers are *-e, -'e* and *-ne,* but the logic behind their distribution is not obvious. What phenomenon can be observed in the forms of the root and the forms of the future marker?

8. Is *feck* in *feckless* a prefix? How can you tell? Is *ric* in *bishopric* a suffix? How can you tell?

PART TWO: Elaboration

CHAPTER 4

Defining the Word-Form

In Chapter 2 we defined word-forms in terms of orthographic words and we noted that this was a matter which would have to receive further attention. As we saw in that chapter (p. 11), there are no gaps between the words in the spoken language as there are in the written language. Many of the languages of the world are still not written languages and, in the history of the world, the majority of languages have not been written. We, thus, need to know how to define word-forms in languages where we do not have an orthography to help or where the orthography is not helpful in this regard. We also need to know whether there is any reason for the division into orthographic words that happens to be used in English (or, mutatis mutandis, any other written language), or whether that is merely convention. On the face of it, this seems fairly unlikely. Speakers of English have, on the whole, a fairly good intuition about what 'a word' is although there are a few marginal cases where intuitions are unclear: cases such as *all right, nonetheless, insofar as*. This, it might be objected, could simply be the result of general literacy in the society. In response, it could be pointed out that even pre-literate children in our society have a reasonable notion of where the words begin and end, as is shown by questions of the type 'What does X mean?', where X represents some string that adults would happily term a word. There is also a certain amount of evidence (though perhaps not enough to make a categorical statement on the subject) that non-literate speakers of unwritten languages know where words begin and end in their languages. It, thus, seems that we are dealing with some fairly clear intuitions in this area. Of course, we need not necessarily expect that word-forms of the written language will overlap exactly with word-forms of the spoken language but we should be surprised if there was no overlap at all.

There are two major sets of criteria which can help us to define a word-form for the spoken language. The first set is phonological and defines what we might term a **phonological word**. However, the phonological criteria, such as they are, do not operate in all languages and, in some languages, define strings which do not correspond to orthographic words or words defined by other criteria.

The best way of defining word-forms turns out to be by morphological and syntactic criteria, and a discussion of them will take up the main part of this chapter.

4.1 PHONOLOGICAL CRITERIA

The phonological criteria that can be used to define the phonological word are a disparate group. They may not all function in the same language and, indeed, may not define the same unit as a word in a single language. Nevertheless, there are a number of phenomena relating to the phonological word which recur across languages. These are dealt with here under three rather broad headings: stress, vowel harmony and phonological processes.

4.1.1 Stress

In many languages there is a tendency for each word-form to carry a single stress. This is to be understood in the following way. If a sentence is said in English as a statement, with falling intonation, there will usually be one neutral place where that fall will come: on the last potentially prominent word in the sentence. It will, however, be possible to move that intonational fall to virtually any other word in the sentence, usually then implying some kind of contrast. But, whatever word the fall comes on in the sentence, there will only be one syllable in each word on which it can come. So, in the sentence below, the intonational fall could, under appropriate circumstances, fall on any word but only on the syllable preceded by a stress mark in those words.

(1) Antidisestablishmen'tarianism 'was sup'posedly 'the 'longest 'English 'lexeme.

In this sense, there is only one stress for each lexeme in English. The same is not true in French, for example, where this criterion defines a phonological phrase.

Notice, however, that the description of English given above is not quite accurate. Other positions are possible for stress within the word-form when there is explicit contrast with another, partially similar word-form. Thus, we can find utterances like:

(2)   I didn't say aw'ful, I said or'chid.
        I said 'replay but I meant 'display.

where the stress apparently falls on 'the wrong syllable'. In cases like this, it is never possible to have two contrastive stresses in the same word-form. So both of these types help to define the word-form.

In some languages, stress regularly falls on a specific syllable in the word. In Czech, Finnish and Icelandic, for example, it regularly falls on the first syllable of a word, in Polish and Swahili on the penultimate syllable of the word. In such languages, stress serves a demarcative function, separating off the words from each other and showing the position of the beginning or the end of the word. It also defines the word-form. Notice, however, that, in a language like Icelandic, prepositions are not stressed and will, therefore, by this criterion, be designated as belonging to the end of the previous phonological word. Nevertheless, stress remains a useful way to help define word-forms.

4.1.2 Vowel harmony

In a language which has vowel harmony, all the vowels in the word-form share some phonetic feature such as backness, closeness or unroundedness. Languages which have vowel harmony include Finnish, Hungarian, Turkish and Twi. Typically, this means that affixes have (at least) two distinct allomorphs, phonetically conditioned by the vowels in the base. Consider the following examples from Finnish:

(3)   otta·a   's/he takes'   pitä·ä   's/he likes'
        otta·vat   'they take'   pitä·vät   'they like'
        otta·vat·ko   'do they take'   pitä·vät·kö   'do they like'

It can be seen from these examples that the morphemes {3rd person singular}, {3rd person plural} and {interrogative} take different forms (have different allomorphs), depending on which root they are added to. If the root contains front vowels, then the affixes also contain front vowels; if the root contains back vowels, the affixes also contain back vowels. (Vowels marked orthographically with an Umlaut are front vowels.) In languages like this, the word-form can be defined in terms of the domain of the vowel harmony.

There are, however, some problems with this. First of all, in Finnish and Turkish (and most languages that have vowel harmony), compounds are defined as sequences of separate word-forms, by this criterion, because vowel harmony only determines vowel quality in affixes. Secondly, some languages with vowel harmony allow a few exceptions to the harmony. In Turkish, for instance, there are a few foreign loan words which do not observe vowel harmony (although most do) and there are a few invariable suffixes which retain their form independent of the vowels in the base.

Despite these few irregularities, in those languages which have it, vowel harmony provides a good way of helping to define the phonological word.

4.1.3 Phonological processes

There are innumerable phonological processes in the languages of the world whose application is determined by the boundaries of units larger than the segment. Some can apply only at the end of a syllable, some only at the beginning of a morpheme and so on. The application of some of these processes is influenced by a unit which, for other reasons, we can identify as a word-form. These processes thus provide an extra way of determining where the boundaries of the word-form fall. It is, of course, not possible to give a complete list of such processes but a couple of examples should suffice to make the point.

In German, the nominative and accusative singular forms of the lexemes RAT 'council' and RAD 'wheel' are homophonous: both *Rat* and *Rad* are pronounced /raːt/. The dative singular forms of these lexemes, however, are pronounced differently from each other. *Rat·e* and *Rad·e* are distinguished in pronunciation in that the former has a /t/ where the latter has a /d/, as shown by the spelling. It is, in fact, a general rule that you never find any voiced obstruent in final position in the word-form in German. This is usually formulated as a phonological rule of obstruent devoicing which applies word-finally. Note that the devoicing does not occur morpheme finally (*Rade*) but only word-finally (*Rad*). Places where this rule of obstruent devoicing apply thus help to determine the final position in the word-form and so help to determine the boundaries of the phonological word.

In Sengseng, a language of Papua New Guinea, geminate consonants occur within the word-form but never across word-form boundaries. When like consonants occur at the end and beginning of adjacent words, they are separated with a schwa. Thus, in (4b) below, there is an inserted schwa, marking the boundaries of the word-forms, although there is no inserted schwa between the identical /t/s in (4a), since these occur within a word-form. Again this allows a phonological definition of a word-form.

(4) (a)   εt·tihon
          she·reflexive
          'herself'

   (b)   εt mihin ə nis
         she head-3rd-person-singular-possessive hot
         'she has a headache'

4.2 MORPHOLOGICAL AND SYNTACTIC CRITERIA

The Bloomfieldian definition of the word-form is 'a minimum free form'. This means that a word-form can stand as an utterance on its own but also that it is the smallest unit which can do this: it is not made up entirely of smaller units which can also stand alone as utterances.

There are cases where elements smaller than the word-form can stand alone as utterances but these are all in contexts such as the following:

(5) A: Did you say 'incur' or 'recur'?
    B: In.

Examples of this type show language **mention** and not language **use**. The same is true of lists of affixes, such as can be found in Linguistics books. In language use, it is not possible for prefixes and the like to occur as isolated utterances.

Even so, many years after this definition was proposed, it is still one of the best definitions of the word-form that are available; but there are some problems with it. The first is that, by this definition, compounds will always appear to be phrases and not word-forms. This is possibly not terribly serious. We have already seen that vowel harmony also treats compound words as sequences of two word-forms rather than as single word-forms. More seriously, it seems that words which can stand alone as utterances are precisely those words which can form a larger constituent by themselves: plural countable nouns, pronouns, intransitive verbs and so on. *Chair, must, consumes* are not minimum free forms in language use, while *chairs, red* and *eat* are. This seems to imply that the definition actually delimits a subset of word-forms and this only by accident. In particular, there are a number of items that we would normally consider to be word-forms (and that we would treat orthographically as word-forms) which will be completely excluded by this definition. These are words such as articles, conjunctions and prepositions, especially in their unstressed forms. You cannot simply walk up to someone and say 'The'. Nor will the form *the* be a suitable part of a dialogue, except in mention contexts like (5) and extraordinarily rare instances of contrast. By Bloomfield's definition, therefore, they will not be considered word-forms. Bloomfield himself was not very happy with this result and tried to avoid it by saying that such words were paradigmatically commutable with units which were minimum free forms. So the word-form *the* could be isolated by parallelism with *that*, which can stand in isolation. There are various problems with this kind of approach, perhaps the most striking of which is that affixes could be claimed to be word-forms using the same kind of arguments and this would be undesirable. Consider the following examples, for instance:

(6)   ex·president   metal(l)·oid
        former president   metal-like

It is perhaps better to conclude that forms like *the* are not word-forms according to Bloomfield's definition. There are then two possibilities. The first is that orthographic words do not coincide with word-forms in the spoken language; the second is that Bloomfield's definition needs to be improved upon. Attempts to improve upon this definition though, have not provided a better formulation of the definition but discussed a number of criteria which units must meet in order to be considered word-forms. There are three major criteria which are discussed in this context:

(a) Positional mobility
(b) Uninterruptability
(c) Internal stability

These three aspects of the word-form are interrelated.

Positional mobility means that the word-form as a whole can be moved, relatively easily, within the sentence. In some languages, this mobility is greater than in others. In English, the mobility is mainly seen in sentences, like those in (7), where one particular part of the sentence comes under focus.

(7)   This we must see.
        Plums I love.
        Shorts you'll never get me into.

In such cases (and also in cases like passivisation where, on some analyses, noun phrases swap positions) it is always at least a word-form which is moved, it is always a whole number of word-forms that are moved and the word-form is always moved so that it does not interrupt other word-forms. In a language like Latin, word-forms show much greater positional mobility than they do in English. For example, under appropriate conditions, any of the following would be an acceptable sentence of Latin:

(8)   Bru:tus Caesarem occi:dit.
        Caesarem occi:dit Bru:tus.
        Occi:dit Caesarem Bru:tus.
        'Brutus killed Caesar.'

Not only is it the case that major constituents may occur in any order but the elements of those constituents need not always occur together, as is illustrated by the following example from Classical Greek (Herodotos, I, 30, 3):

(9)   nun o:n   himeros epeiresthai moi   epe:lthe   se
        now therefore a-desire to-ask   to-me has-come you

        ei tina   e:de: panto:n eides   olbio:taton
        if someone   already   of-all   you-have-seen most-fortunate

        'Now therefore a desire has come over me to ask you whether you have already seen someone who is most fortunate of all.'

Uninterruptability means that extraneous material cannot be introduced into the middle of the word-form. Consider the examples below from Danish, which illustrate this point. In Danish, there are two forms of the definite article, one preposed and one postposed. The postposed definite article forms a single word with the noun it is attached to, while the preposed one does not. (10a) is a piece of genuine literary Danish and (10b-e) provide variant orderings of morphs to illustrate the point.

(10) (a) Lærer·en kunde se ud, som om han spiste smaa Børn ristede
         teacher·the could look as if he ate small children grilled

'The teacher might look as though he ate small children grilled'.

(b) de smaa Børn ristede
    the small children grilled

(c) Børn·ene ristede
    children·the grilled

(d) de smaa ristede Børn
    the small grilled children

(e) *Børn ristede -ene
    children grilled the

This criterion is actually very difficult to formulate precisely. It is clear that there is a sense in which word-forms can be interrupted.

(11)   *Czech:*   zpívám   zpívávám
                  'I sing'   'I am accustomed to sing'

       English: sensationism   sensationalism
                  kings   kingdoms

       French: arrivions   arriverions
                  'we were arriving' 'we would arrive'

       Latin: amat   ama:bat
                  's/he loves'   's/he used to love'

The point, according to Lyons, is that one can insert material between word-forms 'more or less freely' and that one cannot insert material into the middle of word-forms with the same degree of freedom. Matthews says that 'the point is that [the word-form] cannot be interrupted by rearranged material from elsewhere in a given sentence'. Even these general constraints appear to be broken by the exceptional case of the expletive insertion rule in English that gives rise to forms like *absobloodylutely* and so on.

Internal stability means that the ordering of items within the word-form is usually fixed and non-contrastive, as opposed to the ordering of word-forms within the sentence. Given a Latin word such as that in (12), it is not possible to rearrange the order of the morphs.

(12)   reg·e:·b·ant·ur   'they were being ruled'

Reg·b·ur·e:·ant is simply not possible in Latin. The word-forms in a sentence, however, are much more moveable (the criterion of positional mobility discussed above), so that all of the sentences in (8) are perfectly grammatical.

There are languages where the ordering of elements within the word-form does appear to be contrastive and meaningful. Some examples are given below.

(13) *Japanese:* nag·ur·ase·rare
                   hit·present·causative·passive
                   'is made to hit'
                   nag·ur·are·sase
                   hit·present·passive·causative
                   'causes to be hit'

      English: bibl·ic·ist   arm·chair
                  bibl·ist·ic   chair·arm

      Turkish: misafir·se·ler
                  guest·be-conditional·plural
                  'if they are guests'
                  misafir·ler·se
                  guest·plural·be-conditional
                  'if they are the guests'

It appears, however, that even here examples like this are rare. Languages such as Eskimo, which appear to provide regular counter-examples, turn out not to provide genuine ones. In Labrador Inuttut, the following two examples, differing only in the order in which the morphemes are realised, have clearly different meanings (the allomorphy for the 3rd person singular is irrelevant here). What is more, the example is fairly typical.

(14) pi·guma·jau·juk
      empty-base·want·passive·3rd-person-singular
      'He is wanted'

      pi·jau·guma·vuk
      empty-base·passive·want·3rd-person-singular
      'He wants it done to him'

However, in this case, there are simply a number of positions in which the passive morph can occur and it may occur in more than one, as is shown by:

(15) taku·jau·tit·tau·gasugi·jau·juk
      see·passive·cause·passive·believe·passive·3rd-person-singular
      'He was believed to have been made to be seen.'

These three criteria of positional mobility, uninterruptability and internal stability could be classed together as defining the **internal cohesion** of the word-form. But to go no further than to consider these three criteria is to miss a very important point – namely that they, as well as several others, are criteria which are generally used to determine constituency in syntax. What we seem to be saying, therefore, is that word-forms are special kinds of constituents. In the classical languages, it appears that this special kind of constituent can be defined reasonably well in terms of the three criteria already discussed. In other languages, including probably English, they are not, it seems, sufficient. Under these circumstances it is worth considering other tests for constituency and seeing whether they are also helpful in defining the word-form.

Most such tests, while they agree in isolating the word-form as some kind of constituent, do not isolate it uniquely: either they show that the word-form and units larger than the word-form are constituents or they show that the word-form and units smaller than the word-form are constituents, or, most frequently, both. One test, however, does seem to be useful, namely that, under appropriate discourse conditions, a constituent may be omitted. For example, word-forms can be deleted in conversations like the following:

(16)   A: Chris can't come.
        B: But Jean can [sc. come].

        A: Did you see the red file?
        B: No, only the blue [sc. file].

        A: Did you see her in January?
        B: No, [sc. in] February.

It appears that affixes cannot be omitted under similar discourse conditions. The following are thus impossible conversations:

(17)   A: I think it's disgraceful
        B: *And [sc. dis]gusting

        A: I think it's disgraceful.
        B: *But hope[sc. ful].

There are two points to note about this criterion for English. The first is that it does allow us to isolate words like *the* as word-forms. As far as I can make out, most people seem to find the following a perfectly possible conversation:

(18)   A: We saw the engine.
         B: And [sc. the] guard's van

Secondly, this test does marginally allow a base to be deleted when that base is a potentially free morph. The following conversation is perhaps a little odd but perfectly comprehensible.

(19)   A: Have you learnt to encode?
         B: And de-[sc. code].

This last criterion thus seems to allow us to define the word-form in English as the smallest unit which can be omitted when it would be identical with another element which occurred earlier in the discourse. This does not prove, of course, that this criterion will work for all languages. In fact, as far as I can see, it will not work for French, in the sense that it will not isolate articles in that language. (We might conclude that articles are less word-like in French than in English.) Nevertheless, it does seem to indicate that word-forms are particular types of constituent and this may explain why they are isolatable by pre-literate speakers.

An interesting question, but one that we shall not attempt to answer here, would be whether the way of defining a word-form for a given language correlates in any significant way with other syntactic facts about that language. It seems likely that a language in which positional mobility is a defining factor will be a language with a fairly free word order and this is likely to be a language which is fairly highly inflected. In this context, it would be very interesting to know just how the word-form can be defined in a language like Eskimo (see, for example, the word-form from Labrador Inuttut in (15) above) and to what extent the criteria that have been discussed in this chapter are useful there.

REFERENCES AND FURTHER READING

The source of the comment on speakers of unwritten languages on page 57 is Sapir (1921: 34).

Stress and intonation are very complex areas and no attempt has been made here to be systematic in introducing the topics. Indeed, even the use of the term 'stress' is controversial. For an introduction to these areas, Brown (1977) is recommended.

Details of Finnish vowel harmony (which is presented here in a slightly simplified form) can be found in Karlsson (1983: 21). For details of Turkish vowel harmony, see Lewis (1967: 15–20). Suomi (1985) gives a clear discussion of the problems of isolating word-forms in Finnish despite demarcative stress and vowel harmony in that language.

The data on Sengseng is from Ann Chowning (personal communication).

The definition of a word-form as a minimal free form can be found in Bloomfield (1935: 178) (it is called there simply a 'word'). This definition is also discussed in Lyons (1968: 201–2) and the three criteria on page 62 are also discussed by Lyons. Lyons also makes the use/mention distinction and discusses it again (rather briefly but with references) in Lyons (1977: 6).

Some of the examples in (11) and the quotation on page 64 are taken from Matthews (1972: 98, footnote). The quotation from Lyons on the same page is from Lyons (1968: 204).

On the rule of expletive insertion in English, see Bauer (1983: 89–91) and McMillan (1980).

The examples from Labrador Inuttut are from Smith (1982a).

For a discussion of constituency in syntax, see, for example, Chapter 2 of Radford (1981).

EXERCISES

1. For English or for any other language with which you are familiar, find cases where native speakers can be in doubt as to how many words are involved. Do such instances fall into a small number of types or are they random across the language? How frequent are such cases? What do you conclude about how well people know where the ends of words fall?

2. Find examples of writing from children who are just learning to write. (A suitable example can be found in Kress 1997: 81 if you do not have access to the writings of local children.) On the basis of their writing, how far do you think children's notion of a word corresponds to the adult notion of a word? What can you conclude on the basis of this?

3. Note that, even at the end of this chapter, we do not seem to have a particularly good definition of a word-form, even less one which we know a priori will be of immediate use in the next language we happen to investigate. Various conclusions might be possible on this basis, including (a) there is no such thing as a 'word' defined

universally, only language-specific words; (b) there is no such thing as a word in any language; (c) the notion of 'word' may be useful in some pre-theoretical sense but linguists should avoid it because they can never know what they are talking about; (d) there is a universal notion of word, we just have not quite managed to specify it properly (perhaps because we expect phonological, morphosyntactic and semantic criteria to delimit the same unit and they do not); (e) 'word' is a culturally-determined construct, not a linguistic given. Argue a case for any one of these positions or for your own alternative.

4. What would a language with no words be like? How would it function? Do you know any language which comes close?

CHAPTER 5

Productivity

In recent years, productivity has come to be seen as one of the key issues in the study of derivational morphology. It is also traditionally viewed as being one of the factors which separates inflection from derivation, as we shall see in Chapter 6. Yet, despite its importance, it is still poorly understood and the issues have not all been worked out. In this chapter, I shall present a rather idiosyncratic view of productivity, though one which I believe is becoming more generally accepted in the linguistic community as a whole.

There are two important things to notice about productivity. The first is that productivity is not all or nothing, but a matter of more or less, and the second is that it is a synchronic notion. These two points are actually entwined and frequently confused in discussions of productivity, but an attempt will be made here to keep them apart.

5.1 PRODUCTIVITY AS A CLINE

Any process is said to be productive to the extent that it can be used in the production of new forms in the language. Let us illustrate this with some phonological processes and then go onto some morphological examples.

In Middle English, there was a general tendency to shorten stressed vowels which were in the antepenultimate syllable of words. This applied particularly to words of foreign origin but was to a lesser extent true of native vocabulary too. As a result of this process we today have a short vowel in each of the words listed in (1a) below, despite the long vowel in the related word in (1b).

(1) (a) cavity   (b) cave
      cranberry   crane
      gratitude   grateful
      heroine   hero
      holiday   holy
      legacy   legal
      Michaelmas   Michael
      natural   nature
      situate   site
      solitude   sole
      specify   species
      tyranny   tyrant

This rule was probably never fully productive. That is, it was probably never the case that this rule applied to all words of three or more syllables which were stressed on the antepenultimate syllable. Words such as *favourite* are probably genuine exceptions. Modern inventions and loan words, however, do not necessarily fit with this rule. Examples are presented in (2).

(2)   ˈautocite
        kurchaˈtovium
        peneˈtralium
        ˈTethian
        ˈvirion
        Zaˈirean
        Zhdaˈnovian

In other cases, though, the rule is still adhered to by some or all speakers. In words like ˈ*Piscean* and *paraˈcetamol* there is variation between a long and a short vowel in the stressed syllable, despite long vowels being the norm in the related *Pisces* and *acetic*, and in ˈ*negritude* the short vowel is in general use. This shortening rule has, thus, gone, in the course of the last 500 years or so, from being extremely (though not necessarily entirely) productive to being of limited productivity.

At the other end of the scale, we have a rule which is currently very productive. It is the rule determining the distribution of /n/ and /ŋ/ before a velar stop, that is, before /k/ or /g/. The rule governing this process varies slightly from one variety of English to another and is dependent to a certain extent on formality and so on, as well as on geographical variety. However, we can say that /ŋ/ is always found before a syllable-final /k/ or /g/ but may not be found before a word-boundary, a morpheme boundary or a syllable-boundary. That is, in the list in (3), in any given style or variety, there is more likely to be /n/ at the top of the list and bound to be /ŋ/ at the bottom of the list:

(3)   John Gielgud
        can go
        in case
        incredible
        incoherent
        syncopated
        finger
        blink

This rule is still productive so that new words which fit the input conditions, that is which can be subject to the rule, are automatically included in the rule in the same way that existing words are included in that style or variety. This can be seen in words and expressions like those in (4).

(4)   Piscean guy
        in-crowd
        incapacitant
        oncogene
        rinky-dink
        funky

Here, therefore, we have a process which is extremely productive in current English.

Note, of course, that both these processes are productive in modern English: the shortening rule is used to produce some new forms, the rule determining the distribution of /ŋ/ is used in determining comparatively many forms. To make a terminological distinction, we can say that both of these processes are **available** but the second one is much more **profitable**. (Availability and profitability can be seen as different types of productivity.) At the same time, providing any quantitative measure of profitability is extremely controversial. We cannot easily attach numbers to the degree of productivity. Neither does just saying that something is 'available' tell us a great deal because we need to know how profitable the process is before we can tell what that implies. This is extremely unsatisfactory but the best we can do at the moment. Productivity has to remain a comparative notion. Theoretically, we might be able to talk about complete or full or total productivity if we could guarantee that the process would apply without exception every time its input conditions were met.

Unfortunately, we cannot even do that. Firstly, it is rare that we can state anything with that degree of certainty in Linguistics. Secondly, and less trivially, in morphology it is often extremely difficult to state the input conditions with the requisite degree of accuracy. We shall return to this point.

Turning now to morphology, consider the case of the suffix *-th* which creates abstract nouns. Here it is possible to give an exhaustive list of the lexemes of English which clearly contain this suffix, and also an exhaustive list of those lexemes which may contain it, but there is doubt in the minds of many speakers. Lists are provided below as (5) and (6).

(5)		(6)	
	breadth		(after)math
	coolth		berth
	dearth		birth
	depth		breath
	girth		broth
	greenth		death
	growth		drouth
	health		faith
	highth		filth
	length		girth
	ruth		mirth
	spilth		month
	stealth		mowth
	strength		sloth
	tilth		troth
	truth		worth
	warmth		wrath
	wealth		wreath
	width		youth

Some of the words in both these lists may be unfamiliar and not all of the words in (6) are etymologically derived with the *-th* suffix. This is, however, irrelevant for the present purpose, which is to show that the distribution of this suffix can be stated in terms of lexemes. It is not possible, except as a joke, to coin a word such as *newth* on the basis of *truth* and speak of the newth of the growth in spring. *Greenth* is, in any case, extremely rare and old-fashioned but, on that basis, you would not speak of the *blackth* of coal or of the night. This suffix is now not available or is non-productive.

At the other end of the scale, it seems that the suffix *-able* is extremely profitable when added to transitive verbs. It would not be possible in principle to make an exhaustive list of all cases of -*able* suffixed to a base which is a transitive verb because, every time a new transitive verb is formed, -*able* can also be added to it. You may not know what it means to *Koreanise* the US economy (because I have just this moment invented the word) but, given that it exists, you know that it is possible to discuss the degree to which the US economy is *Koreanisable*. This is an extremely productive (profitable) suffix.

As with the phonological cases, we have no uncontroversial measure of how profitable a particular morphological process is and this remains an unsatisfactory state of affairs. But we can say that one process is more profitable than another or, in one limiting case, is not even available. Again, it would theoretically be possible to say that a process was fully productive but that involves us in specifying the productive rule with great precision and that we probably cannot do properly. In fact, it is not clear whether we could say that any morphological process is fully productive in this sense. We shall see later in this chapter why it is so difficult to tell. Even inflectional affixes, which are frequently assumed to be fully productive, usually show some exceptions (see below, section 6.4).

5.2 PRODUCTIVITY AS SYNCHRONIC

It was stated above that the suffixation of -*th* to form abstract nouns in English is no longer available. Yet clearly it was available at some stage in the history of English, otherwise the relevant words in (5) and (6) could not have been formed. The process used to be available (or productive) but no longer is. We cannot sensibly talk about the productivity of a morphological process without implicitly talking about the time at which this process is productive. When we say nothing about the time, the implication is that we are speaking of productivity in the current state of the language we are dealing with. If we were discussing sixteenth-century English, we would have to conclude that -*th* suffixation was productive although there might be severe constraints on the bases with which it was productive, so that there were never very many words formed in -*th*. That is, we can speak of productivity in synchronic terms, or of changes in productivity in diachronic terms, but not of productivity as such in diachronic terms.

But this creates problems. The -*th* suffix in the words in (5), at least, can be clearly recognised, even in current English. The linguist can analyse the words which contain this suffix and thereby, isolate the suffix. This suggests that we have to draw a clear distinction between morphs which are productive and those which are **analysable**. All productive morphs are also analysable but not all analysable ones are necessarily productive. Furthermore, we need to be able to distinguish between the degree to which something is profitable and the degree to which it is analysable. Let us speak of the extent to which the remains of a morphological process are analysable in the established words of a language as the extent to which that process is **generalised**. We can now say that the degree of generalisation of an affix in the vocabulary of a language is a reflection of the past productivity (past profitability) of that affix. The -*th* affix is not widely generalised: there are relatively few words in (5). But other affixes are widely generalised, even if they are not productive. One possible example is the suffix -*ment* that is found in words like *chastisement, government, shipment, treatment*. There are hundreds of established words of English that are formed with this suffix, as can be seen from a reverse dictionary of English, and yet there is some evidence that this suffix is no longer productive in English. If this is true, we can say that -*ment* is highly generalised but no longer available. The fact that it is so highly generalised shows that, at some stage, it was also available and highly profitable. Generalised affixes are the result of past profitability and the more widely generalised the affix, the more highly profitable the affixation process has been.

With an affix that is still productive, it is usual, but not necessary, for the affix to be generalised as well. This is the case with -*er* forming subject nominalisations such as *baker, camper, killer, proposer, singer, walker* and so on. These words, and hundreds of others established in English usage, indicate the past profitability of the suffix. It is a highly generalised suffix. But more than that, it is still highly profitable so that nearly any verb can form a subject nominalisation in -*er*. Some more recent examples are *lander, inducer, converger, scrambler* and so on; and if you invent a new word like *Koreanise*, a person or instrument which does it becomes fairly automatically a *Koreaniser*. The other case is illustrated by the English prefix *a*- as in *ablaze, aflutter, atremble*. This is still available and occasional new words are found using it, words such as *aclutter*. There are, though, relatively few established words which show this pattern (so it is not widely generalised) and it is used relatively infrequently to create new words (so it is not very profitable).

Note that, in theory at least, it is possible to give some measurement of generalisation. This could be done, for example, by counting the number of occurrences of the process in some reasonably representative word-list or (more accurate, no doubt, but correspondingly more difficult), by counting the number of examples of the process in some large word-list as a percentage of the potential bases available for the process.

Notions such as counting word-lists, however, raise other questions about generalisation and productivity which we also have to consider.

5.3 POTENTIAL WORDS AND PRODUCTIVITY IN THE INDIVIDUAL

Until fairly recently, it has been usual for morphologists to discuss derivational morphology in terms of words which 'exist' and words which do not 'exist'. 'Existence' has usually been assumed to be defined by a listing in, for example, *The Oxford English Dictionary*. Such a procedure is dangerous for a number of reasons.

Firstly, words which are included in the *OED* are, in some senses, included pretty much at random. This is not true of a host of common words which the readers for the dictionary could not avoid finding but, with rarer words, a listing in the dictionary depends to a certain extent on a suitable occurrence of the word having been found in the works the readers were considering, and not only found but recognised as a word worth noting. Without wishing to cast any slur upon the ability of the people who have read so assiduously for the *OED* over the years, I am sure that they would be the first to admit that they cannot cover everything, cannot note every attested word, cannot find suitable examples of every attested word. That this is in fact true, and that there are many words which have not made it into the *OED* (or by extension any other dictionary), is easily illustrated. You can probably find words yourself in any journalistic text which are not in the *OED*. For instance, none of the words in (7) was listed in the first edition of the *OED* and, yet, they have all been attested in writing and repeated. *Erraticness, scaredness* and *well-roundedness* are still not in the *OED*.

(7)   apartness
           belongingness
           cunningness
           erraticness
           givenness
           maleness

scaredness
showeriness
well-roundedness

The second reason for treating the lists from any particular dictionary with care is that some of the words which are included in dictionaries are included more or less by mistake. You might like to consider some of the words in (5), for example. *Greenth* is listed in the *OED*, yet it has never been a particularly frequently used word, and it appears to be listed mainly because it occurs in the works of George Eliot. It is, therefore, the case that some of the words entered in a dictionary like the *OED* are in extremely limited use (and have possibly never been widely used) while other words which are not listed are not listed for equally random reasons. To take a list such as that given in the *OED* as the gospel on what the words of English are is to do an injustice both to your data and to the editors and readers who are not, and would not claim to be, infallible.

Thirdly, and most importantly it seems to me, deciding on the basis of some list whether or not a word 'exists' is to cut derivational morphology off from both syntax and inflectional morphology, and to claim an entirely separate condition of relevance for this part of the grammar. If this is to be done, then it should be as a major conclusion of research carried out, not as a premise. But most morphologists today seem to feel that such a separation is, in fact, not justified. We shall return to this problem in Chapter 6.

The point can be made in relation to syntax in the following way. Syntacticians discuss sentences which are possible but not necessarily occurrent. Only in rare cases do they limit themselves to actually attested sentences. Most syntacticians would find the following example to be a perfectly well-formed sentence, even though it has, I take it, never occurred in language use and is unlikely to.

(8) The Minister of Education announced that a sum of forty million dollars per year was being set aside to boost research in Linguistics, particularly Morphology, over the next ten-year period.

If a sentence like (8) is a perfectly acceptable object of study in syntax, why should possible but non-occurrent words not be perfectly acceptable objects of study in morphology? We know that, just as it is possible to create new sentences, it is possible to create new words. We, thus, know that not all the potential words of any language can be attested, just as we know that not all the potential sentences of any language can be attested. It is true that we appear to remember more words than sentences as complete units but, as words and sentences have different functions, this should be expected. In general, it seems to me, morphology and syntax are much closer to one another than would be realised by reading the range of literature that exists on each.

This is even more evident when it comes to the distinction between inflection and derivation. With only a few exceptions, it is often assumed that all potential inflectional forms will be realised in a language but that not all potential derivational forms will be realised. In languages with complex inflectional systems, this may or may not be true. Who is to say whether the first person plural negative future inferential conditional reciprocal causative passive ('if, as they say, we were not about to cause to be VERBed to one another') of any hundred verbs of Turkish chosen at random is actually attested? The difference between inflection and derivation is not necessarily as great as one might conclude from a superficial reading of the literature, either.

One possible objection to the points I have raised here is that they confuse words which 'exist' in the society and words which may or may not be found in the idiolects of particular individuals. Only the former type, it might be claimed, is of relevance to Linguistics. This is a serious point and requires some consideration.

Let us assume that some speaker of English, familiar with the novels of George Eliot, produces the following utterance:

(9) If I had been impressed with the greenth of the beech trees in the spring, I was even more impressed with their brownth that particular autumn.

The linguist/analyst might easily dismiss the coining of *brownth* as a case of analogical formation of no general interest. Assume, however, that the same speaker, taken with this type of word, goes onto use words like *blackth, greyth, pinkth, indigoth* and even *cyanth*. Are all of these also to be dismissed as analogical formations rather than the result of a productive rule? The answer is not clear. I suspect that many would dismiss them in this way, although the use of *-th* then looks more like productivity than analogy (always assuming that the two can be distinguished). But these words would probably not (except in exceptional circumstances) pass into the general vocabulary of English. Even if we wanted to say that *-th* suffixation had become productive for this individual speaker, we would probably not wish to say that, as a result of this, it had become productive 'in English'.

That is, we need to distinguish between productive for the individual and productive within the speech community. Only if a particular morphological process is productive for a large enough number of members of the speech community will that process be said to be productive for the speech community. On the whole, it is productivity within the speech community which is understood by the term 'productivity' and it is this type of productivity which gives rise to listings in dictionaries and the like. What we might call **individual productivity** will occasionally give rise to dictionary entries (as possibly with the example of *greenth*), will frequently give rise to *hapax legomena* (words with only a single attestation) and will even more frequently never come within the scrutiny of the professional linguist, grammarian or lexicographer.

The main problem with making a distinction between individual productivity and societal productivity is in drawing the line between the two. Clear cases at both ends can be recognised but there is a middle ground where it may not be clear whether there is a case where individual productivity is the same for several individuals or a marginal case of societal productivity. The dominating criteria distinguishing the two in our society are probably wide-spread use in the written and spoken media and listing in dictionaries. In a pre-technological society it would probably be much harder to draw the distinction and, indeed, in very small speech communities there may not be any distinction to be drawn.

Notice that, even if we draw this distinction between what an individual does and what is generally accepted in the society as a whole, it does not affect the basic point that there are potential words as well as potential sentences which are not attested in the variety being described. The distinction between productivity tout court and individual productivity makes it possible to state definitively what words have been produced and accepted by the society (on the basis of the *OED* or some equivalent). Nevertheless, more words will have been produced and accepted by individuals and there will be many words which might have been produced but were not, both in the society and by the individual. For instance, *princess·dom* must have been a possible formation at some stage in the history of English, if not still today, but it is not listed in the *OED*. For languages that do not have an equivalent lexicographical tradition, not even this pseudo-definitiveness is possible.

5.4 BLOCKING

One of the main reasons why very few morphological processes show total productivity is a phenomenon which is known as pre-emption or, more usually, by the rather unflattering title of **blocking**. Blocking refers to the non-existence of a derivative (in the societal sense discussed in section 5.3) because of the prior existence of some other lexeme. Some statements of this constraint formulate it so that only a previously existing derivative, formed from the same root (possibly base), can block the production of a new derivative but this is probably too restrictive. It should be noted that this formulation of what blocking is refers only to derivational morphology. While there seems to be no a priori reason why blocking could not also be applied to inflectional morphology, in general use, the term has been restricted to derivational morphology. In many instances, blocking appears to be the derivational analogue of suppletion in inflectional systems. This is something of an over-simplification and there are differences between inflectional and derivational morphology in this regard. Before any further discussion, however, we need an example of how blocking works.

The suffixation of *-er* to create subject nominalisations in English is, as we have already seen, extremely productive. Yet there are times when nominalisations in *-er* seem to be avoided. These are the occasions when there is already a word in existence which means just what the *-er* nominalisation would mean if it were used. So, in (10) below, we tend not to use the word listed in (a) but, rather, to use the corresponding word from (b). The existence of the (b) word blocks the productivity of the *-er* suffixation rule and prevents the general use of the (a) word.

(10) (a) cycler   (b) cyclist
       batter [in cricket]   batsman
       typer   typist
       studier   student
       raper   rapist
       stealer   thief
       deliverer   delivery boy (etc.)
       shop assister   shop assistant
       lift attender   lift attendant

There are a couple of important points to note about this blocking. First of all, blocking does not entirely prevent the coining of words like those in (10a) by individuals if, for example, they temporarily forget what the (b) word is or that there is one. All that is blocked is the **institutionalisation** of these words, that is, their coming into general use in the society and so being listed in dictionaries.

Second, blocking of this type only applies as long as the word like the ones in (10a) is genuinely synonymous with the word like those in (10b). When Shakespeare talks of the 'ten stealers' meaning the fingers, 'stealer' is no longer synonymous with 'thief'. Similarly, it is quite normal for *batter* and *deliverer* to be available in other uses (for baseball and in a religious sense, respectively) because there they are no longer in competition with the word which would otherwise block them.

Third, blocking appears not to apply in so-called **synthetic compounds**. It is quite possible to speak of a *sheep-stealer* even though it would be abnormal to speak of a *stealer* if thief is meant.

Finally, blocking does not always work. There is a general case where the failure of blocking to apply can be explained in a principled way and then a few individual cases which are far harder to explain. The general case is that blocking frequently fails to work with the most productive morphological processes. The affixation of *-ness* in English is a good example. The existence of *productivity* does not prevent us talking about *productiveness*, even though the two things mean exactly the same thing in morphology. It is true that *-ness* and *-ity* do not always produce synonymous words: most people would probably distinguish between *monstrousness* and *monstrosity*, for example, but there are cases where the two words from the same base are synonymous and, yet, are not blocked. If the words were on different style levels, this might also account for lack of blocking. Clipping always provides synonymous words from the same base but here the different style level (not the different meaning) allows both to co-exist.

As an example of an individual case, consider *normalcy*. *Normalcy* means the same as *normality* (and possibly the same as *normalness*) and yet has become, especially in American English, a perfectly usual word. It has not been blocked by *normality*. In this particular case, *The Oxford English Dictionary* lists first uses for both *normalcy* and *normality* at about the same time, but this cannot be a decisive factor since the dominance of *normality* in the period since the coining would have been expected to oust *normalcy*. It would not be surprising for two synonymous words created with different affixes to come into being at about the same time and for one of them eventually to win out over the other, but this is not the whole story in this instance. This is what happened with pairs such as *to doctor ~ doctorise, complemental ~*

complementary, expectance ~ expectancy. In other cases, though, blocking can be seen to have failed. *Coloner* is an earlier word than *colonist*, *computate* is an earlier word than *compute*, *conspicuity* is an earlier word than *conspicuousness*, *heterogeneal* is an earlier word than *heterogeneous*. Current disputes about *disinterested* taking over an area earlier occupied by *uninterested*, and prescriptive debates about *orient* and *orientate*, *use* and *utilise*, *adaption* and *adaptation*, *deduce* and *deduct* show that such changes are still occurring.

Blocking can also be invoked by an embarrassing homonymy, as well as by synonymy. In French, there is a productive suffix *-eur*, which is added to verbal bases to produce subject nominalisations like the English ones in *-er* discussed earlier. We find examples like the following:

(11) destruct·eur   'destroyer'
      emprunt·eur   'borrower'
      imitat·eur   'imitator'
      livr·eur   'delivery person/company'

and so on. However, corresponding to English *flier*, there is no French word *voleur* from *voler* 'to fly' because *voleur* already exists, with the meaning 'thief', and this would cause an embarrassing homonymy. In English, you would not expect to find someone who sues called a *suer* (except as a joke) because of the embarrassing homonymy with *sewer*.

In fact, it rather looks as if blocking is not strictly relatable to derivational morphology. Rather there seems to be a restriction on new words from whatever source to the effect that they should not mean the same as existing words or cause an embarrassing homonymous clash. Blocking in this wider sense does not always work, either, as is shown by the existence of synonyms such as *kudos*, *prestige* and *mana*, or, indeed, by the existence of synonyms in general. However, many people argue that absolute synonyms rarely, if ever, exist. Blocking because of homonymy can be illustrated without reference to morphological processes in the introduction of *rooster* in many varieties of English to replace the earlier *cock*, or the discomfort many people feel in using the word *sod* to mean 'turf' because of its homonym.

5.5 DEFINING THE PRODUCTIVITY OF A PROCESS

One of the major problems for the linguist who is trying to give a description of some morphological process is to state, in a coherent way, just what bases may be used in the process. Normally only a limited number of bases, defined by phonological, morphological, syntactic and semantic criteria, are available for any given process. Discovering just what bases are available and specifying the ways in which those bases may be defined are, in fact, extremely difficult tasks for the linguist.

This leads to problems in discussions of 'full productivity', which have already been mentioned above. Consider two possible definitions of full productivity, one of which is much wider than the other:

(a) A process is said to be fully productive if it applies to every possible base and those bases are defined solely in terms of their major category (noun, verb, adjective).
(b) A process is said to be fully productive if it applies to every relevant base, defined in terms of a number of specific restrictions of types that will be illustrated below.

Of these, (a) demands much more of full productivity than (b) and is correspondingly far less frequently found (not least because of blocking). Strangely enough, it is (a) that is usually understood as a definition of productivity in the literature and this is partly why productivity has become the issue it is today.

In the literature, the fact that a particular process virtually never applies completely without exception has been discussed under two headings, both of which are probably misleading. The first is 'limitations on productivity' and the second is 'semi-productivity'.

5.5.1 So-called limitations on productivity

The reason for the label 'limitations on productivity' is fairly clear. Suppose there is a morphological process (call it p), which can apply to only a very small number of bases, and another process (call it q), which can apply to a very large number of bases. It is probable that a smaller number of forms produced by p will be attested than forms produced by q. As a result, it appears that p does not apply often and that is taken to mean that p has limited productivity. This does not necessarily follow. If a process can apply to a limited, finite set of n bases and is actually attested having applied to all of those bases, then that process is fully generalised and has, correspondingly, been fully productive, whether n is equal to 200,000 or to 10. That is, judgements about how productive some process is, or has been, should not be made before it is discovered which bases could provide input to the process. If this is not done, then the term 'productive' is being used in a rather different and, I believe, ultimately misleading way. The fact that virtually no studies of productivity in the sense in which it is being defined here have been carried out is a nuisance for the theorist but irrelevant to the theoretical discussion.

Although it is not my intention to spend a great deal of time considering individual examples here, it is perhaps worth illustrating briefly the kinds of ways in which the bases available for certain morphological processes may be restricted. The particular examples chosen are random, illustrating a range of kinds of restriction.

In German the suffix -*tum* is now only productive with bases which denote people. Forms such as *Abenteurertum* 'the collection of adventurers', *Bürokratentum* 'the collection of bureaucrats', *Hegelianerium* 'the collection of Hegel scholars', *Ignorantentum* 'the collection of ignoramuses', *Sklaventum* 'the collection of slaves' and so on are found but forms, such as *Altertum* 'antiquity' and *Besitztum* 'property', are **lexicalised** relics, no longer possible formations today. This, then, is a case where there is a semantic restriction on the type of base that is used for this affixation process.

In English, the inflectional suffixes -*s* and -*ing* can be added to virtually all verbs except modal verbs. The few exceptions (such as *beware* and *quoth*) must be specially marked and genuinely prevent the claim of full productivity for these affixes. Modal verbs are frequently defined in terms of this aberrant morphological marking but can also be defined in terms of syntactic criteria (they are followed by a verb in the stem form without *to*, they are always the first verb in the verb group and so on). Here, there is a limitation on the bases which are available for these particular affixation processes and that limitation can be expressed in syntactic terms.

In Russian, the suffix -*ant* can be used to create new words (that is, it is a Russian suffix, it does not just appear in the borrowed words where it originated) but the base to which the suffix is attached must be a foreign base. The following are examples of Russian-coined words using the suffix:

(12)	kurs	'course'	kursant	'student'
	diversija	'sabotage'	diversant	'saboteur'
	spekuljatsija	'speculation'	spekuljant	'speculator'

Whether a base is foreign or native is ultimately an etymological question but it acts synchronically in the same kind of way as declension or conjugation class operate, that is as a morphological feature. This, therefore, is an instance of a morphological restriction on the set of bases available for this affixation process.

In Turkish there is a suffix -*de*- (-*da*- depending on vowel harmony) which is added only to onomatopoeic words ending in /r/ or /l/ to form verbs from imitative words. Some examples are given below, with the final -*mek* (-*mak*) marking the infinitive of the verb.

(13) gıcır   'creak!'   gıcır·da·mak   'to creak'
      hırıl   'growl!'   hırıl·da·mak   'to growl'
      horul   'snore!'   horul·da·mak   'to snore'
      kütür   'crunch!'   kütür·de·mek   'to crunch'
      takır   'tap tap!'   takır·da mak   'to tap'

Here, there are two types of restriction on the bases available for the process. The first is a semantic one, in that the base must be an onomatopoeic word; the second is a phonological one, in that the segments that the base may end in are specified.

The most common kinds of restrictions on bases are those which specify the part of speech of the base or, for inflectional endings, the declension or conjugation class of the base. These are so common as to require no exemplification: examples can easily be found from English, German, Latin and so on.

The fact that there are so many different possible types of restriction on bases available for morphological processes is just one of the reasons why it is so difficult to say how productive a particular process is. Since many kinds of limitation may apply to the bases available for a single morphological process, and the limitations have to be determined by the analysis of attested forms, the job of the linguist is an onerous one. Indeed, it is not clear whether anyone has ever stated, in any clear way, all the restrictions applying to the bases for any process: we simply do not know what such a statement would look like and cannot tell whether all relevant variables might have been taken into account.

5.5.2 So-called semi-productivity

A process is generally said to be **semi-productive** if it does not apply without exception to all bases defined by a certain part of speech. It has just been pointed out, though, that virtually no process applies in this fashion. There are a number of possible reasons for this.

(a) Some bases may not be available for the morphological process for some of the reasons discussed in the last section.

(b) The process may no longer be productive, which is equivalent to saying that the bases to which it can apply can be listed.

(c) The process may be productive, and the base a potential base, and yet the process may not actually be attested with that base. This output of the process might then be said 'not to exist'. This type of argument was discussed earlier in this chapter.

Semi-productivity is frequently taken to be one of the criteria that distinguishes between inflectional and derivational morphology. (See Chapter 2, p. 15 and also below, Chapter 6.) However, the arguments that have been presented here cast considerable doubt on this analysis and on the notion of semi-productivity as a whole.

5.5.3 Measuring productivity

Sometimes it would be nice to compare accurately the productivity of, say, *en-* and *-ify* or to be able to answer questions as to whether *-er* in English is more or less productive than *-er* in German. Such questions presuppose a reliable measure of productivity and there is no such measure which is uncontroversial. Clearly, if we wish to measure comparative productivity, we are talking about profitability rather than availability but, even then, there are problems involved in giving a robust measure which have already been referred to: a measure of availability depends not only on the number of words that are made by a particular morphological process but also on the number of words which might have been made. Similarly, a measure of availability depends on words which are known to have been created and not on words which might have been created but for which we have no evidence.

Two types of measure have been proposed: measures based on dictionary listings and measures based on textual attestation. The first type depends on a suitable list of attested words being available. Where English is concerned, the list in *The Oxford English Dictionary* is usually used (despite all the problems we have seen with such lists in 5.3). Presumably, such measures would not be possible in a language which does not have a history of lexicographic excellence. In any case, measures built on word-lists of this type have to be careful to distinguish between what is productive and what is generalised. The second type of measure is based on the analysis of large collections of text called **corpora**. Here it has to be assumed that any large enough corpus will reflect a typical distribution of words formed by any given morphological process. These measures usually depend upon the relation between the number of words formed by the relevant process which occur once only in the corpus (these are called **hapax legomena** or just **hapaxes**) and the total number of lexemes formed with that same process in the corpus. Although the hapaxes themselves may not be productive uses of the process involved (they may be perfectly familiar words), they are taken as an indirect measure of the number of new words the process can form: it is assumed that, when a process is highly available, a lot of new words will be coined and thus there are more likely to be words which occur only once in a large corpus while, if a process is not available, then all the words formed with that process should be familiar and thus likely to occur several times.

In either case, the precise mathematical formulae used for calculating a measure of productivity are complex and take quite a lot of explanation, which it is not my intention to go through here. Enough has already been said to show that the assumptions underlying the calculations are, in themselves, likely to be open to challenge and that, as such, the measures are controversial. This becomes even more obvious if we note that the two types of measure do not necessarily agree with each other. This is an area in which a great deal of work is currently being done.

REFERENCES AND FURTHER READING

The examples in (1) are taken from Jespersen (1909: 122–7, 139–40). The rule is Chomsky & Halle's rule of Trisyllabic Laxing (Chomsky & Halle, 1968).

The examples in (2) and (4) are all taken from Barnhart et al, (1973).

Reverse dictionaries of English are Lehnert (1971) and Muthmann (1999). Similar dictionaries exist for Danish, French, German and other European languages but rarely for other languages. The argument about the productivity of -ment can be found in Bauer (1983: 55).

The examples in (7) are taken from Williams (1965), a paper which is interesting in that it shows that the productivity of a suffix may be much greater than one might expect from consulting one's intuitions. However, in the course of citing examples to prove how undesirable the over-use of -ness has been claimed to be, Williams also cites, as neologisms, some words which have a long history documented in *The Oxford English Dictionary*. In any case, the prescriptivism in this paper should be ignored.

On the comparative productivity of morphology and syntax, see Bauer (1983) and works referred to there.

The main source on blocking is Aronoff (1976), updated in Aronoff (1994a). The term 'pre-emption' is from Clark & Clark (1979). For comments on synonymy, see Lyons (1977). Homonymics was developed with reference to French by Orr (1962) but this book cannot be recommended to undergraduate students without considerable guidance. There are some brief comments on the subject in Samuels (1972: 67–75) and Trudgill (1974: 29–32).

In section 5.5.1, the data on the German suffix -tum is taken from Fleischer (1975), the data on the Russian suffix -ant is taken from Townsend (1975: 175) and the Turkish example is taken from Lewis (1967: 231). Many more examples of limitations on bases that can undergo various morphological processes may be found in virtually any book that deals with derivational morphology in any detail (for example, Bauer 2001b).

For more detailed discussions of morphological productivity see Bolozky (1999), Plag (1999) and Bauer (2001b). These books discuss, among other things, the notion of measurement of productivity, though the fundamental papers in this area are Baayen (1992) and Baayen & Lieber (1991).

EXERCISES

1. Marchand (1969) lists, among many others, the following words using the prefix be-, grouped here according to the patterns Marchand describes: *become, beget, behold; bemoan, besprinkle, bewail; behead, beland, belimb; becalm, befoul, benumb; becrown, bemire, besmut.* Which, if any, of these patterns are productive and how can you tell?

2. Following on from your answer to question (1), how would you want to describe the use of this prefix in a description of current English?

3. Consider the verbs in -en in the list below. Can you see any restrictions which appear to have been in effect with this suffix or still to be in effect with this suffix?

blacken	deaden	harden
brighten	deafen	lengthen
broaden	fatten	lessen
cheapen	flatten	lighten

loosen	roughen	strengthen
madden	sadden	sweeten
moisten	shorten	thicken
quicken	sicken	tighten
quieten	slacken	weaken
redden	soften	whiten
ripen	straighten	widen

4. Choose a twenty-page section of *The Oxford English Dictionary* at random, making sure that you have not chosen a section with very few extremely common words which take many pages to describe. For each verb in your section look for the nominalisation or nominalisations listed. Nominalisations are words meaning 'the action/fact/state of VERBing': for example, the nominalisations of *appraise, expose, laugh, reduce* will include *appraisal, exposure, laughter, reduction* respectively. Where more than one nominalisation is listed for a verb, what has happened historically? Is it always the earlier nominalisation which persists or does the newer one sometimes come to be the usual nominalisation? Are the two semantically distinct? How does this relate to blocking?

5. Make a list of twenty adjectives, trying to ensure that the adjectives you choose come from different semantic fields and show a variety of different suffixes (including no suffix). Choose a dictionary to consult and determine which of these adjectives has a corresponding noun in *-ness* in your dictionary. Which of the adjectives has a corresponding noun in *-ity* in your dictionary? Do you agree that your dictionary is giving a fair picture of 'the English language' in the words it lists? At this stage, what would you conclude about the relative productivity of *-ness* and *-ity*? Do any adjectives have both types of corresponding noun and, if so, do the nouns mean the same thing or not? How does this relate to blocking? Now divide your adjectives into two groups, group A of native adjectives and group B of non-native adjectives. If you do not have enough etymological information in your head or in your dictionary to make this distinction, draw the distinction as in the table below. If you look at the correlation between your two groups of adjectives and the use of *-ness* and *-ity*, does this give you a different picture of their relative productivity? If you made even finer distinctions, would this change your mind even more? Is the suffix *-able* listed in the right place below?

A: Native	B: Non-native
Adjectives ending in the suffixes *-ed, -en, -ful, -ing, -ish, -less, -like, -ly, -some, -y.* Monosyllabic adjectives with no suffixes or adjectives whose base is monosyllabic if there are prefixes involved. Disyllabic adjectives made up of a single morpheme and ending with a written consonant (including <y>).	Adjectives ending in the suffixes *-able, -al, -ar, -ary, -ant, -ate, -ent, -ic, -ine, -ive, -ory, -ous.* Disyllabic adjectives made up of a single morpheme which end with a written vowel.

6. On page 80 it was stated that 'blocking appears to be, in many instances, the derivational analogue of suppletion in inflectional systems'. Explain the comment and discuss whether or not you would wish to agree with it and why.

CHAPTER 6

Inflection and Derivation

A s we have already seen in Chapter 2, morphology is traditionally divided into two branches inflection and derivation. These two are usually visualised as being entirely separate; inflection is a part of syntax, while derivation is a part of lexis. In fact, as was stated in Chapter 2, that is the basis of the distinction inflection provides forms of lexemes, while derivation provides new lexemes. In recent linguistic theory, this distinction has often been held to have implications for the organisation of the grammar. Rules for inflectional morphology are thought of as being a part of the same system as syntactic rules, while derivational rules are thought of as being in the lexicon or, at least, not in the same section of the grammar as the inflectional rules. For example, while several linguists have suggested that the difference between forms of German like *finde* '[I] find' and *findest* '[you, singular] find' might be accounted for in the grammatical derivation of sentences by the use of features such as [+ 1st person], [+ 2nd person] and [+ singular] as markers on the lexeme FINDEN 'to find', it has not, to my knowledge, been suggested that a form like *Häus·chen* 'house, diminutive' should be accounted for by the use of a feature like [+ diminutive] on the lexeme HAUS 'house'.

All this assumes that it is a fairly simple matter to distinguish between those processes which are inflectional and those which are derivational. This is also the impression that was given in Chapter 2. But it needs to be recognised that many of the definitions that allow us to draw the distinction are based on a prior definition of the lexeme, while most definitions of the lexeme depend on a prior definition of inflection (definitions such as 'an abstract unit of vocabulary which occurs in different inflectional forms', for instance). It would, therefore, be highly desirable to draw a distinction between inflectional and derivational processes without having to make reference to the lexeme but it is actually very difficult to do so. There are a number of criteria which are frequently given as a basis for this distinction and the most important of them will be discussed in this chapter. But we shall see that they are not all easy to apply and neither do they individually always give the intuitively 'correct' results. They do not even always agree on which processes are inflectional and which derivational.

6.1 MEANING

Basically, we are trying to decide when we have a new lexeme and when we just have a form of an old lexeme. On the face of it, this ought to be a fairly simple matter: we probably have reasonably clear intuitions about what are forms of a lexeme and what are new lexemes in any language we speak. However, it is not really as easy as it looks. To see this, consider the data in (1), where causative formations from three languages are put side by side. The second form in each of the languages illustrated means something like 'to make something or someone do what the first form says'.

(1)   *Turkish*
       öl·mek   'to die'
       öl·dür·mek   'to kill'

     Swahili
       chelewa   'be late'
       chelewe·sha 'delay'

     Finnish
       elä·ä   'live'
       elä·ttä·ä   'provide for'

In accounts of the morphology of these languages, the affix in the Finnish example is considered to be derivational, while the affixes distinguishing the two forms in the other two languages are considered to be inflectional. From this it is clear that we cannot rely on meaning to distinguish inflection from derivation. We require some other criteria.

This is a pity. It is otherwise very tempting to say that certain meanings or morphological categories will be inflectional. For instance, we might expect that morphological categories such as number, person, gender, case, tense, aspect, voice and the like will be inflectional where they are marked morphologically at all. This is probably because we expect such categories to be marked on all nouns or verbs as the case may be. It is, thus, linked to the productivity criterion which was mentioned in Chapter 2 and which will be taken up again below. And this kind of approach would probably work fairly well in the majority of cases. However, there are a number of instances where categories which would be classed as derivational by such a criterion are usually considered inflectional. The Turkish and Swahili examples cited in (1) provide simple examples and, in the Nigerian language Fula, diminutives ('a little ____'), augmentatives ('a big ____') and pejorative diminutives ('a nasty little ____') are apparently inflectional categories. There are also a few cases which would be classed as inflectional by such a criterion but which are usually considered to be derivational. For instance, in Diyari (a South Australian language) and Kwakiutl (a language spoken on Vancouver Island), it appears that the marker of plurality is considered derivational. In Kwakiutl, Keresan (a language of New Mexico) and Quileute (a language spoken in Washington State), aspect is described as derivational and, in Kwakiutl, tense is too.

We, thus, still need other criteria for distinguishing between inflectional and derivational processes. Three were mentioned in Chapter 2, and they will be considered first.

6.2 DERIVATION MAY CAUSE A CHANGE OF CATEGORY

If we add the affix -s to the form car to give car·s, we have started out with a noun and finished up with a noun. There is, thus, a sense in which we have not changed the part of speech or the **category** of the base in the affixation process. In contrast, if we add -al to the form person to give person·al, we have changed a noun into an adjective in the process of affixation and, so, have changed the category.

Unfortunately, matters are not quite as simple as this seems to suggest because we do not have a close enough definition of a category. Categories are determined by distribution: if two items have identical distributions, they will be considered to belong to the same category. But it is not clear just how closely a distribution is to be defined. For example, if we define a distribution as being the frame 'Determiner ____', then all nouns belong to the same category. If, on the other hand, we say that the frame is 'Indefinite Article ____', uncountable nouns are excluded. And, if we say the frame is 'a ____', then only countable nouns beginning in a phonetic consonant are included. Each of these might be taken as a category, depending upon the use it was wished to make of the categorisation. Now consider the morphological examples in (2):

(2)

appear	dis·appear
bishop	bishop·ric
boy	boy·hood
green	green·ish
king	king·dom
likely	un·likely
lingual	tri·lingual
lion	lion·ess
Marx	Marx·ist
poet	poet·ry
song	song·ster

In all of these examples, the word coined by the affixation process is of the same major category as the word which is its base. Although most of the examples in (2) show suffixation, the same would be true to a much greater extent with prefixation in English. Have the affixes illustrated in (2) caused a change of category, then? On one level, the answer is obviously 'no' but, on a more delicate level, the answer is equally obviously 'yes'. After all, *boy* is an animate noun, while *boyhood* is not, *lioness* is specifically marked as female, while *lion* is not, and so on. Even with the prefixation cases, there is a change of distribution and thus of category:

(3)   That is a lingual muscle/*child.
        That is a trilingual *muscle/child.

In fact, on an extremely delicate analysis of what a category is, even the affixes which we consider to be inflectional can be seen to cause a change of category. One of the properties of the set of words of which *person* is a member (which could thus be used to define its distribution) is that it can take an -*al* suffix. Once it has changed category, however, it cannot take that same affix so that *person·al·al* is not a possible word in English. Similarly, though, one of the things which defines the category to which a word like *car* belongs is its ability to take an -*s* suffix. Since *car·s* cannot take that same suffix (you cannot have *car·s·s*), *car* and *cars* must belong to different categories and the affixation process must have caused a change of category. On this analysis, it is only the affixes in formations like the German

Ur·ur·gross·vater 'great-great-grand-father' which do not cause a change of category.

So, before we can say that derivational affixes may cause a change in category but that inflectional ones never do, we need a closer definition of category. If we define category at the coarse level of noun, verb, adjective, then the criterion isolates some derivational affixes but fails to distinguish between the other derivational affixes and inflectional ones. If we work with an extremely delicate notion of category, it is not clear that the criterion will work at all.

One suggestion is that only derivational processes can change subcategorisation features associated with the base. For example, the derivational prefix *re-* can change subcategorisation:

(4)   They all act parts.
       *They all react parts.

but inflectional affixes can never make such a change so that the following is a typical pattern:

(5)   They act parts.
       He acts parts.
       Acting parts comes naturally to her.

This allows some way of defining what a change of category means.

This is not the only problem with this criterion, though. Another can be seen by considering a form like *shooting*. We would probably say that in the sentence

(6)   Evelyn was shooting clay pigeons.

the affixation of the -*ing* was inflectional: *shoot* and *shooting* on a coarse analysis are both verbs. But what about *shooting* in the sentences in (7)?

(7)   I saw Lee shooting clay pigeons.
       His shooting clay pigeons didn't worry me.
       The shooting of the clay pigeons was dramatic.

Here there is an indefinite borderline between what is a verb and what is a noun. At some point, however, we would probably agree that *shooting* had become a noun. Do we then say that the affixation of -*ing* in that case is derivational, although in other cases it is inflectional? On the face of it, that is not a particularly satisfactory solution since precisely the same affix, with precisely the same set of allomorphs, is added to precisely the same set of bases in the two cases and, yet, appears to be doing two rather different jobs. Do we say that there are two homophonous affixes -*ing*, one of which is inflectional and one derivational? This seems just as bad, at first glance, since precisely the same set of forms is always produced by what would then be considered two distinct processes. One alternative may be to say that at some stage *shooting* has undergone conversion or zero-derivation and turned into a noun. That is an analysis which is adopted by some linguists although it is open to the theoretical problems involved in conversion (see section 3.4). Another alternative is to say that perhaps, after all, inflection can change category.

6.3 INFLECTIONAL AFFIXES HAVE A REGULAR MEANING

All inflectional affixes have a regular meaning while not all derivational affixes do. The difficulty with this criterion is that many derivational affixes also have a perfectly regular meaning. This is particularly true of the most productive affixes — which is probably not surprising. You have to know what a word is going to mean before you coin it. So, the productive suffixation of -*er* and -*able* show quite regular meaning, even though we would probably want to say they were derivational rather than inflectional.

A thornier problem with this criterion, though, is that it is not clear how we specify the meaning of an affix. Consider the affix -*ette* in English. Some examples are given below.

(8)   beaver·ette
        flannel·ette
        maison·ette
        kitchen·ette
        suffrag·ette
        usher·ette

At least three ways of dealing with the meanings are possible here.

(a)   There are three distinct meanings:

    i.   small (as in *kitchenette, maisonette*),
    ii. female (as in *suffragette, usherette*) and
    iii. mock material (as in *beaverette, flannelette*).

(b)   There are two distinct meanings here,

    i.   mock material
    and

ii. diminutive.

Because women tend statistically to be smaller than men, and because men feel protective towards women, the diminutive meaning is also applied to women although it is the same meaning. Note that this is stated as a hypothesis and is not intended to condone such an interpretation.

(c) There is only one meaning here, diminutive. Diminutive has as its primary meaning 'small in size' but that can, in our society, imply one of two things:

    i. delicacy (as with women) or
    ii. inferior quality (as with the materials and – possibly – with the women).

As a second example, consider the English suffix -*ment*. Under one interpretation, this has a host of meanings, including

(9) (a) state of being VERBed   employment
    (b) that in which one is VERBed employment
    (c) thing which VERBS   payment
    (d) act of VERBing   encouragement

Each of these meanings is illustrated in the corresponding sentence below:

(10) (a) My employment ceases on the 31st.
     (b) My employment takes me all around the world.
     (c) I enclose payment.
     (d) Her constant encouragement was a boon.

Another possibility is that there is only one meaning for the suffix involved and that is 'noun formed from a verb', and that everything else is left to the interpretation of the word in context.

From these two examples, it can be seen that the more delicate the analysis of meaning that is provided, the larger the number of meanings that will be discovered. With the -*ette* example, we might conclude that there was only one meaning and that -*ette* was, therefore, at the inflectional end with regard to this criterion; or that there were three meanings and that -*ette* was clearly derivational with regard to this criterion. More subtly, perhaps, we might claim that there were indeed three meanings, but that each of these meanings was connected with a different suffix and that there just happened to be three homophonous suffixes -*ette*.

The result is that, if we are willing to postulate enough homophonous suffixes, or if we are willing to talk in rather coarse terms when it comes to defining meaning, we can probably claim that every affix has a regular meaning. Under such circumstances, this criterion becomes vacuous. If it is to have some content, then it will first be necessary to establish independently some way of defining the meaning of an affix appropriately.

6.4 INFLECTION IS PRODUCTIVE, DERIVATION SEMI-PRODUCTIVE

We have already seen in Chapter 5 that the notion of semi-productivity may rest on some fundamental misconceptions of productivity. The criterion that inflection is productive but derivation only semi-productive is correspondingly under a cloud before we begin. It was, in effect, argued in Chapter 5 that derivation is more productive than is generally thought.

The reverse is also true. Inflection is less productive than is frequently believed. The phenomenon of 'defective verbs' illustrates this well and will be familiar to anyone who has studied Indo-European languages, as well as to students of some other languages.

In French, for example, the verb *choir* 'to fall' is only common in the past participle, *clore* 'to close' has no first person singular forms and is only common in the past participle; *gésir* 'to lie' has no future and no perfect and is only usual in the third person; *quérir* 'to look for' is only found in the infinitive and so on.

In Latin, *memini:* 'I remember' and *o:di:* 'I hate' only have perfective forms; *inquam* 'I say' only has third person forms in the imperfect; and *fa:ri:* 'I speak' has no perfective forms.

In English, the modal verbs have no special third person singular present tense form, no present participle, no past participle and no infinitive; and *must* has no special past tense form, either. Verbs such as *abide, beware, pending* and *quoth* also do not have full paradigms.

In Russian, the verbs *pobedit'* 'to conquer' and *multit'* 'to stir up, muddy' have no first person singular of the present tense.

Such examples could be multiplied from other languages.

If it is not true that derivational morphology is semi-productive and not true that inflectional morphology is fully productive in either of the senses discussed in Chapter 5, then this criterion is not particularly useful as it stands. This does mask the point, though, that, on the whole, bases for inflectional processes are more likely to be specified simply in terms of their part of speech, and that bases for derivational processes are more likely to require some further specification, of the type that was illustrated in section 5.5.1. A reformulation of the criterion along these lines still does not represent more than a tendency and is not as strong a statement as the original formulation.

Even this reformulated version might be disputed. When considering markers of, say, the plural in English, many authors take it that the three regular markers of plurality, /s/, /z/ and /ɪz/ and the various irregular plural markers, such as *-en, -ren, -im*, vowel change and the like, are all allomorphs of the same morpheme {plural} (see further Chapter 7). When considering nominalisations of verbs in English, the same authors would almost certainly take it that *-ment, -th, -ation, -age* and so on realise different morphemes, not that they are allomorphs of the morpheme {nominalisation}. This is a direct result of the assumption that a morpheme is defined as much by the form of its morphs as by its meaning: an assumption which seems well motivated when you consider that, without it, we would be led to the conclusion that *liber* in *liberty* was an allomorph of *free* in *freedom*. Nevertheless, it might well be possible to build up an argument that the plural markers and nominalisation markers ought to be treated in the same way, not in different ways, in which case, even the reformulated criterion would fail to hold.

6.5 DERIVATIONAL AFFIXES ARE NEARER THE ROOT THAN INFLECTIONAL ONES

It is frequently stated that derivational affixes are found closer to the root than inflectional affixes. Across languages, this criterion appears to have a certain statistical validity although, as we shall see, it is no more than a tendency. Despite this, it is not a criterion which allows us to determine whether a given affix is inflectional or derivational. It is simply an observation based on a prior division of affixes into inflectional and derivational. This can be illustrated with the examples in (11).

(11) (a) *French*:   arriv·er·i·ons
        arrive·future·imperfect·1st-person-plural
        'we would arrive'

   (b) *English*:   palat·al·is·ation

   (c) *English*:   black·en·ed

(d) *German*:   Forsch·ung·en
                 research·nominalisation·plural
                 'research' (plural noun)

In (11a), there is a sequence of affixes, of which -*er* is closer to the root than -*ons*, yet all the affixes would usually be classified as inflectional. In (11b), there is a sequence of affixes, of which -*al* is closer to the root than -*ation*, and yet all of these affixes would normally be considered to be derivational. It is only where we have affixes which we take to be inflectional and derivational in the same word, as in (11c and d), that we can see that the derivational one is closer to the root than the inflectional one.

In any case, as was stated earlier, the criterion does not always work. Even in the familiar Indo-European languages, we find examples like the following:

(12)   *German*:   Kind·er·chen
                     child·plural·diminutive

        Welsh: merch·et·os
                     girl·plural·diminutive

        Dutch: scholier·en·dom
                     pupil·plural·abstract-noun
                     muzikant·en·dom
                     musician·plural·abstract-noun

        English: interest·ed·ly
                     exaggerate·d·ly
                     report·ed·ly
                     accord·ing·ly
                     lov·ing·ness
                     bound·ed·ness
                     for·giv·ing·ness
                     startl·ing·ness
                     speckle·d·y
                     folk·s·y
                     new·s·y
                     sud·s·y
                     better·ment
                     less·en
                     more·ish
                     most·ly
                     worse·n

The German example here is no longer productive but the fact that it was productive at one time shows that this criterion is not necessarily met all the time. The English examples are productive, though it is interesting that the affixes which are most commonly ordered 'wrongly' are the ones involving suppletion, irregular allomorphs and -ed, -ing, -ly and -ness: the most derivational of the inflectional affixes and the most inflectional of the derivational affixes. It might appear that the English examples could be 'rescued' by the use of the zero-derivation option, mentioned in section 6.2, but this is not the case. Even if zero-derivation is presumed to change the inflectional form into a different part of speech before the next derivational process applies, the inflection would still be closer to the root than the derivational zero.

6.6 DERIVATIVES CAN BE REPLACED BY MONOMORPHEMIC FORMS

The idea of this criterion is that it is possible to replace a derivative in a sentence with a monomorphemic form and the sentence will still make sense, but it is not possible to do the same with an inflected form. Thus, parallel to

(13)   Patriot·ism is good for a nation.

a sentence like

(14)   Oil is good for a nation.

is also possible, in which *oil*, which is made up of only one morpheme, has replaced *patriot·ism* and *patriotism* is correspondingly shown to be a derivative and not an inflected form. On the other hand, parallel to

(15)   Lee always arrive·s at noon.

we cannot have

(16)   *Lee always come at noon.

in which the single morpheme word *come* has replaced *arrive·s* and, thus, it can be seen that *arrives* is an inflected form and not a derivative.

The first thing to note about this criterion is that it is a test for specific words in context, not a definition. However, it can be rephrased as a definition since it is more or less equivalent to a statement that inflectional affixes are obligatory while derivational ones are not, where obligatory is to be understood as obligatory to the sentence. More important is the fact that it does not work. It fails in many highly inflected languages because it is hard to find monomorphemic words at all. In Russian, for example, the only apparently monomorphemic form of a feminine noun is the genitive plural (see example (31) in section 3.4). This means that in (17a) there is an apparently monomorphemic form of the noun for 'car' (a monomorphemic feminine noun), despite the fact that it is a genitive plural, while in (17b) it is impossible to replace the word for 'pilot' with a monomorphemic form, despite the fact that it is a derivative (literally, 'fli·er').

(17) (a) koljosa   maʃin   vraʃtʃalis'
         wheel   cars'   were-spinning
         'the cars' wheels   were spinning'

   (b) on dal   ljot·tʃik·u   instruktsii
       he gave pilot·dative-singular instructions
       'he gave the pilot instructions'

This gives the wrong answers for the test but in no way denies the obligatoriness of inflections.

In Kanuri, a language of Nigeria, however, nominative and accusative case endings are optional where no ambiguity results. It, thus, seems that obligatoriness is not always a reliable test.

Even in English this criterion will often give the wrong, or even conflicting, results, as is shown in the following examples:

(18)   They always arriv·ed on time.
         They always come on time.

(19)   She is bright·er than I am.
         *She is bright than I am.

(20)   I bought a dear·er watch.
         I bought a dear watch.

The conclusion must be that this criterion is not very useful.

6.7 INFLECTION USES A CLOSED SET OF AFFIXES

It is not generally possible to add a new inflectional affix to a language or to take one away. We could not, for instance, wake up one morning and start using in English a dual marker such as is found in Greek or Maori. Neither could we ignore the singular/plural distinction. It is possible, on the other hand, suddenly to start using a new derivational affix, as is shown by the success of forms in -*nomics* over recent years (*Nixonomics, Thatchernomics, Reaganomics, Rogernomics, Clintonomics* and so on). Furthermore, it is usually said that the set of inflectional affixes will be considerably smaller than the set of derivational affixes.

First, this must be a synchronic statement although that is frequently not made clear. Diachronically, languages do lose and gain inflectional affixes over time. English has lost its second person singular marking on the verb since the sixteenth century (although it is retained sporadically in the language of religion) and Mandarin is commonly said to be in the process of gaining morphological structure, including inflections.

Second, it is not clear that all languages can add derivational affixes freely. While it does not have a great deal of derivation to begin with, Maori is a language which does not appear to be adding new derivational affixes, although this could be a result of the fact that there are very few monolingual speakers of Maori left alive or even speakers for whom Maori is a first language.

Third, it is not clear that inflectional affixes always form a considerably smaller set than derivational affixes. Little research has been done on this aspect of Maori but, again, it seems likely that the numbers of inflectional and derivational affixes in that language are much closer to each other than they are in, say, English. At the other end of the scale, it seems that a highly inflecting language like Finnish has far more distinct inflectional affixes than derivational ones.

Although this criterion works, to a certain extent, for English, it may not work for all languages. In any case, if you meet a new affix for the first time, you have no means of telling, from this criterion, whether that affix is inflectional or derivational. This is another observation that depends upon a prior classification.

6.8 INFLECTIONAL MORPHOLOGY IS WHAT IS RELEVANT TO THE SYNTAX

This is, basically, just a reformulation of the statement that inflection produces forms of lexemes, while derivation produces new lexemes. However, a reformulation can sometimes be useful, in that it allows you to look at the problem from a different angle. In this case, though, it is not as useful as might be hoped.

The main problem is that it is not clear what 'relevant to the syntax' means. If it means 'what is specified in naming the grammatical word' it is true but circular, since you only need specify the lexeme and the inflectional morphemes in a grammatical word. It can be made non-circular by saying that anything which marks agreement is inflectional. This is true but does not define all the processes which we would probably want to call inflectional. It is not even clear that it would show tense affixes to be inflectional, for instance.

In a wider sense, this criterion as worded depends crucially on what the syntax is or does. Many models of syntax have come and gone over the last twenty-five years and any two of them might define different processes as inflectional if this criterion were taken seriously. For example, if a grammar were developed based on the system used by Jespersen, we might want to say that *extreme·ly* in *extremely tall tower* was the 'adverbial form of *extreme*'. Such a grammar would, no doubt, have problems associated with it but it is not an inconceivable way of looking at syntax. And it would have as its result that the affix -*ly*, normally considered derivational, would be seen as relevant to the syntax and, thus, inflectional. Similarly, in a different kind of grammar, it might well be argued that *advance·ment* was just the nominal form of *advance*. Such a grammar is, indeed, implied in some relatively recent work on morphology. This would make the affix -*ment* inflectional by the same line of argumentation. A general statement such as 'syntax is concerned with the interrelations of words within larger structures' does not help here since, in both the examples cited, this could be argued to be the case: *extremely* is the form of *extreme* required when it modifies an adjective; *advancement* is the form of *advance* which can take articles and adjectives and function in nominal positions in the sentence.

If the argument in the last paragraph seems too forced to be convincing, a different argument from Eskimo is perhaps clearer. In Labrador Inuttut, the marker of the passive is described as a derivational suffix. This classification is based on a number of arguments, including criteria which have been discussed in this chapter. Yet, this suffix appears to have an effect on the syntax, as can be seen from the examples in (21).

(21)   angutik   anna mik   taku·juk
        man-absolutive   woman·modalis   see·3rd-person-singular
        'the man sees a woman'

annak	anguti·mut	taku·jau·juk
woman-absolutive	man·terminalis	see·passive·3rd-person-singular

'the woman is seen by the man'

The presence of the passive marker has an effect on the co-occurring case marking and word order. Here, then, a derivational affix is necessary for the syntax.

Although this criterion is aiming at defining a common and valuable intuition, it is not sufficient as it stands to define the precise area it wishes to capture.

6.9 A FIRST CONCLUSION

These are not the only possible criteria for distinguishing between inflection and derivation but they are probably the most important ones; and the others, in any case, are open to the same kinds of objection. What, then, should be concluded on the basis of these criteria? None of the criteria has appeared satisfactory so there is certainly no simple way of drawing a distinction.

There are two possible answers to the question. The first is simply to discard the distinction. This is being done by many linguists in contemporary morphological theory. If we discard the distinction then, by implication, we also discard the notion of the lexeme and we are left simply with roots, affixes and word-forms. This would mean a total reconsideration of the notion of 'lexeme', to see whether we are willing to discard it or not. It certainly has some useful practical applications in terms of lexicography, for instance, although perhaps it could be replaced there with lexical item.

The alternative is to keep the distinction between inflection and derivation, but to view it in another light. In the discussion of the various criteria for distinguishing between the two, it was often the case that the criterion worked in a large number of cases but failed in others. The criteria were also, in general, less useful as a universal list than in particular languages. One solution to this type of problem has been proposed by language typologists, with the notion of **prototype**. A prototype is what the most typical member of a class is like across languages and individual languages will be expected to have actual types which diverge from the prototype to a greater or lesser extent. In this sense, we might say that a prototypical inflectional affix will not change major category, will have a regular meaning and will be added to every base in the appropriate part of speech; it will be ordered after all derivational markers, will be a member of a small closed set of affixes and will be relevant for the syntax in all models of syntax. A prototypical derivational affix will create new lexemes, change major category, have an irregular meaning on a fairly delicate analysis of meaning, especially in established words, come closer to the root than any inflectional affixes, belong to a large open set of affixes and will not play a role in the syntax of the sentence as a whole. Actual inflectional and derivational affixes in real languages will diverge from these prototypes, possibly to such an extent that we can be in doubt as to which class they belong in. However, in any particular language, we would expect to be able to make a distinction based on one or more of the criteria we have listed. It will turn out that the decision made for any particular language will often be related to the notion of paradigm for that language. In highly inflecting languages, a derivational affix will predict the existence of a whole paradigm of inflections beyond the derivational affix, while an inflectional affix will predict the existence of a much smaller range of forms or none at all. For example, in English the fact that a word ends in -*ise* predicts that there will also be forms ending in -*ise·s*, -*ise·d* and -*is·ing*, whereas the existence of a form ending in -*ing* makes no further predictions about the existence of other forms. In languages which are relatively poor, morphologically speaking, this predictive ability is less striking than it would be in a highly inflecting language but is still a guide in some cases.

Just how prototypes are to be built into a grammar is an interesting and difficult question – if, indeed, they are to be seen as parts of the grammars of individual languages. But the notion of prototype allows us to speak of inflectional and derivational affixes in particular languages and to show how the classes are set up.

6.10 AN ALTERNATIVE CONCLUSION

An alternative conclusion, albeit one which is compatible with much that has been said above, is that the main difficulty with an inflection/derivation split is that it assumes only two categories, when there are really more than two. In particular, a distinction is drawn between **inherent** and **contextual inflection**.

Contextual inflection is the kind of inflection that is determined by the syntactic structure: agreement for person, gender/noun class and number, case-marking. Inherent inflection is the kind of inflection that is not entirely determined by the syntax although it may have some syntactic relevance. Examples would be tense and aspect marking, number marking on nouns, comparative and superlative marking on adjectives and adverbs. This distinction was foreshadowed in section 6.8 with the comment that agreement is inflection: it is always a case of contextual inflection.

Once we have made this kind of distinction, we can revisit the criteria we have looked at for distinguishing between inflection and derivation and see that some of them distinguish between derivation and contextual inflection, some between derivation and inherent inflection. The meaning criterion, for example, does not necessarily distinguish between derivation and inherent inflection but marks contextual inflection as separate. Inherent inflection, but not contextual inflection, can be argued to cause a change of category, when we look at things like the *-ing* forms cited in (6) and (7). In general, only inherent inflectional affixes will be able to occur closer to the root than derivational ones; contextual inflectional affixes will be peripheral. And contextual inflectional affixes are the ones which (by definition) are clearly involved in the syntax.

This is not to say that a distinction between inherent and contextual inflection immediately solves all the problems that have been raised in this chapter. Problems of defining a category and replacing derivatives by monomorphemic forms still remain and, inevitably, there are new border disputes, with individual languages apparently doing things which go against the general tenor of the classification. Nevertheless, introducing this further distinction does seem to clarify why some of the problems we have met should arise and explain some of the difficulties we have been trying to deal with here.

REFERENCES AND FURTHER READING

The data on Swahili is taken from Ashton (1944), that on Turkish from Lewis (1967), that on Finnish from Karlsson (1983) and that on Diyari from Austin (1981). Note, however, that it is not absolutely clear from Austin's description why the plural affix in Diyari should be considered derivational and not inflectional. This is stated to be the case, and may well be justified, but it does not appear to be argued for in that book. The information on Fula is from Anderson (1982), that on Kwakiutl, Keresan and Quileute is from Bybee (1985). Kwakiutl is also mentioned by Anderson (1982) under the name Kwakwala.

The argument about category being defined in terms of recursion is from Lyons (1977).

The argument from subcategorisation is from Scalise (1984: 110).

The examples of Russian defective verbs are from Halle (1973).

The distinction in the way in which the markers of the plural and nominalisation are treated, discussed at the end of section 6.4, is directly relevant in some modern writings on morphology. Anderson (1982: 587) draws attention to the anomaly here. Others (for example, Beard, 1982) have suggested that English plurals may be derivational rather than inflectional.

The example *Kinderchen* is discussed by Fleischer (1975). The Welsh example is from Robins (1964). The Dutch examples are from Booij (1977). The facts about Kanuri come from Lukas (1937: 17). For other examples of unexpected ordering see Bochner (1984), Chapman (1996), Perlmutter (1988), Rainer (1996).

The comment about the relative numbers of inflectional and derivational affixes in Finnish on page 103 is based on a study of Karlsson (1983). Such a method is, of course, likely to have underestimated the number of derivational affixes to be found in the language but the discrepancy in numbers is so great that it does not seem likely that the comment is unjustified.

The title of section 6.8 is a quotation from Anderson (1982). The relatively recent work referred to in section 6.8 in which *advancement* might be taken to be the nominal form of *advance* is, in particular, Chomsky (1970). The definition of syntax provided in the course of the discussion on page 104 is taken directly from Anderson (1982: 587). The examples from Labrador Inuttut are from Smith (1982b).

Works that do not distinguish between inflection and derivation include Lieber (1981) and Van Marle (1996). For an introduction to prototypes in typology, see Comrie (1981: 100–4).

I am indebted to Kate Kearns for the notion of paradigm prediction.

For further discussion of the distinction between inflection and derivation, see Anderson (1982), Dressler (1989), Matthews (1991), Plank (1981: Chapter 2; 1994), Scalise (1988). On inherent and contextual inflection see Booij (1993; 1996) and, on one implication of that, Haspelmath (1996).

EXERCISES

1. For one of the following (sets of) markers, construct an argument to prove that it is inflectional OR that it is derivational in English. Does

the inherent/contextual distinction help you? The plurals of nouns, ordinal -*th* (for example, in *fourth, eighth*, etc.), superlative -*est*.

2. If the categories of inflection and derivation are prototypical categories, we might expect individual processes in any given language to form a cline from the most inflectional to the most derivational. The alternative would be that the criteria provided (or some subset of them) would provide a firm dividing line between inflection and derivation for any particular language. For any language you know well, use a sample of half-a-dozen affixes to determine which of these two outcomes applies. What do you conclude?

3. For any language you are familiar with which marks infinitives morphologically (this excludes English), determine whether the infinitive marker is inflectional or derivational and, if inflectional, whether it is a case of inherent or contextual inflection.

4. Consider the instances of unexpected ordering listed for English in (12). Look for other similar examples. How many of these examples can you explain away as not being 'real' counter-examples and why? How many real counter-examples are left?

5. 'The difference between inflection and derivation may not, in fact, have any foundation outside of the theory of grammatical structure, that is, it may be seen as corresponding to an aspect of the internal organisation of grammars, and thus as being strictly theory-internal rather than being susceptible of independent definition.' (Anderson, 1982: 587)

How does such a view of the distinction between inflection and derivation fit with the facts presented in this book? If such a view is adopted, what are the implications for 'the ordinary working linguist' (to use Fillmore's phrase)?

CHAPTER 7

What is a Morpheme?

The term 'morpheme' was introduced in Chapter 2. There we saw that a morpheme is an abstraction away from a number (possibly only one, possibly more) of morphs which share meaning and form and are in complementary distribution. It was perhaps implicit in Chapter 2, but not stated explicitly, that morphemes must analyse a word exhaustively: there can be no bits of the word left over which do not belong to any morpheme. This is actually a very narrow definition of morpheme and few practising linguists today would wish to adhere to it strictly. The reason is that there are a number of problems with such a definition. Some of the problems particularly those relating to recognising shared form and meaning, will be taken up in Chapter 9. Here we will consider some of the problems and discuss some of the ways in which the notion of a morpheme has been modified to avoid the problems. At one theoretical extreme, we will consider a position in which the morpheme is eliminated as a unit of analysis.

7.1 PROBLEMS WITH MORPHEMES

The whole notion of morpheme works best when each word is easily divisible into one or more discrete morphs, as in (1). This divides each word up into self-contained units which are adjacent in the word, and is sometimes called the 'beads-on-a-string' approach to morphology.

(1)   person·al·iti·es
        dis·em·power·ment
        in·coher·ent·ly

While analyses of this type are possible in large proportions of many languages, there are also many places where this kind of analysis simply will not account for the data. Some such examples have already been discussed.

Portmanteau morphs or **cumulation** was discussed in examples (4)–(6) in Chapter 3. There it was shown that we could have distinct meanings which could not be attributed to separate morphs but which had to be piled up on a single morph. The standard notion of a morpheme requires that each morpheme should have its own form and this is not true with cumulation. This is a case where there is meaning but no form.

The converse is also found: the situation where there is form but no meaning. This can be illustrated with the French adverbial formations in (2). It can be seen that the adverbs are consistently derived from the feminine form of the adjective but there is no feminine meaning in adverbs. Accordingly, we have a form (to which we would normally be able to attribute a meaning in a straightforward way) but the meaning associated with that form is lacking in these instances. Interfixes, discussed in section 3.1.5, were another example of such empty morphs.

(2)

Gloss	Masculine	Feminine	Adverb
'complete'	kɔ̃mplɛ	kɔ̃mplɛt	kɔ̃mplɛtmã
'cool'	fʁɛ	fʁɛʃ	fʁɛʃmã
'frank'	fʁɑ̃	fʁɑ̃ʃ	fʁɑ̃ʃmã
'gentle'	du	dus	dusmã
'happy'	œʁø	œʁøz	œʁøzmã
'hasty'	atif	ativ	ativmã

Examples of Ablaut, like those in (3) were also cited in Chapter 3. Here, there are a number of possible modes of analysis, none of which seems entirely satisfactory.

(3)

sing	sang
stand	stood
swing	swung
take	took

One option would be to analyse these forms as having infixes. Apart from being typologically odd (English is not a language which typically uses infixes), this runs into trouble with the meanings of the infixes. For instance, the /eɪ/ in the middle of *take* cannot easily be glossed as 'present tense' when it also appears in *taken*. An alternative analysis, perhaps even more theoretically dubious, is to see the replacement of /ɪ/ in *sing* by /æ/ as being a morph. This, however, is playing with the theoretical concepts: a morph is defined as a form, not as a process of replacement (see above, p. 36). Finally, we might simply refuse to analyse words such as those in (3) into more than one morph and see (at least some of) the words as further cases of cumulation.

Similar problems attach to the cases of zero or subtraction discussed in Chapter 3. If a morph is a form, calling a lack of form (a zero) a morph is again extending the notion (perhaps justifiably, perhaps not). But calling the removal of formal material a morph is a clear case of treating a process as a form and seems to take things too far.

These are just some of the places where the beads-on-a-string view of morphemes does not seem to work very well. The result of such problems is a dissatisfaction with analysing words in terms of morphemes because, in some languages, the analyses can only be partial. This has led scholars both to avoid morphemes where possible but also to try to redefine the morpheme. Since problems of different kinds have also provided pressure for a redefinition, there have been a number of alternative views of what precisely a morpheme is.

7.2 SOME OTHER VIEWS OF THE MORPHEME

We have already considered the allomorphy illustrated in (4), showing how the different allomorphs of the morpheme are phonologically conditioned.

(4)
singular	plural
ʤɪrɑːf	ʤɪrɑːfs
kæt	kæts
ræbɪt	ræbɪts
bæʤə	bæʤəz
dɒg	dɒgz
skwɪrəl	skwɪrəlz
fɪntʃ	fɪntʃɪz
fɒks	fɒksɪz
hɔːs	hɔːsɪz

But we also have other ways of making nouns plural in English, some of which are illustrated in (5). What do we want to say about the relationship between the plural markers in (4) and those in (5)?

(5) | singular | plural |
|----------|---------|
| guːs | giːs |
| ʧerəb | ʧerəbɪm |
| əlʌmnʌs | əlʌmniː |
| ɒks | ɒksən |
| ʧaɪld | ʧɪldrən |
| fənɒmɪnən | fənɒmɪnə |
| tempəʊ | tempiː |

According to what we have said so far, the only conclusion we can come to about the words in (5) is that they contain morphs belonging to morphemes which are synonymous with the {s} plural morpheme shown in (4). They must be separate morphemes because they do not (or do not clearly) share form with the markers which are found in (4). An alternative view, which gives priority to the semantics rather than to the form, sees this as unhelpful. Just as the plural markers in *cats* and *dogs* are in complementary distribution, it is argued, so the plural markers in *children*, *geese* and *oxen* are in complementary distribution with each other and with the various allomorphs illustrated in (4). The meanings are identical and, in each case, the markers place the word-forms in comparable places in a restricted paradigm. Therefore, we should say that at least the markers for the plural on *children*, *geese* and *oxen* and probably all the plural markers in (5) are allomorphs of the same morpheme {plural} that is illustrated in the second column of (4). The difference is that the choice of allomorphs is lexically conditioned for the data in (5), not phonologically conditioned, as it is in (4).

This argument has been widely accepted and this view of the morpheme is better accepted than the first one I provided you with in Chapter 2. It does raise some questions although they are probably fairly easily dealt with. First, note that, while the *-en* in *oxen* and the *-s* in *cows* are genuinely in complementary distribution, the same is not true of all the plural markers illustrated in (5). Both *cherubs* and *cherubim*, *tempos* and *tempi* are possible plurals in English. This can be answered in two ways. It is possible that *cherubs* and *cherubim* belong to separate lexemes in English, *cherubs* being the plural of CHERUB[1] 'innocent-looking child' and *cherubim* the plural of CHERUB[2] 'attendant of God'. If this is the case (and you can decide for yourself whether it is true in your English) then it remains true that the allomorphs of {plural} are lexically conditioned. If this is not the case, we can fall back on a second explanation. While *tempos* and *tempi* are both possible plurals of *tempo* in English, they are used in different registers, *tempi* being more or less restricted to use in musical contexts. Different registers equate, it might be argued, to different dialects, and our aim is not to provide an explanation of variation between dialects but simply to provide a grammar of a single dialect. So we choose our dialect and choose our plural. This is idealisation of the data but perhaps not excessive idealisation. Second, we might argue that the same set of arguments could be used to make the *-ter* in *laughter* an allomorph of the same morpheme as the *-ion* in *division*. This conclusion is usually rejected, probably on the grounds that only in inflectional morphology (which the plural is taken to be) is there a tight enough paradigm to ensure that the meanings really are the same. You can decide for yourself how convincing you find this particular argument. One of the great advantages of this view of the morpheme is that it allows suppletion to be dealt with in a relatively simple manner: given the two French forms *all·ait* 's/he/it was going' and *ir·ait* 's/he/it would go' (see section 3.9), we can class *all* and *ir* as allomorphs of the same morpheme, despite the fact that they have no phonological similarity.

There are other, less widely accepted, definitions of the morpheme, which are important only in that you may come across them in your reading. For example, some writers fail to make a consistent distinction between morph and morpheme and call the occurrent forms 'morphemes'. For some Francophone linguists, 'morpheme' is used only for inflectional morphology. And some writers solve the cumulation problem by making the morpheme more or less equivalent to a morphosyntactic feature, so that there is, in a Latin nominal paradigm like that in (4) of Chapter 3, a morpheme {plural}, even though it has no consistent representation in form and does not occur in isolation. This makes direct representation of morphemes by morphs a little difficult to formalise and, as such, is clearly an extension of the original insight. One result of this has been a divorce between the semantic side of a word and the formal side of the word, with the form being derived indirectly from the meaning rather than by linking individual meaningful elements as was done in (1) above. We will return to this kind of approach below in section 7.4.

One alternative definition of the morpheme is rather more important, however, having been adopted by many in the last part of the twentieth century, sometimes without any apparent recognition of how controversial it is. Again, whether or not you wish to define the morpheme in this way for your own use, you need to be aware of this understanding of the term when you read the relevant literature.

To understand this extended use, consider first the data in (6).

(6)

verb	noun	verb	noun	verb	noun
conceive	conception	confer	conferral/ conference	commit	commission
deceive	deception	defer	deferral/ deference	demit	demission
				emit	emission
perceive	perception			permit	permission
receive	reception	refer	referral/ reference	remit	remission

If we first look at the verb columns in (6) and compare across them, it might appear that we need to divide each of the verbs into two morphs, each representing a morpheme: *con* and *ceive* and so on in each case. However, given our definition of a morpheme so far, this is hard to motivate and the reason it is hard to motivate is the meaning. It is very difficult to see what *con* means that is the same in *conceive* and *confer* or what *re* means that is the same in *receive, refer* and *remit*. Similarly, it is very difficult to see what *ceive* means that is the same in *conceive, deceive, perceive* and *receive* (and similarly for the other putative elements). While we have previously seen that, in sufficiently constrained circumstances, we can feel justified in establishing a morpheme where the meaning is constant but the form is not, there has been nothing to suggest that we can keep the form constant but not the meaning and still establish a morpheme. Indeed, just the opposite would normally be taken to be the case: given *Wasp* 'White Anglo-Saxon Protestant' and *wasp* 'stinging insect' we would normally associate them with different morphemes, on account of their meaning, even though they form their plurals in precisely the same way (see also the discussion of *cherub* just above). However, in the *conceive* set there is a further consideration. All the verbs ending in *-ceive* form their corresponding nouns in the same way (by changing *-ceive* to *-ception*) and this is not a regular way of forming nouns in English. All the *-fer* words have similar nouns and all the *-mit* words have similar nouns. If we find a word ending in *-it* which does not contain the element *-mit* (for example, the verb *edit* or *orbit* or *solicit*), such a word does not make its corresponding noun in the same fashion (we do not find *edission, *orbission or *solicission). The way of forming nouns seems to have something to do precisely with the *-ceive, -fer* and *-mit* elements. Rather than say that the noun corresponding to *commit* ends in *-ission* and that the noun corresponding to *demit* ends in *-ission* and so on (with each an independent piece of information), it would be more economical if we could relate this behaviour to the element -*mit*. And so it has been suggested that, where an element like -*mit* has formal implications of this kind, even if it has not semantic unity, it should be seen as a morpheme.

7.3 FROM MORPHEME TO MORPHOME

This leaves us with a term 'morpheme' which is potentially multiply ambiguous. We cannot avoid this ambiguity in already published works and so readers have to take care in their interpretation of what they read. But we can avoid some of the ambiguity by the judicious use of extra terminology.

Let us agree to retain the term 'morpheme' in the sense it was used in Chapter 2, so that the -*s* on *cats* and the -*en* on *oxen* belong to synonymous, but different, morphemes. We now need a new term for the wider sense whereby -*s* in *cats* and -*en* in *oxen* belong to the same unit. This unit has been termed the 'morphome'. We can define the **morphome** as a set of morphemes which perform the same function.

In fact, the morphome is used in a slightly wider sense still. To see the value of this sense, consider the past participle of English verbs. Grammarians, acting as morphologists, will usually give three principle parts of modern English verbs: the infinitive (or present stem), the past tense and the past participle. Other forms of the verb are predictable from these (for example, the third-person singular of the present is always made by adding -*s* to the present stem). The parts of a few verbs of English are given in (7).

(7) come   came   come
     hit   hit   hit
     spoil   spoilt/spoiled spoilt/spoiled
     swim   swam   swum
     walk   walked   walked

The principle parts listed in (7) correspond to the uses in sentences like those in (8):

(8)   I come to Edinburgh every year. / I didn't want to come to
        Edinburgh.
        He came to Edinburgh last week.
        We have come to Edinburgh to see the tattoo.

Note in (7) that sometimes the past participle is homophonous with the stem, sometimes with the past tense, sometimes with both and sometimes with neither.

That is the view of the morphologist but the view of the syntactician is rather different. The syntactician sees a use for past participles in sentences like those in (9) but also a use for passive participles in sentences like those in (10).

(9)   She has just swum the Channel.
        He has already walked the dog.

(10)   The Channel has just been swum.
        The dog has already been walked.

The crucial thing about past participles and passive participles in English is that they are always the same. This is just a fact about English, not something which we would necessarily expect to find, any more than we would expect to find the passive and the imperative with the same forms (as they have in Maori for transitive verbs). In a language like Finnish, the past participle and the passive participle would not be homophonous (*sano·nut* 'say·past-participle-active' versus *sano·ttu* 'say·past-participle-passive'). But, in English, even if you are not sure of what the past participle of a particular verb is, the passive participle will be just the same. For example, you might not know which alternative to choose in (11a) but, whichever you choose, it will also be the one you choose in (11b). You will not have one word-form for one function and another for the other for any verb in the language.

(11) a.   He has cleft/cloven/cleaved the log in two.
     b.   The log has been cleft/cloven/cleaved in two.

The morpheme is defined so as to include such variation. Whether the form has a suffix in *-ed* or *-en*, or illustrates Ablaut or lack of change from some other form, whether the meaning is the past participle or the passive participle, it is all part of the same morpheme.

This leaves us with the case of *-mit* in *commit*, *remit*, etc. Since these instances deal with a form without relation to meaning, it seems appropriate enough to use the existing term **formative**. Formative is sometimes used to mean just the same as a morpheme, sometimes used to avoid a commitment as to whether something is or is not a morpheme, but is often used vaguely enough for the lack of precision not to be an issue. Here we seem to have a suitable match between a name requiring a meaning and a meaning looking for a name.

Accordingly, we can use an extended terminology to straighten out the confusion that has been wrought by assigning too many different meanings to the term 'morpheme'. Care still has to be exercised in reading older texts but you should be able to keep the different situations distinct.

7.4 CAN WE HAVE MORPHOLOGY WITHOUT MORPHEMES?

It has been pointed out above that some scholars are so dissatisfied with the notion of morpheme that they reject it completely. This seems to give rise to some kind of paradox: if the morpheme is the fundamental unit of morphology and you want to reject the morpheme, this might seem to imply that you reject the whole notion of a morphological level of analysis.

This is far from being true. Rather it is a matter of what unit is given priority. For theories which do not accept the morpheme, the central unit is the word-form rather than the morpheme. Given a word-form like *elephants*, a morpheme-based theory is going to say that it is made up of two elements, *elephant* meaning 'elephant' and *s* meaning 'plural' so that the whole word means 'more than one elephant'. In a word-form-based theory, in contrast, *elephants* is first and foremost seen as being 'the plural of ELEPHANT', that is in terms of its place in the paradigm of the lexeme to which it belongs. While a morpheme-based account has to go onto explain how the appropriate allomorph of the relevant plural morpheme is chosen, the word-form-based theory has equally to account for the way in which the plural form is derived from the stem of ELEPHANT (ELEPHANT has only one stem but, in other cases, it might be a matter of choosing the appropriate stem in the first place). This involves noting the generalisation of patterning that unites *elephants* and *bandicoots, bats, cats, goats, marmosets, rabbits, rats, stoats* and so on, in the same way that the morpheme-based account notes the conditioning of the particular allomorph that is found on *elephants*.

So far there is no great difference, except a difference of point of view. The difference lies in two things. In the word-form-based theory, it is no particular surprise that different lexemes make their plurals according to different patterns, as long as there is a suitable word-form in the appropriate place in the paradigm. In a morpheme-based account, we might ask why it should be that there are synonymous morphemes (or, equivalently, allomorphs of a morpheme like {plural} which do not share any form). More importantly, in the word-form-based account, we cannot say that the final -s in elephants 'means' 'plural': all we can say is that elephants is 'the plural of ELEPHANT' while elephant is 'the singular (or unmarked form) of ELEPHANT'.

It might seem at this point that we are splitting hairs: the two boil down to much the same thing. Of course, both approaches are attempting to deal with precisely the same set of data so this is not all that surprising. Nevertheless, there are differences between the two which may be rather more important.

The first of these is that a morphemic theory can only pay attention to morphemes, while a word-form-based approach is, in principle, free to look at similarities between word-forms which are not morphemic. This becomes relevant in the discussion of phonaesthemes. Many speakers feel that the series of words given in (12) share some kind of vague meaning as well as some kind of partial phonetic resemblance: in the words in (12a), this might be something to do with faint light; in those in (12b), something to do with being disreputable or dirty.

(12) a.	glare	b.	slime
	glimmer		slink
	glimpse		slop
	glint		slovenly
	glisten		slug
	glitter		sluggard
	glory		slum
	glossy		slump

The gl- and sl- sequences in (12) cannot be morphs because morphs have to analyse words exhaustively, and there are no recurrent elements (with appropriate meanings) -are, -immer; -ime, -ink and so on. Nevertheless, it is possible that speakers of English use these forms to help them interpret such words and find that these sequences motivate the words in a similar way to the way in which morphs motivate the structure of words.

The second point of difference between a morpheme-based theory and a word-form-based one comes in relation to derivation. While we might not object to the notion that elephants holds the place in the paradigm for 'the plural of ELEPHANT', we have already seen (p. 99) that there is less reason to think that greenness fills the slot 'noun of GREEN' or that greenery fills 'collective of GREEN'. It is, therefore, far less clear just how derivational morphology is to be approached in such a theory. Now, in some cases, this may be a positive advantage. If we contrast *ignorance* with *perseverance* we might not want to say that they derive their meanings directly from their bases and the same morpheme {-ance}. Certainly, the meanings of the two words do not relate to the meanings of the bases in precisely the same way in the two cases. But these examples are lexicalised and, to a certain extent, their meanings are due to semantic drift away from any productively derivable meaning. On the other hand, the words in (13), all recent words of English, are interpretable precisely because we know what *-ism* means when attached to appropriate bases. In productive uses like this where there are, nevertheless, relatively few words in the established paradigm, it seems less likely that we recognise the whole word and are, thus, able to see the pattern linking it to words like *ageism*, *sexism* and so on. We will see further arguments for this in Chapter 16.

(13)   ableism
        beardism
        bodyism
        handism
        sizeism

REFERENCES AND FURTHER READING

On the subject of this chapter see Mugdan (1986), Anderson (1992), Matthews (1993; 2001) and Bauer (1999), with the final version of the morpheme introduced in section 7.2 coming from Aronoff (1976).

For the morphome, and the example of the past participle, see Aronoff (1994b).

For the Finnish data, see Karlsson (1983).

For phonaesthemes, see Marchand (1969) under the heading of 'phonetic symbolism'.

The example of *ignorance* and *perseverance* is from Lyons (1963: 78).

The examples in (13) are from Knowles (1997).

EXERCISES

1. Consider the forms of the past tense illustrated in the data below and provide at least two distinct analyses into morphemes and allomorphs, distinguished in terms of the way in which these notions

are interpreted. How would you deal with this data if you had a morphome as well as a morpheme? How would you deal with this data in a theory which did not recognise the morpheme?

fɒləʊ	fɒləʊd	rʌn	ræn
hɪt	hɪt	spɪt	spɪt/spæt
kʌm	keɪm	spend	spent
kɔːl	kɔːld	trʌst	trʌstɪd
lɑːf	lɑːft	wɒnt	wɒntɪd
pʊt	pʊt	wɔːk	wɔːkt

2. While the notion of morphome clarifies some matters, it leaves others unclear and may even cause problems. Discuss the notion of morphome, contrasting it with the notion of morpheme (in any acceptance), and paying particular attention to points which require further clarification.

3. In relation to the words in (12a), consider the two sets of words provided below. How do these affect your understanding of the phonaestheme or its relation to the morpheme?

glad	glair
glade	glaucous
gladiolus	gley
gland	gloat
glen	glob
globe	gloomy
glove	gloop

4. If you were reading an introductory physics textbook, you would not expect to find warnings that a term such as 'gravity' or 'ohm' was subject to different definitions in different texts and that you would have to take care in interpreting anything you read. Do the problems associated with the term 'morpheme' indicate that Linguistics is not scientific in its approach?

CHAPTER 8

The Domain of Morphology

In Chapter 3, it was pointed out that the central domain of morphology is affixation but that there are a number of other processes which at least impinge on morphology and may or may not belong to morphology proper. The reason for this is that other processes have certain things in common with affixation processes, while differing from them in other ways. There are thus links of variable strength binding affixation processes to other processes and, the weaker these links become or the greater the number of intermediate steps in these links, the less likely it is that a particular process should be considered to be morphological. In this section, I should like to illustrate this state of affairs. Since it is not clear to me that such an exercise makes any sense in a universalist kind of way, I shall illustrate it purely from English. It may be that other languages display other patterns; though, if they do not, this is, of course, a very interesting discovery. Towards the end of this section, I shall try to show that some processes are less centrally morphological than others, though no definite conclusion on where to draw the boundaries of morphology will be reached. I shall do this by drawing parallels between various kinds of process and then trying to summarise them diagrammatically.

(a) Prefixation resembles suffixation because both deal with the addition of obligatorily bound forms to forms which, in the majority of cases, are potentially free.

(b) Prefixation resembles compounding because both prefixes and the first elements of compounds can, under appropriate circumstances, be coordinated in English. This is not the case with suffixes, in particular. This is illustrated in (1).

(1)   summer and winter holidays
         girl- or boyfriends
         in- and output
         pro- or antivivisection
         psycho- and sociolinguistics
         *adviser and -ee
         *normalcy or -ity
         *aeroplane or -drome

(c) Prefixation is like neoclassical compounding because:

  i.   Many of the same items can act as first elements in neoclassical compounds and as prefixes, such as *socio-* in *sociology* and *sociolinguistics*;

  ii. Both prefixes and the first elements of neoclassical compounds can be coordinated under some circumstances and not under others.

(2)   pre- and post-natal care
         Anglo- and Francophilia
         *re- and decode
         *phon- and graphology

         The precise circumstances under which coordination is possible are not well understood, and do not appear to be easily formalised, so they will not be enlarged upon any further here. Suffice it to say, for present purposes, that this similarity exists.

(d) Prefixation is like back-formation because both can deal with the same elements: prefixation adds them, back-formation deletes them, and the end result may be indistinguishable. In a sentence like *I don't know if Jillian was nonplussed but she certainly wasn't plussed*, we have a case of back-formation. In a sentence like *The PC connectives behave in non-normal worlds precisely as they do in normal ones*, a case of prefixation. However, in both instances, the same element *non-* is involved.

(e) Suffixation is like neoclassical compounding because the same elements may be used as suffixes and as the second elements in neoclassical compounds, such as *-ology* in *Kremlinology* and *psychology*.

(f) Suffixation is like conversion because they both regularly cause changes to the major category to which the word belongs.

(g) Suffixation is like back-formation because the same elements may be involved in both, and the final results may be indistinguishable (see the discussion above with regards to prefixation and back-formation). An example is *edit* versus *editor* as opposed to *exhibit* versus *exhibitor*.

(h) Back-formation is like conversion because:
    i.   Neither of them involves overt affixes, yet both can cause changes of major category.
    ii. The two are extremely important ways of forming compound verbs in English and compound verbs in English are rarely formed except by one of these two processes.

(i) Back-formation is like clipping because both involve a shortening of the base.

(j) Neoclassical compounding is like compounding because
    i.   The same kind of variable meaning relationship holds between the elements in neoclassical and ordinary compounds.
    ii. It can be argued that both are involved with the collocation of roots, even if the roots in the one case are not always English ones.
    iii. The first elements of compounds and neoclassical compounds can (at least under some circumstances) be coordinated, see examples (1) and (2) above.

(k) Neoclassical compounding is like blending because both involve the fusion of two elements neither of which is potentially free, occasionally to the extent that the one is indistinguishable from the other. The form *autocide*, for example, has two meanings: 'self-destruction' (neoclassical compound) and 'suicide in an automobile' (blend).

(l) Blends are like acronyms because they are both made up of non-meaning-bearing parts of other words.

(m) Compounding is like syntax because they are both concerned with the collocation of lexemes.

There may well be other possible links that could be drawn and other reasons for the links that have been made here. These various similarities can be mapped to form a network like the one illustrated in Figure 8.1

In Figure 8.1 there appears to be a central core of strongly morphological processes, made up of prefixation, suffixation, back-

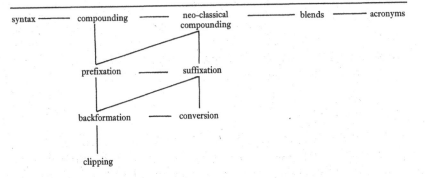

Figure 8.1 Network of various processes in English

formation and neoclassical compounding. Outside that central core, clipping, blending and forming acronyms appear as processes which are much less morphological. This does not mean that there is a firm line between morphology in the central core and non-morphology outside it. Rather, morphology shades off into other things and the central core is probably the area which is most clearly within morphology. It should, of course, be remembered that Figure 8.1 is drawn up on the basis of English only and that other languages (some of which use other processes such as reduplication and infixation) might well give rise to different networks.

This indicates that there are no firm boundaries to morphology. Correspondingly, what is treated as morphology in any particular theory will depend on other facets of that theory. This is made even more complex by the fact that there are, in any case, close links between morphology and phonology, on the one hand, and morphology and syntax, on the other. The links with phonology are seen in the whole area of morphophonemics. The links with syntax are shown particularly in clitics and compounds. These three areas will be treated in turn below.

8.1 LINKS WITH PHONOLOGY

What is phonology? The dictionary definition is that it deals with the sound systems of particular languages. There are, however, a number of ways in which this can be done. Consider, for example, the [n] in the word *in* in the two sentences in (3).

(3) (a)   I read it in the newspaper.
    (b)   I saw it in a book.

The [n] in (3b) is an alveolar nasal while the [n] in (3a) is a dental nasal. Most phonologists would probably agree that this variation is part of the sound system of English and should be part of the field of phonological study. Now consider the examples in (4).

(4)   long
        leng·th

We can probably agree that *long* and *leng* are allomorphs of the same morpheme, {long}. Is the phonological distinction between these two allomorphs to be explained as part of the field of phonological study or is it simply the phonological result of a morphological difference? Different phonologists would give different answers to this question.

The distinction between the two types illustrated in (3) and (4) is not as great as might appear at first glance. If the difference between alveolar and dental [n] illustrated in (3) has a phonological explanation, what about the alveolar and dental [n]s in *ten* as opposed to *ten·th*? Many scholars distinguish between assimilation in the first instance and similitude in the second and, thus, do not equate the two, but it is clear that similar processes account for the dental [n] in both cases. If assimilation like that mentioned above is to be explained phonologically, so presumably is the alternation between [s] and [ʃ] in the word *this* in

(5)   this kind
        this year

Note that the [j] may disappear entirely, giving [ðɪʃɜː]. The same phonetic change is found in the pairs in (6).

(6)   express   expression
        regress   regression.

If we assume that *-ion* has a basic phonological form something like /jən/, the same rules can account for both cases. If the forms of allomorphs which depend on assimilation or similitude are to be explained phonologically, presumably alternations due to vowel harmony are also to be explained in that way. So the alternations between *-a* and *-ä*, *-vat* and *-vät*, *-ko* and *-kö* in the Finnish examples in (7) will be given a phonological explanation.

(7)   otta·a   's/he takes'   pitä·ä   's/he likes'
        otta·vat   'they take'   pitä·vät   'they like'
        otta·vat·ko   'do they take'   pitä·vät·kö   'do they like'

If examples like this, where the segmental form of one part of the word is determined by the segmental form of another part of the same word, are to be explained phonologically, what about cases where the segmental form of a word is determined by suprasegmental form? For example, the difference in the segmental form of the first morph in *tele·graph* and *tele·graph·y* is determined by the position of the stress. Should this also receive a phonological explanation? And, if so, what about the differences between the pairs of English words in (8)? Here the difference between the allomorphs of the root is determined partly by stress, partly by the position of the appropriate vowels in the word and partly by lexical listing (in that not every word which fits the phonological criteria shows the same alternation, consider *obese/obesity* as a contrast with the examples below).

(8) divine   divin·ity
     obscene   obscen·ity
     profound   profund·ity

If such allomorphy is to be given a phonological explanation, then why not the purely lexically determined allomorphy in *long* and *leng·th*?

The dominant approach to phonology in the last part of the twentieth century was generative phonology. The standard approach in generative phonology is to see the phonology as a component which links the output of the syntactic component to pronunciation (usually fairly grossly specified). The output of the syntactic component is seen as a series of morphemes, whose precise phonetic shape is to be supplied by the phonology. In the vast majority of cases, each morpheme is given a single deep-structure phonological representation and phonological rules have to apply to this to specify all cases of allomorphy which are observed in that morpheme. The limiting case is suppletion, where two (or more) deep-structure phonological representations are specified. The general trend in phonological studies has been to minimise suppletion and to derive as much as possible by phonological rules.

But consider the situation in Welsh (and comparable data can be found in other Celtic languages). In Welsh, many consonants can undergo mutation – that is, a change to another consonant. There are three patterns of mutation: soft mutation (which provides a lenited form of the original consonant); nasal mutation (which provides a nasal corresponding in articulation to the original consonant); and spirant mutation (which provides a fricative at the same place of articulation as an original stop). Each type of mutation can clearly be described in phonological terms and, indeed, must be so described.

But the conditions under which the various mutations apply have to be described in syntactic and morphological terms. For instance, different prefixes condition different types of mutation in the initial consonant of a base. The initial consonant of an adjective undergoes soft mutation after a feminine noun, but not after a masculine one. The initial consonant of a noun undergoes soft mutation after an inflected preposition. The second element of one type of compound also undergoes soft mutation. In all these cases, there is a morphological trigger for the phonological process and any explanation cannot be entirely phonological.

Similar conclusions apply in cases where morphological change is indicated by internal modification of a base. To remain with Welsh, consider the following examples:

(9)	*masculine*	*feminine*	*gloss*
	byr	ber	'short'
	crwn	cron	'round'
	gwyn	gwen	'white'
	trwm	trom	'heavy'

The feminine forms in (9) will also undergo soft mutation, so that their final form will not be identical with that given above. In cases such as these, it may be possible to give a phonological description of the change of form but any description of the way in which that change of form operates will also include morphological information. Conversely, of course, any morphological description of the changes illustrated here will involve phonological facts as well as purely morphological ones.

Another example of the way in which morphology and phonology interact is provided by the effect of English suffixes on the stress of derivatives. There are some English derivational affixes which, like all English inflectional affixes, do not affect the stress of the base. For example, when the suffix -*less* is added to a base, the stress on the new word remains on the same syllable that it was on in the base. This is illustrated below.

(10)	'humour	'humourless
	'meaning	'meaningless
	'character	'characterless
	de'fence	de'fenceless
	re'morse	re'morseless
	ex'pression	ex'pressionless

However, there are other derivational affixes which do affect the stress of the base. They do this either by attracting stress onto themselves (11a) or by attracting stress onto a specific syllable defined in relation to the suffix (11b).

(11) (a) 'journal   journa'lese
          Ja'pan   Japa'nese
          o'fficial   officia'lese

     (b) 'acid   a'cidic
          'poet   po'etic
          'algebra   alge'braic
          'telescope   tele'scopic
          im'perialist   imperia'listic

In either case, the fact that one of these affixes is present has a phonological effect on the base of the new word. Again morphology and phonology can be seen to be closely related.

The extreme view would be that there is no distinction to be drawn between phonological and morphological processes. There are only phonological processes. The actual arrangement of morphs, on this view, is determined syntactically, with the result that there is no separate morphological component of a grammar. This view is implicit in some versions of transformational-generative grammar. More recent theories tend to reject this extreme view but precisely where the distinction between morphology and phonology is drawn varies from theory to theory. In the light of the close connections, this variation is only to be expected.

There is also a sense in which the effect of phonological processes on morphological strings can make morphological analysis much more difficult. Consider the following data from Sanskrit:

(12)   viːna   iːrṣjaja   vinerṣjaja
       without   jealousy   without-jealousy
       saː   uːvatʃa   sovatʃa
       she   spoke   she-spoke

In (12) we see that an open vowel followed by a close vowel across a word-boundary merge as a mid vowel. Which morph does that mid vowel then belong to? Clearly, it belongs entirely to neither but, in some sense, to both. We can carry out a morphological analysis in terms of the word-forms as they would be spoken in isolation but phonological processes then mask the morphological structure. In practice, this kind of problem is dealt with in a generative grammar by allowing underlying forms of the morphemes such as {saː} and {uːvatʃa} in (12) and then having phonological rules apply to those underlying forms to produce the **sandhi** phenomena, such as those illustrated above. Some sandhi phenomena are relatively simple, such as assimilation processes mentioned earlier, others far more complex, such as the vowel fusion illustrated in (12). In some cases, morphological information is needed to know whether sandhi will occur or not. For example, some speakers of English have an intrusive /r/ in (13a), where a new word immediately follows, but not in (13b), where another morpheme in the same word-form immediately follows:

(13) (a) We want to draw /r/ and paint.
    (b) We are draw*/r/·ing a house.

Different varieties of English have different rules for sandhi at this point. Once again, though, the close relation between phonology and morphology is illustrated.

8.2 LINKS WITH SYNTAX

The links between syntax and morphology are at least as close as those between phonology and morphology. In many structuralist grammars (and, following this tradition, in early transformational-generative grammars), the syntax was the part of the grammar which dealt with statements concerning the order of morphs (or morphemes). If the phonology dealt with problems of allomorphy, there was no need for a separate morphological component.

Although this view is unpopular today (for reasons which will be discussed in Chapter 10), there is some evidence to support it. First, there are some languages in which morphs and word-forms are largely coterminous. In such languages, dealing with an extra component or level of morphology may complicate the linguist's task unnecessarily. Given a sentence like that from Chrau, a language of Vietnam, in (14), a statement of morphology would only complicate the description.

(14)   Anh nhai nŏq là ănh nhai nhâng
        I speak thus is I speak true
        'I speak like this, that is, truthfully.'

Second, syntactic structure appears frequently to give rise diachronically to morphological structure (see further, Chapter 15). For example, the French adverbial suffix -*ment* and its cognates in the other Romance languages are derived from the ablative form of the noun meaning 'mind', which could appear as a separate word-form in vulgar Latin. This seems to imply that the distinction between morphs in a separate word-form and morphs in the same word-form is relatively unimportant and that, therefore, there is no point in a separate section of a grammar dealing with morphology.

If we are to argue against this point of view, we have to show that words are useful constructs. There are some arguments that seem to show this. However, these arguments do not necessarily show that we must have a level of the word in every language, only that it can be useful in some languages.

First of all, the arguments that were presented in Chapter 4 to show how a word-form can be defined can be turned on their heads. If we have no notion of word, then we cannot state the domains of vowel harmony, cannot state with maximum efficiency the positions where contrastive stress can fall and so on. There is a danger of circularity here but not, I think, an insuperable one.

Perhaps the most telling argument, though, is that morpheme ordering in a word can be obligatorily different from morpheme ordering in a sentence. This may be true even where we are probably dealing with the same morphemes. So, in English comparatives, mono- and disyllabic adjectives, which take the affix -er, take it suffixed to the adjective, while disyllabic or longer adjectives, which take *more*, order it before the adjective. Some adjectives may take either form, quite synonymously. Thus, the two sentences in (15) are synonymous.

(15)   Suffixation is commoner than prefixation.
        Suffixation is more common than prefixation.

This seems to imply (since the only difference is a difference in the way the comparative has been realised and the comparative is probably inflectional) that we are dealing with the same morphemes. Nevertheless, the morpheme {comparative} is ordered differently depending on whether it is in the same word-form as *common* or in a different word-form.

Although there are many reasons for seeing morphology and syntax as closely related and although they may function very largely in similar ways, arguments like this suggest that, at least for some languages, morphology should be kept separate from syntax.

Nevertheless, there are some areas where it is difficult to draw the distinction. In particular, this is true with clitics and compounds.

8.2.1 Clitics

There is a type of obligatorily bound morph which is generally distinguished from an affix. This is the **clitic**, a form which seems to be intermediate between an affix and a word. In the clearest cases (but, unfortunately, not in every case), a clitic is a reduced form of a word with independent existence. The forms *'ve, 'd, 's* and *'ll*, as reduced forms of *have, had, has* and *will* respectively, are instances of clitics in English. Such clitics are called **simple clitics**. Clitics which are not weakened forms of ordinary words are called **special clitics**.

The problem for the morphologist lies in distinguishing clitics from affixes, since both are bound morphs. There are a number of ways of distinguishing between the two, which will be discussed below. Basically, the distinction is that clitics are more syntactic than are affixes. Since the most syntactic of the affixes are inflectional affixes, the distinction that has to be drawn is between clitics on the one hand and inflectional affixes on the other.

The criteria for distinguishing between inflectional affixes and clitics, like the criteria for distinguishing between inflection and derivation, do not always define precisely the same set of morphs as clitics and do not necessarily agree in all cases. Rather, they define the prototypical cases of clitics or inflectional affixes. Actual cases will deviate from the prototype to a greater or lesser extent.

(a) Affixes attach to lexical categories such as nouns, adjectives and verbs. For example, the *-ed* affix, which marks the past tense in English, attaches to bases which are verbs. Clitics may attach to phrasal categories, although they will always be phonologically attached to a single word in that phrase. The *-'s* formative which marks the possessive in English is a clitic and illustrates this point. In (16) below, a number of noun phrases are illustrated, each of which contains a possessive noun phrase before the head noun. In every case the *-'s* is attached to the last word in the possessive noun phrase, not simply to the noun.

(16)   a dog's life
the King of Spain's daughter
the woman in white's face
the woman we saw's coat
the cat which came in's fur
the man I saw yesterday's hat

(b) As is also evident from the examples in (16), the category of the word to which a clitic attaches itself is usually irrelevant. In the examples above, the clitic is attached to a noun, an adjective, a verb and an adverb. Where a clitic is a reduced form of a freely occurring word (such as *'ve* for *have*), the clitic simply occurs wherever the non-reduced word could occur. In contrast, affixes tend to attach to specific categories: the past tense *-ed* marker in English attaches specifically to verbs. This criterion, however, is not always met, since some languages have specific clitic positions where any clitic must be placed. For example, in West Greenlandic, clitic particles usually follow the first sentential constituent, as illustrated in the example below where the particular clitic illustrated indicates that the information expressed was gained at second-hand:

(17)   tassa·guuq   Kangirlussuatsia·kkut   umiar·passuit
       that-is·clitic   (place-name)·case-marker   boat·many
       ilummukaa·pput
       move-inwards·3rd-person-indicative
       'Well, it is said many boats came inland by way of
       K.(fjord).'

(c) Clitics do not show lexically conditioned allomorphy, while affixes frequently do. The plural in English, on one analysis, shows lexically conditioned allomorphy with lexemes such as CHILD, OX, SERAPH, WOMAN and so on. In contrast, the possessive -*'s* does not show lexically conditioned allomorphy.

(d) Finally, while clitics can attach freely to bases containing affixes or clitics, affixes cannot attach to bases containing clitics. This is illustrated below:

(18)   I'd've come.
       Girls've been seen here.
       The dogs' dinners are there, but the cats' 've been eaten.
       *cat'ds
       *the man who walk'sed feet

Clitics are divided into **proclitics**, which are attached before their base, and **enclitics**, which are attached after their base. An example of a proclitic is the French direct object pronoun in sentences like *Claude l'a fait* 'Claude did it'. An example of an enclitic is Latin *que* 'and' attached to the second of two conjoined words, as in *Patriam re:gnum·que meum repetere* 'to reclaim my country and my kingdom'.

8.2.2 Compounds

As was seen in Figure 8.1 on page 125, compounding has links with syntax as well as links with morphology. Some scholars have tried to distinguish, even within English, between those compounds which are the result of morphological processes and those which are the result of syntactic processes. For example, there are some compounds which appear to have a single stress (in the sense discussed in section 4.1.1), while others have two. For example, *apple cake* is generally agreed to have a single stress, while *apple pie* has two. To a large extent, this coincides with an orthographic distinction between those compounds written as a single orthographic word and those written as two. There seems to be some feeling, amongst both lay people and linguists, that this orthographic distinction reflects a genuine linguistic distinction of some kind. Since it always comes up in this context, it is worth making the point that hyphenation in English is totally random and does not necessarily prove anything at all about the linguistic status of strings of elements. To illustrate this, consider the following spellings, found in three different dictionaries:

(19)   girlfriend (*Hamlyn's Encyclopedic World Dictionary*)
         girl-friend (*The Concise Oxford Dictionary* (7th edition))
         girl friend (*Webster's Third New International Dictionary*).

Presumably we would not want to decide that *girl-friend* is a lexeme for the editors of the Hamlyn's dictionary, but not for the editors of the Webster's, although it is a lexical item for both. Some linguists seem happy enough to concede GIRLFRIEND (however spelt) as a single lexeme but are less happy with longer compounds. For example, everyone would probably agree that there is a lexeme TEXTBOOK. What, then, about MORPHOLOGY TEXTBOOK? Is that still a single lexeme? If so, what about MORPHOLOGY TEXTBOOK COVER? And, if we have a box that contains these covers, what about MORPHOLOGY TEXTBOOK COVER BOX? Despite conflicting intuitions caused by factors such as the ones just discussed and despite numerous attempts to provide a scientific basis for these intuitions, it appears that there is no reliable way of drawing distinctions along such lines; for example, none of the criteria discussed in Chapter 4 make any distinction between these different kinds of compound. That is not to say that none can be made and, indeed, some recent work in Lexicalist Morphology suggests that a distinction between root and synthetic compounds might be drawn on the basis of morphology versus syntax but this result is not yet generally accepted.

There are at least two arguments in favour of seeing compounding as more closely allied to morphology.

(a) Like derivation, compounding creates new items of vocabulary (that is, lexemes, if this hypothesis is adopted), which appear to be learnt as wholes and used just like any other kind of derived or simplex lexeme. In particular, it is noticeable that speakers do not analyse the internal structure of familiar compounds. To use the noun *hedgehog* you do not have to be aware that its elements imply 'pig which lives in hedges'. In a similar way, to use the derivative *carriage*, you do not have to be able to analyse it as 'nominalisation from CARRY'. Occasionally, you get instances where a speaker realises that a compound, which has been considered as a unit, has an analysable structure, and this is commented on with remarks such as 'I've never thought of that before.'

(b) Like derivatives, compounds provide names for entities, properties or actions. This is opposed to providing descriptions, which is the function of syntax. A derivative like *judo·ist* and a compound like *judo·man* both provide a name for the person concerned, as opposed to a syntactic phrase like 'an expert in judo', which provides a description.

There are other arguments in favour of seeing compounding as being more closely allied with syntax.

(a) Compounds are sequences of lexemes. Any other sequence of lexemes (with the possible exception of idioms, though even they are not totally excluded) is dealt with as syntax and not as morphology. Particularly strong motivation is, thus, required if one type of lexeme sequence is to be called morphology.

(b) While there are many instances where a compound is remembered and used as an unanalysable unit, as discussed above, there are plenty of other cases where items which are formally indistinguishable are not learned as wholes but are created on the spur of the moment and forgotten again immediately. This effect is more noticeable in some languages than in others; for example, it is clearly true of the Germanic languages but far less true in the Romance languages. A quick glance at any newspaper written in a Germanic language should show the truth of this. An advertisement for a linguistics book, on my desk as I write, speaks of 'the main issues raised by second language acquisition research', thus, coining a compound which is unlikely to be treated as an unanalysable whole.

(c) It is frequently the case that the meaning of a noun plus noun compound is indistinguishable from the meaning of an adjective plus noun phrase. Consider, for example:

(20)   atom bomb   atomic bomb
        gold ring   golden ring
        language development   linguistic development
        sea life   marine life
        verb paradigm   verbal paradigm

In cases like those illustrated here, the two constructions appear to be entirely equivalent alternatives. Traditionally, the noun plus noun alternative is seen as part of morphology, the adjective plus noun alternative is seen as part of syntax. While it is possible that there should be such a distinction, it has generally not been as well-motivated as it ought to have been.

(d) In other cases, a sequence of noun plus noun is equivalent to a sequence of possessive plus noun. Again similar arguments apply. The latter is usually seen as part of syntax, the former as part of morphology. If there is a genuine distinction, it needs to be well-motivated. Generally, no such motivation is provided. The probability remains, therefore, that they are both structures of the same kind, and that is most likely to mean syntactic structures not morphological ones. Some examples from English to illustrate the parallelism are given in (21).

(21)   birdfoot   bird's foot
        dog house   dog's house
        rat-tail grass   rat's-tail grass
        student evaluations   students' evaluations
        summer day   summer's day

and contrast, too:

        cat gut   cat's-eye
        cowhide   cow's milk

There are also supporting parallels from other languages. Some of the interfixes used in other Germanic languages are historically derived from (and in some cases are still homophonous with) allomorphs of the morpheme {genitive}. Finnish and Sanskrit both have compounds with genitive first elements.

(e) While it is quite common to find compound prepositions and compounds in other minor categories, it is extremely rare to find prepositions which are created derivationally except by conversion (I know of no such examples). Prepositions may inflect in some languages (for example, Welsh) but there are no derivational affixes for producing them. Examples of compound forms in minor categories are given below:

(22)

English	French	Indonesian
an·other	le·quel	di·belakang
because of	the·which	at·back
any·one	'which'	'behind'
when·ever	pour·quoi	ke·belakang
in·to	for·what	to·back
Finnish	'why'	'behind'
ett·ei	mal·gré	di·samping
that·not	bad·liking	at·side
ell·ei	'despite'	'beside'
or·not		di·muka
'unless'		at·front
		'in front of'

This suggests that compounding and derivation may be rather different in kind.

There are, thus, a good many reasons for seeing compounding as being more closely allied with syntax than with derivational morphology. When the linguist builds compounding into a grammar, the relative importance placed on these arguments and the arguments, which show the link between morphology and compounding, will determine where compounding is dealt with. In current theories, compounding is nearly always dealt with as part of morphology. In either case, the point is made that the dividing line between morphology and syntax is a very fine one and not necessarily easily drawn.

8.3 CONCLUDING REMARKS

In this chapter, more questions have been asked than answered. In part, this is because many of the questions cannot be answered definitively in a theoretical vacuum but only in relation to a particular model of grammar. At the moment, as we shall see in the next Part, there are a large number of different models of grammar being used and a correspondingly large number of ideas about how morphology is to be dealt with in a grammar. In theory, these could range from dealing with morphology entirely as a matter of phonology to dealing with morphology entirely as a matter of syntax. In this chapter, it has been hinted that at least for some languages, it is going to be far more satisfactory to deal with morphology on its own terms. The models that will be considered in the next Part all do this. What has been shown here is that any morphological component in a grammar cannot be entirely autonomous: it must have close links with both phonology and syntax. How these links are established may well differ from theory to theory. They must exist to account for the rather fuzzy boundaries that morphology seems to have on both sides.

REFERENCES AND FURTHER READING

The matter of when prefixes and the elements of neoclassical compounds can be coordinated is dealt with briefly by Quirk et al. (1972: 610), where it is discussed in terms of whether the elements concerned are 'loosely' or 'tightly attached'. For further discussion of this phenomenon, see Booij (1985), Okada (1999) and Smith (2000).

The two sentences illustrating the use of *non-* on page 123 are genuine examples: the first from Lawrence Block (1978), *The Burglar in the Closet*, London: Robert Hale; the second is cited in the Supplement to *The Oxford English Dictionary*.

The discussion of Welsh mutation is based on Williams (1980). For further details and for the syntactic uses of mutations, see that work or any other grammar of a Celtic language.

The matter of affixes and stress is dealt with in considerably more detail in Fudge (1984).

The data on Sanskrit sandhi is taken from Lass (1984). For further discussion of sandhi from a morphological point of view see Matthews (1991: Chapter 8).

The Chrau data in (14) is taken from Thomas (1971). The data from West Greenlandic in (17) is from Fortescue (1984).

For arguments that morphology should not be equated with either phonology or syntax, see Aronoff (1994b). The arguments are based on paradigm structure and form an interesting extension of the discussion given here.

The main source on clitics is Zwicky & Pullum (1983). This paper argues interestingly that English *n't* is an inflectional affix and not a clitic. There is also a problem in distinguishing between words and clitics, which is not relevant in the present context. This is treated in

Zwicky (1985a). Another useful reference on clitics is Anderson (1985b: 154ff).

The Lexicalist Morphology work on compounds mentioned on page 134 is Botha (1984b).

The point about the lack of distinction between noun plus noun constructions and adjective plus noun constructions is made within Hallidayan grammar, where both count as Classifiers, and is also argued extensively by Levi (1978). She concludes that the appropriate adjective plus noun constructions are types of compound. The alternative conclusion is the one hinted at here that noun plus noun constructions are syntactic, phrasal constructions. For a discussion of the distinctions, see Bauer (1998).

The data from Finnish is from Karlsson (1983), that from Indonesian is from Kwee (1965). The data from Turkish in exercise 1 is taken from Lewis (1967).

EXERCISES

1. In Turkish, there is a suffix which is semantically equivalent to the English *-er* in *traveller, photographer*, etc. This suffix occurs in a number of different forms: /ʤi/, /ʤy/, /ʤɯ/, /ʤu/, /ʧi/, /ʧy/, /ʧɯ/, /ʧu/. *For the purposes of this exercise, ignore the differences in the vowels, which are caused by vowel harmony.* On the basis of the data below, explain what kind of sandhi process is operating.

iʃ	'work'	isʧi	'worker'
syt	'milk'	sytʧy	'milkman'
diʃ	'tooth'	diʃʧi	'dentist'
kaʧak	'contraband'	kaʧakʧɯ	'smuggler'
orman	'forest'	ormanʤɯ	'forester'
jol	'road'	jolʤu	'traveller'
jalan	'falsehood'	jalanʤɯ	'liar'
statyko	'status quo'	statykoʤu	'conservative'
ʃaka	'joke'	ʃakaʤɯ	'joker'

2. A few base nouns and their diminutives in Dutch are illustrated below (diminutives mean 'a (nice) little X'). If your model of grammar demanded a single form for each morpheme, what would you postulate as the single underlying form for the diminutive morpheme? What kinds of sandhi rules would you have to postulate to get the appropriate surface forms?

Base	Gloss	Diminutive
haːrɪŋ	'herring'	haːrɪŋkjə
ʋœrm	'worm'	ʋœrmpjə
tœyn	'garden'	tœyncə
streːp	'stripe'	streːpjə
leːpəl	'spoon'	leːpəlcə
kɪkər	'frog'	kɪkərcə
trœy	'sweater'	trœycə
baŋərik	'scaredy cat'	baŋərikjə
rœyf	'manger'	rœyfjə
ʋerəlt	'world'	ʋerəlcə

3. Consider the list of putative compounds given below. Are they always stressed the same way? (You can check in pronouncing dictionaries and dictionaries or you can listen to speakers of English – perhaps even ask them directly.) Are they always written the same way? (You can check in dictionaries or search the internet.) Does the spelling correlate with the stress in any way? Are any of them freely interruptable? Can you coordinate another head with the head of the compound (the right-hand element) in any of them? Can you replace the head of the compound with the word *one* (for example, is a sentence such as *He threw up his girlfriend and got a boy one* possible?) in any of them? Do any of these criteria correlate with each other or with any of the others?

apple pie	cherry cake	kitchen garden
apron stage	churchwarden	nightwatch
boyfriend	cottage cheese	peanut butter
bus driver	flour mill	wage earner
buttercup	iron fence	windmill

4. Look in newspapers and advertisements for long compounds (with more than three elements). What is the longest you can find? Is a longer compound conceivable? Why do you think that people might be less ready to accept long compounds as lexemes than things like *buttercup*? How important should this feeling be for the linguistic description of compounds?

5. Consider *n't* in English, as in *isn't*. Test it against the criteria discussed in the chapter to see whether it is best treated as an affix or as a clitic.

6. One question that was raised in this Chapter was whether it is possible to distinguish between those compounds that belong to the

morphology and those that belong to the syntax. Botha argues that, in fact, synthetic compounds are very like other morphological formations. Consider whether the division between morphological compounds and syntactic compounds could be equated with the division between synthetic and root compounds. To answer this question you will have to read Botha (1981) and Botha (1984b). You might also like to consider whether synthetic compounds could be seen as a special type of incorporation.

7. In Figure 8.1 on page 125, a network is drawn up of various morphological processes in English. One could extend the network shown there, for example, by pointing out that acronyms and clipping have in common the facts that they both involve shortening and that neither involves the deletion of morphs. How does this affect the figure and the conclusions drawn from it? Are there any other links which could be drawn? How would a language with infixation and/or reduplication affect the network shown in Figure 8.1?

PART THREE: Issues

CHAPTER 9

Recognising Morphemes

One of the major problems in morphology is knowing when you are dealing with two realisations of the same morpheme and when two morphs realise different morphemes. At first blush, this may appear to be a trivial matter: the form *cat* realises the morpheme {cat} and the form *dog* realises the morpheme {dog} and it is intuitively quite clear that these are completely separate morphemes. If one were asked to justify this intuition, one would probably say that the two morphs differ from each other in form and meaning. Unfortunately, this is not enough.

First of all, it must be realised that neither form nor meaning alone is a sufficient criterion. On the basis of form alone, we might propose that *cargo* was related to {car} and {go}, that *piety* was related to {pie} or that *bear* (the animal) and *bare* ('naked') represented the same morpheme. Conversely, on the basis of form alone we might very well deny that the forms *accident·al* and *event·ual·ity* could share any common morpheme (particularly in varieties of English where a word-final /l/ is vocalised to give [æksɪˈdentʊ] or something similar). On the basis of meaning alone, we might propose that forms such as *little, small, tiny, petite, minuscule* shared some morpheme in common. Conversely, we might deny that *escapee* ('one who escapes') and *trainee* ('one who is trained') share any morpheme in common. Yet all these conclusions would be unsatisfactory, if not downright wrong.

More importantly, however, it is not clear how much form or how much meaning must be shared before two morphs can be seen as realisations of the same morpheme. The problem as it relates to meaning has already been illustrated with reference to the suffix *-ette* in section 6.3. The problem as it relates to form will be illustrated repeatedly in this chapter. A simple example is provided by the forms *mother, maternal, matron, mum, mummy* and *mama.* All contain an initial /m/ but they have nothing else in common (although various pairs of these forms have rather more in common). Is this sufficient for us to say that a single morpheme is involved? If not, how many are involved? Problems of this kind become particularly acute where neither the form nor the meaning is unambiguously shared between morphs.

The question, thus, turns out to be far from simple. In the long run, decisions on these matters are likely to be the result of the theoretical approach taken by the individual linguist. However, some guidelines are possible although the guidelines for affixes and bases are not quite the same.

9.1 AFFIXES

To make the discussion here more concrete, three sets of data are presented below. In each case, a single form is discussed and, in each case, it is intuitively fairly clear that the single form represents at least two distinct affixes or morphemes. The clear distinctions are indicated by the columns in which the words are listed. The discussion will then centre on the arguments which support the intuition that we are dealing here with distinct affixes despite the similarity of form.

(1) (a) earth·en (b) broad·en
         flax·en   damp·en
         gold·en   dark·en
         lead·en   deaf·en
         silk·en   hard·en
         wheat·en   light·en
         wood·en   sick·en
         wool(l)·en   soft·en

(2) (a) in·come   (b) in·dependent
         in·door   in·direct
         in-house   in·edible
         in·land   in·eligible
         in·lay   in·eloquent
         in·put   in·equality
         in·set   in·sociable
         in·shore   in·solvent
                        in·tangible
                        in·transitive

location   *neg*

(3) (a)   apple·s   (b)   build·s
          cabinet·s   consider·s
          car·s   expect·s
          cat·s   hear·s
          curtain·s   observe·s
          lawn·s   provide·s
          pigeon·s   write·s
          sump·s   yield·s

The first, and most obvious, way to distinguish different affixes of similar form is by meaning. In (2b), for example, the *in-* means something like 'not, negative' while, in (2a), it means something like 'location within'. In (3a), the final *-s* indicates plurality while, in (3b), it indicates '3rd person singular present tense'. A clearly distinct meaning difference, with no possibility of overlap (as in these cases), usually indicates separateness of morphemes. Results are not always so clear, though. In (1), it might be difficult to specify precisely what the meanings are (although something like 'made of' versus something like 'cause to be' seem probable candidates). In other instances, notably in the case of nominalisations of verbs, it can be difficult to specify the meaning of the affix and to decide what constitutes a distinction in meaning. Recall from the discussion in section 7.3 that a difference in meaning of this type shows that we are dealing with a different morpheme, though not necessarily that we are dealing with a different morphome.

A second, again fairly obvious, way to distinguish between affixes is in terms of their function. In (1a) the *-en* suffix creates adjectives, while the suffix in (1b) creates verbs. The suffix in (3a) creates nouns, that in (3b) creates verbs. Again this is a useful and fairly easily applied criterion but, again, it breaks down in some cases. First of all, the majority of prefixes in English, like the prefixes in (2b), do not have any clear function in terms of creating a particular part of speech: the category of the derivative is the same as the category of the base. This criterion is, therefore, not always of value when dealing with prefixes in English or languages like it. Secondly, it may not always be clear what the function of an affix is. This can be seen with relation to the *in-* in (2a). *Land* is a noun (possibly a verb but much more probably a noun in this context) and *inland* is not. The prefix, therefore, has some function in changing category. But *inland* may be an adjective (as in the phrase *inland revenue*) or an adverb (as in *They walked inland for three kilometres.*). Should we postulate two distinct morphemes {in-}, one for each of these uses? In general, the answer will be no, as long as the dual function of the derivative is a regular phenomenon. This is the case here with *inboard, inshore*. We might, however, wish to set up other subdivisions of (2a) on the basis of this criterion. Alternatively, we might decide that other uses of these forms were the result of conversion, since English allows widespread conversion.

As well as the category of the new derivative being relevant, the category of the base is also a guide. In (1a), the base is in each case a noun while, in (1b), the base is always an adjective. In (3a), the base is always a noun and, in (3b) the base is always a verb. The different categories of base help to suggest that different affixes could be involved. Again, however, care is required in applying this criterion. In (2b), the prefix *in-* has been applied to adjectives (in the majority of the words listed) but also to nouns. In the case of *inequality*, the most likely analysis is that the prefix has been added to the noun *equality* and not the adjective *equal*, since the established adjective is *unequal* rather than *inequal*. Thus, some affixes may permit classes of base which are wider than a single part of speech. In English, this is particularly noticeable with prefixes. In other cases, it may not even be clear what the category of the base is. The prefix *de-* creating verbs such as *delouse, decipher, demast* is generally said to be added to nouns (thus, Marchand, 1969 following *The Oxford English Dictionary*). But, in virtually every case, a verb homophonous with that noun, albeit rarely as common as that noun, can be found listed in the major dictionaries of English.

It is not only the major category of the base which may be of importance but also the restrictions on the base. For instance, all the bases in (2b) are Latinate, while all of those in (2a) are Germanic in origin. In other cases, there may be phonological or semantic restrictions on bases, as discussed in section 5.5.1.

The range of allomorphs displayed by an affix can also be relevant. The prefix *in-*, illustrated in (2b), has a number of different allomorphs, both in the written and spoken forms, (the allomorphs in the written forms do not correspond in a one-to-one manner with allomorphs in the spoken forms but that is irrelevant for present purposes). In particular, there is an allomorph *il-* (/ɪ/) which occurs before bases beginning in /l/, as in *illegible, illegitimate*. The prefix illustrated in (2a) has no such allomorph, as can be seen from *inland, inlay*. The different range of allomorphs, in similar conditioning environments, seems to indicate fairly clearly that two distinct affixes are involved here. On the other hand, the parallel sets of allomorphs shown in (3a) and (3b) do not, in themselves, indicate that the same affix is involved in the two cases.

As well as the range of forms an affix may take, the form it imposes on the base can be a relevant criterion. There are two examples of this in (1) and (2) but neither of them is particularly convincing. The first concerns the stress on *in-house*. There is greater stress retained on the second morph of this word than there is in any of the others listed (*inshore* is the one that comes nearest to it). This difference in the stress pattern apparently caused by the prefix may be sufficient to indicate that this word does not realise the same {in-} as the others in (2a). Indeed, it may be a compound rather than a prefix. The example is not particularly convincing because there could be other explanations for the difference, always assuming that the difference is a consistent one in the first place. The other example concerns the word *earthen* in (1a). The voiceless dental fricative at the end of the base is voiced here for some speakers, apparently under the influence of the affix. In words which may contain the same suffix as that illustrated in (1b) (despite the major category of the base), such as *lengthen* and *strengthen*, there is no corresponding voicing of the dental fricative. This suggests that, for these speakers, a different affix is involved. For speakers who pronounce the word /ɜːθən/ – the majority of speakers – this evidence of difference is missing. In both these cases, the examples would be more convincing if it could be shown that the condition was general over a wide range of examples. Really good examples are hard to find from English but consider the case of two distinct -*y* suffixes. The first of these forms adjectives from either nouns or verbs, as in *summery, jittery*. The second forms nouns, especially from learned words, and especially from nouns, as in *democracy, diplomacy, spectroscopy*. Now, with this second suffix, the stress shifts away from the place where it would fall on the base (*democrat, diplomat, spectroscope*, respectively). With the first -*y* suffix, the adjective-forming one, this does not happen even in the rare cases where the word becomes long enough to allow stress-shift, as in the forms *coronetty, other-worldy*. This shows a case where homophonous suffixes impose a different form to the base, in that the first does not alter the stress pattern of the base, while the second does. For further discussion of stress in English word-formation see, for example, Fudge (1984). Note further that, if we analyse *diplomacy* as being made up of the morphemes {diplomat} and {y}, this {y} has caused a morphophonemic change to the base, changing a /t/ to an /s/. The adjectival -*y* does not have the same effect, as is shown by words like *carroty, sooty, throaty*. Again, a difference in the form imposed on the base by affixes of the same form provides an argument that we are dealing with distinct affixes.

Different affixes may also potentiate different subsequent affixation. **Potentiate** in this context is a technical term which means 'create a base suitable for'. In most cases, this potentiation will be a by-product of the major category of the derivative. For example, the suffix in (1b) potentiates subsequent -*ing* affixation because it creates verbs. In other cases, potentiation may be more subtle and, correspondingly, more useful in distinguishing between affixes. For instance, the prefix *en-* which creates verbs from adjectives as in *endear* and *ennoble* appears to potentiate -*ment* suffixation (*endearment, ennoblement*), whereas the prefix with the same form, which creates verbs from verbs, such as *enclose, encounter* and *entreat*, does not always potentiate -*ment* in the same way (?*enclosement,* ?*encounterment,* ?*entreatment*).

Finally, different affixes may show different degrees of productivity. The negative *in-*, illustrated in (2b), is now of very restricted productivity (at least when added to adjectives) and the prefix *un-* tends to be used instead (Marchand, 1969: section 3.26). The prefix or prefixes illustrated in (2a), on the other hand, are still productive, as can be seen by consulting any dictionary of new words. In (3a) and (3b), the two affixes are both extremely productive (possibly fully productive in the more restricted sense of this term, see above section 5.5), without that indicating that they are the same affix.

On the other side of the coin are affixes which are not homophonous and which, at first glance, are likely to be judged separate affixes. Homophony in itself, however, is not sufficient to allow a decision to be made one way or another. If homophony were the only reason for judging relatedness, the prefixes in the Indonesian examples, in (4) below, would have to be seen as realising separate unrelated morphemes.

(4)   men·duga   'to suspect'
         meng·gunting   'to cut (with scissors)'
         mem·buru   'to hunt'

The fact is that all these prefixes realise the same morpheme. There are, thus, extra factors which have to be taken into account: distribution and conditioning.

The general rule is that only forms (putative allomorphs) in complementary distribution can be taken to realise a single morpheme. This is the case for the examples in (4), where *men-* occurs before *d*, *meng-* occurs before *g* and *mem-* occurs before *b*. The final nasal of the prefix is homorganic with the voiced stop which follows it and the allomorphs are, thus, in complementary distribution. Complementary distribution on its own, naturally enough, is not sufficient. The prefix *de-* in English is added only to verbs (*decapacitate*, *demagnetise*) while the prefix *a-* (*amoral*, *atypical*) is added only to adjectives. They are, thus, in complementary distribution but would not be seen as allomorphs of the same morpheme. For morphs to be viewed as allomorphs of the same morpheme, they must not only be in complementary distribution but also fit all the other conditions that have already been discussed in this section. It is easier to see forms as allomorphs if the reason for the change in form is apparent; that is, if the allomorphy is phonetically conditioned. Lexical conditioning is possible but usually restricted to very specific circumstances.

Lexical conditioning is generally accepted within the morphome, rather than within the morpheme as it has been defined here (see section 7.3). Thus we find data like that in (5), where we have a plural morpheme and where a number of different morphemes are used. The morphemes used are lexically conditioned, though not always in perfect complementary distribution, as is made clear in (5).

(5)

?alumnuses	alumni
brothers	brethren
bureaus	bureaux
campuses	*campi
*childs	children
fishes	fish
formulas	formulae
indexes	indices
*mans	men
octopuses	octopodes
*oxes	oxen
seraphs	seraphim
?stratums	strata
tempos	tempi
*thesises	theses
ultimatums	?ultimata

(for other examples see Quirk et al., 1972: 181 ff.). Note that implicit appeal is being made here to a distinction between inflectional and derivational morphology. It seems unlikely that such a disparate range of suffixes would be attributed to a single morpheme if that morpheme was derivational (though Anderson, 1982: 585, does make such a suggestion: see the brief discussion at the end of section 6.4 above). Those scholars who do not distinguish between inflection and derivation are, thus, likely to face problems in relation to points such as this.

9.2 BASES

It might appear that the problems with bases would be very similar to the problems with affixes. There is a major difference, though, which effectively means that bases are a separate problem: while affixes are generally recognised because they recur with a range of bases, bases are far more idiosyncratic in their behaviour and do not show regular patterns of occurrences with affixes. The same basic point remains true with bases as with affixes: generally speaking, a single morpheme will retain a constant shape (or a limited range of related forms) and a constant meaning (or a limited range of related meanings). This, however, is open to a wide variety of interpretations.

Interestingly enough, most of the work in this area has been done not by morphologists but by phonologists, since it is of importance to the area of morphophonology, where the two overlap. Discussion of this area, therefore, demands some basic knowledge in a rather wider area of linguistics than just morphology. Most of the phonologists working in the tradition of generative phonology accept some version of the Unique Underlier Condition (the term is from Lass, 1984). This states that every morpheme has a single underlying morphophonemic representation, except in cases of suppletion. The reasons for this were discussed briefly in section 8.1. This view of the phonology implies that the analyst knows which morphs should be classed together as a single morpheme. In many languages, there is no problem here but English has a particularly complex morphophonology, with the result that many conflicting suggestions have been put forward. These are usually discussed in phonology texts under the heading of **abstractness**. Underlying phonological representations (underliers) which differ from the surface morphs are considered to be more abstract than those which have the same form as the surface morphs. The greater the difference between the underliers and the surface morphs or the greater the proportion of morphs that have abstract underliers, the more abstract the phonology is deemed to be. Underliers which are identical to the surface morphs are said to be **concrete**, in contrast.

The abstract end in this debate is represented by Lightner (1975, 1981, 1983). Lightner's position is basically that the underliers for English morphemes should be at least as abstract as the reconstructed morpheme in Proto-Indo-European and that more abstract analyses would be permissible if we knew more about the history of the language. As he says (1981: 96):

> To do a synchronic analysis of N[ew] E[nglish] – at least for phonology and D[erivational] M[orphology] – we have to return to 3000 B.C. It is painfully clear that those who thought PIE a primitive form of language were in error. Yet without older texts than we have or without some new concept we cannot go further back.

Yet the reconstruction of underliers as abstract as this is supposed to be based not primarily on etymological knowledge but on a form of internal reconstruction. It will, according to Lightner, become clear to the analyst that there are forms in English which are related in meaning and also by regular sound correspondences. For example, the pairs listed in (6) would be partial evidence for a correspondence reflecting Grimm's Law.

(6) | canine | hound |
|---|---|
| cornucopia | horn |
| decade | ten ✓ |
| dental | tooth |
| genus | kin |
| paternal | father ✓ |
| pedal | foot |
| pipe | fife |
| triple | three ✓ |

Lightner would then build Grimm's Law into his phonology and say that morphs like *foot* and *ped* (in *pedal, pedestrian* and the like) realise the same morpheme. (Note that the fact that *pipe* and *fife* are not historically related by Grimm's Law in the same kind of way as the other examples is irrelevant, since internal and not historical reconstruction is involved.) The result of this position is that the meaning of morphemes has to be extremely widely specified and has to allow for metaphorical extension and diachronic change. For example, Lightner (1975: 621) suggests that all the words in (7) below and many others should be derived from a morpheme {reg} with a meaning something like 'lead straight, guide, conduct'.

(7)   direct
        ergo

incorrigible
regal
regular
reign
right
rule

A position at the other extreme is taken by Vennemann (1974). He claims that no roots or affixes should be listed in the lexicon at all but the smallest item listed in the lexicon as an underlier should be a word-form. This position is motivated by arguments internal to the phonological theory which Vennemann espouses but is basically an attempt to give a specified level of abstraction which underliers may not exceed.

From the morphologist's point of view, neither of these extremes appears very attractive. Lightner's extreme abstractness seems to stretch what is meant by 'morphology' so far beyond its traditional boundaries that it becomes unrecognisable. In particular, if Lightner's position is accepted, it becomes impossible to formulate firm guidelines on the level of semantic relatedness required before two morphs can be said to realise the same morpheme. This would mean that relatedness of form would be the only available criterion and yet it was argued above that it is not enough to consider relatedness of form without relatedness of meaning. It also seems to be the case, within Lightner's view of the grammar, that the only way to distinguish the positions in which the various allomorphs of a super-abstract Lightnerian morpheme can occur is by means of lexical listing: there is no phonological or morphological way of distinguishing between a *semidemisemiquaver* and a *hemidemisemiquaver*, for example, the distinction must be marked lexically. This implies that Lightner's lexicon will need a full list of lexemes as well as a full list of morphemes, and the list of morphemes will be entirely redundant. Economy (the guideline of linguists such as Lightner), thus, argues against such a solution.

On the other hand, Vennemann's extreme concreteness appears to deny morphological productivity by listing productively generated forms on a par with non-productive and suppletive forms. Since it is the basic insight of morphology that word-forms can be analysed into morphs with a consistent form-meaning correlation, this viewpoint seems to negate everything that morphology is concerned with. The morphologist, therefore, is really looking for some degree of abstractness which is intermediate between the two extremes.

The difficulty is that there is no obvious and clearly defined middle ground. In a series of publications, Derwing (1973, 1976; Derwing & Baker, 1979) has shown that there is a cline of relatedness on both phonetic and semantic axes, so that words may be more or less closely related either semantically or phonetically. Abstracting from examples given in the works referred to above, the kind of pattern that can be seen in Table 1 emerges.

Table 1 is not very finely graduated. It would be possible to motivate many more steps on both scales. Yet even with the small amount of data given here it becomes clear that there is no obvious point at which a cut-off line can be drawn, so that the forms on one side of it are said to realise morphemes in common, while those on the other side are said not to. While it might be possible to go through any such list of words and say 'I personally feel that these contain/do not contain realisations of the same morpheme' or even (following Derwing) to test whether a sample of native speakers of English feel that there is a common morpheme involved or not, this does not provide any motivated way of drawing a distinction.

Part of the problem with discussions of this area is that any conclusions depend crucially on the individual researcher's notion of what Linguistics as a whole is doing. Again there are two extreme positions. At one end of the scale there are instrumentalists or 'hocus-pocus' linguists. Such linguists think that their description of a linguistic phenomenon has simply to provide an account of forms that are or have been or could be produced by native speakers of the language, with no implication whatsoever that the account provided will bear any relationship to the way in which speakers actually use the language themselves. Perhaps the extreme formulation of this point of view was Householder's (1966: 100) celebrated (or notorious) remark that 'A linguist who could not devise a better grammar than is at present in any speaker's brain ought to try another trade'. At the other end of the scale are the realists or 'God's truth' linguists, who feel that any description is correct to the extent that it is congruent with the way in which native speakers actually use their language. For such linguists the 'psychological reality' of the units and mechanisms they postulate is of prime importance.

Lightner is fundamentally an instrumentalist, while Derwing, with his insistence on testing the actual behaviour of native speakers, is a realist. Their different approaches to morphology are partly, at any rate, determined by these underlying philosophical attitudes. Any compromise position between the extreme abstractness of Lightner

Table 1 Semantic and Phonetic Relatedness of Words

Examples from the works of Derwing cited in the text. The most clearly related words on both axes are at the top left, the least related at the bottom right.

Phonetic relatedness	Clear	Intermediate	Unclear
Semantic relatedness			
Clear	quiet	sheep	father
	quietly	shepherd	paternal
	erase	berry	cat
	eraser	strawberry	kitten
Intermediate	skin	spin	beard
	skinny	spider	barber
	wonder	fable	sister
	wonderful	fabulous	sorority
Unclear	bug	gypsy	lead
	buggy	Egyptian	plumber
	ear	crane	lean
	eerie	cranberry	ladder

and the extreme concreteness of Vennemann is also going to be conditioned by the philosophical attitude of the linguist. Instrumentalists will search for a compromise which shows maximum generality and theoretical coherence; realists will look for a compromise which can best be shown to reflect native speaker behaviour. The two compromises may have little in common. In addition, not only is a compromise between abstractness and concreteness possible, but also one between extreme realism and extreme instrumentalism. It is, thus, rather dangerous to attempt to formulate a compromise position for theoretical as well as practical reasons. Nevertheless, this will be attempted in the next section.

9.3 A PROPOSAL FOR LIMITING ABSTRACTNESS

The proposal to be put forward in this section is one which I have advanced in a number of publications (Bauer, 1978a, 1978b, 1983, 2001b), and it is controversial. It is basically a compromise solution, and one which suffers the drawbacks of all compromises: it pleases no-one entirely. On the other hand, it does permit a motivated line to be drawn, limiting abstractness without going to either of the extremes discussed in the last section.

The proposal is that no underlier may be more abstract than is required to handle productive processes. Only productive processes should be handled by rules. Non-productive processes should not be acknowledged in the grammar but their products listed separately in the lexicon.

This means that the examples listed in (6) would not be related by the grammar because Grimm's Law is no longer a productive process in modern English. Forms like *foot* and *ped* would, correspondingly, not be derived from a single underlier: they would not be considered to be allomorphs of the same morpheme. As a result, FOOT and PEDAL can be considered separate lexemes, related in meaning but not related in the morphology. On the other hand, the process, illustrated in (8) below, is still a productive one. Names with *-on* /ən/ in their last syllable are pronounced with /əʊn/ rather than /ən/ when the suffix *-ian* is added to produce an adjective from those names. So, if a Mrs Robinson left a bequest to fund an art gallery, it might well be called the *Robinsonian Gallery*, pronounced /rɒbɪnsəʊnɪən/. The underlier for a name like *Robinson*, thus, has to be abstract enough to allow this allomorphy by rule, and *Robinson* and *Robinsonian* are related by the morphology in a grammar.

(8)   Amazon   Amazonian
         Babylon   Babylonian
         Bacon   Baconian
         Bergson   Bergsonian
         Johnson   Johnsonian

The big advantage of this proposal is that it provides a motivated level of abstractness between the two extremes previously discussed. It was shown, in Table 1 on page 156, that there is no obvious way that a line can be drawn between related and unrelated morphs in terms of meaning or phonetic shape, so some other measure is required. Productivity provides this alternative measure. Moreover, any discussion of morphology is going to have to make appeal to productivity for other reasons anyway (as was seen in Chapter 5). For realists, there is the added attraction that productivity appears to have correlates in actual linguistic behaviour. Speakers are sensitive to productivity when asked to judge the acceptability of new words (Anshen & Aronoff, 1981; Aronoff, 1980). Aphasics sometimes replace unproductive affixes with productive ones and one of the signs of language death appears to be a confusion between productive and unproductive processes which are otherwise kept apart (Dressler, 1977).

The major disadvantage of this proposal, from the point of view of the instrumentalist at least, is the loss of generalisation. Many affixation patterns in a language like English are analysable without being productive (see the discussion in Chapter 5). One example from English is the variations in form of bases arising from the results of the Great Vowel Shift. Some examples are given in (9).

(9)   chaste   chast·ity
       divine   divin·ity
       jocose   jocos·ity
       profound   profund·ity
       serene   seren·ity

This root allomorphy is widespread in English and is, to a large extent, predictable (as witness the discussions in Chomsky & Halle, 1968 and other studies within the same framework), yet it is no longer productive. Correspondingly, if the proposal in this section is adopted, this allomorphy will not be dealt with in the morphology but each of the words in (9) will be listed separately in the lexicon.

From the realist's point of view, it must also be admitted that there is a certain amount of evidence that language users are not always sensitive to productivity. Wheeler & Schumsky (1980), for example, found that informants failed to segment even forms such as *baker*, *citizenship* and *kingdom* into morphs, despite the fact that all the suffixes in these words are productive. The evidence is suggestive rather than conclusive but indicates that even realists might not be completely happy with the proposal being made here.

The discussion in this section has been in terms of limiting abstractness (and, thus, grammatically acknowledged allomorphy) in bases but there are also implications in terms of affixes. Affixes which are no longer productive would, on this proposal, no longer be acknowledged as forming separate morphemes. Thus, all words containing the nominalisation suffix -*th* (see examples (5) and (6) in Chapter 5) would be listed in the lexicon on a par with monomorphemic lexemes. Note again that the distinction between analysable and productive is crucial here. This may seem counter-intuitive, in that the suffix is clearly analysable in a word like *warmth*. However, it was shown earlier that there are words ending in -*th* where the affix is far less obvious to the naive speaker of English (words like *dearth*, *month* and so on), and we have also seen in this chapter that it is hard to draw a motivated line between those morphs which should be seen as related to a single morpheme and those which should be seen as related to more than one morpheme (or indeed as not realising a morpheme at all). Using productivity as a guide allows a clear decision for all these words. It also allows us to explain in some sense why so many of these words should show unpredictable root allomorphy (*long/length, moon/month, wide/width*). If there is no rule generating a set of alternations and the words are individually listed in the lexicon, there is no longer a link in the grammar between the base forms and the variant allomorphs, so that this is no longer grammatically predictable but only predictable in terms of internal reconstruction; also, it is then possible for the words to change their form diachronically without reference to the form of the original base word.

In conclusion, although it would be naive to suggest that the proposal for limiting abstractness and grammatically recognised allomorphy presented here can solve all the problems associated with this area of enquiry, it does provide a coherent point of view with a level of abstractness that is well-motivated from the morphological side. In that sense, it is, perhaps, one of the most hopeful developments in the search for a limit to abstractness in grammar.

9.4 WHAT ARE THE ALTERNATIVES?

If words are not related by sharing a morph or by belonging to the same morpheme, what are the possibilities? One of the possibilities is, of course, that the two words are not related at all: we are back to the *cat* and *dog* examples with which we started this chapter. We have seen that the borderlines of a morphological relationship may be drawn for theoretical reasons; there are other types of relationship, however, which may be easier to see. Once we know what the alternative types of relationship are, it may be easier to distinguish between them and morphological relationships. Hockett (1987) calls these relationships **resonances**, a term which I find particularly apt: hearing one word makes you think of another because of some similarity between the two. Different types of resonance will be considered in what follows.

9.4.1 Phonological

Some words remind us of others because they share some

phonological similarity. The similarity may be in the number of syllables, the stress pattern (or tone in languages where that is relevant) because they have the same segments in a particular syllable (for example, *provision* and *visual*), because they alliterate (for example, *petty* and *politics*), assonate (for example, *goose* and *food*) or rhyme (for example, *intense* and *pretence*). When I say that a word is 'on the tip of my tongue', it frequently means that I have some outline phonetic framework of what the word looks like in precisely this kind of term and I can sometimes make some of the details overt ('it starts with *c* and is about four syllables long'). While the tip-of-the-tongue phenomenon does not always accurately reflect the sought word, it shows the kinds of phonetic (and orthographic) categories which are familiar to us and which we can use to judge similarity to other words.

Where a lot of words share some phonological structure and also some vague semantic structure, we talk in terms of phonaesthemes (see section 7.4). *Bump, clump, dump, jump, thump* are sometimes said to be related in this way. Phonaesthemes can usually be seen as the result of post hoc analysis of existing words, rather than the motivation for creating new words, and the boundaries of the phonaestheme are typically rather fuzzy: for instance, do *frump, galumph, hump, lump* or *slump* belong to the same phonaestheme as *bump* and so on?

In a set of words like *automaton, krypton, micron, phaeton, phlogiston, photon*, it may be difficult to tell whether the resonances are purely phonological or whether they are also morphological (or whether there is a mixture of the two types).

9.4.2 Semantic

Clearly, semantically similar words resonate with each other – cryptic crosswords rely on this fact (and on other points). Words like *red, yellow, puce* and *khaki* resonate because they are all colour terms; *alsatian, corgi, dachshund, labrador* and *poodle* resonate because they are all names for dogs, but they do not share a morpheme {dog} because they do not share form. Words may resonate semantically because they are synonyms, antonyms, complementaries (like *lend* and *borrow*) or just because they are in the same semantic field.

The difficulty comes in distinguishing words which are semantically related (and no more) from words which share a common morpheme. *Prettier* and *more intelligent* probably have a morpheme in common. *Advice, division, laughter, measurement, mixture* and *procrastination* are usually treated as though they are related only semantically.

9.4.3 Syntactic

Words may resonate because they are common syntactic companions. They are then usually said to form a **collocation**. So when you hear *red* you might think of any one of *admiral, cabbage, head, light, see, wine* or a host of others. Words may resonate because they co-occur in compounds, in idioms, in familiar proverbs or quotations or in much looser constructions. Because these are syntagmatic relationships, they are unlikely to be confused with morphological relationships, which are paradigmatic.

9.4.4 Etymological

Words may resonate because they share a common historical source. Here the degree of resonance may depend on the speaker/hearer's individual knowledge. It takes specialised knowledge to link *Guinevere, Jennifer* and *Winifred* and you can use your language perfectly well without being aware of any relationship. Similarly, you can function in English perfectly well without being aware of the relationship between *dear* and *dearth* or that between *foul* and *filth*. Other relationships appear to be more intrusive than these two sets seem to be. For example, many speakers seem to feel that there is or must be a relationship between *predict, prefer, presume* and *pretend*, even if they can find no reason for assuming that there is any meaning of 'before' in *pretend*. There is, indeed, a relationship: in each case the *pre-* comes from Latin *prae*. But it is difficult to see that as a matter of morphology (although it might be a matter of formatives, in the sense of section 7.3) – it is fundamentally a relationship of form due to a historical relationship.

Another example is presented by the words *phonecard, phonetic, stereophonic, symphony* and *telephone*. It is an open question how many of these words share a morpheme, though note that the meaning in *phonecard* is not the same as the meaning in *symphony* and that, if we are to analyse these words into morphs, the *-et-* in *phonetic* has to be accounted for somehow. There is, however, an etymological connection: all of these eventually go back to the same Greek root. Again etymology is not necessarily morphology.

Sometimes speakers feel that words do resonate in this way, even though there is no genuine etymological connection. In such instances we talk of **folk etymology**, although the label is not particularly enlightening. Folk etymology (sometimes called 'popular etymology') is better seen as the remotivation of a form which has become semantically opaque by reinterpreting it as though it contains morphs. The obvious cases of this are foreign loans, which get reinterpreted as though they had an English basis. For example, the *musk* in *muskrat* seems to be a serendipitously appropriate-sounding element for English speakers, since the word is derived from Abnaki *muskwessu*. The now obsolete word *popinjay* 'vain and conceited person' has nothing to do with *pop* or with *jay* but was, originally, the same word as the modern German *Papagei* 'parrot'. And the modern *penthouse* comes from Middle English *pentis*, related to Old French *apentis* 'lean-to shed' and Latin *appendicium* 'an add-on'. But even native words can get reinterpreted: *slowworm* was not considered to have anything to do with *slow* until the sixteenth century; the meaning of the *slow* element is obscure but its cognate in other languages is simply the name of the lizard. What folk etymology seems to show is that people expect words to be made up of meaningful parts (morphs) and try to interpret them that way even when they are monomorphemic.

9.4.5 Back to morphs

There are thus many types of resonance. Morphs, it can be argued, are also a type of resonance: the type that occurs when there is simultaneous formal and semantic resonance over recurrent units which analyse a word exhaustively. The crucial point is not to confuse this type of resonance with the others.

REFERENCES AND FURTHER READING

The problem of the meaning of affixes, and that of the meaning of nominalisation affixes in particular, is discussed in Bauer (1983: section 6.7).

The discussion of potentiation of *-ment* by *en-* is based on Williams (1981: 250), from where the term 'potentiation' is also taken. However, matters are more complex than is revealed there. First, *en-* added to a nominal base does not always potentiate *-ment* suffixation (*encouragement* is quite normal, but ?*enrobement*, ?*enwallment*). Second, it is frequently difficult to know whether the prefix has been added to a noun or a verb (*enlist*). Third, even with adjectives the potentiation does not appear to work all the time: *ensurement* does not seem usual to me. Fourth, there are problems anyway with *-ment*, which may no longer be productive (Bauer, 1983: 49, 55). This means that we may be dealing with a historical potentiation, which no longer holds. The basic point, however, remains true: if the same form in different uses potentiates different subsequent affixation, it is an argument for seeing two distinct affixes.

Dictionaries of new words include Barnhart et al. (1973, 1980), Mish (1983), Butler (1990), Green (1991), Tulloch (1991), Knowles (1997) and the Supplement to *The Oxford English Dictionary*.

The Indonesian example in (4) is from Kwee (1965). The situation in Indonesian is actually more complex than is illustrated in (4) because base-initial voiceless stops are deleted after the assimilation has taken place and because [s] is treated for the purposes of the assimilation as a palatal consonant. The basic complementary distribution holds, though.

The question of affixes being recurrent forms is an interesting one. Consider forms of English such as *laugh·ter, bishop·ric*. To all intents and purposes the suffixes here do not recur and, yet, we would probably wish to call them suffixes despite that. Words which start off as non-recurrent parts of other words turn into suffixes diachronically *alcoholic* gives rise to *workoholic, chocoholic, spendaholic* and so on. It, thus, seems that affixes need not be recurrent for us to analyse them as affixes. Precisely what qualities they do need is an open question. Note, though, that, if the proposal for limiting abstractness discussed in this chapter is adopted, all unique morphs will only be listed in the lexicon as parts of larger words.

The use of productivity as a guide to what should be listed in the lexicon is also adopted within Functional Grammar (Dik, 1980: 25–8), although in that framework it is not restricted to morphology. I would subscribe to Dik's position here that unproductive syntactic structures should also be lexically listed (for example, *if you please* is not derived by productive syntax and should be listed in the lexicon as a unit). This takes us beyond what is directly relevant to this chapter. The same position on productivity and the lexicon can be read into the work of Aronoff (1976), but it is not usually specifically allowed for in Lexicalist writings.

On resonance, see Hockett (1987) and Bauer (1999).

EXERCISES

1. Assuming that all the words in Column A below contain the same morpheme {ful} and also that all the words in Column B contain the same morpheme {ful}, is the same morpheme illustrated in Column A and in column B? Explain ALL your evidence.

Column A	Column B
awful	cupful
careful	houseful
merciful	mouthful
skilful	pipeful
truthful	spoonful

2. There is some disagreement as to whether the suffix -*able* which occurs in the words in column A below represents the same morpheme as the suffix -*able* which occurs in the words in column B. Provide three arguments which consistently provide evidence either in favour of them being the same morpheme or in favour of them being two separate morphemes. State clearly whether your arguments support the one morpheme solution or the two morpheme solution.

Column A	Column B
comfortable	acceptable
honourable	agreeable
knowledgeable	commendable
marriageable	desirable
objectionable	reliable

3. Which of the words in Column A can be analysed as containing as a morph the corresponding form from Column B? If such an analysis is possible, provide a justification in the form of parallel examples which illustrate each morph in different environments. If no such analysis is possible, state what kind(s) of resonance (if any) hold between the two forms.

	Column A	Column B
(a)	distress	dis
(b)	compromise	promise
(c)	professorial	profess
(d)	history	his
(e)	parsonage	parson
(f)	telekinesis	tele

4. In the following set of words, say whether each is morphologically analysable or not. For those which are morphologically analysable, divide the words into morphs and morphemes, giving parallels with other words containing the same affixes. For those that are not morphologically analysable, say what kind (or kinds) of resonance are found between the various words listed.

preamble, prejudge, prelude, pressure

5. Consider the pairs of words below. Which of them would you want to see as morphologically related to each other? Is there some objective criterion which can be applied to select precisely that set from the rest of the pairs given?

evolve	evolution
fast	fasten
germ	cognate
hole	conceal
holy	holiday
live	liver
ride	ridden
right	rectitude
rise	raise
steal	stealth
suspect	suspicion
wide	width

6. In the first edition of *The Categories and Types of Present-Day English Word-Formation*, Marchand makes the following statement:

The prefix *in-*, however, can claim only a restricted sphere [in comparison with *un-*]: it forms learned, chiefly scientific, words and *therefore has morphemic value with those speakers only who are acquainted with Latin or French*. [Stress not in the original.]

In the second edition (Marchand, 1969: 170) the phrase 'morphemic value' is replaced by 'derivative value'. To what extent would you agree that a formal element can have different morphemic value (or derivative value) for different speakers? Take care to explain your reasons clearly and to make reference to the definition of a morpheme, as well as to realist and instrumentalist ideas about grammar.

CHAPTER 10

Lexicalist Morphology

In the aftermath of the introduction of transformational-generative grammar in the mid-1950s, morphology was virtually ignored by linguists for almost twenty years. As we have previously seen, morphology was dealt with in that period partly as a matter of syntax and partly as a matter of phonology (see section 8.2). There is, thus, a certain irony in the fact that the main reason for the resurgence of interest in morphology after that period was almost certainly the amount of attention paid to morphology – especially derivational morphology – by linguists of the same school. While several approaches to morphology have arisen as a result of this renewed interest, there is one set of approaches which holds that derivational morphology at least (and possibly also inflectional morphology) must be dealt with in the lexicon. We can accordingly refer to this general way of approaching morphology as Lexicalist Morphology. For fuller discussion of this school of morphological thought and the way it has developed, see Kiparsky (1982), Scalise (1984) and McMahon (1994).

10.1 WHY THE LEXICON?

In the early days of Transformational Grammar, it was axiomatic that two sentences or parts of sentences which were related in meaning but differed from each other formally in terms of order of elements or presence versus absence of a few specifiable morphemes were transformationally related to each other. The classic example is the passive transformation, which relates pairs of sentences such as

(1)   The fat cat swallows the milk.
        The milk is swallowed by the fat cat.

These two sentences, obviously related in meaning, were related formally by a series of operations which could be generalised and summarised in a transformational rule of the following kind:

(2) NP   V +   tense   NP
     1   2   3   4 $\Rightarrow$ 4 BE + 3 2 + ed BY 1

This rule changes the order of the elements numbered 1, 2, 3 and 4 but also specifies the morpheme {past participle} (shown by *ed* in (2)) and the lexemes BE and BY. Given this general approach to such matters, it was inevitable that pairs such as those in (3) which involve morphological considerations should also be treated in the same way:

(3)   Robin is devoted to her mother.
       Robin's devotion to her mother.

Pairs such as these were also derived from a common underlying structure by different sets of transformational rules. This is the approach that was taken in Lees (1960).

However, it gradually became clear that there were problems with this kind of approach, some of which were discussed in Chomsky (1970). Chomsky considered the case of derived nominalisations in English such as *destruction, marriage, trial.* He argued that such nominalisations were irregular both semantically and morphologically. They were irregular semantically in that there was not precisely the same change of meaning between the verb and the nominalisation in each case. That is, the semantic relationship between *destroy* and *destruction* is not the same as that which holds between *marry* and *marriage* or *try* and *trial.* Yet it was fundamental to the Chomskyan approach that transformations do not change meaning (a corollary to the position that paraphrases are related by transformation). If these derived nominalisations were to be created by syntactic transformation, they would thus be breaking a constraint on such rules. Thus it was argued that the rules which create nominalisations are not just like other transformations.

This conclusion is supported by the fact that, for some verbs, there are two nominalisations which do not mean the same thing:

(4)   approve   approval   approbation
       commit   committal   commitment
       employ   employ   employment
       join   junction   juncture

In pairs like these there is no fixed correlation between the meaning and the form of the nominalisation, so that any transformation that tries to link form and meaning will prove impossible, even without considering the more general constraint.

Chomsky also pointed out that further problems arise from the transformational analysis of derived nominalisations because there are many sentences which do not have a corresponding derived nominalisation. For instance, although (5a) corresponds to (5b), there is no (5d) to correspond to (5c).

(5) (a) Kim was amused at the children's antics.
    (b) Kim's amusement at the children's antics.
    (c) Robin amused the children with stories.
    (d) *Robin's amusement of the children with stories.

To this we can add that there are a number of nominalisation affixes whose distribution is not predictable, that there are verbs which have no derived nominalisation at all (verbs such as *come, eat, open, see*) and that some words which look like nominalisations, have no corresponding verb: *exigency, invultuation, notion, tutelage*.

All of this makes it very difficult to postulate any transformations which have general applicability. Yet one of the aims of writing transformational rules should be precisely to make sure that they apply to as many potential input strings as possible (ideally all potential input strings). Again the conclusion is that these nominalisations should not be generated by ordinary syntactic transformations.

There are also other reasons for saying that the rules of morphology are different in kind from the rules of syntax. It is generally accepted that rules of syntax do not make appeal to phonological structure and do not need to make reference to the output of phonological rules. In contrast, there are many instances of morphological rules requiring phonological information before they can apply. One example was given in section 5.5. Another concerns the German diminutive suffix *-chen*, which is not added to bases ending in /x/ or /ŋ/ (Fleischer, 1975: 179). Siegel (1974: 163ff) gives several similar examples from English, including a particularly nice example (although a rather marginal one in terms of the English system as a whole) involving formations including *-bloody-* or other expletives. The expletive is always added immediately before a stressed syllable (sometimes a secondary stress, but never before a zero-stressed syllable). Thus *absobloodylutely* is perfectly normal, but not *abbloodysolutely, absolutebloodyly*. This example is striking because most generative phonological theories would see stress as being generated by a series of phonological rules. In such theories, therefore, the stressed syllable cannot be identified until after the appropriate phonological rules have been processed. This is then a very clear case of rules for word-structure depending crucially on phonological structure and, thus, being markedly different from syntactic rules.

If nominalisations are not to be derived from their corresponding verb by a syntactic transformation, then some other way must be found of stating in the grammar the relationship between strings such as those in (3) and (5a, b). Clearly there are at least semantic relationships which hold between the members of such pairs. There are also close parallels of subcategorisation of a type which were traditionally captured in the transformational relationship. If we consider a verb and its corresponding nominalisation, it is frequently (though not always) the case that the same kind of subject and object can occur with both and that, where the verb takes a direct object, the nominalisation takes the preposition *of* (this is a typical pattern, but not an exceptionless one: Bauer, 1983: 81). This is illustrated below:

(6) (a) Kim caroused until the stars faded from the sky.
  (b) Kim's carousal lasted until the stars faded from the sky.
  (c) *Kim caroused the whole bottle/his friends.
  (d) *Kim's carousal of the whole bottle/his friends.
  (e) Pat refused entry to everyone.
  (f) Pat refused to come home.
  (g) *Pat refused that he would come home.
  (h) Pat's refusal of entry to everyone.
  (i) Pat's refusal to come home.
  (j) *Pat's refusal that he would come home.
  (k) Sam laughed at the joke.
  (l) *Sam laughed the joke.
  (m) Sam's laughter at the joke.
  (n) *Sam's laughter (of) the joke.

Relationships like these need to be captured somehow and Chomsky's answer is that they should be captured in the lexicon. He suggests that there should be a 'neutral lexical entry', which is neither completely specified as a verb nor as a corresponding nominalisation, and that such matters as subcategorisation should be dealt with in this neutral entry. In such a system, it seems natural that the rules relating the form of the verbs to the form of the nominalisation should also be somewhere in the lexicon, possibly as redundancy rules as suggested by Jackendoff (1975).

Most subsequent work in Lexicalist Morphology appears to have by-passed the suggestion for a neutral lexical entry, while adopting the suggestion that derived nominals should be dealt with in the lexicon. In either case, there does not seem to be any pressing need to handle nominalisations in the lexicon rather than, say, in a separate morphological component of the grammar. There may not be any distinction between these two suggestions: it is perfectly possible to have a morphological component which is relatively autonomous and yet seen as being within the lexicon. There are various possibilities here for alternative ways of organising the grammar. The alternatives may look extremely different from each other without differing substantially or making any different empirical claims. What is crucial is that (a) the rules which form nominalisations are not ordinary syntactic transformational rules and (b) they must still allow generalisations to be made about verbs and their nominalisations.

It should be noted that this discussion has been carried out purely in terms of verbs and their nominalisations. The assumption is made in Lexicalist Morphology that the argument extends to all derivational morphology. This could be seen as controversial, given that the morphology of nominalisations (at least in English) is considerably less regular than that found in other constructions; but generally this assumption has been accepted without comment. It should also be noted that the discussion is carried out over a body of established words, not over productive uses of morphological processes, which would be a considerably smaller and more regular set of processes.

10.2 THE FUNCTION OF A MORPHOLOGY

The goal of a morphology is set out by Aronoff (1976: 17–18) in the following terms:

> Just as the simplest goal of a syntax is the enumeration of the class of possible sentences of a language, so the simplest task of a morphology, the least we demand of it, is the enumeration of the class of possible words of a language.

Or, in rather different terms (1976: 19):

> It [is] the task of a morphology to tell us what sort of new words a speaker can form.

This means that, theoretically (although regrettably not always in practice, see above), the study of actually attested words is, for the

Lexical Morphologists, only a guide to potential words, the real subject of their study. This is precisely the viewpoint that was espoused in section 5.3. In the jargon of Lexicalist Morphology, this means that we need an **overgenerating morphology** (Allen, 1978), that is, one which generates more words than are familiar to any particular individual or than are to be found in any particular reference book, even words which are not likely to be found because of blocking. The basic idea behind an overgenerating morphology is that it should allow everything to be generated that is not excluded by some principled restriction on the form of a rule.

10.3 FULL ENTRY THEORY

Despite (or perhaps rather, because of) the acceptance of the idea of an overgenerating morphology, most Lexicalist Morphologists seem to operate with some version of a **full entry theory** of the lexicon. According to this, every word which 'exists' is listed in the lexicon. For some Lexicalist Morphologists (for example, Lieber, 1981; Selkirk, 1982) stems and affixes are also listed in a lexicon (not necessarily in the same list as the 'existing' words), while for others (for example, Aronoff, 1976) this is not a requirement. Precisely how the full entry lexicon is used varies from scholar to scholar. For Halle (1973), the lexicon is preceded by a filter on the output of word-formation rules (usually abbreviated as WFRS) and makes sure that only 'existing' words are entered in the lexicon and, thus, used in sentences. For Jackendoff (1975), the full entry lexicon acts as a domain in which lexical redundancy rules operate, linking verbs with their nominalisations in non-generative ways, for example. For Aronoff (1976) the WFRS act as 'once only' rules, generating forms which are then listed in the lexicon. According to this theory, WFRS are distinct from syntactic rules in that, while syntactic rules apply every time the appropriate construction is used, WFRS do not – they apply only when a word is originally coined. The full entry theory of the lexicon has certain advantages if it is considered in realist terms, since it explains why it is perfectly possible for an individual speaker to know two words and be able to use them without being aware of the derivational relationship that holds between them. *Dear* and *dearth* would come into this category for many people (see the discussion in section 9.2 in general). Even if no realist claims are to be made for the model, this remains a very sensible approach to dealing with non-productive morphology. But what about productive uses of morphology?

Jackendoff (1975) is not primarily concerned with productive morphology, but he does make some relevant comments. For example he admits (1975: 667) that 'it is quite common for someone to invent a new compound noun spontaneously and to be perfectly understood' and, yet, from there he goes onto state that 'the normal mode for syntactic rules is creative, the normal mode for lexical rules is passive'. Jackendoff's idea is that morphology is used productively so infrequently that the few occasions when this does happen can be dismissed as exceptional cases of analytical redundancy rules being turned on their heads and used abnormally. The norm is for morphological rules to be used to analyse 'existing' forms. This deserves further comment. It is ironic that Jackendoff should have cited compound nouns as his test case, since some figures are actually available on these in German and they do not support his contention. Thiel (1973) reports on a count of compound nouns from the weekly paper *Die Zeit*, where in a corpus of 1331 compound nouns only 37.9% were found listed in dictionaries, while 62.1% were neologisms. This scarcely supports the notion that the creative use of compounding rules is in some way not normal. It has, of course, been shown that there are reasons for saying that compounding is a very syntactic kind of process (see above, section 8.2.2). Jackendoff's point would undoubtedly be more effectively made with respect to derivatives. Even here, though, Jackendoff appears to be dismissing the quite considerable productivity that various types of affix show. This is striking enough in English, but even more striking in a language like Eskimo, where derivational affixes abound and the chance of a speaker having heard or used a particular derivative in his or her previous experience becomes vanishingly low. Consider, for example, a West Greenlandic example like the following, where all the affixes except the last one are derivational (Fortescue, 1984):

(7) puu·ssa·qar·ti·nngil·ara
bag·future·have·causative·negative·1st-singular·3rd-singular-indicative
'I have no bag for it.'

This dismissal of productivity is even more striking with reference to inflectional affixes. Following Halle (1973), Jackendoff (1975: 665) suggests that:

> paradigmatic information should be represented in the dictionary. As a consequence, the lexical insertion rules must enter partial or complete paradigms into deep structures, and

the rules of concord must have the function of filtering out all but the correct forms, rather than that of inserting inflectional affixes.

For a language like English, such a proposal seems entirely plausible. In Finnish, however, the maximal nominal paradigm contains about 2,000 distinct forms, and the maximal verbal paradigm over 12,000 when cliticised forms are included, and 150 and 850 respectively if cliticised forms are excluded (Karlsson & Koskenniemi, 1985: 210–1), and in Archi the maximal verbal paradigm contains over one and a half million forms (Kibrik, 1998: 468). In cases like this, Jackendoff's proposal seems computationally inefficient, whether it is intended as a psychologically real statement of speaker behaviour or simply as an instrumentalist model. It is worth quoting Karlsson & Koskenniemi (1985: 212) at length in this context:

> For analytic languages such as English, [the Full Entry Hypothesis] is perhaps possible to defend, the main reason being that lexemes have so few forms. Now consider the situation in morphologically rich languages like Finnish. It makes little sense to claim that all the 150 nominal and 850 verbal paradigm members (of all nouns and verbs, respectively) would be independent lexical entries. First, this would amount to the strange claim that the Finnish lexicon is hundreds of times larger than the English one. Second, there would be no convincing account of how language users are capable of acquiring, understanding and producing forms of new words they have not heard before. One would have to hypothesize e.g. that it happens by internally generating and storing all the core forms. But this would imply storing some 850 forms upon learning a new verb. Only a handful of these are likely to be used at all. Some 800 forms would be strange inhabitants of the lexicon: never heard and never used in speech production.

It, thus, seems that the Lexicalist model needs to be modified to deal appropriately with productive morphology, perhaps particularly in languages like Finnish and Archi but probably in general.

10.4 STRATA IN THE MORPHOLOGY

It is a well-known fact about English that it contains two distinct types of affix. The first type, generally Germanic in origin, does not affect the stress-pattern of the base to which it is attached. This type of affix is, therefore, sometimes termed 'neutral' (Chomsky & Halle, 1968). In generative phonology it is associated with a strong '#-boundary'. The other type of affix is called 'non-neutral' and associated with a weaker '+-boundary'. It is generally Latinate in origin and is associated with a change in stress-pattern in the base to which it is attached. This difference is exemplified in (8).

(8) | base | neutral affix | non-neutral affix |
|---|---|---|
| 'curious | 'curious#ness | curi'os+ity |
| pro'ductive | pro'ductive#ness | produc'tiv+ity |
| 'patriarch | 'patriarch#y | patri'arch+al |
| 'finite | non#'finite | 'in+finite |

Notice, too, in (8) that only the non-neutral affixes have an effect on the segmental form and this can also be seen in (9).

(9) | base | neutral affix | non-neutral affix |
|---|---|---|
| profane | profane#ness | profan+ity |
| organ | organ#ise | organ+ic |
| expend | expend#able | expens+ive |

Also, only non-neutral affixes appear to show obligatory phonetically conditioned allomorphy:

(10)   in+   il+legal, ir+relevant
       un#   un#lawful, un#reasonable

The best way to account for these differences seems to be to order the phonological rules (including, crucially, the stress rules) after the rules introducing affixes with +-boundaries, but before the rules introducing affixes with #-boundaries. In that way, the phonological rules will determine the segments and stress pattern of *curious*, for example, before {#ness} is added, so that the segmental shape and stress of *curious* remains the same in *curiousness*. However, {+ity} is added before the phonological rules apply, so that the segmental form of *curiosity* and its stress pattern are determined in the presence of the whole string and not just by the base. Siegel (1974), therefore, suggests that these various processes are ordered in the following way:

(11)   Roots

|

Rules for addition of
+-boundary affixes

|

Appropriate
phonological rules,
including stress
rules

|

Rules for addition of
#-boundary affixes

Since no inflectional affix in English affects stress or regularly causes segmental changes in a base, all inflectional affixes have a #-boundary. The organisation of rules in (11) thus predicts that all +-boundary affixes (which are all derivational) should occur closer to the root than inflectional affixes. This is, in fact, the case. There are words of the form *formal+iti#es* but none of the form **profane#s+ity*. The model in (11) also predicts that there should be strings of the form *root+affix#affix* but not of the form *root#affix+affix*, where both affixes are derivational. This is less clearly true but it is certainly true that there are innumerable words which fit this constraint and relatively few which break it. For example, all words which end in *+al#ly* (e.g. *industrially*), *+al#ness* (e.g. *exceptionalness*), *+ive#ness* (e.g. *prescriptiveness*), fit the constraint, and there are no established words ending in, for example, *#ness+al* (Lehnert, 1971), despite the fact that other nominalisation markers occur before *-al* (*sculpt+ur+al*).

I have discussed this ordering hypothesis purely in terms of English and it might appear that the ordering of the types of affix is a result of the very mixed history of English and has ultimately an etymological explanation which would be uninteresting cross-linguistically. It is thus important to note that similar differences have been found in a wide range of languages, including Dutch, Italian, Japanese, Kannada, Malayalam, Russian and Tagalog (see the references in Aronoff, 1983: 363 and Scalise, 1984: 99). The classes of affixes appear to behave in similar ways to the English ones, having similar phonological effects and ordering restrictions. In most, possibly all (I do not have access to all the appropriate papers) of these cases, the distinction is a result of etymologically diverse sources of vocabulary. It is interesting that this kind of language mixture should have such similar effects in so many different languages.

The ordering hypothesis presented in (11) is extended by Allen (1978) to include compounds. Allen argues that compounding is carried out in a third stratum, which applies after the two strata given in (11). This predicts that there will be no cases of derivational affixes using compounds as their base. That is, there will be no derivatives of the form *[[war-hero] ic], *[[street-music] al], *[mis [fuel-injected]] (Allen, 1978: 215). Such an analysis implies that inflectional affixes must be separated from other #-affixes, since inflectional endings occur regularly outside compounds. In English this can only be illustrated clearly with compound nouns (compound adjectives never take synthetic comparison in -er, and so are never inflected; compound verbs, which do carry inflections, are usually formed by conversion or back-formation, which might be seen as providing an intermediate step, distancing the inflection from the compound) but it could be illustrated with other types of compound in other languages. The plural marker comes outside the compound in forms like [[text·book] s] and [[red·skin] s]. This can be seen particularly clearly with the last example. *Redskins* are not a number of skins which are red (that is, the plurality is not applied purely to the *skin*-element) but a number of the entities each of which would individually be a *redskin*. Secondly, if we consider a compound such as *Walkman*, it seems that most speakers make the plural by adding -s. If the plurality were added directly to the element *man*, internally, the result would be *Walkmen*. The more usual plural form demands the bracketing [[Walk·man] s].

Given this conclusion, the form of the ordering constraints on the rules must be as in (12).

(12)   Roots
                   |
          Rules for addition of   Stratum I
           +-boundary affixes
                   |
              Appropriate
            phonological rules,
           including stress rules
                   |
          Rules for addition of   Stratum II
              #-boundary
           derivational affixes

Rules for	Stratum III
compounding	
Rules for inflectional	Stratum IV
affixes	

10.5 HEADS AND FEATURE PERCOLATION

As was seen in section 3.6, endocentric compounds in English are hyponyms of their right-hand element. A *seabird* is a type of bird, a *heffalump trap* is a kind of trap, if you *trickle-irrigate* some land, then you are irrigating it and so on. This means that the semantic information associated with the right-hand element in the compound is also associated with the compound as a whole (although the compound as a whole will focus on some special type of entity denoted by the right-hand element). The same is true of some information which can be seen as grammatical rather than, or as well as, semantic. For example, if we consider *seabird*, we find that the compound as a whole, like its right-hand element *bird* is animate, countable and a noun. In a language like German, it is the right-hand element which determines the gender and declension class of the compound as a whole. This is illustrated in (13) below:

(13)	*def sing*	*indef sing*	*gender*	*gloss*
	der Beamte	ein Beamter	*m*	'official'
	der Staats·beamte	ein Staats·beamter	*m*	'government official'
	der Tag	ein Tag	*m*	'day'
	der Geburts·tag	ein Geburts·tag	*m*	'birthday'
	das Brot	ein Brot	*n*	'bread'
	das Butter·brot	ein Butter·brot	*n*	'sandwich'
				lit. 'butter bread'

where *Staat* is masculine, *Geburt* and *Butter* feminine and where data for plural forms would provide similar results: see any good German grammar.

The element which determines such matters for the whole compound we can term the **head** of the compound. There is a generalisation here, namely that the compound as a whole must be marked for many of the same features as the head of the compound. That is, given a tree such as (14), where X is an endocentric compound and Y and Z are the two elements that make up the compound and where Z is the head of the construction X, X must carry many of the same grammatical features as Z.

(14)

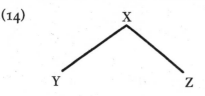

This is ensured by a principle known as **feature percolation**. There is more than one version of it in the Lexicalist literature but a simple picture of how it works can be given quite easily. In any tree, features from all the daughters are available to the mother node. In some cases those features will be in agreement, in other cases they will conflict. For example, in the compound *seabird* the features of both *sea* and *bird* will agree in that the parts are nouns, but conflict in that *bird* is animate whereas *sea* is inanimate. Where there is no conflict, the mother node is marked for the features in common. Where there is conflict, the mother node takes the feature of the head element. In two-element compounds, this means that all grammatical features from the head are taken for the mother node. If we consider a German compound such as *Butter·brot* this will give the following picture:

(15)

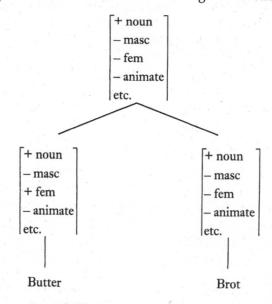

Butter   Brot

All the agreeing features are the same on all three nodes and, where there is disagreement, as in the value for the feature [feminine], it is the value for the head which is repeated on the mother node.

Purely semantic features (if, indeed, meanings are represented in terms of features) do not work in precisely the same way, since the meaning of the compound is a function of the meaning of both parts of the compound and it is not simply a matter of agreement or conflict.

It is suggested within Lexicalist Morphology that the notion of feature percolation is generalisable from endocentric compounds to all cases of word-formation and, possibly, to all morphological processes, including inflectional ones. Exocentric compounds provide a problem but they are frequently assumed by Lexicalist Morphologists all to be lexicalised and not generated by productive rules. They will accordingly not be considered further here. In derivational morphology, though, it is fairly clear how feature percolation will work. The head in a suffixal derivative will be the suffix because it is the suffix which determines, for example, which part of speech the derivative as a whole belongs to. In most cases of prefixal derivation in English, the base will be the head because the prefix does not determine the part of speech of the derivative as a whole, but there are a few exceptions such as *be·witch, de·plane, en·train* where the prefix does determine the category of the entire derivative and, thus, is the head. We, therefore, have trees like those in (16)–(20).

(16)

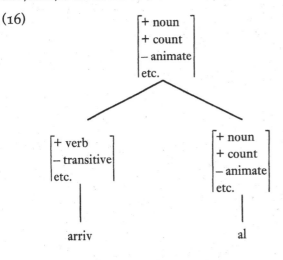

(17)

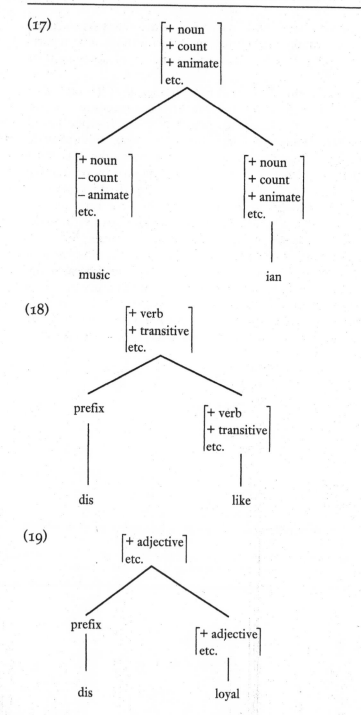

(18)

(19)

(20)

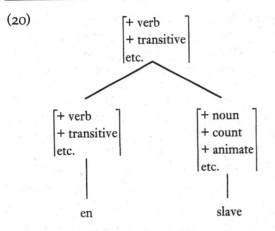

In cases of inflectional morphology, it is less clear what the head is and this is a matter of some disagreement; but, whether it is the affixes or the stem, we can generalise feature percolation in the way illustrated in (21) (a French example is used to make the point more clearly).

(21)

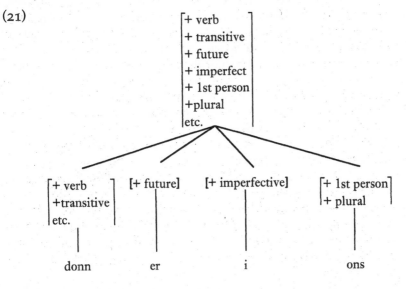

There is a certain amount of dispute in the literature on how to recognise a head element. The main paper on this topic is Williams (1981), where it is argued that, at least for English, this can be decided in the unmarked cases by the Right-hand Head Rule. This states that (other things being equal) the head in an English word is the right-hand element in that word. There is plenty of evidence that such a rule is not suitable across languages and it is not even clear how valuable it is in English, given the number of exceptions to it (words like *bewitch* and so on, cited above, exocentric compounds, compounds including particles such as *by-pass* and *in-put* and also a few other compounds like *who(m)ever* and *Model-T*). A full discussion of this topic would go far beyond the bounds of this book. It is an important area for Lexicalist Morphology and one that requires serious consideration. But it seems likely that any final answer to this problem will be far more complex than the Right-hand Head Rule.

10.6 OTHER CONSIDERATIONS

I have outlined in this chapter those facets of Lexicalist Morphology which seem to me to be most central to that school of thought and also those facets where there seems to be a reasonable amount of agreement between different scholars. Lexicalist Morphologists have dealt with far more topics than have been included in this brief survey, some of which are still extremely contentious. For instance, there is still a great deal of discussion on the topic of whether inflectional rules are to be found in the lexicon with other morphological rules, or whether they rightly belong in the syntax. Another topic on which there does not yet seem to be general agreement is the way in which WFRs interact with subcategorisation rules (that is, rules which state what syntactic environments words can occur in). In particular, there are a number of attempts to constrain WFRs, so as to rule out, by some general principle, large numbers of non-occurrent constructions. This book does not allow space to explain all the arguments that lie behind such constraints and all the arguments against them. Nevertheless, it is, I think, worth listing some of the postulated constraints, to show the kind of work that is being carried out in Lexicalist Morphology. These have the status of working hypotheses, which may require considerable modification in the light of further data, and many (if not all) of them are contentious.

The Word-Based Hypothesis (Aronoff, 1976: 21):

All regular word-formation processes are word-based. A new word is formed by applying a regular rule to a single already existing word. Both the new word and the existing one are members of major lexical categories [defined as adverb, adjective, noun and verb].

There are a number of constraints implicit in this one, one of which has been rephrased as:

The No Phrase Constraint (Botha, 1981: 18):

Morphologically complex words cannot be formed (by WFRs) on the basis of syntactic phrases.

Another constraint is:

The Unitary Base Hypothesis (Aronoff, 1976: 48):

The semanticosyntactic specification of the base, though it may be more or less complex, is always unique. A WFR will never operate on either this or that.

In other words, an affix may be added to a nominal base or to a verbal base, but it will not be added to either a nominal or a verbal base. In such cases, Aronoff claims, it will always be the case that there are two affixes, presumably distinguishable on other grounds.

Multiple Application Constraint (Lieber, 1981: 173):

No word formation process ... can apply iteratively to its own output.

This constraint prohibits the formation of words such as *person·s·s* or *king·dom·dom* with the same affix repeated. This constraint will be considered again in section 12.3 below.

Generalised Lexicalist Hypothesis (Lapointe, 1981: 22):

Syntactic rules are not allowed to refer to, and hence cannot directly modify, the internal morphological structure of words.

This constraint says, for example, that it can never be the case that an underived noun can take part in a syntactic transformation while a morphologically complex noun cannot do so. Also, the form of a word cannot be determined by its syntactic environment. The second part of this is controversial (see for example, Anderson, 1982) but the first is not.

The Adjacency Condition (Allen, 1978: 155):

No rule of word formation can involve X and Y, unless Y is uniquely contained in the cycle adjacent to X.

This constraint says that it is never possible to have a morphologically complex word of the form

(22)   [[[[root] affix W] affix X] affix Y]

where the form of affix Y is determined by any property of the root or affix W; only affix X can affect affix Y.

This list of postulated constraints, which is far from exhaustive, gives some idea of the type of work being done in Lexicalist Morphology, in particular the level of abstraction at which the work is being carried out.

10.7 A CLOSER LOOK AT STRATAL THEORIES

The stratal theory of ordering of processes, which appears to be central to much Lexicalist Morphology, has a number of problems associated with it. To see this, it is important to ask first how it is possible to tell what the structure of a word is.

The most obvious clue is meaning. Consider the following passage from the Dr Seuss book *Fox in Socks*, which is aimed at pre-school children:

What do you know about tweetle beetles? Well...
When tweetle beetles fight, it's called a tweetle beetle battle.
And when they battle in a puddle, it's a tweetle beetle puddle battle.
AND when tweetle beetles battle with paddles in a puddle, they call it a tweetle beetle puddle paddle battle.
AND...When beetles battle beetles in a puddle paddle battle and the beetle battle puddle is a puddle in a bottle they call this a tweetle beetle bottle puddle paddle battle muddle...

Consider the compound from this *tweetle beetle puddle paddle battle*. This compound describes a kind of paddle battle, so 'paddle' and 'battle' belong together. We know that the creatures having these battles are tweetle beetles, so those two elements must belong together. This is a special kind of paddle battle, so the element which tells us what kind must go closely with paddle battle, and we have, as a result, the following structure.

(23)

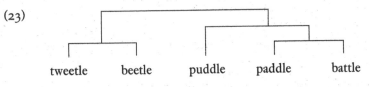

    tweetle   beetle   puddle   paddle   battle

There is no reference in this compound to a beetle puddle or a puddle paddle, and this is shown by the structure, which reflects the meaning. The same kind of exercise can be carried out with derivatives. If we consider *encouragement* we can see that it contains three morphs, *en·courage·ment*. These could be structured [[en·courage]ment] or [en[courage·ment]]. The first of these is supported by the semantics. *Encouragement* means 'act of encouraging' and *encourage* means something like 'put courage into'. The second is excluded for semantic reasons and also on distributional grounds: although the prefix *en-* is added to nouns (as the existence of *encourage* shows), none of the patterns that this process regularly gives rise to are ones which are relevant here. This prefix added to nouns can have one of the following meanings:

    (a) 'Put into NOUN', as in *encage, entomb. Encouragement* does not mean 'put into couragement'.

    (b) 'Make into a NOUN', as in *enslave. Encouragement* does not mean 'make into a couragement'.

    (c) 'Put a NOUN on a person or thing', as in *encrown. Encouragement* does not mean 'put a couragement on a person or thing'.

(Meanings taken from Marchand, 1969: 162f.) Thus the meaning of an affix or affixation process is relevant: other things being equal, we expect to find an affix having one of a fairly restricted number of possible meanings, otherwise the notion of a WFR will not make sense. Furthermore, if it is the case that *-ment* affixation is no longer productive (and there is some evidence that this is so: see Bauer, 1983: 55), then the fact that *couragement* is not an established form in its own right may also be relevant. There is nothing else available which could have been the base for the *en-* prefixation if the structure [[en·courage]ment] is rejected. We also have the evidence that *-ment* has probably never been used as a suffix on a noun base (Marchand, 1969 says that all the words like *devilment* which appear to come from nouns are actually formed on the basis of obsolete verbs). We thus expect *-ment* to be added to a verb, such as *encourage*, but not to a noun, such as *courage*. All these reasons support the analysis in (24).

(24)

There may still be cases where it is difficult to make a decision about the structure of a derivative. Consider the cases of *enliven* and *misshapen*. The prefix *en-* is regularly added to adjectives, as in *enable*, *enlarge*, *enrich* with the meaning 'make ADJECTIVE', so it could be added to *live*. But the suffix *-en* is only added to adjectives, as in *darken*, *straighten* and not to verbs. The prefix *en-* can be found added to verbs (although this use seems not to be productive), as in *enclasp*, *enclose*, *entrust* but, then, it means 'VERB in', which is not appropriate for *enliven*. The only structure that can really be motivated for *enliven* is:

(25)

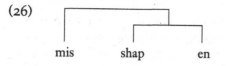

The problem with *misshapen* is that there is no regularly occurring form *misshape* (verb) or *shapen* in current English. Only the extra etymological information that *shapen* was the past participle of the verb *shape*, until the fourteenth century, allows us to assign the following structure to *misshapen*:

(26)

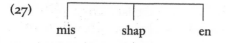

If the use of etymological information is excluded in making a synchronic decision, there is no strong evidence to indicate that the structure is anything but

(27)

Examples like this are unusual since, in most cases, it seems to be perfectly possible to assign a structure to English words where every branch in the tree is binary. Dvandva compounds with more than two elements such as *Cadbury-Schweppes-Hudson* are the only regular exceptions to this principle. Again historical (non-linguistic) information may allow a decision to be taken on a binary structure but that kind of information should not be relevant for linguistics. For those theories that see binary tree structure as some kind of language universal, it is unfortunate if such structure has to be imposed randomly.

On the basis of this, we can now turn to consider the stratal ordering hypothesis. The problem here is that the hypothesis is apparently not supported by the data. It seems to be possible to find ordering relations amongst elements from the four strata put forward in (12) which are not predicted by the stratal ordering hypothesis. This is shown in Table 2, where the kind of analysis discussed in the preceding paragraphs has been undertaken. It can be seen that, of the possible orderings of the strata set up in (12), only one does not seem to occur. The patterns predicted not to occur by the stratal theory in (12) are marked with two asterisks in Table 2.

It should be noted that the Lexicalist Morphologists themselves are aware of problems with the stratal ordering hypothesis and have tried to overcome them in many ways. As a result, the form of the hypothesis presented in (12) is not the only form to be found. Other versions merge Strata III and IV, allow suppletive forms to be introduced in Stratum I, suggest that the stratal ordering applies only to the affixes on one side of the root, so that a +-boundary prefix outside a #-boundary suffix does not constitute a violation and so on. And there are a number of sub-regularities among the violations. For example, most of the cases of derivational endings occurring further from the root than inflectional endings involve the derivational affixes *-ness* and *-ly*, which are extremely productive and very much at the inflectional end of the cline of derivational affixes, and the inflectional affixes *-ed* and *-ing*, which are very much at the derivational end of the cline of inflectional affixes. In fact, many scholars (notably Allen, 1978) argue that the suffixes *-ed* and *-ing* are derivational in some of their functions, so that examples involving them do not constitute violations of the stratal ordering hypothesis. Although the distinction between inherent and contextual inflection (see section 6.10) has not been taken into account in formulating the stratal theories, it might be that it would make a statement of the real generalisations easier. Even when such cases are taken out of consideration, however, there remain some unexplained violations of the hypothesis. The ordering hypothesis may explain the majority of cases in English but these exceptions still jeopardise it as a general explanation of the facts. The

Table 2 Possible Orders of Four Classes of Rule

	non-neutral derivational inside neutral derivational	[[im+[[pi]+ous]]#ness] [[[mysteri]+ous]#ness] [[[commerc]+ial]#ism]
**	non-neutral derivational outside neutral derivational	[[[govern]#ment]+al] [[[develop]#ment]+al] [[un#[[[grammat]+ic]+al]]+ity] [[[arch#[angel]]+ic]+al]
	non-neutral derivational inside inflectional	[[[quant]+ifi]#ed] [[[quant]+iti]#es] [[[oper]+ate]#d]
**	non-neutral derivational outside inflectional	NO EXAMPLES FOUND IN ENGLISH
	non-neutral derivational inside compounding	[[job] [[secur]+ity]] [[[satur]+ation] [point]] [[[quant]+ity] [surveyor]]
**	non-neutral derivational outside compounding	[[[set] [theoret]]+ic] [[[party]-[[polit]+ic]]+al] [[[[common][sens]]+ic]+al]
	neutral derivational inside inflectional	[[[develop]#ment]#s] [[[walk]#er]#s] [[[[comput]#er]#is]#ing]
**	neutral derivational outside inflectional	[[[accord]#ing]#ly] [[[interest]#ed]#ly] [[[lov]#ing]#ness] [[[folk]#s]#y] [[more]#ish] [[most]#ly]
	neutral derivational inside compounding	[[[govern]#ment] [offices]] [[[lectur]#er] [scale]] [[[own]#er]-[[occupi]#er]]
**	neutral derivational outside compounding	[ex#[[frog][man]]] [un#[[self]-[sufficient]]] [[[laid]-[back]]#ness] [[[skate][board]]#er]
**	inflectional inside compounding	[[[universiti]#es] [yearbook]] [[[suggestion]#s] [box]] [[[shoot]#ing] [stick]] [[least][ways]]
	inflectional outside compounding	[[[black][bird]]#s] [[[bath] [towel]]#s] [[[test]-[market]]#ing] [[[hang]-[glid]]#ing]

actual word-forms we can attest in English do not support simple adherence to the stratal ordering hypothesis. If this were merely a research strategy, acknowledged as an overgeneralisation, this might not matter. But it is often taken as a fixed point of reference. In one case (Williams, 1981) it has even been suggested that other principles should be abandoned to allow the ordering hypothesis to be maintained. This seems to be methodologically unsound, as well as a distortion of the basic data.

Another criticism that has be levelled against stratal ordering theory is that most English affixes show evidence of being on more than one stratum. To understand this we need to know what would count as evidence that an affix is on a particular stratum. Since we are here concerned purely with derivational affixes we can restrict our attention to the difference between Strata I and II.

We have already seen the first piece of evidence: the relative order of affixes. If an affix regularly occurs outside another affix which we know from other evidence to be on Stratum II, it must also be on Stratum II. Equally, if an affix appears inside a Stratum I affix, it must itself be on Stratum I. The second criterion concerns an affix's behaviour in respect to stress. If an affix is regularly stress neutral, it must be on Stratum II, while if it is involved in stress-shift, it must be on Stratum I. Note that affixes which themselves are stressed must, thus, all be on Stratum I. As a practical point, note that some words – even words with affixes – are not long enough to show whether there is stress shift or not, so that lack of movement in a particular case may not be critical. The third piece of evidence is attachment to obligatorily bound roots. Only Stratum I affixes can attach to these. A fourth piece of evidence is a major morphophonemic change to the base; generally speaking, only Stratum I affixes impose major allomorphy on their bases (though there are a few rare counter-examples to this). Some authorities add a criterion of semantic specialisation to this list but this cannot be right. Semantic specialisation is a matter of lexicalisation and lexicalisation can apply to words containing affixes from any Stratum. For example, although -er and -ness are fairly regular Stratum II affixes, words like lover (not just anyone who loves, but a person in a close, usually sexual, relationship) and highness (a title, not a quality) are semantically specialised just as much as monstrosity (an object not a quality) or dramatic (striking in effect as much as having to do with drama) which contain Stratum I affixes. It is not only words with Stratum I affixes which can become semantically specialised.

Given all this, the behaviour illustrated in (28) is typical and establishes -y]$_N$ (that is, the -y suffix which forms nouns) as a Stratum I affix and -y]$_A$ (that is, the -y suffix which forms adjectives) as a Stratum II affix.

(28)	-y]$_N$	-y]$_A$
Ordering	colloqu·i+al[†]	govern#ess·y
Stress	an'tonym·y	'governess·y
Obligatorily bound bases	energ·y (compare energetic)	NO RELEVANT WORDS
Morphophonemics	accura/s/·y	velve/t/·y

† There are not many words which make this point with this suffix, so a rare one has to be used. *The Oxford English Dictionary* lists both *to colloque* and *colloquy*.

Against this background, Giegerich (1999) argues that virtually any affix of English can appear either on Stratum I or on Stratum II. Giegerich illustrates this at length for a number of affixes but a few examples will make the general point. The prefix *pre-* usually behaves like a Stratum II prefix but, in a word like *premature*, it takes the stress and so must be a Stratum I affix. Also, in words like *preference* and *prevention*, it occurs inside Stratum I *-ence* and *-ion*, respectively, and so must be a Stratum I affix. The suffix *-less* usually behaves like a Stratum II affix, as is shown by ordering in *lead#er·less*, but, in words like *feckless, gormless* and *hapless*, it appears attached to an obligatorily bound base and so must be a Stratum I affix. In terms of ordering in words like *consum#er·ism*, the suffix *-ism* looks like a stratum II affix but, in *albin·ism*, it seems to attach to an obligatorily bound base and, in *Catholi/s/·ism*, the morphophonemics make it look as though it is a Stratum I affix. Some of these apparent anomalies can be explained in a number of ways: for example, it was argued in section 7.2 that *prefer* does not contain a morpheme {pre}, which would make the evidence of a word like *preference* irrelevant. It can be argued (Bauer, 1990b, 1992) that the four factors in (28) do not necessarily co-occur but that they are independent of each other. Indeed, sometimes the same affix in the same word may show facets of a Stratum I affix and simultaneously of a Stratum II affix. Consider the word *commentate*. To this we can add the suffix *-or* to give *commentator*, without any change in stress, so *-or* must be behaving like a Stratum II affix; yet we can add *+ial* to give *commentatorial* (with a change in stress), so the *-or* is ordered like a Stratum I affix. Much of this may be solved by appeal to the notion of lexicalisation but even that may not account for all the problems with level-ordering (Bauer, 1992).

A different kind of problem with level-ordering is that it accounts for such a small proportion of the data. Fabb (1988) looks at the behaviour of 43 suffixes in English. If suffixes could combine freely, he says, there would be 43^2, giving 1849, different two-suffix combinations possible from these suffixes in English. We know, however, that affixes do not combine freely: some can be added only to nouns, some can be added only to bases with final stress and so on. If we take account of these major restrictions, the number of possible combinations of 43 suffixes is 614. The level-ordering hypothesis rules out another 155 further potential affix combinations, leaving 459 which appear to be theoretically possible within the predictions of the theory. In fact, there are only 50 two-suffix combinations attested. The restrictions on combination must be far stricter than is accounted for simply by level-ordering. While criticising the details of Fabb's argumentation, Plag (1998, 1999) takes the argument further and suggests that we should not look at suffixes selecting their bases at all; rather we should consider how bases select their affixes. Thus, rather than saying, for instance, that *-ity* selects (among other things) bases that end in *-able*, we should say of bases ending in *-able* that they permit subsequent affixation with *-ity*. Precisely the same conclusion is arrived at (not entirely independently but using different evidence) by Giegerich (1999). While such conclusions do not do away with the requirement for level-ordering, they may weaken the case.

10.8 REVIEW: LEXICALIST MORPHOLOGY

This does not exhaust the things we might say about Lexicalist Morphology. In particular the place of productivity within such a model needs to be considered. The goal of morphology was said above (section 10.2, see also section 5.3) to be the description of the possible words of a language. This implies that the actual words of any language have only a restricted role to play in a morphology. That role is mainly concerned with providing a database which can be used as a basis for a grammar of words. The grammar of words will then predict that other words than those in the original database are possible. If subsequent new words attested fit the predictions of the grammar, the grammar is at least observationally adequate. (In fact, this is a simplification, since new rules can be added to a grammar at any time, but it will suffice for present purposes.) But not all existing words can be used as a basis for working out what the WFRs are because some of them may be lexicalised; that is, the WFR which produced them is no longer productive (see Chapter 5). The database thus has to be considered with great care.

There can, I think, be little doubt that the Lexicalist Morphologists are right that the lexicalised words have to be listed in the lexicon. The question then arises as to what should be done with those words which are established in the community and those potential words which are not established in the community, whether they are attested or not. Is there any difference in principle between *unleadedness*, which I have just this moment invented, *scaredness*, which is attested but not in, for example, *The Oxford English Dictionary* (Williams, 1965; section 5.3) and *boundedness* which is listed in the *OED*? Such difference as there is seems to be a difference between the number of people in the community who are familiar with the words, rather than a difference inherent in the words themselves. It, thus, seems to me that any theory which gives a particular status to *boundedness*, as opposed to other *-ed·ness* words, is to that extent misleading. Lexicalist Morphology falls into this category. The particular status is given to *boundedness* because only *boundedness* is listed in the permanent lexicon. In Aronoff's version of Lexicalist Morphology, *scaredness* and *unleadedness* are treated in the same way: the WFRS generate *scaredness* and *unleadedness* when the words are first used by means of once-only rules; the two new lexemes are then stored in the user's lexicon on a par with other lexemes; both are, thus, part of my personal lexicon (since I have just used these words) though other people's will be different. This too seems misleading. It implies that, if I do not use the word *unleadedness* for the next two years but then get involved in a discussion of whether petrol should be leaded or not, I will not have to generate *unleadedness* from scratch for that discussion, it will already be listed in my personal lexicon as a familiar item. It is hard to see just how this claim could be tested empirically but, a priori, it does not seem to be correct, at least not for a real native speaker of this language as opposed to the ideal speaker-listener. For real speakers, there seems to be some link between familiarity (based on regular exposure) and the possibility of something becoming established in the lexicon. Hapax legomena are not established words.

This is linked with the fact that regular new words are coined all the time without being listed in dictionaries. Evidence of this can be found in the numerous articles in the journal *American Speech* which list attested words that have some formative, or method of formation, in common. It is rarely the case that all such words later appear in standard dictionaries. If we are talking about real speakers of the language, it is quite clear that they cannot have all these words in their lexicons. If we are talking about the ideal speaker-listener, who might be expected to have all these words in the lexicon, the only way to ensure that they are all there is to include the maximum potential output from all WFRs. If that is done, there should be no distinction between *unleadedness*, *scaredness* and *boundedness*. I, therefore, conclude that some further clarification of the role of the permanent lexicon within Lexicalist Morphology is required.

Lexicalist Morphology has brought about a new era in the study of morphology. Because of work done within this school, it is now generally accepted that at least derivational morphology is quite distinct from syntax. More and more people also seem to be coming to see morphology as distinct from phonology. There are very few linguists who would still wish to see those lexemes which can be analysed in terms of non-productive processes generated by rule rather than listed in the lexicon. Lexicalist Morphologists have also started a search for formal universals in word-formation processes of a very different kind from anything that has gone before. The abstract principles and conditions that they operate with and attempt to elucidate are very clearly influenced by the type of work that has previously been done in syntax. As yet, the results of their search for universals and abstract principles have been rather disappointing, in that there is data readily available to show that the conditions do not hold. It is to be hoped, however, that successive refinements will lead to a more exact picture of the kinds of abstract universals that can be maintained in morphology. However, a fundamental review of their position on productivity and the permanent lexicon, a rather more realistic approach to the Stratal ordering hypothesis, and a clarification of some other principles such as rules for determining headedness in derivatives would seem to be essential if this theory of morphology is to have a sound foundation.

REFERENCES AND FURTHER READING

The best introductions to Lexicalist Morphology are Scalise (1984) and McMahon (1994). The only other source is the original works. The paper which gave the main impetus to Lexicalist Morphology is Chomsky (1970). Halle (1973) was the first important article stimulated by the ideas there and that was followed by Jackendoff (1975), although much of the content of these two papers has not become part of the accepted basis of Lexicalist Morphology. Three theses, Siegel (1974), Aronoff (1976) and Allen (1978), form the real basis of Lexicalist Morphology and since their appearance, there has been an explosion in the amount of work done in this framework. For a review of the work done by Lexicalist Morphologists on compounding, see Botha (1984b).

The 'general acceptance' that syntactic rules do not require access to phonological information, mentioned on page 168, is rather overstated although, as a very broad generalisation, it holds within writings in the Chomskyan tradition. For some suggestions as to where it might fail to hold, see W. Bauer (1982: 334 ff.) and Plank (1984).

In (8) the prefix *non-* is listed with a #-boundary. Allen (1978) argues that it must actually contain a sequence of two such boundaries. This does not influence the points made about the data in (8). The general principle holds.

Although the examples in (10) are presented in the text in more or less the terms in which they are usually presented by Lexical Morphologists, they require further comment. On the face of it, it is quite simply wrong that {in+} has phonetically conditioned allomorphs and {un#} does not. Pronunciations like *u[ŋ]#kind*, *u[m]#moved* are common, if not the norm. It looks as though the Lexicalist Morphologists are misled by the orthography. However, there is a difference between the two types, in that the phonetically conditioned allomorphs of {in+} are obligatory in all styles, while those of {un#} are optional in some styles. It is in this much more abstract sense that only +-boundaries demand obligatory phonetically conditioned allomorphy.

For fuller discussion of headedness in morphology see Anderson (1980), Baldi (1983), Zwicky (1985c), Di Sciullo & Williams (1987), Bauer (1990a), Lieber (1992), Bauer & Renouf (2001).

The criticisms presented in section 10.8 with reference to productivity are not as true of the model presented in Allen (1978) as they are of other versions of Lexicalist Morphology. Allen's model does not appear to have been universally adopted, however, and even it is not immune to criticism. Allen suggests that, as well as the permanent lexicon, there should be a conditional lexicon. The conditional lexicon contains the output of all WFRs which has not yet become lexicalised (that is, made unpredictable in some way, phonologically, morphologically or semantically). This makes the conditional lexicon infinite in extent since, for example, N + N compounding is recursive and there is, therefore, no longest compound in the English language. A grammar with an infinite component in it is not particularly explanatory: if the grammar is infinite, it could simply contain a list of grammatical forms without any explanation as to why they are grammatical.

EXERCISES

1. Below is presented a list of English words which end in the affix -*ism*. Some of these words are not helpful in deciding whether this suffix must be on Stratum I or Stratum II, others present relevant data. Which words present relevant data? What is the relevant data? If there is doubt about the relevance of the data, explain why. What conclusion about the class of this suffix would you arrive at, based on each individual word? What overall conclusion do you arrive at or what extra information would you need to arrive at an overall conclusion?

æbsən'tiːɪzm	absenteeism
æg'nɒstɪsɪzm	agnosticism
'ælkəhɒlɪzm	alcoholism
'bæptɪzm	baptism
juːtɪlɪ'teərɪənɪzm	utilitarianism
kriː'eɪʃənɪzm	creationism
rɪ'pɔːtərɪzm	reporterism
'sɪmbəlɪzm	symbolism

2. What is it about *Model-T* which makes it an example of an unexpected headedness pattern?

3. Consider the examples of asterisked categories given in Table 2. Can you find more examples parallel to the ones given? How far would you take these examples to be genuine counter-examples to the level-ordering hypothesis?

4. Draw structural trees for the following words: *bepatched, completion dates, disengagement, enlightenment, polarised, unhappier.*

5. Find some more examples of verbs and their nominalisations where the subcategorisation patterns for the two are the same, and some examples where they differ. Which are easier to find?

CHAPTER 11

Word-and-Paradigm Morphology

If Lexicalist Morphology deals primarily with derivational morphology, Word-and-Paradigm morphology concentrates on inflectional morphology. While it seems reasonably clear that the methods of Word-and-Paradigm (henceforth WP) could be extended to cover derivational morphology as well (and statements are occasionally made to that effect by the proponents of WP, for example, Robins, 1959: 125), WP has been developed to deal with the inflectional morphology of morphologically complex languages and it is here that its strengths are most apparent. As will appear below, the focus of theoretical attention in WP morphology is also rather different from that in Lexicalist Morphology. Some versions of Lexicalist Morphology and WP approaches are perfectly compatible with each other and may, indeed, supplement each other.

In the discussion in this chapter, I have avoided the specialised terminology used in WP in favour of the terminology already introduced in this book. Some translation will, thus, be required to read the original works in this area.

11.1 THE DISTINCTIVENESS OF WP

The WP approach to morphology is a reaction to the usual simplistic notion that words can be analysed into sequences of morphs each of which is in a one-to-one correspondence with a morpheme (the 'beads-on-a-string' approach discussed in section 7.1). While such a model of morphology may be largely applicable in some languages, there are many more where it is grossly inadequate. We have already seen many difficulties with the notion of morpheme in section 7.1.

The situation also arises (and this, too, has already been illustrated) where a single morpheme is realised by a number of morphs, which may be discontinuous. All of this is illustrated in the diagram in (1), which can be taken as a summary and revision of earlier discussion. (1) shows the patterns of realisation involved in the Italian word-form *canterebbero* '[if] they would sing'. The *-bb-* occurs only with forms which are both third person and conditional, the stressed *-e-* following the *-r-* occurs consistently only in conditional forms, the *-ro* occurs only with the third person plural, the *-r-* occurs with futures and conditionals (Matthews, 1970: 107–8).

(1)

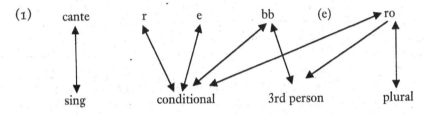

In a situation of this kind, whether we take the semantic units marked in the bottom line of the diagram to represent morphemes or whether we attempt to associate the individual morphs with bundles of meanings, there is no easy way to equate the formal units with semantic units (and, thus, no obvious direct relation between morph and morpheme) and no easy way to view words as realising ordered sequences of morphemes. Rather, the morpho-semantic elements (let us call them, following WP morphologists, **properties**) have an influence on the way in which the word-form is made up, either individually or in combination with other similar elements.

In WP morphology the word-form is, therefore, taken as the basic unit of syntax, even though it is not minimal. The word-form is derived by a number of processes or operations which apply to the lexeme. The properties other than the lexeme which influence the form of the word-form determine which processes apply. The linguist as analyst can deduce what these processes are by consideration of the entire paradigm in which the lexeme appears and by contrasting the word-forms which appear in that paradigm. In this way, syntax and morphology are kept clearly distinct, which is not necessarily the case in a system which takes the morpheme as its basic unit. Since the word-form and not the morpheme is the basic unit of analysis and there is no expectation that there will be any minimal unit of form within the word-form, morphs have no status within this theory. This has led to the WP being renamed **a-morphous morphology**, in a piece of morphological reanalysis that has stuck (Anderson, 1992). The two labels can be taken as being synonymous. I shall retain the more conservative label of WP here.

Morphologists working with WP point in particular to two advantages of the theory. First, there are many cases where a single formative appears to realise different morphemes in different parts of a paradigm. As an example, consider the -b- which occurs in Latin *ama:bo* 'I shall love' and *ama:bam* 'I was loving'. It appears to be a function of either the future tense or the imperfect, since it is missing in the present *amo:* 'I love', the perfect *ama:vi:* 'I loved', the future perfect *ama:vero* 'I shall have loved', the pluperfect *ama:veram* and all tenses of the subjunctive. It is not simply a non-present marker because other non-present tenses do not show it. There is no reasonable analysis according to which it realises a single morpheme or even a single property. Rather than say that there is a single morph which realises two distinct morphemes, it seems preferable to say that the -b- is generated by operations in the two partial paradigms, but is not related, that is – if we wish to reformulate this in the old terminology – it represents two homophonous morphs. In other cases, the position of a morph relative to others can define the value of the morph. In Finnish, the suffix -in can indicate the superlative nominative singular of an adjective or be an allomorph of the illative case. Thus, in (2a), -in means 'superlative' but, in (2b), where it occurs after another affix, it means 'illative' (that is, 'into') (Karlsson, 1983):

(2) (a) selv·in
       clear·superlative
       'clearest' (nominative singular)

   (b) selv·imp·i·in
       clear·superlative·plural·illative
       'clearest' (illative plural)

Since WP is concerned with the word-form as a whole rather than with the shape of individual morphs within the word-form, it can easily deal with features such as this. It should be noted, however, that any theory which allows homophonous morphs to belong to different morphemes can also cope with such data. WP is not the only possibility.

The second advantage of WP is that it can cope with cumulation of morphemes in a single morph. For example, the Latin *bon·us* shows the number, gender and case of the adjective 'good' in the -us suffix, and these various properties (singular, masculine, nominative) cannot be assigned to independent formal elements within the affix. Any theory which demands that each morpheme should be spelt out in turn independently of others cannot deal with this type of realisation. WP, however, allows clusters of properties to determine the shape of the word-form as a whole and can thus deal with such data. (We shall see precisely how in the next section.)

Anderson (1977: 30 ff.) provides an example from the Algonquian language Potawatomi to show the necessity for a WP type of approach to the morphology of at least some languages. Later (1982), he provides a similar example from Georgian, so the problem is not isolated. In Potawatomi the paradigm for a transitive animate verb with first and second person subjects is, in part, as in (3).

(3)   n·wapm·a   'I see him'
         k·wapm·a   'you (singular) see him'
         n·wapm·a·k   'I see them'
         k·wapm·a·k   'you (singular) see them'

In this paradigm, the n- prefix marks the first person singular, the k- prefix the second person singular, the -a suffix marks a transitive verb and the -k suffix marks the third person plural object. The root is *wapm*. However, when the subject is in the third person, the initial prefix marks the object of the verb, not the subject, and the final suffix marks the subject, not the object, as we see in (4).

(4)   n·wapm·uk   'he sees me'
         k·wapm·uk   'he sees you (singular)'
         n·wapm·uko·k   'they see me'
         k·wapm·uko·k   'they see you (singular)'

Here the -uk(o)- appears to mark the changed status of the verb. The n- and k- prefixes still mark first and second person singular respectively, but these are objects in (4) while they were subjects in (3). Anderson claims that any system of morphology that assigns morphs to morphemes (or meanings to forms) and then provides formulae for combining morphs will be in grave difficulty in describing this kind of phenomenon. Only in WP, which allows the cumulation of properties to determine the shape and order of affixes, will such a language not create difficulties of description.

WP, it should be clear, is a morphological theory which has its origins in the traditional grammatical treatment of the classical languages. This is (or used to be) seen as a disadvantage by some scholars, who attributed to WP the lack of formalness and lack of universality that were associated with traditional grammar.

Morphologists working within WP have been quick to argue that, for the traditional style to have remained dominant for so long, it must at least have reflected something of the way in which speakers felt their languages functioned. These morphologists, thus, feel that it is worthwhile providing the formalness that traditional grammar lacked in an attempt to bring this approach to morphology up-to-date.

The biggest potential disadvantage of WP is that it may not be the most suitable model to apply to all languages. For example, although Turkish has quite complicated morphology, it seems that it can be explained without any of the complexities of WP. That is because in Turkish there is generally a one-to-one relation between morpheme and morph; cumulation, the kind of situation illustrated in (1), or the inversion, shown in (3) and (4), are not found. At the other end of the scale, a language like Chinese has very little inflection at all. Robins (1959: 123) argues that, even in a case like this, WP may have some contribution to make in allowing compounds, for instance, to be treated as single word-forms. He claims that, even in such cases, 'the word as formally established is the most profitable unit to be taken as basic in the statement of…sentence structures'. This is obviously open to empirical verification. While it looks as though WP may not have much to offer in such languages, this cannot simply be presupposed.

11.2 AN EXAMPLE

As an example of the way in which WP morphology works, I have taken the forms of neuter nouns in German, although many of the rules I shall mention would also be used in generating the forms of nouns of other genders. German noun morphology is not nearly as complex as, say, Italian or Latin verb morphology, so the full extent of the way in which WP works cannot be illustrated using this example. Enough detail can be given, however, for it to be reasonably clear how such extensions would work. For a full discussion of Latin verb morphology in this framework see Matthews (1972). In several places in this exposition it will be seen that there is more than one way to deal with a given phenomenon within WP. This is not necessarily a disadvantage for the theory. In some cases a decision about which of two competing ways is best could be taken on the basis of a larger sample of data. In other cases decisions would, in the long run, be made in terms of the relative economy of the options –

something which cannot be seen from such a small section of the morphology of a single language.

German has several distinct classes of neuter noun from a morphological point of view. Some of these classes are extremely large, some are restricted to a single noun. Nouns typifying these classes are listed below in their nominative singular and plural forms. Other forms will be considered subsequently. The numbers attributed to the classes are entirely random.

(5)

Class	Singular	Plural	Gloss
1	Mädchen	Mädchen	'girl'
2	Ufer	Ufer	'bank (of a river)'
3	Kloster	Klöster	'monastery, convent'
4	Kind	Kinder	'child'
5	Bein	Beine	'leg'
6	Bett	Betten	'bed'
7	Buch	Bücher	'book'
8	Floss	Flösse	'raft'
9	Herz	Herzen	'heart'
10	Auge	Augen	'eye'
11	Konto	Konten	'account'
12	Prinzip	Prinzipien	'principle'
13	Auto	Autos	'car'

Even a superficial glance at the forms in (5) makes it clear that a number of processes are involved in specifying the forms of German neuter nouns. These processes can be expressed as a number of rules, as in (6):

(6) Rule 1 Suffix -e to the base.
　　　Rule 2 Suffix -er to the base.
　　　Rule 3 Suffix -en to the base.
　　　Rule 4 Suffix -n to the base.
　　　Rule 5 Suffix -s to the base.
　　　Rule 6 Suffix -i to the base.
　　　Rule 7 Delete the final vowel in the base.
　　　Rule 8 Umlaut rule (discussed below).

Each of these rules could be stated more formally, using some suitable notation, but the prose versions are sufficient for present purposes. The Umlaut rule requires further discussion, however. In orthographic terms, it takes as its input a, o and u and turns them into ä, ö and ü, except where there is a diphthong au, which is changed to äu. (This last case is not illustrated in (5), but is shown by das Haus, *die Häuser* 'house'.) No other vowels are affected by Umlaut. The phonology of this operation is complex for a number of reasons but the complexity is not enlightening for the morphology. It is easier simply to stick with the orthographic version (as was implicitly done in the other rules in (6)) and say that the Umlaut rule is:

(7)
$$\begin{Bmatrix} a \\ o \\ u \\ au \end{Bmatrix} \rightarrow \begin{Bmatrix} ä \\ ö \\ ü \\ äu \end{Bmatrix}$$

It is now necessary to consider a format for morphological statements within the WP model. What the morphological rules are doing is building the phonological structure of the word-form from information about what lexeme is involved and from information about what morphological properties are necessary for the word-form in the sentence in which it appears. The first piece of information we need, therefore, concerns the lexeme which is involved in the word-form. Since the lexeme may be realised by any one of a number of word-forms, we need to know the irreducible form which belongs to the lexeme and to which phonological alterations may be made in order to specify the form of the word-form. In the terms we have used in this book, we need to know what the base is to which the affixes will be added and, since we are discussing the base of the lexeme, we might call this the **lexical base**. However, since the morphology which is to be encoded on this base is inflectional, WP morphologists usually use the more precise term **stem**. Stem traditionally refers to that morphological unit to which inflectional affixes are added, so that a stem is a sub-type of base. We will continue to use this terminology here, though you need to be aware that 'stem' is used in a different sense by some linguists, particularly those working within Lexicalist Morphology.

In many languages, inflectable lexemes may have more than one stem. We have already seen this with regard to suppletion (see section 3.9) but the point is a more general one than that. Some analysts see the Ablaut series in Germanic verbs as being cases of alternative stems for the same lexeme (Lieber, 1981): so, for example, the German verb TRINKEN 'to drink' has the principal parts *trinken, trank, getrunken,* and the stems which occur in the past tense and past participle also arise in *der Trank* 'beverage' (and possibly *das Getränk* 'beverage') and *der Trunk* 'drink, drinking'. An alternative analysis would derive all of these from the stem *trink*. The point is that we may need a way of choosing a particular stem from among many and we shall, in any case, see that we end up with intermediate (incomplete) stems.

Stems are presented in morphological rules of the type we shall be considering in a phonological transcription (normally between phonemic slashes) which must be listed in the lexicon. As has already been noted, the example to be worked through here will use orthography rather than phonology (though one corresponds to the other quite well) so that orthographic transcription symbols ('<...>') will replace the normal phonemic brackets in the examples below.

In order to know what processes to apply to the chosen stems, we need to know the relevant word-form's place in the paradigm for that lexeme. This is given in terms of morphological properties: things like [1st person], [+ past], [+ plural] and the like. It is assumed that these properties are derived from the syntactic tree in which the word-form is to appear, although they are clearly also meaningful in terms of the paradigms involved. These properties look as though they might equate to morphemes in other models, and we have seen in section 7.2 that this is one way in which the term 'morpheme' has been used, but this is not an equation that is made within WP. One oddity of this system is that the properties typically include a marker of word-class such as [+ Noun] or [+ Adjective], which are not obviously of the same nature as the other properties.

Having specified the class to be affected by our structure-building rule, we need to specify how the structure of the stem is to be modified. In the easiest cases, we will be adding some phonological material and we will be adding the same phonological material independent of the structure of the stem. Under such circumstances, we would need a rule of the form in (8).

(8)
$$\begin{bmatrix} +\text{Noun} \\ +\text{Feature x} \\ -\text{Feature y} \end{bmatrix}$$

$$/X/ \quad \rightarrow /Xn/$$

Rule (8) says that any nominal stem which, by virtue of its syntax, carries the properties [+ Feature x] and [- Feature y] should have an /n/ added after it. Note that since we do not care about the phonological structure of the stem, we have represented it with a variable, X. If different processes applied, depending on the phonological structure of the stem, we would have to specify the relevant bits of stem phonology to the left of the arrow.

Now let us come to the example of German neuter nouns. In this example, we will use the following properties: nom[inative], acc[usative], gen[itive], dat[ive], sing[ular] and pl[ural]. Since we are only dealing with neuter nouns, a marking for gender is implicit rather than explicit. We use the class numbers from (5) as further features to specify which sets of lexemes are affected by particular rules.

We can begin with the singular forms of these nouns. Although some of the case forms of the singular are not homophonous with the stem, the nominative and accusative forms are in most cases and, in all instances, the genitive is derived from the nominative/accusative form. The only class we need to worry about is Class 11. Since -*en* is a widely used plural marker, it seems that we should probably take the stem of *Konto* as being *Kont*. This is a neat solution for that lexeme but other words, apparently in the same class, do not end in -*o* in the nominative singular: examples are *das Album*, pl. *Alben*, *das Datum*, pl. *Daten*, *das Museum*, pl. *Museen*. Either we need to set up more classes (perfectly possible), one which adds -*o* in the singular and one which adds -*um*, or we need to use a rule like rule 7 in (6) to form the plural after all. Let us elect to set up the extra classes. The general rule we need will look like that in (9).

(9)
$$\begin{bmatrix} +\text{Noun} \\ +\text{sing} \end{bmatrix}$$

        <X>   → <X>

The '<X> → <X>' notation, in effect, says 'make no change to the form'. But this is not going to give us a good account of the nouns in class 11; here we need to add something to the stem to get the singular forms. We need a rule like (10):

(10)
$$\begin{bmatrix} +\text{Noun} \\ +\text{sing} \\ +\text{class 11} \end{bmatrix}$$

        <X>   → <Xo>

Rule (10) deals with nouns like *Konto*; we will need another version for words like *Album* which will have the same set of properties as shown in (10) but whose final line will be <X> → <Xum>.

For (9) and (10) to work properly, we need (10) to apply just for class 11 nouns and (9) to apply everywhere else. What is more, once (10) has applied to a class 11 noun, (9) is not required. This is achieved by means of a principle of disjunctive rule order known as the **Elsewhere Principle**, formulated by Anderson (1992: 132) as:

Elsewhere Principle:

Application of a more specific rule blocks that of a later more general one.

Note, first, the implication that these rules are ordered; we shall return to this point. Then consider (9) and (10). (10) is identical to (9) except that it includes an extra specification for the class of noun to which it applies. It, thus, affects a more specific sub-set of the forms which would otherwise be affected by (9). This is precisely the case that the Elsewhere Principle is set up to solve. As long as (9) is ordered after (10), (10) will apply to class 11 nouns and, then, the later rule, rule (9), will not apply to those nouns but only where rule (10) has not applied.

We can also use the Elsewhere Principle to predict the form of the genitive singular of these nouns. The most general rule is that you form the genitive singular of these nouns by adding an <s> to the stem. However, when the stem ends in <s> (whatever class the noun belongs to: so *Mass* 'measurement' is a class 5 noun, while *Floss* 'raft' is a class 8 noun), the genitive singular is formed by adding <es>. There are two ways of arranging this. The first is to use the Elsewhere Principle to guarantee the correct application of rules; the second is to allow sequences of <ss> to be generated but, then, to split them up by a phonological (or orthographic) rescue rule. Either of these is justifiable and the choice between them might be determined by factors in the wider grammar of German. Class 9 has an irregular genitive singular. Thus, we need a set of rules (11)–(13) to generate the genitive singular forms of our nouns.

(11)
$$\begin{bmatrix} +\text{Noun} \\ +\text{gen} \\ +\text{sing} \\ +\text{class 9} \end{bmatrix}$$

<X>   → <Xens>

(12)
$$\begin{bmatrix} +\text{Noun} \\ +\text{gen} \\ +\text{sing} \end{bmatrix}$$

      <X>   = <Ys> → <Xes>

(13)
$$\begin{bmatrix} +\text{Noun} \\ +\text{gen} \\ +\text{sing} \end{bmatrix}$$

      <X>   →<Xs>

The notation in (12) is to be read as 'as base of any form, where that form is something followed by a final <s> adds <es> to the base'. The Elsewhere Principle ensures that rule (13) does not apply to something which has already undergone (11) or (12). Notice, however, that, since rules (9) and (10) are ordered before rule (11), they are not subject to the Elsewhere Principle and the changes they made to stems persist. Thus the genitive <s> is added to the stem + <o> (or, for the other subtype, <um>) in class 11.

As well as having an irregular genitive singular, class 9 also has an irregular dative singular. In all other cases, the dative singular is the same as the nominative singular. This is an oversimplification of the actual state of affairs. In reality, an earlier dative singular marker <e> has been in the process of vanishing for some time in German and is retained optionally for stylistic purposes on some nouns and obligatorily in some fixed phrases. Here we shall adopt the simplified version because dealing with the more complex true picture would not help us understand WP any better. Given that, we need the rule in (14). All the other dative singulars have already been provided by rules (9) and (10).

(14)
$$\begin{bmatrix} +\text{Noun} \\ +\text{dat} \\ +\text{sing} \\ +\text{class 9} \end{bmatrix}$$

      <X>   → <Xen>

Now let us consider the plural forms. First we need to notice that some nouns have Umlaut in the plural (and this applies to all their plural forms). We can write a simple rule (15) which makes reference to the more complex form in (7) to provide Umlauted forms. The features inserted between braces ('{...}') are options (we could equally have listed these options vertically rather than horizontally): we choose one of these; the rule works just as well with any one.

(15)
$$
\begin{bmatrix}
\text{+Noun} \\
\text{+pl} \\
\{\text{+class 3, + class 7, + class 8}\}
\end{bmatrix}
$$

<X>   = <YVZ> → <YV̈Z>

An alternative approach here would be to say that some of the other classes also undergo Umlaut but, because their vowels are not in the list in (7), the rule cannot apply to them and nothing changes (that is, to use the jargon, the rule applies vacuously). We need not get involved in the relative strengths of these different approaches.

If we look at the plural forms, they are the same in all cases for some nouns and different only in the dative for some others. In those cases where the dative is different, it can be formed by adding <(e)n> to the basic plural form. So again we can use rule-ordering to get the appropriate answer. First we need a set of rules to provide the most widespread plural forms.

(16)
$$
\begin{bmatrix}
\text{+Noun} \\
\text{+pl} \\
\{\text{+class 1, + class 2, + class 3}\}
\end{bmatrix}
$$

<X>   → <X>

(17)
$$
\begin{bmatrix}
\text{+Noun} \\
\text{+pl} \\
\{\text{+class 4, + class 7}\}
\end{bmatrix}
$$

<X>   → <Xer>

(18)
$$
\begin{bmatrix}
\text{+Noun} \\
\text{+pl} \\
\{\text{+class 5, + class 8}\}
\end{bmatrix}
$$

<X>   → <Xe>

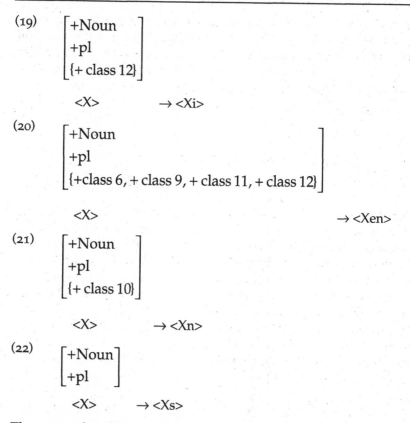

(19)

$$\begin{bmatrix} +\text{Noun} \\ +\text{pl} \\ \{+\text{ class 12}\} \end{bmatrix}$$

      <X>   → <Xi>

(20)

$$\begin{bmatrix} +\text{Noun} \\ +\text{pl} \\ \{+\text{class 6}, +\text{ class 9}, +\text{ class 11}, +\text{ class 12}\} \end{bmatrix}$$

      <X>   → <Xen>

(21)

$$\begin{bmatrix} +\text{Noun} \\ +\text{pl} \\ \{+\text{ class 10}\} \end{bmatrix}$$

      <X>   → <Xn>

(22)

$$\begin{bmatrix} +\text{Noun} \\ +\text{pl} \end{bmatrix}$$

      <X>   → <Xs>

There are a few things to note about rules (16)–(22). The first is that, except for (22), they are rules of equal generality (in any instance of application, applying only to nouns of one class) and so they do not block each other on the Elsewhere Principle. Rule (22) does work according to the Elsewhere Principle and it might seem an odd form to leave to apply 'elsewhere' given how few words are in this particular class. The point about this is that there is evidence that a final <s> plural is the **default** for all nouns in German (Clahsen *et al.*, 1992; Marcus *et al.*, 1995; Wiese, 1996): it is replacing irregular forms in a number of words (for example, *Konten* is giving way to *Kontos*), it is used for making the plurals of new loan words, it is used to make acronyms plural (for example, *LKWs* < *Lastkraftwagen* 'lorries, trucks') and in a number of other places where the plural of the noun might be in doubt. Rule (19) is used to insert the <i> in *Prinzipien*, which is, then, by rule (20), given the more general <en>. An alternative would be to add <ien> as a separate ending. This would have the pleasing effect of making the endings <n> and <en> rather more in complementary distribution (<en> following a consonant, <n> following a vowel), but the distribution is not completely complementary even so and it is probably better to keep the two classes.

Finally, we need to provide for a dative plural form where this is different from the form which occurs in the rest of the plural. This can be achieved by the rule:

(23)
$$
\begin{bmatrix} +\text{Noun} \\ +\text{dat} \\ +\text{pl} \end{bmatrix}
$$

$$
<X> \qquad = <Y \begin{bmatrix} +\text{sonorant} \\ -\text{nasal} \end{bmatrix}> \rightarrow <Xn>
$$

We might add a final rule saying that otherwise the dative plural is the same as the general plural. Rule (23), in effect, rules out final combinations of *<nn> and *<sn>, where the plural is the same for all cases, and adds an <n> to all other stems which, as it happens, will always end in a sonorant (including a vowel) other than <n>. This has to be specified in phonological terms, since letters do not have phonological content and cannot be spelt out in terms of distinctive features.

It should now be possible to apply the rules (9)–(23) (with rules (9) and (10) in the reverse order) to any of the stems given in (5) and get the appropriate number + case forms of these nouns. You need to realise that, although the exposition here has been artificially limited to just neuter nouns, basically the same rules apply to nouns of all genders in slightly different ways, so that some economies might be possible if we looked at the complete system. You also need to realise that, when, in these rules, we say that if you find a particular set of properties marking a noun you add such and such a piece of phonological (or orthographic) material, we are specifically not saying that the phonological material thus added has a meaning in isolation: we are simply trying to spell out the phonological shape of the relevant word-form.

11.3 SYNOPSIS

The WP approach to morphology is mainly concerned with providing a theoretical framework and, with that, a notation for escaping from a simplistic view of morphology in which there is a one-to-one correspondence between morph and morpheme. In doing this, its practitioners have concentrated mainly on the inflectional morphology of a small number of morphologically highly complex languages. Derivational morphology and the morphology of other, morphologically simpler, languages have tended to be ignored. However, there is no reason to suppose that the general approach taken in WP could not account for derivational morphology. It does seem likely, however, that precisely those facets of WP descriptions which make them so well suited to languages such as Latin or Potawatomi would remain largely unexploited in the description of languages such as Turkish or Yoruba. There is a suggestion that WP may, nevertheless, provide useful insights in the description of such languages but it remains to be clearly exemplified.

WP descriptions are most useful in cases where:

(a) there is a regular paradigm;

(b) there are cumulative realisations of meaning (portmanteau morphs);

(c) a single morpheme is realised by a number of formal elements, which are possibly not even contiguous;

(d) an analysis into morphs is complicated by the many-to-many realisation rules involved;

(e) there is morphological inversion, as in the Potawatomi example discussed earlier;

(f) rules of affixation and rules with phonological content (such as vowel lengthening, Umlaut and so on) are used side-by-side with similar effects.

There are also some disadvantages to WP. Some of these are problems with the notation rather than with the ideas behind WP. For instance, in some versions of WP it is possible to say that a particular form is created by performing an operation on another specified form (for example, the dative plural is created by adding /n/ to the nominative plural). While the notation given above allows you to do that, it does not allow you to make that generalisation: rather than saying that you should start with a particular form, the notation given here forces you to arrive at the appropriate surface form by ordering rules in such a way as to arrive there without having stopped on the way through and said 'at this point we have a new intermediate stem which is useful for other purposes'. This means that some generalisations will be impossible to capture using this notation.

Another problem comes from the properties which arise in a syntactic tree. It is easy to see why properties marking contextual inflectional categories should arise from the syntax: they are there specifically to allow the syntax to do its job. But it is far less easy to see why a marking such as [+ past tense] should arise in the same way. Some inherent inflection, such as gender on nouns, arises in the lexicon, not in the syntax. It is hard to see why tense marking should, in principle, be in either place, except in a few subordinate constructions. It is generated as a property not because this is a particularly well-motivated option in terms of the way language is used, but because tense marking is so tied up with person and number marking in a language like Latin that it would not be feasible to give rules for person and number markers without making reference to tense. This is an argument of a rather different order.

The major disadvantage of WP morphology is that the mechanisms it employs appear to allow almost anything as a morphological operation. This is, in part, due to the very powerful mechanism of allowing extrinsic rule-ordering in descriptions, but is also due to the fact that there appear to be no constraints on what rules may do phonologically. Like transformational grammar, therefore, WP probably requires constraining in some way in order to exclude rules which are universally impossible. At the moment it is probably not possible to proceed far in this direction since we have too little knowledge about precisely what is possible in language. The way forward in WP morphology lies in attempting to discover what constraints are possible and this involves WP descriptions of rather more data than we currently have available.

REFERENCES AND FURTHER READING

For the background to WP morphology, see Hockett (1954) and Robins (1959) Most of the recent development of WP, and in particular the development of a notation, has been undertaken by Matthews, see especially Matthews (1972). Even more recently, WP morphology has been taken up by Anderson (1977, 1982, 1992). Another version of basically similar ideas, although with some additions, is put forward by Zwicky (1985b) and another by Stump (2001).

My exposition of WP differs from the originals in a number of ways but, particularly, in matters of terminology. In keeping with the terminology used elsewhere in this book, I have talked in terms of realisation, where the usual term in WP is **exponence**. Similarly, what I have termed formal elements or phonological representations are usually called **exponents** of the various morphological properties, to use Matthews' terminology. I have totally ignored here the notion of morphological **categories**, which is actually an extremely useful one. A morphological category is a class whose members are morphological properties. For example, in some languages the morphological properties of present, past and future may be the options within the morphological category of Tense, the morphological properties singular, dual and plural may be the options within the morphological category of Number and so on. Morphological categories are, then, such things as Person, Number, Gender, Case, Aspect, Mood, Tense, and so on. (Matthews writes categories with a capital letter to distinguish them from properties but this usage is not general). One use of these categories will be seen in Chapter 13. As far as notation is concerned, I have basically adopted that used by Anderson, which seems to be the most usual. One refinement which did not arise in the material considered here is that it is possible to introduce an environment for the application of a particular rule, using the usual notation of generative phonological statements.

The data in exercise 4 is from Lockwood (1993: 201).

EXERCISES

1. Take as a stem any form listed in the 'Singular' column of (5) (if you choose the word *Konto*, use the form *Kont* as the stem instead). Choose singular or plural and one of nominative, accusative, genitive and dative and follow the rules (9)–(23) through, checking that an appropriate form is produced. Remember to take the Elsewhere Principle into account. You may decide that you need at least one extra rule. If you do, where would the rule or rules be ordered?

2. Would it possible to rewrite the rules for the generation of German nominal forms without using rule-ordering? How would you go about it?

3. Look in an Italian grammar to see how the word-form in (1) is constructed. How would you deal with this in a morpheme-based grammar?

4. Languages can sometimes do things which you might not expect. The data below is from the language Clallam, once spoken on the northwest Pacific coast of the United States. Note the relationship between the second and third segments in these words. Can you write a rule deriving the form in the third column from the form in the first?

ʧkʷut	'shoot'	ʧukʷt	'shooting'
xʧʔit	'scratch'	xiʧʔt	'scratching'
mtəqʷt	'put in water'	mətqʷt	'putting in water'

CHAPTER 12

Non-linear Approaches to Morphology

We have already seen how the sequence of morphs in a word has been likened to a series of beads on a string (see section 7.1). Any approach to morphology which deals with things in this way can be considered a **linear** approach: the morphs are accounted for in terms of their ordering in time (or on the page). Similar approaches were also taken to phonology in the mid-twentieth century: utterances were seen as being made up of a number of more or less independent segments placed adjacent to each other and influencing each other by their proximity. But, from the 1970s onwards, new approaches to phonology started to appear which rejected this fundamental premise. In particular, attempts to deal with stress and tone seemed to show that there were phonological systems for these things which were parallel to but not directly associated with the segments that had been dealt with earlier. Not only did we need to account for these parallel processes, we also needed to show how they matched up with each other: how tones or stresses were mapped onto sequences of segments. This brought out the need for hierarchies of phonological structures: not only did we need segments, we also needed moras, syllables, feet, prosodic words and so on.

When these 'non-linear' approaches to phonology proved to be valuable, it was inevitable that attempts would be made to extend them to morphology as well. Some types of morphology proved to be very suitable for descriptions cast in non-linear moulds and these will be considered in this chapter.

12.1 SOME CONCEPTS AND TERMINOLOGY

The first type of non-linear phonology to be extended to morphology was Autosegmental Phonology. In order to understand what is going on in the morphology, we need to see something of the way in which the phonology works and become familiar with some of the terminology that is used.

Consider the data from the Nigerian language Margi in (1):

(1) (a) fĭ + ani   →   fjàní
        swell   causative   cause to swell

    (b) bdlĕ + na   →   bdlèná
        forge   forge

where ´ indicates high tone, ` indicates low tone and ˇ indicates rising tone (low followed by high).

We can explain (1b) fairly readily: a sequence of high and low tone, which are both attached to the same syllable when there is only one syllable, is split up over two syllables when the next syllable does not have its own tone. (1a) is harder, though. The [i] becomes a glide and, thus, is not capable of carrying the tone, which accordingly moves to the first position where there is something which can carry it. We can illustrate this as (2):

(2) a)   L H   L H
          \\/   \ /
         fi   +   ani   →   fjani

    b)   L H   L H
          \\/   \ |
         bdle   +   na   →   bdlena

where L indicates low tone and H indicates high tone.

This kind of behaviour is taken as evidence that tone and segments are (to a large extent) autonomous – whence the blended term **autosegmental**. We can view the tonal pattern as a separate and independent entity from the segmental pattern. The two are dealt with as being on separate levels or **tiers**, as indicated by the double line of the transcription in (2).

The moment we do that, we have to put in place a mechanism for relating the appropriate part of the tonal transcription to the appropriate part of the segmental transcription. This is done by drawing in a number of **association lines** between tones and appropriate tone-bearing units (in this case, the vowels). Such association lines have to be drawn in in an appropriate way and they are governed by a number of principles. The **initial association** line is drawn in by a rule which is either language-specific or, in the default case, links the left-most tone to the left-most tone-bearing unit. Other tones are then linked to tone-bearing units in a one-to-one manner starting from the initial association line and working outwards (which usually means working from left to right). If at the end of the process there are tones left over, they are **dumped** onto the last vowel (as in the roots in (1)); if there are vowels left over, the final tone **spreads** to those vowels (as in the outputs in (1)). In most cases (though there may be language-specific exceptions) you will end up with every vowel being related to at least one tone and every tone being related to at least one vowel, but anything which is not associated at the end of a derivation is not pronounced (in effect, is deleted). An important constraint, the **well-formedness condition**, states that association lines may not cross. The association lines are drawn in (2). As a notational device, fixed association lines are shown as solid lines, while association lines, which are in the process of being established, are shown as dotted lines.

Although in (2) the association lines have been shown linking the tonal tier directly to the melodic tier (on which the segments are found), in principle these are mediated by the **skeletal tier**, on which segmental positions only are marked. Here we will mark these as being C(onsonants) or V(owels), although examples like (1a), with the change from a vowel to a glide, provide evidence that, for some purposes at least, it might be better not even to specify that much about each segment.

12.2 ARABIC TRANSFIXES OR ROOT-AND-PATTERN MORPHOLOGY

To see how this all applies in morphology, let us first consider how Arabic verbal morphology works. An Arabic verbal root consists of a number of consonants (we will, here, deal only with tri-literal roots) which are frequently segmentally discontinuous in the verbal word-forms. These consonants have, interspersed among them, vowels which provide derivational or inflectional information. There may also be affixes involved in these processes. The pattern of consonants and vowels in any particular word-form, and the choice of vowels, is determined by the paradigm or **binyan** (plural: **binyanim** – the term is actually Hebrew, not Arabic) that the verb-form belongs to. Thus the second binyan is associated with the pattern CVCCVC and, in the perfective active, the vowels are both [a]. Each binyan is associated with a particular meaning, for example, the third binyan is reciprocal. A partial paradigm is provided in (3) for *ktb* 'to write':

(3)

	perfective		imperfective		participle	
	active	passive	active	passive	active	passive
II	kattab	kuttib	ukattib	ukattab	mukattib	mukattab
III	kaatab	kuutib	ukaatib	ukaatab	mukaatib	mukaatab
IV	?aktab	?uktib	u?aktib	u?aktab	mu?aktib	mu?aktab

Binyan II: causative ('cause to write')
Binyan III: reciprocal ('correspond')
Binyan IV: causative ('cause to write')

Consider the form /kaatab/ 'he corresponded'. The morpheme {write} is represented by the discontinuous consonant string /k...t...b/; the perfective and active are represented cumulatively by the discontinuous vowel string /aa...a/; and the morpheme {reciprocal} is represented by the pattern of consonants and vowels CVVCVC. Thus there are three morphs (called morphemes in the literature, though that may depend on your definition) realised in this word-form and none of them is a prototypical morph (continuous and stringable). In Autosegmental Morphology, each of these morphemes (and, as a general rule, every morpheme) is put on a separate tier. The various morphemes are then connected by appropriate association lines, which can be seen as instructions for the precise articulation of the word-form. So we start with the morpheme {reciprocal}, which acts as a base for the others, providing the skeletal tier. Onto this we can now map the root, by associating the consonants from left to right with the consonantal positions in the skeletal tier, as shown in (4) where μ indicates the morphemic status of the root.

(4)

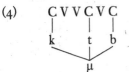

To this we can add the tense/aspect. Here we only need specify one vowel and, by the conventions of association, it will automatically spread to fill in the other positions, as shown in (5).

(5)

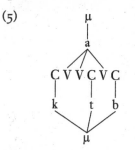

This looks insightful. It allows us to view the (superficially) discontinuous morphs as (underlyingly) continuous and explain why the particular qualities end up where they do. Where prefixes are involved (and, in one case in the Arabic binyanim, an infix) they appear on a separate tier and are associated early in the piece (this is sometimes called **pre-association**), and then the normal rules apply from then on.

But the data in the (3) shows some problems. For example, why do we find the form *kuutib* rather than *kuitib*? If the vowels associate regularly from left to right, we ought to get the latter not the former. One solution, which has not been canvassed in the literature as far as I know, is that the correct template is not CVVCVC but CV:CVC, which would provide the correct output. Suggestions from the literature include that association should not take place left to right but from the outside in, so that the first [u] and the final [i] are associated first, leaving the middle [u] to be associated by usual spreading rules. Another theory is that geminates are universally preferred to splitting up adjacent skeletal elements between items from a melodic tier. Thus, [aa] is preferred to [ai], [uu] to [ui]. Note also the geminate [tt] in binyan II, which equally causes a problem that has given rise to all sorts of solutions, including the two mentioned above.

Although I have pointed out that there are problems in transferring the autosegmental model to Arabic morphology, it would be misleading to suggest that the model is unworkable or that it is not worth applying it to such data. Much work has been done on the Arabic binyanim, with the result that we now have a much better picture of the ways in which they work and a much better appreciation of how the theory needs to be able to deal with complex data of this kind.

12.3 REDUPLICATION

Consider the examples of initial reduplication from Maori in (6).

(6)	base	distributed plural	gloss
	kino	kikino	'bad'
	nohi	nonohi	'small'
	nui	nunui	'big'
	pai	papai	'good'
	roa	roroa	'long'

What we see in (6) is that the form of the prefix added to the base depends on the form of the base itself. Accounting for this involves a copying of the relevant piece of form, something which would have been assumed in earlier grammars to require rules with transformational power. What we need is a way to derive the appropriate form yet preferably without using a procedure which is quite as powerful as transformations. Nonlinear morphology allows us to do this.

To begin with, we note that the constant in reduplication is the phonological structure which can be defined in terms of the skeletal tier: from the data given in (6) we can make the provisional assumption that this constant is CV. Next we remove variability in copying by allowing only the whole base to be copied: since some of the base will not be associated with a position in the skeletal tier, that part of the base will not be pronounced. We then associate the copied melodic tier with the affixed skeletal tier, as in (7), matching left-to-right.

(7)
```
k    i    n    o    k    i    n    o
|    |              |    |    |    |
C    V              C    V    C    V
```

In (7) the prefix is given a form in terms of C and V slots but, in principle, we could reduplicate any prosodic constituent. We can see from the data in (6) that it is not syllables which are reduplicated in Maori, since *pai* 'good' is monosyllabic while the other words are disyllabic. There is plenty of evidence that the fundamental unit of reduplication in Maori is the mora (for Maori, a unit equivalent in length to an optional consonant and a short vowel; W. Bauer, 1981a). The examples in (8), all showing the same pattern of final bimoraic reduplication, although not all clearly showing the same synchronic morpheme, illustrate the point.

(8)

base	gloss	reduplicated form	gloss
aahua	'appearance'	aahuahua	'resemble'
hiikei	'step'	hikekei	'hop'
maakuu	'moist'	maakuukuu	'rather moist'

In (8), *aahua* ends in a disyllabic sequence, *hiikei* ends in a monosyllabic sequence (a diphthong) and *maakuu* ends in a long vowel, yet they all reduplicate in the same way. Ideally, therefore, the phonological constant would be given not in terms of C and V, but in terms of the number of moras. Other languages may reduplicate other phonological constituents which may, of course, include the phonological word. The interesting point about this proposal is that the constituents to be reduplicated are predicted to be phonological ones.

12.4 INFIXATION

If we now return to Arabic, in binyan VII, the form for the perfective active of 'write' is *ktatab*. At first glance this looks as though it breaks the rules but this is misleading. The first /t/ is not one of the consonants of the root, but an infix of constant consonantal value independent of the verb root to which it is added. Because it is a separate morph and not part of the root morph, according to the **morphemic tier hypothesis**, it is placed on a separate tier, so that we find the situation in (9).

(9)

For this to work, the /t/ has to be **preassociated** with the second C of the skeleton before the *ktb root is associated with the skeleton. This is how Autosegmental Morphology deals with morphs which have a fixed shape in a fixed place and, as indicated above, it includes prefixes and suffixes as well as infixes.

A very different approach to infixation is provided within Optimality Theory (OT). In order to explain how this works, a little background on OT is required.

OT is a theory that does away with rules. What used to be done with rules is now done with constraints. These constraints differ from rules in two crucial ways: (a) they are universal and (b) they are violable.

The idea is the following. You cannot say anything without breaking some constraint or another. However, not all the constraints are equally strong and, other things being equal, you will break a weak constraint rather than a strong one. The constraints are organised in a hierarchy of strength. This hierarchy of the universal constraints is defined anew for each language. To solve any particular linguistic problem, there may be huge numbers of possible outputs (perhaps an infinite number). Most of these will break strong constraints. The output that is actually used (which appears on the surface) is the one which breaks the fewest or the weakest constraints. That is, you must violate constraints but you choose the optimal path which breaks only the weakest constraints.

There are three parts to the model to allow you to do this. The Generator, usually called GEN, generates all the possible candidates to solve a particular problem (this will be illustrated below). The Evaluator (EVAL for short) determines which of these candidates is the best one. And the constraints (CON) are a universal set of statements about preferred structure (equating to statements about markedness or naturalness in other theories) which are ranked for every variety and which allow EVAL to do its work.

Let us start with a fairly simple example of a phonetic insertion rule: in Arabic, words which phonologically begin with a vowel actually begin with a [ʔ], so that 'the pen' is [ʔalqalamu] (a similar phenomenon is found in a number of other languages as well). A rule of epenthesis like this breaches one major constraint type called Faithfulness: Faithfulness constraints demand that the output should be just the same as the input. On the other hand, this kind of epenthesis guarantees that the initial syllable in the word will have an Onset. So we can now formulate two constraints which interact in dealing with forms like the Arabic one. They are given in (10).

(10) (a) ONSET. This constraint says that every syllable should have an onset.

(b) FAITH. This constraint says that input structure must correspond to output structure.

The problem is that, in the crucial cases, these two constraints conflict, as shown in (11), where syllable divisions are marked by full stops (periods).

(11)

Candidates	Onset	Faith
.al.qa.la.mu	*	
.ʔal.qa.la.mu		*

In (11) we have a tableau which presents the candidates and the constraints and shows whether or not the candidates breach the constraints. An asterisk is added in the appropriate cell in the matrix for every breach of the constraint. In (11), however, we have not ranked the constraints (and this is indicated in the tableau by the fact that the line between the two constraints is a dotted one, not a solid one. If we rank the constraints, then we can see that we get a preferred outcome, as in (12)

(12) Constraint tableau Onset >> Faith

Candidates	Onset	Faith
.al.qa.la.mu	* !	
☞ .ʔal.qa.la.mu		*

The shaded part of the tableau in (12) is supposed to indicate that nothing in that part of the table is relevant for coming to a decision (this has no theoretical status but makes it easier to see what is going on). The exclamation mark indicates a fatal breaking of a constraint, that is one which rules that candidate out of contention. The little hand at the left-hand side indicates the optimal candidate, the one that is eventually chosen. Note also that the ranking of the constraints is shown not only in the heading to the tableau, but by the solid line between them in the tableau.

Of course, the candidates I have listed in the tableau are not all the possible candidates, just the shortlisted ones (as it were). Other possible candidates would have glottal stops between every syllable, epenthetic vowels between the /l/ and the /q/, spurious extra syllables – anything you can think of. Some of these would involve extra contraventions of the Faith constraint but, in such cases, even multiple breaches of the Faith constraint would be overruled by a single breach of the Onset constraint.

This ordering of Onset and Faith is, of course, language specific.

Other languages, for example, Spanish, may have them ordered the other way round. In such languages you can get empty onsets because FAITH is more important than ONSET. This is illustrated in (13) where the Spanish word *aún* 'still, yet' is under consideration.

(13) Constraint tableau FAITH >> ONSET (Spanish)

Candidates		FAITH	ONSET
☞	.a.un		**
	.ʔa.un	*!	*
	.ʔa.ʔun	*!*	

The double breach of ONSET in the optimal candidate does not matter since other candidates are excluded by virtue of breaking a higher-ranked constraint.

In order to go on and look at infixation, we need two further constraint types. The first is a series of constraints of Alignment. Alignment constraints are there to guarantee that certain bits of structure start or end in the same place (for instance, that prefixes come at the beginnings of words or that suffixes come at the end of words). Prefixes are aligned to the left, suffixes are aligned to the right with the word-boundary. We will not need more complex types of alignment here. The second constraint we need is a restriction against codas: this makes open syllables the preferred syllable type, in line with their predominance in natural languages. So we will use the two constraints in (14).

(14) (a.) *CODA: Syllables should not have a coda; that is, a syllable does not end in a consonant. (The asterisk indicates the undesirability of having a coda and is used in much the same way as it is used to show ungrammatical sentences.)
(b.) ALIGNL: Make the affix align with the left-hand edge of the word (that is, create prefixes). Removal of the prefix from the leftmost edge of the word by any one segment is a violation of this constraint.

Let us consider how OT deals with infixation in Tagalog. We have seen examples of Tagalog infixation in section 3.1.4, with examples such as *sulat* 'write', *sumulat* 'wrote', and so on. When the root is *aral* 'teach', though, we get *umaral*. As far as OT is concerned, the prefixation in one case but infixation in the other is a matter of improving syllable structure, though such an observation cannot be captured in most other theories. If we say that *CODA dominates ALIGNL, we get the pattern in (15) for *um + sulat*:

(15) Constraint tableau *CODA >> ALIGNL (Tagalog)

Candidates	*CODA	ALIGNL
UM.su.lat	**!	Ø
☞ .sU.Mu.lat	*	s
.su.UM.lat	**!	su
.su.lU.Mat	*	su!l
.su.la.UMt	*	su!la
.su.la.tUM	*	su!lat

Note that although *sumulat* breaks the *CODA constraint, all other candidates which break the *CODA constraint only once break the ALIGNL constraint more often than *sumulat* does. In (16) we see what happens if we try the same thing for *um + aral*.

(16) Constraint tableau *CODA >> ALIGNL (Tagalog)

Candidates	*CODA	ALIGNL
☞ .U.Ma.ral	*	Ø
.a.UM.ral	**!	a
.a.rU.Mal	*	a!r
.a.ra.UMl	*	a!ra
.a.ra.lUM	*	a!ral

In (15) and (16) we see that the difference in underlying structure of the root makes a difference to whether we end up with prefixation or infixation. The same technique can be extended to show what happens in words with initial cluster, like *gradwet* 'graduate'.

(17) Constraint tableau *CODA >> ALIGNL (Tagalog)

Candidates	*CODA	ALIGNL
.UM.grad.wet	***!	Ø
.gUM.rad.wet	***!	g
☞ .grU.Mad.wet	**	gr
.grad.wU.Met	**	gra!dw
.grad.we.tUM	**	gra!dwet

Clearly, in Tagalog both the constraints *CODA and ALIGNL are violated regularly. Nevertheless, their influence is still visible. We find out that this particular infixation is less a morphological constraint than a phonological one.

12.5 TAKING IT FURTHER

What we are seeing in all of these examples is the close interplay between phonology and morphology, such that the morphological structure of words is, to some extent at least, determined by the phonology. The principle is far from new, of course. Phonologically conditioned allomorphs of morphemes are using the same principle. Now, however, the principle is being taken that much further. The question is how far this principle can be taken.

One type of word-formation which might be expected to yield to this kind of analysis is blending (see section 3.7). In blends, we merge the first part of one word with the last part of another to provide a result which is usually no longer (in terms of number of syllables) than the longer of the two base words. What is more, the switch point between the two words seems to be determined by the phonology of the bases, so that, in *slang + language > slanguage*, we avoid the phonological repetition of /læŋ/ and this would seem to be a phonological constraint. The final word must also conform to the phonological constraints affecting all English words (we could not, for example, derive */sllæŋgwɪʤ/ with a geminate /l/ because such geminates are impossible in English except over morphological boundaries – and, even there, they tend to get simplified). And we appear to be dealing with Alignment Constraints in that the first element provides the start of the new word, while the second element provides the end of the new word.

Unfortunately, while all of this looks plausible, it has not yet (to my knowledge) been satisfactorily done. Not only does it turn out to be rather more difficult to state the constraints or rules than one might expect, especially when a lot of data is considered, there are also questions of how we know which base word to order first (something which appears not to be entirely a phonological matter). Some attempts have been made which provide starting points for such work but it remains to be shown that there is a set of phonological constraints which determines the form of blends.

Going even further, though, if the form of blends is determined to some extent by the phonology of the resultant word, might the same not be true of affixed words? Plag (1999) argues that in one case, at least, this is true. He considers the phonology of English derivatives in *-ise* and those in *-ify*, claiming that the two are synonymous and in complementary distribution. He suggests constraints such as those in (18), giving rise to the tableaux in (19).

(18) (a.) ALIGNR-STRESS: Put the stress on the rightmost syllable of the word.

(b.) *STRESSCLASH: Do not permit stress (primary or secondary) on adjacent syllables.

(c.) FAITHAFFIX: The output must contain the full form of the affix.

(19) Constraint tableaux FAITHAFFIX >> *STRESSCLASH >> ALIGNR-STRESS (English)

Candidates	FAITHAFFIX	*STRESSCLASH	ALIGNR-STRESS
☞ rán.do.mìse			**
rán.do.mi.fỳ			***!
rán.dom.fỳ	*!		**
bourge.ói.sìse		*!	*
☞ bourge.ói.si.fỳ			**
mý.thìse		*!	*
☞ mý.thi.fỳ			**

The tableaux in (19) do not account for all possible types of derivative using one of these two suffixes; to do that would require too much exposition. But they do indicate the kind of approach that is being taken and the general notion that it is constraints on the output which determine the ultimate shape of derivatives.

We can see this type of approach being generalised in morphological studies. It has been argued that some subtractive morphology might be best accounted for in terms of constraint interaction (Golston & Wiese, 1996) and the use of output constraints as a way of determining allomorphs is becoming more fashionable.

REFERENCES AND FURTHER READING

For a textbook introduction to Autosegmental Morphology (albeit from a phonologist's viewpoint) see Durand (1990). For more detail see Goldsmith (1990), McCarthy (1994), McCarthy & Prince (1995) and McCarthy & Prince (1998).

The Margi examples in (1) are from Williams (1976). The Arabic paradigms in (3) are extracted from Durand (1990: 258).

On reduplication specifically, see Marantz (1982, 1994) and Wiltshire & Marantz (2000).

The Maori examples in (6) are from W. Bauer (1997); those in (8) are from Bauer (1981a).

On OT, see Archangeli & Langendoen (1997) and Kager (1999). Tagalog infixation is dealt with in both books in rather different ways. For more Tagalog data, masking the distinction between C-initial and V-initial stems, but showing the interplay of reduplication and infixation, see Gleason (1955: 32). The Arabic, Spanish and Tagalog examples were taken from a lecture by Alan Prince in Nijmegen in December 1995.

On blends, see Bat-El (1996, 2000) on Hebrew, and Kubuzono (1990) and Kelly (1998) on English.

Plag (1999) points out that there are places where we find synonymous derivatives in -ise and -ify: for example, dandyise and dandify are both found. His rules lead to these being equally good candidates.

EXERCISES

1. Using the kind of analysis provided in (7), how would you generate the reduplicated forms in (8)? What do you have to change to get the right outputs?

2. The morphemic tier hypothesis, according to which each morpheme (or possibly, each class of morpheme) is on a different tier, allows the analysis of infixation without crossing association lines by putting the infix on a separate tier. Under such circumstances, does the constraint against crossing association lines have any empirical value?

3. The data set presented below is made up of some Ablaut-motivated 'compounds' in English. (The term 'compound' is often used to describe these, though they are different from normal compounds in many ways.) On the basis of the data given below, which element of these words do you think is the base and which the reduplicant? (That is, do we have initial reduplication or final reduplication and how can you tell?) How would you have to account for the changing vowel qualities in an Autosegmental approach to these words?

chitchat	clipclop
fiddlefaddle	flipflop
pitterpatter	pingpong
riffraff	slipslop
tittletattle	ticktock

4. As well as having infixation, Tagalog also has reduplication. The future forms of 'write' and 'teach' are, respectively, *susulat* and *aaral* (where the double *a* indicates a sequence of two syllables not a long vowel). The continuous forms ('is writing', 'is teaching') are *sumusulat* and *umaaral*. Extend the analysis from (15)-(17) to cover these new forms. Is the position of the *-um-* still correctly accounted for? Can you see how the reduplication will be dealt with?

5. Below are some English blends from recent dictionaries of neologisms. What are the base words involved? Is it possible to predict the form of the blend from the forms of the two bases?

acupressure
advertorial
bikeathon
biopreneur
breathalyser

computeracy
docudrama
faction
glasnostalgia
glocal
instamatic
Reaganomics
Sloane Ranger
slurb
workaholic

CHAPTER 13

Morphological Typology and Universals

There is considerable irony in the fact that, although we have available morphological descriptions of numerous languages, we know very little about morphological typology or morphological universals. No doubt there are good reasons for this. The study of morphological typology appears to have become stuck in a rut, historically, and the study of language universals is, in any case, quite new; and, so far, syntactic universals have received more attention than morphological ones. Furthermore, when researchers start looking for morphological universals, it seems that they are extremely difficult to formulate precisely (Carstairs, 1984b). Thus, however much we may suspect that morphology is potentially a rich field for typological and universalist studies, we are in no position to demonstrate it. This, of course, means that the potential for research in these areas is enormous. Before we go onto look at typology and universals in more detail, a few comments on each are required.

Language typology is concerned with possible patterns of covariation throughout the languages of the world. Suppose, for example, that in the languages of the world there are two ways of marking syntactic relation A – call them A1 and A2 – and two ways of marking syntactic relation B – B1 and B2. If it is the case that languages which use A1 always use B2 and languages which use A2 always use B1, this is a possible domain for a typological statement. Typology is specifically not interested in genetic language relationships but in links which exist despite the lack of any known common source for the languages concerned. The idea is that a typological statement should express a limitation on the range of possible variation which can occur in the structures of languages. Perhaps the most successful known language typology is in terms of the order of the elements Subject (S), Verb (V) and Object (O) in a sentence. Languages which have the basic order VSO all seem to use prepositions and not postpositions (there is a postposition in the Turkish *adam için*, literally, 'man for', 'for the man' as opposed to the preposition *for* in the English equivalent).

It can be seen, therefore, that typological studies can lead us to formulate statements of implications which are believed (we can never be absolutely sure) to hold for all languages. Such statements are called **implicational universals**. An implicational universal is a statement of the form 'If a language has feature *a*, then it also has feature *b*', without any implication that the reverse is also true unless this is specifically stated.

The term 'universal' itself looks as though it refers to things which are true in all languages. There are such statements, such as 'All languages have vowels' which are true of all languages (as far as we know, but, of course, in this case omitting sign languages). Such statements are called **absolute universals**. But there are also, perhaps more commonly, **universal tendencies**. A universal tendency is a statement such as 'If a language has only one fricative, it is /s/' which is true for the vast majority of languages but not for all. In the case in point, it is not true for Maori, whose only fricatives are /f/ and /h/. A universal tendency, then, is a statement which we expect to be true, and which we know to be true of most languages, but one to which we know there are exceptions. Such statements are still important because they are statements of ways in which actual language structures differ from purely random patternings, even if there are known cases which contravene them. Tendencies may or may not also be implicational. An example of an implicational tendency is 'If a language has SOV basic word-order, it will have postpositions' which is not true of Persian, for example.

Armed with this small amount of terminology, we can now go onto consider the details as applied to morphology. We shall deal with typology first and then with universals.

13.1 MORPHOLOGICAL TYPOLOGY

Morphological typology is fraught with confused terminology, inconclusive results and the emotive appeals of linguistic imperialists, who were convinced that the language they favoured represented some kind of linguistic or aesthetic ideal. Yet students of linguistics tend to come across the terms **isolating**, **agglutinative** and **fusional** early in the study of the subject and they are part of the standard and widely-used terminology of linguistics. Accordingly, they are discussed here, though not without a kind of Editorial Health Warning: morphological typology, in the present state of the art, should be taken in small doses, diluted with a great deal of scepticism. Illustrating the terminological confusion of this area, it should be noted that 'agglutinating' is sometimes used in place of 'agglutinative', and 'inflective', 'flectional', 'inflecting' or 'inflectional' (despite the possible confusion) are sometimes used in place of 'fusional'. Some authors use the terms 'analytic' and 'synthetic' as meaning 'isolating' and 'non-isolating', for others these terms have different implications.

The three-way division of languages into isolating, agglutinative and fusional goes back to the work of Friederich and August von Schlegel in the early years of the nineteenth century. Their ideas were developed by others in the course of that century, frequently in an attempt to show that the fusional languages, such as Classical Greek and Latin, were the acme of human linguistic endeavour. It was this type of misuse which led this *trop fameuse classification* (in the words of Meillet) into disrepute and led Sapir (1921: 124) to make the following acerbic statement:

> A linguist that insists upon talking about the Latin type of morphology as though it were necessarily the high-water mark of linguistic development is like the zoologist that sees in the organic world a huge conspiracy to evolve the race-horse or the Jersey cow.

Sapir (1921) and, following him, Greenberg (1954) attempted to rehabilitate the typology but without any notable success. Indeed, part of the confusion in terminology appears to stem from their disparate attempts to clarify and enlarge on what they felt to be misused labels.

What, then, do the categories refer to? A pure isolating language would contain no obligatorily bound morphs, so all words would be invariable. Languages usually cited as being close to this ideal are Chinese and Vietnamese. A pure agglutinative language would have obligatorily bound morphs, each of which realised a single morpheme, and, ideally, where the obligatorily bound morphs always appeared with precisely the same form. Turkish is frequently cited as a fairly typical agglutinative language, although the obligatorily bound morphs there are not of fixed form. Swahili is another example. A fusional language does usually contain obligatorily bound morphs but there is no simple one-to-one correspondence between morphs and morphemes. Examples are the Classical languages: Greek and Latin.

To this three-way division, some scholars of Native American languages felt the need to add a fourth category, the category of **polysynthetic** languages. This is one in which there is a high density of obligatorily bound morphs and these are semantically more important than would be expected of an affix, even a derivational one, in other language types. For example, in West Greenlandic there is a single word-form meaning 'You simply cannot pretend not to be hearing all the time' which is made up as follows (Fortescue, 1984):

(1) tusaa·nngit·su·usaar·tuaannar·sinnaa·nngi·vip·putit
hear·negative·intransitive·participle·pretend·all-the-
time·can·negative·really·second-person-singular-indicative

The Eskimo languages are frequently cited as the main examples of polysynthetic languages but many others, especially North American languages such as Kwakiutl, are also included. Some authors are quite scathing about this category. Sapir (1921: 123) calls it 'an uncomfortable "polysynthetic" rear-guard to the agglutinative languages'; and Bazell (1966) is dismissive, saying that the category 'deserved the self-contradictory definition of the Oxford Dictionary: "characterized by combining several words of a sentence [...] into one word"'.

Part of the difficulty with this category is that it encompasses a great deal of variation (Fortescue, 1994) and should probably be broken down into a series of categories, each of which would be amenable to closer definition. However difficult this category may be to define and however awkwardly it fits into the system of classification, it is again a term in current use.

One of the important things to notice about this typology is that there are very few pure types, if any. Consider, for example, a sentence of English like:

(2) Obscenity can be found in every book except the telephone
directory.

In this sentence, many of the words appear to present an isolating type of morphology: *can, be, in, book*, for instance. Others appear to show agglutination: *obscen·ity, direct·ory*. And *found* shows the fusional type, since it represents both the lexeme FIND and the morpheme {past tense} but no simple analysis into morphs. This

Table 3 Breakdown of three main types into two parameters

		number of morphomes per morph	
		low	high
morphomes per word-form	low	isolating	fusional
	high	agglutinative	

result is typical, not only of English but perhaps of all languages. Sapir stresses that it is even possible to mix isolating and polysynthetic types in the same language. We are thus not dealing with absolutes when we speak of these types but with tendencies.

It is probably possible to break the three main types down into two simpler parameters: the ratio of morphomes to word-forms, and the number of morphomes to morphs (especially, but not necessarily exclusively, obligatorily bound morphs). This is illustrated in Table 3. In this table the qualitative terms 'high' and 'low' are used rather than any precise quantities to show that we are dealing with tendencies. The number of morphomes per word-form may be high or low in an fusional language, since *led* is fusional (realising the two morphomes {lead} and {past tense}) just as much as *regentur* (Latin, 'they will be ruled', realising the morphomes {rule}, {3rd person}, {plural}, {future}, {passive}). Nevertheless, fusional languages are usually considered to have a relatively high number of morphomes per word-form. The polysynthetic category does not fit easily into Table 3 since it is distinguished from agglutinative largely by the semantic importance or density of the elements involved.

The average number of morphomes per word does seem, in general, to distinguish isolating languages and polysynthetic languages from others. The following figures are given by Greenberg (1954) on the basis of passages of running text one hundred words long:

Vietnamese	isolating	1.06
English	mixed	1.68
Old English	fusional	2.12
Swahili	agglutinative	2.55
Eskimo	polysynthetic	3.72

My own figures over smaller samples are broadly comparable:

Yoruba	isolating	1.09
English	mixed	1.69
Turkish	agglutinative	2.86
Russian	fusional	3.33

The average number of morphomes per morph, on the other hand, does not appear to give the same kind of spread:

Yoruba	isolating	1.00
English	mixed	1.37
Turkish	agglutinative	1.31
Russian	fusional	1.58

This seems to be because the number of morphs which show cumulative exponence, even in an fusional language, is, in fact, a rather small proportion of the total, because of the number of indeclinable prepositions and particles, and the number of roots and derivational affixes which do not allow cumulation. The English total is boosted by a few very common words, such as *has, is, him*, and so on, which are portmanteau morphs.

Once we have set up a typology of this type (however satisfactory or unsatisfactory it may be) we are left with the vital question asked by Kroeber (1954: 297): 'What do we do with a morphological classification of the world's languages when we have it?' Basically, a typology is not of much value unless it predicts other things about the various types of language. For instance, a typology in terms of the relative order of Subject Verb and Object is useful since it allows you to predict (not with total accuracy but with a fair degree of success) the relative order of nouns and adjectives, of main verbs and auxiliaries, of adpositions and noun phrases, and so on. Now, as far as can be discovered from most of the research specifically in this area, a typology in terms of isolating, agglutinative and fusional does not correlate with anything else in the morphology at all. There is some slight correlation with syntax, in that isolating languages use word-order to distinguish subjects from objects more centrally than do fusional languages and the languages with the freest word-order tend to be of the fusional type. It also seems that agglutinative languages tend to be SOV languages. It should, however, be noted that there are fusional languages with fairly fixed word-order and isolating languages can use adpositions to indicate function. The value of the typology qua typology is, thus, very much in doubt.

Nevertheless, the categories may say something useful about the type of grammar required to deal with languages which belong to them. Hockett (1954) distinguished between three 'models' of grammar (morphology and syntax): Item and Arrangement (IA), Item and Process (IP) and Word-and-Paradigm (WP). Hockett saw these as reflecting a different approach on the part of the linguist to the data to be described. He pointed out that a description given in terms of one of these models can (with a certain amount of contrivance) be reformulated in terms of one of the others. While this is true, the models do not all allow the same statements to be made with the same degree of ease. IA allows only statements of lists of items and the positions in which the items can be found; IP allows dynamic statements in terms such as adding one thing to another or turning one thing into another; WP allows statements of much greater complexity in terms of operations, input conditions and the like. Generally speaking, IA is the simplest type of model, IP is rather more complicated and WP the most complicated. It seems, in general, that isolating languages can be dealt with adequately with an IA type of grammar. Some facets of agglutinative and fusional languages are more easily dealt with in terms of an IP grammar. And some facets of fusional languages require the power of a WP grammar to be dealt with most effectively.

To illustrate this, let us start with a sentence of English which is made up of monomorphemic word-forms and is, thus, isolating in type.

(3)   The dog can see the rabbit.

In an IA grammar we can say that this sentence is made up of three constituents, a noun phrase, a verb group and another noun phrase; that the noun phrases are made up of determiners and nouns; that verb groups are made up of auxiliaries and main verbs; and that determiners are words like *the*, nouns are words like *dog* and *rabbit*, auxiliaries are words like *can* and main verbs are words like *see*. Using this set of statements, we can see that we have accounted for the distributions of the various items that occur in sentence (3). In an isolating language there is, of course, no need to make any morphological specifications because there are no obligatorily bound morphs.

Now consider a partial paradigm for a Turkish noun EL 'hand'.

(4)		Singular	Plural
	accusative	el·i	el·ler·i
	genitive	el·in	el·ler·in
	locative	el·de	el·ler·de
	ablative	el·den	el·ler·den

This partial paradigm can also be described perfectly well using an IA grammar. The root is the leftmost item in the word-form, following that comes the plural marker (if the word is plural) and following that comes the appropriate case marker. If we add that the morph realising {3rd person possessive} is *-in-* and it comes before the case marker, we can work out that other words of Turkish must be *elinde* 'in his/her/its hand', *ellerinden* 'from his/her/its hand' and so on.

But now consider the following partial paradigm from Turkish, which shows the same case forms, but this time of a word whose root ends in a vowel, GECE 'night'.

(5) | | Singular | Plural |
|---|---|---|
| *accusative* | gece·yi | gece·ler·i |
| *genitive* | gece·nin | gece·ler·in |
| *locative* | gece·de | gece·ler·de |
| *ablative* | gece·den | gece·ler·den |

Here the sequence of two vowels in the accusative and genitive singular has been broken up by a consonant: *y* in one case, *n* in the other. We can, of course, still describe this in terms of an IA grammar, by saying that there are two forms of the accusative and genitive endings and the first occurs after a consonant, the second after a vowel. If we go further, though, we see that this is a regular feature of Turkish. The third person singular possessive marker after a vowel is *-sin-* so that 'of his/her/its night' is *gece·sin·in* but 'in his/her/its nights' is *gece·ler·in·de*. And, so far, we have not taken vowel harmony into account, which makes the ablative plural of TARLA, 'field', *tarla·lar·dan*. At this point, rather than listing all the possible allomorphs and the places where they occur, it might seem simpler to use a dynamic notation and say that the plural marker becomes *-lar-* when it follows a back vowel, that a consonant is introduced if adding a suffix gives rise to a sequence of vowels (or, alternatively, that a consonant is deleted after a consonant-final base) and so on. At this point, we have started using an IP type of grammar.

Now consider the following two nominal paradigms from Russian, GAZETA 'newspaper', a feminine noun, and STOL 'chair', a masculine noun:

(6) | Singular | | |
|---|---|---|
| *nominative* | gazet·a | stol |
| *accusative* | gazet·u | stol |
| *genitive* | gazet·i | stol·a |
| *dative* | gazet·e | stol·u |

instrumental	gazet·oi	stol·om
prepositional	gazet·e	stol·e
Plural		
nominative	gazet·i	stol·i
accusative	gazet·i	stol·i
genitive	gazet	stol·ov
dative	gazet·am	stol·am
instrumental	gazet·ami	stol·ami
prepositional	gazet·ax	stol·ax

The problem with describing a paradigm like this is that the inflectional suffix -*e* can realise {feminine dative singular} or {prepositional singular}, the suffix -*u* can mark {feminine accusative singular} or {masculine dative singular} and the ending -*i* can mark {nominative plural}, {accusative plural} or {feminine genitive singular}. This can still be done in an IA grammar, by listing all the possible affixes and all the classes of base to which they can attach and under what circumstances, but it is extremely cumbersome. It could be done with an IP grammar, by saying which affixes can be added to which bases to produce which forms. But a WP grammar is specifically designed to cope with the case where the presence of a number of properties together triggers a specific (but non-unique) affix (see Chapter 11). In a WP grammar, the list of properties which create the input conditions are listed, along with the base which is required and the operation which is carried out on that base. Of course, this model could be applied very easily to the paradigms in (4) and (5), as well as to the type of structure illustrated in (3), but it would no longer be efficient, since more information would be demanded by the rule format than is strictly necessary.

We can thus conclude that, while the classical typology in terms of isolating, agglutinative and fusional languages does not appear to be helpful as a typology of the languages of the world, it may be helpful in determining the complexity of the grammar that is required to provide an account of that type of language.

13.2 UNIVERSALS CONCERNING ORDER

We shall begin this section with a list of a few putative universals concerning order in morphology and then go onto consider what generalisations can be drawn on the basis of these. The discussion is based primarily on Bybee (1985). The universals listed here are not in any particular order and those which are known to be tendencies and not absolute universals are marked with a parenthesised т.

(7)   Number is marked closer to the root than case (т).

(8)   Aspect is marked closer to the root than tense.

(9)   Aspect is marked closer to the root than mood.

(10) Aspect is marked closer to the root than person (т).

(11) Tense is marked closer to the root than mood (т).

(12) Tense is marked closer to the root than person (т).

(13) Imperative markers (where these occur) come closer to the root than person/number markers (т).

(14) Interrogative affixes occur as the final suffix on a verb (т).

(15) Languages which are exclusively suffixing use postpositions.

(16) Languages which are exclusively prefixing use prepositions.

Most of these universals can be condensed into a statement that there is a tendency for the following ordering of morphs in a word-form:

(17) Verbs: root – aspect – tense – mood – person
      Nouns: root – number – case

or the precise reverse in prefixing languages. This is assuming, of course, that all of these categories are realised morphologically, which they may very well not be. But those which are realised morphologically, and which are realised consistently on one side of the base, will tend to show this ordering. (The case where, say, aspect is realised as a prefix but tense as a suffix is not directly covered by this generalisation.) The question is whether there is any particular reason for this tendency.

Bybee (1985) makes a convincing case for this being governed by principles of relevance and lexical generality. By relevance, she understands the degree to which the morphological category affects the lexical content of the base (1985: 15). For example, if we compare aspect and person agreement with reference to a base which is a verb, we can see that verbs typically show actions or states, and aspect represents ways of viewing the internal make-up of the action or state: this is clearly extremely relevant. Person agreement, on the other hand, is far less relevant, since it refers to an argument of the verb, and not to the verb itself. By lexical generality is meant low semantic content, so that the category can apply to a large class of bases. The more relevant a category is the more likely it is to be expressed either by forming a completely separate lexical item, or by derivation, or by inflection, and these three show a decreasing level of perceived relevance (relevance being, in the final instance, a cultural property). The more lexically general a category is, the more likely it is to be shown by inflectional morphology. There is, thus, a tension between these two factors which, between them, determine how a particular category is marked.

This can be illustrated with the notions of number and case. The case marking on a noun shows its relationship to other elements in the sentence, the role that noun plays and so on. This is of low relevance to the noun, since it does not directly affect the lexical content of the noun base. It is, however, of high lexical generality, since it can apply to virtually any noun. Number, on the other hand, is of far greater relevance. It has a much greater effect on the lexical content of the noun, while still being of high lexical generality. We would, therefore, make the prediction that number would occur closer to the root than case does, and this is precisely what is observed (see (7) above). One result of this is that, even in English, we can find some words with a special form (probably a separate lexeme) for the plural or collective: words such as *people, cattle* and possibly, nowadays, *brethren*. Other languages do this far more commonly. Note also that according to Greenberg (1963) all languages mark plurality on at least some nouns. Not all languages mark case.

The same principle can be argued to be operating in the ordering of elements within the noun phrase in English. The difference between *a pretty little girl* and *a little pretty girl* is a matter of whether we are dealing with a group of little girls or a group of pretty girls. Culturally, it seems to be more normal to deal with a class of little girls, so that the first order is the more natural out of context. Similarly, Greenberg (1963: 68) notes that the order of items in the noun phrase across languages tends to be:

(18)   Demonstrative – Numeral – Adjective – Noun
        OR
        Noun – Adjective – Numeral – Demonstrative

Bybee is able to argue convincingly that, on the basis of relevance, one would expect precisely the order given in (17). While she lists several examples of languages which break this pattern to a greater or lesser extent, the weight of the evidence is overwhelmingly on her side.

If this principle has general applicability, it ought to be possible to extend it quite simply. For example, we would predict that causation would have a greater lexical effect on the verb base than aspect does and that it would, thus, occur closer to the root than any of the other categories mentioned so far. In English causatives are shown either by lexical paraphrases, by the use of separate lexemes or by derivation, as is shown below:

(19) (a) He made the horse swallow the pill.

    (b) She killed the fly. [caused it to die]

    (c) He ran the horse round the field.

    (d) She lightened my load.

If we consider what happens in languages with overt morphological causative markers, this is what we find. In some languages, like Kanuri and Swahili, the causative marker is not on the same side of the root as the other affixes under consideration, so these do not provide any relevant data. In Finnish, the causative marker is considered to be derivational and occurs inside all inflectional markers. In Hixkaryana (a Carib language spoken in Brazil) the causative affix is closer to the root than the cumulative affix which marks tense, aspect and (to some extent) person. This is illustrated in the following example:

(20) w·eny·ho·no
      1st-sing-subject-3rd-sing-object·see·causative·immediate-past
      'I showed it'

In Diyari, which does not mark aspect, the causative morph occurs closer to the root than the tense morph.

(21) ṭana ṇari·ṇanka·ṭadi·yi
      they dead·causative·reflexive·present
      'They kill themselves'

And in Turkish, the morph realising causation also occurs closer to the root than the morphs for tense, mood, and so on:

(22) tanı·ş·tır·ıl·ay·dı·k
      know·reciprocal·causative·passive·subjunctive·past·1st-person-plural
      'Would that we had been introduced to one another!'

Thus Bybee's hypothesis about relevance is again vindicated in this random sample of languages from very different language families.

One important fact about Bybee's hypothesis here is that it allows her to account for the frequently noted tendency (not, pace Greenberg, 1963, absolute universal: see above section 6.5) for derivational affixes to be closer to the root than inflectional ones. In fact, many of the characteristics of inflection and derivation discussed in Chapter 6 can be explained with reference to Bybee's principles of relevance and generality. For example, the regular meaning of inflectional affixes is related to their generality, the fact that derivational affixes are frequently category-changing indicates relevance and so on.

This leaves us with (15) and (16) to discuss. There is a tendency for the use of prepositions to correlate with the ordering of elements in (23).

(23)   noun – modifying genitive
         verb – object
         noun – adjective

The use of postpositions correlates with the reverse orders. In each case, the order of modifier and head is the same for all four constructions (the three in (23) and prepositional/postpositional phrases). The universals in (15) and (16) can be seen as related to this. If affixes are heads of words (a hypothesis discussed within Lexicalist Morphology), the same generalisation can be seen to be applying within the word and outside the word – heads either precede their modifiers or follow them.

13.3 IMPLICATIONAL UNIVERSALS

There are a number of implicational universals discovered by Greenberg (1963), most of which concern the existence of various categories or the places in which the categories are marked. Again the same procedure will be adopted as in section 13.2, with the universals being listed first and then discussed.

(24) The presence of inflectional morphology implies the presence of derivational morphology.

(25) The presence of morphological gender marking implies the presence of number marking.

(26) The presence of a special property of trial number marking

implies the presence of a dual which, in turn, implies the presence of a plural.

(27) If a verb agrees in gender with either its subject or its object, then adjectives agree in gender with the noun they modify.

(28) If a verb agrees with either its subject or its object in gender, it also agrees with it in number.

(29) If a language marks gender on a noun, it marks gender on a pronoun.

(30) There are never more gender categories in a non-singular number than there are in the singular.

(31) If the pronoun is marked for gender in the plural, it is also marked for gender in the singular.

(32) If a language marks gender on a first person pronoun, it always marks gender on a second and/or third person pronoun.

(33) Morphological marking of either person/number or gender on the verb implies morphological marking of tense/mode on the verb.

Some of these universals can be explained with reference to Bybee's notion of relevance discussed in section 13.2. For example, (24) can be reformulated to state that, if less relevant categories are marked morphologically on a base, more relevant ones will be marked morphologically, too. This is not actually necessary: it would be possible to imagine a case, for instance, where aspect was always shown by using a different lexeme, while tense was marked morphologically. If we assume that Greenberg's universal holds and this type of language is never found, it is presumably because it would be a very uneconomical way of dealing with aspect because of the lexical generality of aspect. (33) can also be explained in terms of relevance, since person/number and gender are both less relevant for a verb than tense/mode and a less relevant category is unlikely to be marked if a more relevant one is not. (28) can also be explained by the same principle. The gender of a subject or object has less direct effect on the lexical content of the verb than the number of entities involved in the action. If the less relevant category is marked on the verb, it would be expected the more relevant category would be marked. Since number is lexically general, it would be expected that number on the verb would be marked inflectionally.

(30), (31) and (32) can all be explained in terms of another general principle but this requires some preliminary discussion of the notion of markedness. The terms **marked** and **unmarked** are used in a number of slightly different ways. Firstly, a property can be said to be marked with relation to another one if it is shown by some morphological marker in the language under consideration. In this sense the English plural *cats* is marked in relation to the singular *cat* by the presence of the -s. This sense of marked is translated into German as *merkmalhaft*. Secondly, something can be said to be unmarked if it has a wider distribution than another category with which it contrasts minimally. In this sense, the English singular is unmarked with reference to the plural since it is also found in generic sentences such as:

(34) The tiger is a ferocious beast.

which actually refer to more than one tiger and, in the first elements of compounds, even if more than one is implied:

(35) He spends his days sewing up trouser legs.
     She has built hundreds of possum traps.

Related to this (but not always identical with it) is that the most commonly occurring form is frequently said to be unmarked with regard to a less commonly occurring partner. These last two senses are translated into German as *markiert*. It is sometimes inconvenient that English does not allow us to distinguish between the various meanings of 'marked'. As can be seen, these three meanings actually coincide in relation to the English singular/plural distinction, where plural is marked in all senses; and this is frequently, but not always, the case. Now consider the three universals under discussion. In each case the universal can be explained by a meta-universal which states that a more marked category will never show a finer division for other categories than its less marked counterpart. This holds in (32) because the 1st person pronoun is generally the one with the most restricted usage (despite royal plurals and editorial *we*) and the 3rd person is, across languages, generally the least marked.

(26) can be seen to be due to another application of the same meta-universal, since you do not have special marking for specific numbers greater than one unless you have a marking for the less marked notion of plural and, while there are several natural phenomena that occur in twos (eyes, ears, legs, etc), phenomena that occur in threes are rarer, and the use of a trial is correspondingly rarer.

(29) may be a result of the same meta-universal if pronouns can be said to be less marked than nouns, but this is less clear.

This leaves (25) and (27). (25) appears to contradict the principle of relevance. Gender has a bigger direct effect on the lexical content of a noun than number does. Amongst other things, this can be seen by the number of instances in English where gender is shown by a separate lexeme (*cow, bull; man, woman; king, queen; hen, rooster/cock*; etc.) or a derived form (*lion, lioness; prince, princess; usher, usherette*; etc.), while it is never shown by inflection, though number is shown predominantly by inflection. (27) does not fit neatly into either category. It is clear that gender is more relevant to nouns than it is to verbs but it is not clear that gender is more relevant to adjectives than it is to verbs. This may be partly explained by a closer link between an adjective and a noun than between a verb and the noun but this is hard to prove without some suitable survey of the way in which languages operate.

13.4 PARADIGM-CENTRED UNIVERSALS

So far no attempt has been made to define the notion of paradigm. This is deliberate, in that a precise definition of the relations embodied in a paradigm is extremely difficult (see Carstairs, 1984b: 167ff for one attempt). This is despite the fact that it takes very little experience of paradigms to allow you to recognise one. We can make some attempt to be more precise, though.

First of all, paradigms are usually inflectional (although some writers do use the term in a rather broader way). This is because a paradigm implies regularity and predictability. The word derives etymologically from a Greek word meaning 'pattern, example' and the idea is that the word-forms for other lexemes should be predictable according to the pattern of the paradigm lexeme. While a few lexically conditioned exceptions to the paradigm are possible (see section 6.4), very few exceptions are usually accepted in a paradigm, which is why it is relatively rare for derivational morphology to be discussed in terms of paradigms. A paradigm, then, lists all the word-forms of a lexeme or those word-forms of a lexeme which are related in sharing a particular morpheme (the term appears to be used with both meanings: in the one case, we would talk about the verb paradigm; in the other, the paradigm for the present indicative). In fusional languages, it is usual for a paradigm to list all the possible word-forms of a lexeme. In an agglutinative language, it is usually impossible to list all the word-forms, so only those which contain obligatory morphs occurring more peripherally (further from the root) than the morph realising the morpheme under consideration are given. Thus, a Finnish paradigm for case endings does not include all the word-forms with more peripheral, but not obligatory, possessive markers. That is, a partial paradigm like (36) ignores possible word-forms like those in (37):

(36)   *nominative*   auto
        adessive   auto·lla
        inessive   auto·ssa
        elative   auto·sta
        genitive   auto·n

(37)   auto·nsa
        car·3rd-person-possessive
        'his/her car'

        auto·lla·ni
        car·adessive·1st-person-singular-possessive
        'in my car'

        auto·sta·si
        car·elative·2nd-person-singular-possessive
        'out of your car'

Isolating languages do not, of course, have paradigms.

Since not all the lexemes of a language necessarily follow the same pattern of inflectional endings, we find various inflection classes (conjugations, declensions, etc.), such as those in (6) above. Each conjugation or declension shows its own paradigm.

What, then, can we say about paradigms and the way in which lexemes fit into them? It seems that there is always a basic form in a paradigm from which other members of the paradigm can be deduced (Bybee, 1985). In verbal paradigms, there is a tendency cross-linguistically for this basic form to be the third person singular of the present indicative, each of these properties being realised by zero more commonly than its more marked counterparts. This fits with Greenberg's (1963: 74) observation that plurality is always marked formally somewhere in a language, while singularity may not be. Children learning inflected languages appear to learn this basic form first and create other forms by applying processes to the basic form. While they may make mistakes in arriving at other, more marked, forms, they do not generally make mistakes with the basic form. In some languages, the paradigms may be so complex that there are, in fact, several basic forms in this sense. In these cases, there is always one which is less marked than the others and, again, mistakes are only made in creating the more marked forms. Bybee (1985) illustrates this from a number of languages and also shows how this principle may constrain historical change

There also appears to be a Paradigm Economy Principle (Carstairs, 1983, 1984c) in operation. To understand this principle, consider the following hypothetical example. Suppose there is a language with four cases and different marking for singular and plural. Suppose, further, that for each of these bundles of morphemes there is more than one affix attested in the language. The affixes might be something like the following:

	Singular	Plural
nominative	-Ø, -s	-n, -ad
accusative	-Ø, -m, -u	-n, -ud
genitive	-a, -r	-ri, -e
dative	-e, -en	-ru

Now, in theory, it might appear that any given noun could 'choose' its case affixes at random from the list given for each of the cases. If that were true, one noun might take the first option for every case/number combination except the accusative singular, where it took the third option, another the last option for every case/number combination except the nominative plural and genitive singular and so on. In fact, one would then have to learn the case/number endings for every noun with the noun itself, because there would be 192 different possible combinations of case endings, far too many to make any other system feasible. In fact, of course, languages do not work like that. In its strongest form, the Paradigm Economy Principle states 'the inflexional resources of a given word-class must be organized into as few paradigms as is mathematically possible' (Carstairs, 1984c: 119). In the hypothetical case illustrated above, the language would have to have no more than three paradigms. While it may not be possible to maintain the Paradigm Economy Principle in this extremely strong form (Carstairs, 1983), it does seem that there is an extremely strong tendency operating here, which has the effect of reducing memory load in the learning of paradigms (however unlikely that seems in the light of your own experience of learning highly inflected languages!).

It seems that there are also constraints on syncretism in paradigms.

Syncretism is homonymy between two forms of a lexeme caused by neutralisation. In the Russian example in (6), for instance, there is syncretism between the dative and prepositional singular of GAZETA. (6) is repeated here as (38) for convenience:

(38)　*Singular*

nominative	gazet·a	stol
accusative	gazet·u	stol
genitive	gazet·i	stol·a
dative	gazet·e	stol·u
instrumental	gazet·oi	stol·om
prepositional	gazet·e	stol·e

Plural

nominative	gazet·i	stol·i
accusative	gazet·i	stol·i
genitive	gazet	stol·ov
dative	gazet·am	stol·am
instrumental	gazet·ami	stol·ami
prepositional	gazet·ax	stol·ax

Carstairs (1984a) points out that, under certain circumstances, syncretisms lead to a reduction in the number of forms that have to be learned. For instance, in the Russian example there is a syncretism between dative and prepositional, which is conditioned by the property singular, and all three are realised in the same portmanteau morph. These are precisely the circumstances where there is a reduction in the number of forms that have to be learned: instead of having to learn two distinct forms of the lexeme GAZETA for the two cases, there is only one form, *gazete* to be learned. In instances where there is no portmanteau morph involved, the situation is rather different. Consider the Turkish paradigm in (4), repeated below as (39) for convenience:

(39)

	Singular	*Plural*
accusative	el·i	el·ler·i
genitive	el·in	el·ler·in
locative	el·de	el·ler·de
ablative	el·den	el·ler·den

If the locative and ablative plurals were to be syncretised as, say, *el·ler·di*, this would not reduce the number of forms to be learned, since you would still have to know that ablative is marked by *-den* in the singular, locative by *-de* in the singular and then the extra form

-*di* in the plural. It turns out that this type of syncretism is, indeed, extremely rare and that there may be some further generalisation to be captured concerning the few cases where it does occur. If the locative and ablative plural were syncretised as *el·ler·de*, with -*de* marking both locative and ablative in the plural, but only locative in the singular, there would be no extra forms to learn and this type of syncretism is correspondingly more common.

It, thus, seems that part of the function of paradigms is to reduce the memory load involved in learning a morphologically complex language and that this is done in a number of ways including paradigm economy and efficient use of syncretism.

To see how some of these constraints function, consider the following data on Tamil noun declensions (Asher, 1982). The set of endings in the noun declensions is as follows:

(40) | | |
|---|---|
| *nominative* | -Ø |
| *accusative* | -e |
| *dative* | -ukku |
| *instrumental* | -aale |
| *comitative* | -ooṭe |
| *locative* | -kiṭṭe, -ile |
| *ablative* | -kiṭṭeruntu, -ileruntu |
| *genitive* | -ooṭa, -u |

Note that the ablative affix could be divided into two morphs, although the form given here is apparently the normal one listed by Tamil grammarians.

Given that there are maximally two choices in any particular slot, the Paradigm Economy Principle predicts that there will be two different declensions. This is, in fact, the case. Plurality is marked by a suffix -*(a)ŋka(ḷ)* where the presence of the /a/ is phonetically conditioned by the previous sound (the /a/ is present after a consonant but not after a vowel) and the presence of the /ḷ/ is partly phonetically and partly grammatically conditioned: the /ḷ/ is present only before a vowel in the same word-form. The plural suffix, which is obligatory for one declension and optional for the other, occurs before the case suffix, in accordance with the statistical universal (7) above. Since number and case morphology is agglutinative, it is not surprising to find that there is no syncretism in the paradigm. The basic form of the paradigm is clearly the nominative form, which has no ending. For some nouns, the stem is not identical with the nominative singular form but the change in form is always predictable from the form of the nominative (although the rules of allomorphy are peculiar to noun stems and do not apply to other classes). Complete paradigms for the singular of nouns PAYYAN 'boy' and MARAM 'tree' illustrating the two declensions are provided below The forms of the plural can be worked out from the discussion above once we know that the form of the suffix is -ŋka(ḷ), the optional /ḷ/ occuring only before a vowel in the same word, and that a stem-final nasal is deleted when this suffix is added.

(41)
nominative	payyan	maram
accusative	payyan·e	maratt·e
dative	payyan·ukku	maratt·ukku
instrumental	payyan·aale	maratt·aale
comitative	payyan·ooṭe	maratt·ooṭe
locative	payaŋ·kiṭṭe	maratt·ile
ablative	payyaŋ·kiṭṭe(·)runtu	maratt·ile(·)runtu
genitive	payyan·ooṭa	maratt·u

From this it can be seen that it is not quite true, as was once thought, that 'languages can differ without limit as to either extent or direction' (Joos, 1957: 228). There are restrictions on the way in which the morphological structure of languages is arranged, although these restrictions are not necessarily obvious at first glance.

REFERENCES AND FURTHER READING

For introductions to universals and typology in general, and to morphological typology too, see Comrie (1981) and Croft (1990).

On the history of morphological typology, see in particular Greenberg (1954) and the works he refers to. For a text-book introduction, see Lyons (1968). A brief, but more modern, introduction is provided by Anderson (1985a), who also provides an outline of how the polysynthetic language Kwakiutl works. Greenberg (1954), as well as calculating the number of morphemes per word for eight different languages, also calculates a number of other statistics, designed to give measures of isolation, agglutination, etc. The match between my figures and Greenberg's own seems to be coincidence. He cites figures for other passages which are more different than the figures I came up with, but which are still in the region of 1.6.

On Item and Arrangement and Item and Process approaches to grammar, see Hockett (1954) and Matthews (1970). For a discussion of Word-and-Paradigm morphology see Chapter 11 and, for references, see the section at the end of that chapter.

The data from Turkish comes from Lewis (1967). The position of the extra consonants is somewhat fudged in the presentation here. They could be seen as empty morphs, separate from the morph to which they are marked as belonging in the text. The *n* in the third person singular possessive is also a problem since it is missing in the absolute case. It, too, might be seen as an empty morph or possibly a subtractive morph. The analysis of these points (and, indeed, of which morph these should be attached to if they are not separate empty morphs) depends on the wider analysis of Turkish and is not of immediate concern here. Note also that a case might be made for dividing the ablative suffix into a locative *-de-* followed by an ablative *-n*. This would fit well with localist theories of grammar but is not generally done in discussions of Turkish. Again, it makes no difference to the points being put forward in this section.

The list of universals in section 11.2 comes from Greenberg (1963) and Bybee (1985). The data on various languages is derived from the following works: Diyari, from Austin (1981); Hixkaryana, from Derbyshire (1979); Kanuri, from Lukas (1937); Swahili, from Ashton (1944); Turkish, from Lewis (1967). In the exercises, data on Mandan is simplified from Mixco (1997), data on Meithei is from Chelliah (1997) and data from Warumungu is from Simpson (1998).

In example (21) in section 11.2, it can be seen that the Diyari reflexive affix comes further from the root than the causative affix. In (22), the reciprocal affix comes closer to the root than the causative affix. In Turkish, the reflexive affix is also placed closer to the root than the causative. It, thus, appears that there is a conflict between the ordering of reflexive and causative in these two languages which might be counter-evidence to the hypothesised principle of relevance. This would, however, be an ungenerous conclusion to draw since the notion of relevance is stated to be culturally dependent. There may simply be a different cultural perception of the relative relevance of these two features. If that is so, we might expect to find them in apparently random order across a number of unrelated languages. The principle of relevance requires further elaboration.

On paradigms and the problems they give rise to, see the papers collected in Plank (1991), and Carstairs-McCarthy (1998). On the extension of the notion of paradigm to derivation, see Bauer (1997).

The 'meta-universal' discussed in section 11.3 derives from the work of Jakobson and is discussed very briefly by Waugh (1976: 97) under the title 'nonaccumulation of marks'. The use of the principle is illustrated in Jakobson (1960).

EXERCISES

1. Given an English sentence such as the one below, find an example of English behaving like an isolating language, an example of it behaving like an agglutinating language and an example of it behaving like a fusional language.

> Let us be thankful for the fools; but for them the rest of us could not succeed.

2. In Mandan, a Siouan language, prefixes and suffixes marking various types of information on the verb are found in the order shown below. What relative orderings are expected or predictable from general principles? What relative orderings are unexpected?

> Negative – Future – Subject agreement – Reflexive – Root – Aspect – Past –Modality

3. Meithei, a language spoken in Manipur state, marks gender, quantification and case on nouns and, among other things, directionality (inward, outward, upward, downward), causation, negation, aspect and mood on verbs. All these things are marked in suffixes. What order might you expect them to occur in?

4. Look at the paradigms in (6)/(38) or look at the paradigms for nouns in grammars of Latin or other fusional languages. In what way (if at all) might they be said to conform to the meta-universal on the nonaccumulation of marks?

5. In the data below you can see partial verbal paradigms for two verbs of the same conjugation class in Warumungu, a language spoken in Australia's Northern Territory. The data is presented in orthography, with morphs marked. Provide an IA and an IP description of this data set. One thing is unusual about this data set. What is it?

gloss	future	present	past punctual	past continuous
'go'	api	apa·n	api·nyi	api·na
'fall'	wanppi	wanppa·n	wanppi·nyi	wanppi·na

6. In Section 13.2, it is claimed that many of the characteristics of inflection and derivation discussed in Chapter 6 can be explained by Bybee's principles of relevance and lexical generality. Test this claim. Are the characteristics discussed in Chapter 6 merely corollaries of these principles? Can you see any other principles which might underlie those characteristics?

CHAPTER 14

Natural Morphology

Natural morphology is not a theory of morphology in the same way that Lexicalist Morphology, Word-and-Paradigm Morphology or Autosegmental Morphology are theories. Whereas those three theories are concerned with building up a formalism which will allow the description of the morphology of individual languages, natural morphology is concerned with providing a partial explanation for patterns of morphological behaviour. As such it is concerned with morphological universals and the way in which these universals interact with general cognitive or semiotic principles. While Lexicalist Morphology and even WP might be said to be concerned with linguistic universals in one sense, there is a difference. Lexicalist Morphology and WP deal with formal universals concerning the way in which a grammar is built up and the types of rule involved. Natural morphology deals with substantive universals such as the range of possible morphological patterns and the categories that are necessary in morphology. The difference is that between the Chomsky and the Comrie approach to the whole question of language universals. Thus, while Lexicalist Morphology and WP tend to concentrate on detailed deliberations of the way in which individual languages work, natural morphology is far more centrally involved with the range of possible variation within morphology. As a result, the study of natural morphology is perfectly compatible with either Lexicalist Morphology or WP or both; but it often provides a different perspective on the data.

It is unfortunate that much of the material on natural morphology is not easily available. Not only has most of the work in this area been written up in German (which ought not to be an excuse for its being virtually ignored), but it has appeared in publications which are not readily available in university libraries, even within Europe. When an English version of one of the major texts did appear (Mayerthaler, 1988) not only was it poorly printed, it was a particularly incompetent translation. It is to be hoped that publications such as Dressler (1985, 1986, 2000), Dressler et al. (1987) and Wurzel (1994) will help to overcome these problems.

14.1 NATURALNESS

Natural morphology came into being in 1977, directly influenced by the then fashionable movement in natural phonology (Dressler, 1985: 321). In phonology, 'naturalness' was often ill-defined, with the result that, although scholars could agree that naturalness was a desirable thing, they could not agree on what it actually entailed (Dressler, 1982: 72; Lass, 1984: 198). A problem for natural morphology, therefore, was that, if it was to be given any solid core content, naturalness had to be properly defined.

Naturalness is defined in natural morphology as the converse of markedness (see above, section 13.3 and, in more detail, Zwicky, 1978; Waugh & Lafford, 1994). That is, a particular morphological phenomenon is natural if:

(a) it is widespread in the languages of the world;

(b) it is itself relatively resistant to language change;

(c) it arises relatively frequently through language change, particularly analogical change;

(d) it is acquired early by children learning languages in which it occurs;

(e) it is left relatively unaffected by language disorders such as aphasia;

(f) it is relatively unaffected by speech and language errors;

(g) it is maintained in pidginisation and introduced early in the process of creolisation;

(h) it has a high frequency and wide distribution in individual languages.

(Mayerthaler, 1980: 29; 1981: 4–5; Wurzel, 1980: 104; 1984b: 165). The appeal to evidence external to the language system itself is striking in this list.

As was mentioned above, naturalness is also determined by general cognitive or semiotic principles. Of these, the most important is the principle of **constructional iconicity** (also called **diagrammaticity**). An **icon** is a linguistic sign which shows a similarity of some kind between its structure and the object the sign represents. In the case of constructional iconicity, that similarity is simply a matter of amount: an extra amount of meaning is represented by an extra amount of form. In the words of other researchers: 'formal complexity corresponds to conceptual complexity' (Haiman, 1985: 147), or 'what is semantically "more" is formally symbolized by "more"' (Wurzel, 1984b: 167). Precisely how semantic 'more-ness' is to be determined is discussed in some detail by Mayerthaler (1980) but is in most cases relatively clear from a purely intuitive point of view. Thus, plural is seen as being 'semantically more' than singular. The addition of an affix to mark plurality, as in *car·s*, is, thus, maximally constructionally iconic. An internal modification as in *mice* as the plural of *mouse* is far less iconic because, although there is a mark of the change in status, it is not an additional mark to reflect the additional semantic structure. An unmarked plural, such as *sheep* as the plural of *sheep*, is non-iconic since there is no marker of the additional semantic structure. A subtractive morph to show plurality, as in the German dialect form *hon* 'dogs' from the singular *hond*, is counter-iconic, in that less formal structure reflects more semantic structure. There is a scale of naturalness here from the most iconic = most natural, down to the least iconic = least natural. The prediction is that, if any language only uses one technique, it will be the most iconic one and that the most iconic one will be the most common kind in any language, independent of whether it also uses other kinds (Dressler, 1982: 74).

14.2 CONFLICTS OF NATURALNESS

There will, inevitably, be cases where there is a conflict between what is natural on one parameter and what is natural on another. Perhaps the most obvious cases of this are those where what is natural in phonological terms is unnatural in morphological terms. For instance, it seems to be fairly natural for a word-final unstressed vowel to be deleted, particularly if that vowel is a close vowel. In some cases, though, this will mean that a whole suffix is deleted. It might then be the case, that as a result of this natural phonological rule, the situation arises where what was once constructionally iconic is no longer so. It seems, in fact, that a great deal of 'unnatural' morphology arises in precisely this way. For example, the feminine plural genitive in Russian, which is striking because it has no overt marker, arose precisely through the deletion of unstressed [u] (Wurzel, 1980: 109). In this particular case, then, it seems that phonological naturalness is more potent than morphological constructional iconicity in determining the outcome of language change. But general statements are required as to what will happen in any given conflict of criteria for naturalness or, at least, of the type of condition which will affect the outcome.

As an example of a case of morphological conflict, consider the naturalness of transparency on the one hand versus the unnaturalness of extremely long words on the other. **Transparency** is the extent to which there is a clear match between meaning and form. To the extent that the relationship between the two is obscured, the construction is said to be **opaque**. Dressler (1985: 330–1) gives the following hierarchy of transparency:

(1) I   Only allophonic rules interfere between form and meaning   excite·ment

II   Phonological rules such as resyllabification interfere between form and meaning   exis$t·ence[a]

III   Neutralising phonological rules, such as intervocalic flapping, interfere between form and meaning   rid·er (in American English)[b]

IV   Morphophonemic rules (but with no fusion) interfere between form and meaning   electri[s]·ity

V   Morphophonemic rules with fusion interfere between form and meaning   conclu[ʒə]n

VI   Morphological rules, such as rules reflecting the Great Vowel Shift, interfere between form and meaning   dec[ɪ]sion

VII   Suppletion creates opacity   be → am

a. The symbol '$' indicates a syllable boundary.

b. *Writer* and *rider* become homophonous in some varieties of American English as [raɪɾɚ], where /t/ and /d/ are both realised as [ɾ].

I is the most transparent, VII the least. I is accordingly seen as the most natural option and is expected to be the most common option across languages. Suppletion is predicted to be (and is) the least common option.

Conflicting with the naturalness of transparency, we have the naturalness of words that are not too long. It is claimed that the optimal size of an affix is a syllable and that the optimal size of a lexical base is one or two syllables (Kilani-Schoch & Dressler, 1984: 52). The source of these generalisations about the size of words and affixes is not clear. Kilani-Schoch & Dressler (1984) cite Ohlander (1976) and Stein (1970). Neither of these is particularly specific and, in any case, Ohlander is dealing specifically with Old English, Stein with English, French and German. The range of languages on which the generalisation appears to be based is, thus, extremely small and typologically unrepresentative. Dressler (1982: 76) admits that 'thorough typological studies are necessary' in this area. In the absence of such studies, we may accept the general statement for the sake of the argument, although it should be noted that at least the precise values quoted are open to question. On this basis, we can conclude that the ideal length of a word-form is somewhere in the region of three syllables, plus or minus two.

In agglutinative languages, where there is in general a one-to-one relationship between form and meaning (see above, section 13.1), transparency is maximised. As a direct result of this, however, word-forms often tend to become long. Fusional languages keep their word-forms relatively short at the expense of transparency. Compare the translations of the phrase 'of our hands' in (2) below, where the citation form of the lexeme for 'hand' in Turkish is EL and in Icelandic is HOND.

(2)   *Turkish (agglutinative)*
el·ler·imiz·in
hand·plural·1st-person-plural·genitive

Icelandic (fusional)
vor·ra hand·a
1st-person-plural-possessive-genitive-plural hand·genitive-plural

The difference between agglutinative and fusional languages can thus be seen partly as a difference in the way various parameters of naturalness have affected particular languages.

One particularly interesting set of conflicts occurs between system-independent and system-dependent naturalness. The factors that have been discussed so far all deal with system-independent naturalness, that is, they may be expected to apply equally in all languages. System-dependent naturalness, on the other hand, applies only to a single language and is determined by patterns peculiar to that language. To exemplify this, we shall consider the plurals of German nouns as discussed by Wurzel (1984a, 1985). First, however, a further terminological digression is required.

In fusional languages, a distinction can be drawn between stem inflection and base form inflection (also called word-based inflection). In Russian, for example, masculine nouns show base form inflection, where the affixes are added to the whole word, as is shown in the following partial paradigm:

(3)   CHAIR   *singular*   *plural*
         nominative   stol   stol·i
         dative   stol·u   stol·am
         prepositional stol·e   stol·ax

Feminine nouns, on the other hand, show stem inflection because the affix is added to the stem, as shown in the following partial paradigm:

(4)   BOOK   *singular*   *plural*
         nominative   knig·a   knig·i
         dative   knig·e   knig·am
         prepositional knig·e   knig·ax

While the distinction looks perfectly clear in these terms, it is not necessarily as clear-cut as it has been made to appear here. As far as I can make out, the term 'base form inflection' is used when the affixes are added to the citation form of the lexeme and 'stem inflection' means they are added to only the base in the citation form of the lexeme. However, in the example quoted, *knig* is a word-form realising the genitive plural of KNIGA and could be reinterpreted as the basic form in the paradigm. The feminine nouns in the Russian example might, therefore, be something closer to base form inflection. Stem inflection would be better illustrated with the Latin DOMINUS, where every case singular and plural is marked by an affix. The distinction is thus clear at each extreme but there may be some mixed cases in between.

Now German plurals are mainly marked by base form inflection.

(5)   *Singular*   *Plural*   *Gloss*
         der Tag   die Tag·e   'day'

der Uhu	die Uhu·s	'owl'
das Brot	die Brot·e	'bread'
das Kind	die Kind·er	'child'
die Hand	die Händ·e	'hand'
die Uhr	die Uhr·en	'clock'

There is, however, a small class of nouns in German which show stem inflection. Some examples are:

(6)

Singular	Plural	Gloss
die Firm·a	die Firm·en	'firm, business'
der Radi·us	die Radi·en	'radius'
das Stadi·on	die Stadi·en	'stadium'

Since base form inflection is the rule in German and stem inflection is very much a minority case, there is pressure to change the stem inflections in German to base form inflections. Thus, while no new words seem to be being added to the class of stem inflections in German, words which previously showed stem inflection are changing class so that they show base form inflection. In some cases these changes are well established, in others they are still limited to informal style levels, non-standard varieties and so on.

(7)

Singular	Old Plural	Innovative Plural	Gloss
das Konto	die Kont·en	die Konto·s	'account'
das Aroma	die Arom·en	die Aroma·s	'aroma'
die Junta	die Junt·en	die Junta·s	'junta'
die Tuba	die Tub·en	die Tuba·s	'tuba'
der Globus	die Glob·en	die Globus·se	'globe'

This change is brought about because one of the **system-defining structural properties** of modern German is the property of using base form inflection. This is a property of modern German but not, say, a property of Russian or Latin or even of Old High German. It is clearly not universal. Neither is this a rule in the generative sense of the word 'rule'. The system-defining structural property is a generalisation available to speakers of a language concerning the morphology of their language. Such generalisations tend to produce unity in the morphological structure of individual languages. They tend to force change in a language even in the face of what would be seen as natural from a system-independent viewpoint.

This can be seen even more clearly with another facet of German plural formation. As was shown above, there is a hierarchy of iconicity such that the addition of an affix is more iconic than internal modification. It would, therefore, be predicted, from a system-independent viewpoint, that plurals created by internal modification would tend to yield to plurals created by affixation. Despite this, there is a group of plurals in modern German where affixation is yielding to internal modification (Umlaut). Examples are given in (8):

(8) | Singular | Old Plural | New Plural | Gloss |
|---|---|---|---|
| der Mops | die Mops·e | die Möps·e | 'pug' |
| der Strand | die Strand·e | die Stränd·e | 'beach' |
| der Zwang | die Zwang·e | die Zwäng·e | 'compulsion' |

The important point to note about the words in (8) is that they are all masculine. Neuter nouns, for instance, show changes in the other (more generally expected) direction:

(9) | Singular | Old Plural | New Plural | Gloss |
|---|---|---|---|
| das Boot | die Böt·e | die Boot·e | 'boat' |
| das Rohr | die Röhr·e | die Rohr·e | 'pipe' |

The point, according to Wurzel, is that most masculine nouns now have this kind of Umlaut plural, while most neuter nouns do not. A criterion of **inflectional class stability** tends to lead to changes which support this pattern. As a result, he says (1984a: 73), incorrect plurals, such as *die Hünde* instead of *die Hunde* from *der Hund* 'the dog', are more acceptable than incorrect plural forms with no Umlaut (for example, an incorrect *die Flusse* instead of *die Flüsse* from *der Fluss* 'the river'). This criterion of inflectional class stability is clearly language specific, not universal, and it appears to take precedence over universal natural patterns. That is, where universal and language specific naturalness criteria conflict, the language specific ones seem to take precedence.

In similar ways, it seems that feminine plurals in German are gradually changing so that they are marked with an -*n* plural, while masculine nouns that used to have an -*n* plural are losing it (Wurzel, 1985: 594–5). Similar factors might explain the resistance to loss of the final -*e* on German feminine nouns (Ohlander, 1976: 170).

14.3 IMPLICATIONS

Perhaps the most important feature of natural morphology is that it attempts to give some kind of explanation of morphological universals in terms of semiotic, and perhaps ultimately cognitive, principles. This is the same kind of approach as that we saw taken by

Bybee in Chapter 13 but generalised far beyond the two principles that Bybee proposes.

Care must, of course, be taken not to get into a vicious circle such that something is claimed to be universal because it is natural and natural because it is universal. It is for this reason that there is stress placed on the need for external evidence of naturalness. This was seen in the list on page 254. It is also the reason that the semiotic background is seen as important by natural morphologists (Dressler, 1985: 323).

So, for example, Mayerthaler (1980: 30; 1981: 28) gives a list of tendencies in morphological marking that look very much like Greenbergian statistical implicational universals. Some of these are repeated below in (10). Mayerthaler says that it is natural for there to be no marking on the category in the first column but for there to be one in the category in the second column. We can reformulate this in Greenbergian terms by saying that a marking for the category in the first column implies a marking for the category in the second column. The difference between the two is that Mayerthaler's list has as an 'explanation' the principle of constructional iconicity, a semiotic principle based, in turn, upon cognitively defined ideas of what 'more meaning' is.

(10)	Singular	Non-singular
	Active	Non-active
	Indicative	Non-indicative
	Nominative	Non-nominative
	Cardinal number	Non-cardinal
	3rd person sing.	Other persons

Clearly, any universals arising from such a list are only statistical, not absolute: the English 3rd person singular present tense -s suffix is a notorious counter-example to the last item on the list, for instance. But natural morphology does not expect to find absolute universals of this type.

The whole notion of constructional iconicity can be taken even further. For instance, Haiman (1985: 137) notes the following 'nearly universal' property of the contrast between what he terms the direct cases (nominative/accusative or ergative/absolutive) and the oblique cases (all others).

In no language will the morphological bulk of a direct case affix *exceed* that of the oblique case affixes, as a general rule. There will be languages, however, in which the morphological bulk of oblique case affixes exceeds that of direct case affixes.

Haiman estimates bulk simply in terms of syllables, although some more subtle way of counting could no doubt be used. This might be extended to endings within a paradigm of oblique cases, too. In Latin, for instance, the dative and ablative plurals show a disyllabic case ending (-*ibus*) and they are doubly marked. Moreover, it would be worth examining whether similar facts hold true (or how far they hold true) for all the pairs listed in (10). Is it the case that, where the indicative is overtly marked, its marker is at most the same size as the marker of the subjunctive? If all affixes in the language under consideration are of the same 'size' (however computed) this may not mean anything but, where there are affixes of different 'sizes', the implication may be found to hold more widely.

Since the general constraints introduced by the Lexicalist Morphologists (see section 10.6) are also statements that are presumed to be universal, they should also fall within the purview of natural morphology. The universals are often of a rather different kind, as was discussed earlier, but this is not necessarily crucial. It is important, though, that, whereas universals in Lexicalist Morphology tend to be formulated as though they were absolute universals, within natural morphology they would rather be seen as statements of relative naturalness. For example, The Word-Based Hypothesis (Aronoff, 1976: 21) is stated as follows:

> All regular word-formation processes are word-based. A new word is formed by applying a regular rule to a single already existing word. Both the new word and the existing one are members of major lexical categories [defined as adverb, adjective, noun and verb].

In natural morphology this would have to be modified. Dressler (1982: 76) suggests that the lexeme is a manageable unit for perception. It must be listed in the speaker's lexicon. Units smaller than the word may not be listed, as is argued within WP. Units larger than the word are assumed to recur as units only if they are idiomatic: so *red herring* recurs because it is an idiom but *this red jersey* is not a learned or fixed unit of English vocabulary. He suggests that is why word-based morphology is preferred. But there is plenty of evidence that not all morphological processes are word-based (for some discussion see Bauer, 1980, 1983: 174ff; Botha, 1981; Carroll, 1979; Scalise, 1984: 71–6). Where Lexicalist Morphology is concerned, this simply indicates that the constraint has been incorrectly stated. In natural morphology, this state of affairs would be expected but it would also be expected that the deviations from word-based morphology would be the exceptions and should, in some sense, cost more in terms of the description or language processing. Similarly, consider the Multiple Application Constraint (Lieber, 1981: 173): 'No word formation process ... can apply iteratively to its own output.' That this constraint is not universal can be seen from Afrikaans diminutives such as *kind·jie·tjie* 'nice little child', Italian diminutives such as *car·in·in·o* 'very nice little' (Scalise, 1984: 133 and note), German forms such as *Ur·ur·gross·mutter* 'great-great-grandmother' and a few English prefixes such as those in *meta-meta-rule, re-rewrite*. Consider also the data from Zulu in (11):

(11)	umu·ntu	'person'
	um·ntw·ana	'child'
	um·ntw·any·ana	'small child'
	um·ntw·any·any·ana	'very small child'

Such examples simply contradict the constraint as put forward by Lieber but, again, such examples would be trivial if the constraint were reformulated as a markedness convention within natural morphology. Under such conditions it would simply be expected that such reapplication would be exceptional in any language (which appears to be the case) and costly in terms of the description required and the processing time required by speakers coping with it. Both of these seem to be true as far as the English prefix *re-* is concerned. There is a brief discussion in Bauer (1983: 68) of the difficulty in deciding which forms in *re-re-* are acceptable and which are not, and the processing difficulty is suggested by the fact that the sequence *re-re-* is usually avoided in terms of a paraphrase with *again* (Stein, 1977: 225).

Similar implications for relative cost apply also to Word-and-Paradigm morphology. One way to simplify a WP rule is to make the operation it describes null. According to the principle of constructional iconicity, however, this should make the morphology less natural, since it would lead to a greater amount of conversion. There is, thus, conflict between what appears to be simplification in a WP rule schema and what should be simplification in the sense of likely language change (that is, becoming more natural). In an ideal grammar, these two would coincide.

There are also implications to be drawn from natural morphology about various questions of description at all levels. For instance, it seems that discontinuous morphs are less natural than continuous ones. This implies that circumfixes, transfixes and infixes should be less usual than other types of affixation. We have seen that this is the case. Most cases of circumfixes can probably be analysed as being made up of a prefix and a suffix (this is true of the German example cited in section 3.1.3, where the *ge-* prefix is not used on all verbs). Infixation, which gives rise to a discontinuous base, is, in any case, extremely rare in the languages of the world. Furthermore, we have seen in section 12.4 that, in some cases, it can be analysed as constrained prefixation. Transfixation should be doubly unnatural: not only does it involve discontinuous affixes, but also discontinuous bases. We know that it is virtually restricted to the Semitic languages, so its general rarity is confirmed. Furthermore, it is not completely generalised there: Semitic languages also have large numbers of suffixes and prefixes. Nevertheless, transfixation is notably dominant in these languages. Even if we assume that this is a system-defining structural property of these languages, the question remains as to why it should be so unnatural in system-independent terms. Kilani-Schoch & Dressler (1984) suggest that transfixation is, in fact, so unnatural that it does not exist and that so-called transfixes are the result of misanalysis. They suggest that a better analysis for Classical Arabic is in terms of a basic form and multiple internal modifications (Ablaut and/or consonant gemination). They base their argument on the patterns that are actually attested, as a proportion of the possible forms if transfixes could have any form. Their argument no doubt needs to be evaluated by a competent scholar of Semitic but is at least superficially persuasive. If their analysis is adopted, the Semitic languages are still not maximally iconic, but they are much more natural than they appear using a transfixal analysis.

At a much more trivial level, consider the problem of the multiplication of homophonous affixes discussed in section 6.3. It was said there that the suffix *-ette* might be seen as one, two or three affixes, depending on one's position with regard to the meaning of a suffix. Haiman (1985) provides a means of solving such quandaries. He gives, what he calls, the Isomorphism Hypothesis which states (1985: 19):

> Different forms will always entail a difference in communicative function. Conversely, recurrent identity of form between different grammatical categories will always reflect some perceived similarity in communicative function.

This hypothesis is formulated for application to syntax but it can be modified for morphology, too. In morphology, it is questionable whether 'different forms always entail a difference in communicative function': do the various nominalisation affixes really have a different 'communicative function', for example? But, within natural morphology, Haiman's hypothesis could be seen as representing the unmarked and, therefore, natural case. If the converse is applied to morphology, then we are under some obligation to take the three meanings of -*ette* as being meanings of the same suffix, unless there is overwhelming evidence to the contrary. In the case of English plural, possessive and third person singular present tense morphemes (all of which have the same allomorphs), I take it that the facts discussed in section 9.1 would constitute such overwhelming evidence.

14.4 CONCLUSION

As yet very little descriptive work has been done using natural morphology. It is to be expected that further research will lead to modifications in the theory and to greater detail in some of the many areas which are currently rather obscure. Of these, perhaps the most notable is the prediction of which parameter will win out under what circumstances in the cases of naturalness conflicts. Also, researchers in this area will have to beware of the temptation to provide ad hoc 'explanations' of apparently unnatural phenomena. It may be that what appears 'unnatural' in one place is actually a lot less unnatural when a lot more data is considered. At this stage, a statement that certain features are currently inexplicable within the framework would be preferable to appeals to loosely-formulated and badly-understood intuitions. Future research will have to concentrate not only on the linguistic side of the predictions made by the theory, but also the semiotic and cognitive and, for this, some input from outside linguistics will be required. The research project that natural morphology represents is, thus, an ambitious one. Nonetheless, natural morphology looks like a very hopeful avenue of exploration in morphological theory.

REFERENCES AND FURTHER READING

The major sources on natural morphology are Mayerthaler (1981) (badly translated as Mayerthaler, 1988) and Wurzel (1984a) (translated as Wurzel, 1989), but neither of these is particularly easy to read. Dressler et al. (1987), Wurzel (1994) and Dressler (2000) provide useful summary statements. For a textbook introduction, see Kilani-Schoch (1988).

The discussion of plurality in section 14.1, while based firmly on publications from the school of natural morphology, appears to leave some questions unanswered. In Turkana, a Nilotic language of North Western Kenya, a morphological distinction is made not between singulars and plurals, but between singulatives and pluratives. Objects which normally occur in isolation have a morphologically unmarked singular form, with a morphologically marked plural form. Thus, the singular of the word for 'road' is e·rot` (where the e is a gender marker) and the plural is ŋi·rot·in` (where the prefix marks gender and the suffix is a plurative marker). On the other hand, objects which normally occur in groups have a morphologically unmarked plural form and a morphologically marked singular. Thus the plural of the word for 'breast' is ŋi·sikin` (where the prefix marks gender) and the singular is ε·sikin·a` (where the prefix marks gender and the suffix is a singulative marker). The data is taken from Dimmendaal (1983), where further details can be found. There is an intuitive sense in which this is a perfectly 'natural' system and, yet, it appears to be at odds with the general presumption that plurality is always (or 'naturally') the marked category. I do not wish to imply that natural morphology cannot deal with such a phenomenon, simply that rather more elucidation is required. Mayerthaler (1981: 51ff) does deal with singulatives, which he sees as being the marked form of collectives. The point about the Turkana data is that both regular singulatives and regular pluratives are found. It is not clear from Mayerthaler's exposition whether the same is true for any of the languages he mentions.

Wurzel's discussion of Umlaut versus lack of Umlaut in German noun plurals requires a little further explanation. Hammer (1971: 7) states not only that plurals with Umlaut and a final -e are most frequent for masculine nouns, but also that this is the preferred way of marking the plural for masculine nouns. However, neuter nouns also prefer an Umlaut pattern, but with the suffix -er (as in das Buch, die Bücher 'book'). It is the pattern with Umlaut and suffix -e which is rare in feminine nouns (some 33 examples) and almost unknown for neuters (only one example, das Floss 'raft', and that used to be a masculine noun). Hammer provides figures for the less common patterns and for the numbers of exceptions to the general rules, which support Wurzel's basic claims.

In regard to the iterative application of affixes as in

Ur·ur·gross·mutter, re-rewrite discussed in section 14.3, Mayerthaler (1981: 117ff) suggests that it may be possible to formulate natural constraints on affixes which can be used in this way. His suggestion is, however, based on far too little evidence to be conclusive. He suggests that iteration of the same affix is constructionally iconic if it marks a scale showing monotonic progression. It is not clear that *meta-meta-rule* fits this category.

The data on Zulu in (11) is from Andrew Carstairs-McCarthy (personal communication).

EXERCISES

1. Test the hypothesis on the bulk of affixes for marked and unmarked categories in any language for which you can find suitable data. It will probably be easiest to look at nominal inflections rather than verbal inflections, if only because it is clearer there what the unmarked categories are likely to be, although the list in (10) provides a starting point.

2. Most of the examples of breaches of the Multiple Application Constraint given in this chapter are diminutives. Is this just coincidence? Look for breaches of this constraint in descriptions of a few languages. (If you do this as a class exercise, pool your results.) If diminutives for some reason belong to a semantic category where multiple application is natural, it might be expected that augmentatives would belong to the same semantic category. Find some languages which have augmentatives and see whether they also allow multiple application. Can you explain your finding?

3. English is a language which generally uses base form inflection. Are there any examples of stem inflection in English? If so, give an example.

4. Return to the data in Table 1 (in section 9.2) and determine to what extent phonetic relatedness, as described there, correlates with phonological transparency as given in (1). Could you use the approach in (1) to justify a ranking for Table 1?

5. Discuss the Isomorphism Hypothesis on the basis of any relevant morphological data.

CHAPTER 15

Diachronic Morphology

A ll living languages change and the linguistic change they undergo affects not only phonetics and phonology and lexis, but also morphology. In this chapter, we will consider some of the ways in which morphological systems can change, including how they can arise and how they can vanish.

15.1 WHERE DOES MORPHOLOGY COME FROM?

Morphology arises when something which once had no morphological structure is suddenly perceived as having morphological structure. This can happen in one of two ways: either a word which was monomorphemic is perceived to be bimorphemic, in which case we talk of **reanalysis**, or a series of words is perceived as being a single word, in which case we talk about **grammaticalisation**. We will deal with each of these in turn, although terminologically we could argue that the term 'reanalysis' would cover both instances.

15.1.1 Reanalysis

If we wish to keep 'reanalysis' as a superordinate term for cases of emergent morphology, then we could term this type of change **resegmentation**. We have already seen resegementation applying in the discussion of folk etymology in section 9.4.4. We might say that, once a folk-etymological analysis becomes generally accepted and starts being used as the basis for the production of new forms, it becomes a case of reanalysis.

A simple example from modern English will make the point. We are used to going out and buying hamburgers, cheeseburgers and, these days, chickenburgers. We may generalise all of these and say we like to eat *burgers*. So *hamburger* is analysed as having an element *burger* within it. This seems to suppose that there is also an element *ham* in *hamburger*, a supposition that could be supported by the fact that some people talk about *beefburgers* and the word *chickenburger* which has already been cited. So a morphological analysis of *hamburger* would give us *ham·burger*. But this has nothing to do with the origin of the word, which is derived from the name of the German city Hamburg. A hamburger was originally a meat patty in the style served in Hamburg, just as a frankfurter is a sausage of the kind served in Frankfurt. The German morphology was thus *hamburg·er*, but that has been reanalysed in English (presumably because of the coincidence of the sequence *ham*) as *ham·burger* and the new morphology has been used to create a new series of words in English. Where once there was no morphology, there now is morphology.

The example may seem trivial and is recent enough that some people still have a feeling for the original meaning of the word; the principle is not trivial, however. The English suffix *-ness* derives from a similar piece of misanalysis in Germanic (Joseph, 1998: 359). The *-n-* at the beginning of *-ness* was originally the last part of the base in words like a reconstructed **ebn·assu-* 'even-ness', but has become part of the suffix in both English and German.

15.1.2 Grammaticalisation

The term grammaticalisation was apparently invented by Meillet, although awareness of the phenomenon predates him. As well as grammaticalisation, grammaticisation is a synonymous term in common usage to avoid the 'heptasyllabic cacophony' (Matisoff, 1991: 383) of the more usual term, which will be retained here.

There are many definitions of grammaticalisation in the literature. The following from Kuryłowicz (cited in Heine et al., 1991: 3) will make the point:

> Grammaticalization consists in the increase in range of a morpheme advancing from a lexical to a grammatical or from a less grammatical to a more grammatical status, e.g. from a derivative formant to an inflectional one.

That is, we speak of grammaticalisation whenever something moves towards the grammatical end of a cline which goes from lexical item at one end to inflectional marker at the other. This is a fairly narrow definition of grammaticalisation (which frequently includes matters such as the historical change from focus-marking syntax to fixed word-order as well as changes from verb or noun to preposition), but it will be sufficient for our purposes here, where we are interested in the way in which morphology arises.

Even this allows for several different subtypes. We have cases where words become derivational affixes, where words become inflectional affixes, where derivational affixes become inflectional affixes. Each of these can be illustrated in turn.

English has many instances where words become derivational affixes. The words *childhood, cupful, kingdom, manly* all illustrate suffixes which were once words. With a word like *childlike* we have something which can be seen as being on the cusp between word-status and affix-status: we might not know whether to analyse this word as being a compound or a derivative. It has been argued that words like *cod* and *mock* are in the process of changing into prefixes in English journalistic writing, where they seem to be in competition with an item like *pseudo-* (Renouf & Baayen, 1998). Although grammaticalisation is usually said to be a one-way process (items change from being less grammatical to being more grammatical, but not in the other direction), there are occasional instances of items apparently going in the 'wrong' direction, from derivational affix to word: the English *-ism*, once only a suffix, is now heard apparently increasingly in isolation as a noun, as in the following example cited by *The Oxford English Dictionary*: 'Democracy could become more dynamic than Fascism or Communism or any other ism or ideology.'

Other examples include the fact that the Zulu diminutive marker (see p. 263) comes from proto-Bantu **gana* 'child' — a pattern which is frequent in African languages (Heine et al., 1991: 94) – and that case suffixes derive from verbs in a number of languages, including Ewe (Heine et al., 1991: 189) and Nez Perce (Rude, 1991: 186): for example, in both of these languages, a dative marker derives from a verb meaning 'give'.

The case of words changing into inflectional affixes is nicely illustrated with future-marking in French. In (1) we can see the future of CHANTER 'to sing' side-by-side with the present tense of AVOIR 'to have'.

(1)

	future of CHANTER	present of AVOIR
1sg	je chanterai	j'ai
2sg	tu chanteras	tu as
3sg	il/elle chantera	il/elle a
1pl	nous chanterons	nous avons
2pl	vous chanterez	vous avez
3pl	ils/elles chanteront	ils/elles ont

Note that the inflectional ending of the future looks very like the present tense of AVOIR added to the infinitive of CHANTER (the *av*-stem is missing in the plural; otherwise they are identical). This is because this is the origin of the future tense in French. The Classical Latin future was shown by an inflection; for example 'I shall sing' was *cantabo*. In Vulgar Latin this gradually changed to the equivalent of 'I have to sing'. If you consider such English expressions as *What do you have to say?* and *I don't have anything to write to you*, you can see that having something to do is pragmatically equivalent to expecting to do something at some time in the future. Accordingly, the Vulgar Latin for 'I shall sing' became *cantare habeo* (literally, 'to sing I have') and the two words eventually merged to give *chanterai*. There is a current French trend to avoid this kind of future marking, though, in favour of *je vais chanter* (literally, 'I go to sing'), so that we might think we can see the entire cycle restarting.

In this example we see two possible sources of future marking: necessity in having to do something and motion in go to do something (if I am currently moving to do something, the implication is that it will soon be done). Other common changes are from markers of ability (I can do it tomorrow), intention (I expect to do it tomorrow) and volition (I will do it tomorrow) to markers of futurity (Bybee et al., 1991). Although we cannot predict with certainty what will become a marker of futurity (or whether or not it will eventually become an inflection), there are well-trodden paths to the future which many languages have already traversed.

As an example of a derivational affix becoming inflectional, consider the fate of Latin *-sc-* in modern Romance languages. In Latin, the *-sc-* marked an inchoative and we should probably count it as derivational on the basis of examples like MATURUS 'ripe', MATURESCO 'I become ripe, I ripen' (Matthews, 1991: 54), although others see it as an aspect marker (Rudes, 1980: 328). In modern Italian and Romanian the descendant of this morph is an empty morph in certain parts of just some inflectional paradigms: compare the present indicative paradigms of the Italian verbs SERVIRE 'to serve' and FINIRE 'to finish' in (2). Some verbs, like MENTIRE 'to tell lies', can be conjugated in either way.

(2)		SERVIRE	FINIRE
	1sg	serv·o	fin·isc·o
	2sg	serv·i	fin·isc·i
	3sg	serv·e	fin·isc·e
	1pl	serv·iamo	fin·iamo
	2pl	serv·ite	fin·ite
	3pl	serv·ono	fin·isc·ono

Whether or not we think that this morph realised a derivational morpheme in Latin, it seems to have become much more inflectional in the modern languages. Interestingly, according to Matthews (1991: 55), this morph was inflectional in Indo-European, so again the change can occur in both directions.

The slogan which summarises this kind of change is 'today's morphology is yesterday's syntax' (Givon, 1971), which contains enough truth to be memorable, even though not all morphology comes from syntax and not all relevant syntax leads to the expected morphology (Anderson, 1988: 338).

15.2 WHERE DOES MORPHOLOGY GO?

Just as we have already seen that folk etymology sees morphological structure where there was originally none, so we have seen that lexicalisation ignores morphological structure. Typically, in lexicalisation, the internal structure of a word is lost sight of (it is frequently only marginally helpful in interpreting the word, anyway) and then phonological change can alter the word so that the identity of its original elements becomes opaque. Some examples will make this clear.

The English word *lord* is derived from a compound, whose elements meant 'loaf' and 'ward [i.e., guardian]'. Only the /l/ is left of the part meaning 'loaf', and we could no longer reconstruct that from *lord* if we had not evidence from older stages of English. What was once a compound has become monomorphemic, losing morphological structure. Similarly, modern *sheriff* derives from a compound whose elements meant 'shire' and 'reeve'. Even if we no longer use the word *reeve* very often, we still could not make a connection between *shire* and *sheriff* without external knowledge. Again, morphological structure has been lost (Joseph, 1998: 357).

More easily reconstructed are words like *health*, *stealth* and German *Drittel* ('third' from an earlier *dritteil* 'third part').

In some cases, a morphological form vanishes because its paradigm ceases to be used. The French simple past, directly derived from the Latin perfect, is no longer used in spoken French and has not been for about 200 years, having had its function taken over by the periphrastic past (the *passé composé*). Originally these two tenses were semantically distinct but became confused from the seventeenth century onwards (Cohen, 1973). Similarly, Old English had not only singular and plural first and second person pronouns, but also dual ('we two', 'you two'). This specific dual form vanished by the thirteenth century and the plural form was used instead (Lass, 1992). We can see all kinds of reasons for the disappearance, including system-dependent factors (see section 14.2), since these were the last remaining dual markers in English (with the possible exception of *both*) but, again, the result is a gradual loss of morphological paradigms.

In other cases, phonological loss leads to loss of morphology. This is the reason usually given for the loss of nominative, accusative and dative marking on the singular of nouns in the passage from Old English to Middle English (Lass, 1992). All these inflections (where there were any — some nouns had no inflectional marker in the nominative and accusative) were vowels; moreover, the stress was on the stem, so that these vowels were in weak positions. By the end of the Middle English period, they had all vanished and we were left with the situation we have today where no noun marks a distinction between nominative, accusative and dative singular (although the descendants of such markers are still found on pronouns). A similar fate attended the Latin case inflections on the way to modern French. In the Spanish of Panama, word-final /s/ is no longer pronounced in the vernacular speech; since Spanish plurals are marked elsewhere in the world by a final /s/, this has the effect of making the singular and plural or many nouns identical (Lipski, 1994). Phonetic erosion, when it happens, does not pay any attention to the semantic value of the sounds it erodes and so morphology can vanish with the sounds.

15.3 HOW DOES MORPHOLOGY CHANGE?

Phonological change can also lead to changes in the appearance of morphological patterns. The Umlaut plurals in Germanic languages originally arose because there was an [i] or a [j] in the following syllable to which the stressed vowel assimilated by taking on a front (and, in the case of /a/, closer) quality. Thus, the development of the German word GAST 'guest' is as given in (3).

(3)
	'guest'	'guests'
Pre-Old High German	*gast	*gastiz
Old High German	gast	gesti
Modern German	gast	gestə

The Umlaut is shown by the /a/ ~ /e/ alternation in the Old High German and Modern German forms; but while that alternation was motivated in Old High German, by the Modern period, the reason for the alternation is obscured. That is even truer in instances where, in Modern German, there is no ending at all, but plural is indicated entirely by the Umlaut (for examples see section 11.2). It is sometimes said that Umlaut in German has become morphologised. Looking at it from another point of view, we can say that what used to be affixal morphology has become morphology by mutation of the base. In terms of natural morphology, we can note that less natural morphology has arisen by natural phonological change.

The same is true in at least some cases of morphological metathesis. Consider the data in (4) from Clallam (repeated from exercise 4 in Chapter 11).

(4)
tʃkʷut	'shoot'	tʃukʷt	'shooting'
xtʃʔit	'scratch'	xitʃʔt	'scratching'
mtəqʷt	'put in water'	mətqʷt	'putting in water'

In this case, we have enough evidence from closely related languages to believe that an earlier version of this process would have looked rather different, as in (5).

(5)
tʃuˈkʷut	'shoot'	ˈtʃukʷut	'shooting'
xiˈtʃʔit	'scratch'	ˈxitʃʔit	'scratching'
məˈtəqʷt	'put in water'	ˈmətəqʷt	'putting in water'

In other words, what now seems to be metathesis began life as the deletion of unstressed vowels in forms which were distinguished in terms of stress. Again, less natural morphology has arisen from a natural phonological process.

Sometimes the form of a morph may be changed without affecting its semantics. One possible source for this is borrowing. This is what has happened in the marker of the third person singular present tense on English verbs. Old English had a form ending in -þ (or -th) and this persists right through Middle English and into Early Modern

English: Shakespeare uses a mixture of the old form and the new. The new -s marker is borrowed from northern dialects of English and spreads from Northumbria southwards, making its first appearance in the south in the fourteenth century (Lass, 1992).

Sometimes the meaning associated with a particular form is changed, but the form itself remains. This can be illustrated with the plurals of some nouns in the history of German. In the Pre-Old High German period, we find paradigms like that in (6), where the -ir is an empty morph.

(6)

	Singular	Plural
Nominative	lamb	lamb·ir·u
Accusative	lamb	lamb·ir·u
Genitive	lamb·ir·as	lamb·ir·o
Dative	lamb·ir·a	lamb·ir·um

By the Old High German period, this had changed to the pattern in (7). Here we see that Umlaut has affected the stem vowel in the plural but that the -ir morph has become restricted to the plural and, is accordingly, reinterpreted as a plural marker. What was once an empty morph, occurring in various places throughout the paradigm, has changed into being part of the plural morphome.

(7)

	Singular	Plural
Nominative	lamb	lemb·ir
Accusative	lamb	lemb·ir
Genitive	lamb·es	lemb·ir·o
Dative	lamb·e	lemb·ir·um

The noun in Modern German is *Lamm, Lämmer* 'lamb', (Class 7 in (5) in Chapter 11), where we can see the -er and the Umlaut between them marking the plurality.

We find changes which appear to be brought about by forces of naturalness. Again, we can look at German noun plurals but at a different period of history. As has already been mentioned, in recent German there has been a movement from such plurals as those marked as 'conservative' in (8) to those marked as 'innovative'. The precise social values of these innovative forms is not always the same: some are widely accepted, others are regional, informal or otherwise marked.

(8)

Gloss	Singular	Conservative pl.	Innovative pl.
'aroma'	Aroma	Aromen	Aromas
'atlas'	Atlas	Atlanten	Atlasse

'climate'	Klima	Klimata	Klimas
'comma'	Komma	Kommata	Kommas
'account'	Konto	Konten	Kontos
'risk'	Risiko	Risiken	Risikos
'schema'	Schema	Schemata	Schemas

Whatever else is going on here, we see that stem-based inflection is giving way to base-form inflection, thus making more of the German declension system fit this system-defining structural property (see above section 14.2; Wurzel, 1989: 87).

As we have seen, it is generally assumed that inflectional processes are all fully productive (see section 6.4); derivational ones, however, are not and they may change their productivity quite drastically over time. The most striking examples are those which suddenly cease to be productive: the compounding process which gave us *cut-throat*, *pick-pocket* and *scare-crow* is no longer productive (we could not have a new word **rob-tourist*); similarly, it seems likely that the suffix *-ment* is no longer productive in twenty-first century English. Less dramatic changes may also be observed, although we have to be careful how we assess productivity at different periods of history. For example, it appears that conversion as a way of forming nominalisations of verbs reached a peak of productivity in the late eighteenth century, whereas the peak of productivity for nominalisations in *-isation* was the late nineteenth century (Bauer, 2001b: 184–6). Both have been productive for at least 400 years but the preference for one or the other (or something else entirely) has changed at different periods of history.

Perhaps the most important mechanism of morphological change is **analogy**. Analogy is the process whereby one morphological form is changed under the influence of another (or, more usually, under the influence of a class of others). The innovative morphological pattern may lead to a reduction of allomorphy (when we talk of **analogical levelling**) or to a greater amount of allomorphy (when we talk about **analogical extension**). These processes are very common and many examples can be found in handbooks. The fundamental mechanism is easy to see.

In analogical levelling, exceptions to a general pattern are lost. In English verbs, the regular way of forming the past tense and the past participle is by the addition of *-ed* (variously pronounced). However, there are numerous, usually very common, verbs which use a different pattern (think of BREAK, BRING, RIDE, SING and so on). Throughout the history of English, verbs with these different patterns have been assimilated to the regular pattern. The past tense of HELP used to be *holp* but has now become part of the regular pattern as *helped*. Two verbs are currently in the process of making this shift: CLEAVE and STRIVE. Speakers are often unsure as to the past tense and past participle of these verbs and forms like *cleft, clove, cloven, strove* and *striven* are all attested. But more and more, people are using *cleaved* and *strived* as the past tense and past participle of these verbs (I came across *strived* most recently in a printed notice in a McDonald's restaurant). You will sometimes see such changes set up in analogical statements like those in (9). In (9) I have chosen to make the analogy with rhyming words, though this is not necessary for the analogy to work; it is the overwhelming weight of the regular pattern aided by the relative infrequency of the changing verbs which allows for the changes. If the verbs were very common ones, we would be familiar with the irregular past tense and past participle and would feel less pressure to change them, as appears to be the case with DRIVE and LEAVE, for example.

(9)   arrive : arrived   ::   strive : ?   (implying a form *strived*)
        heave : heaved   ::   cleave : ?   (implying a form *cleaved*)

Analogical extension, on the other hand, creates extra allomorphs, so that verbs which have changed from being regular to one of the strong patterns illustrate this type of analogy. There are not nearly as many of this type but RING is one. It used to be a regular verb and *The Oxford English Dictionary* shows regular past tense forms being used into the eighteenth century, but today *rang* is general rather than *ringed* (except in the sense 'encircle' and in 'ring the pigeons' which, we may claim, belong to a different lexeme RING, because they have a different paradigm).

Unfortunately, the term 'extension' is used in another sense as well, namely to indicate the situation where a morphological marker escapes from one paradigm into another. There may or may not be a reduction in the number of allomorphs available. While it is clear why this gets called extension (for example, by Samuels, 1972), a different term, such as analogical spreading, would seem to be preferable. As an example, consider the history of the genitive marking in the Scandinavian languages. In Common Scandinavian, some masculine strong nouns and all feminine strong nouns marked the genitive singular in *-ar*, while other masculine strong nouns and all neuter strong nouns marked the genitive singular in *-s*. Weak nouns of all genders and all nouns in the genitive plural had a vocalic marker. In continental Scandinavian, the *-s* suffix for genitive singulars began to spread to other masculine nouns very early, to feminine nouns after about 1400 and to plural nouns by about 1500 (Haugen, 1976: 294). Today the -s is used in Danish, Norwegian and Swedish with only a few exceptions, while Icelandic retains something much more like the Common Scandinavian system (and Faroese appears to be in the process of losing genitives entirely). It has spread beyond its original gender and number paradigms into other paradigms in continental Scandinavian and this, too, must be seen as a kind of analogy.

The outline of analogy and how it works that has been presented here has avoided most of the controversy that surrounds the use of analogy. Analogy is tied into markedness and naturalness: forms from unmarked categories tend to get carried across to marked categories rather than vice versa (with the interesting counter-example of Italian -*iamo*, apparently a subjunctive form influencing an indicative one — see Vincent, 1980). Without such notions, it is not clear that analogy can be properly interpreted. The links are interesting but will not be followed here. Notice also that many of the other changes that have been discussed in this chapter could be termed analogical changes: the instances of reanalysis, for instance. Analogy is potentially a powerful tool but needs to be properly controlled if it is to work well.

REFERENCES AND FURTHER READING

On diachronic morphology in general see Anderson (1988) and Joseph (1998), although neither is easy for beginners. Textbooks on language change or historical linguistics discuss morphological change, though not usually in a coherent way.

On grammaticalisation see Heine et al. (1991), Hopper & Traugott (1993) and the papers collected in Traugott & Heine (1991). On the development of the French future, see Hopper & Traugott (1993: 42–4), from which some of my examples are taken.

The discussion of Clallam in (4) and (5) is based on Anderson (1992: 67) and the data is from Lockwood (1993).

The German sequence in (3) is from Bynon (1977: 79); that in (6) and (7) is from Anderson (1988: 329–31). On the latter, see also Bynon (1977: 102), Joseph (1998: 353).

On analogy, see the textbook coverage in Bynon (1977) and Campbell (1998), the discussion in Kiparsky (1992) and, for the brave, Anttila (1977). The seminal articles by Kuryłowicz (1949) and Mańczak (1958) lead into the relationship between analogy and naturalness.

EXERCISES

1. Check the origins of the words *darling, husband, hussy, lady* and *twine* in any dictionary which provides etymologies. In how many of these cases is any of the original morphology still visible? Were you aware of the original meanings before you looked these words up?

2. In the data below, conservative and innovative past tense forms for a number of English verbs are listed. Some of the innovative forms are regional or nonstandard, some of the conservative forms are very old. What is important here is not their sociolinguistic status, but the fact that they all appear to show change in the same direction. What kind of analogy is involved here? On the basis of this data set, would you wish to comment further on the notion of analogical levelling?

Base form	Conservative Past	Innovative Past
drag	dragged	drug
shrink	shrank	shrunk
sneak	sneaked	snuck
spin	span	spun
stick	stack, sticked	stuck
strike	stroke	struck
string	stringed	strung
swim	swam	swum

3. In Old English, there were many different noun declensions, only one of which was marked in the plural by -*s*. This was one of the masculine noun categories and the most common type of noun. Most of the other markers were vocalic in nature, except in the dative case, where they ended in -*m* (which became -*n* in later periods). By Middle English, there were two main types left, those in -*s* and those in -*n* and, by Modern English, the -*n* plurals have been reduced to a few exceptional nouns (like *oxen*). Discuss the processes of morphological change which appear to have taken place.

4. The word *washeteria* 'self-service laundry' made a brief appearance in Britain in the late 1960s, apparently following the pattern of *cafeteria*. *Sandwicheria* was another coining of the same period. Discuss these results of reanalysis.

5. What might be some possible morphological changes to modern English? Can you think of some changes which would not be possible? Why are they ruled out?

CHAPTER 16

Morphology in the Mind

We have seen many approaches to the study of morphology, from the analysis of words into morphs and morphemes to sophisticated theoretical models which attempt to provide a rigorous account of some part of morphological behaviour across a range of languages. We have not yet asked whether the constructs of any of these theoretical approaches correspond to the way the human mind actually deals with the phenomena concerned. That is the topic of this chapter, though the overall results will be rather disappointing.

We need to be aware that, in moving from the predictions of theoretical morphology to a psycholinguistic view of morphology, we are taking a huge theoretical step. The predictions of theoretical morphology are – with the notable exception of natural morphology – largely based on the internal evidence provided by the morphological systems of a various languages; the results of psycholinguistic approaches to morphology are based on the results of detailed experiments. The results of theoretical morphology frequently stand back from the detail to try to get an overview of the whole field. Psycholinguistic approaches cannot do that: the whole experimental approach is based on trying to rule out factors which might lead to lack of clarity in the results and this means focussing on very small details. An experimental approach also demands a statistical analysis of results which those working outside the paradigm often find not only unfamiliar, but difficult to interpret accurately. This is less important in case studies – for example, those considering the language of individual people with particular language deficits – but is vital where experiments are carried out over a large number of subjects. In what follows, I shall try to provide summaries of the main points rather than get involved with the details of interpretation of experimental result but, to follow up this kind of approach, you have to be statistically literate.

We also need to be aware that the psycholinguists are usually in the position of trying to prove or disprove the reality of constructs provided by the theoretical linguists. Since it takes a long time to set up detailed experiments, the psycholinguists are, understandably, interested in looking at the better established constructs rather than at constructs which may not survive in the theoretical literature. This means that there is an apparent time lag between the establishment of morphological theories and the psycholinguistic testing of those theories. Much psycholinguistic work is still wedded to the notion of morpheme, for example, at a time when may theoretical linguists are giving it up. To the extent that psycholinguistics shows that human beings actually work with morpheme-like constructs, the theoretical linguists should be attempting to retain some version of morpheme: which version of morpheme is the best one, however, remains an open question, until such time as the psycholinguists start testing not only the concept of the morpheme, but the empirical differences between views of the morpheme.

Having said all that, we can begin by looking at one approach to morphology which became very controversial in the last years of the twentieth century, and which has given rise to a whole industry of psycholinguistic experimentation, because it appears to suggest that we can do without any morphology.

16.1 CONNECTIONISM AND THE DUAL ROUTE

How are you supposed to predict that the past tense of GO is *went* and that the past tense of SING is *sang* rather than either *singed* or *sung*? Basically, you cannot. On the other hand, you can predict that the past tense of KOREANISE will be *Koreanised*. So *went* and *sang* have to be learnt, but *Koreanised* need not be learnt – it can be created according to some kind of rule. We can, thus, argue that we have two ways to getting past tenses: a route via look-up and a route via computation. This has become known as a 'dual route' hypothesis. However, just because we could do these things in two different ways, it does not prove that we must do them in different ways. Perhaps there is a way in which these two kinds of past tense could both be generated by the same process.

That way has been set up in what is called a connectionist model, using parallel distributed processing (PDP). In a classic article, Rumelhart & McClelland (1986) report on an experiment in which they attempted to teach a computer to produce the past tense forms of English verbs, given the present tense bases. The model they use can be diagrammed as in (1), where the nodes in the left-hand column represent aspects of the phonology of the input (the present tense base) and the nodes in the right-hand column represent aspects of the phonology of the output (the past tense form).

(1) A pattern associator

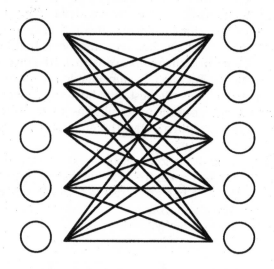

In the first stage of learning, the computer is presented with both the input and the output. The strength of the connections between appropriate input nodes and appropriate output nodes is adjusted until the machine provides the right answer. Eventually, when the machine is producing the right answer to the learning materials, the connection strengths are fixed and the machine is given new verbs to see how well it produces outputs corresponding to those found in English. The pattern associator can be made more powerful by giving it more input features or by giving it an intermediate set of nodes (each connected to every input and every output node). Such an intermediate set of nodes has no meaning associated with it; it is simply a way to make the connection between input and output more reliably predictable.

Notice what the pattern associator is doing. It is matching one phonological string to another phonological string according to a set of instructions which it is taught in the course of exposure to relevant data sets. It does not attribute any meaning to the matched patterns, it does not divide them into regular and irregular, it does not see any pair as different from any other pair. In terms of our introductory paragraph, it does not treat *went* any differently from *Koreanised*.

In the original experiment reported by Rumelhart & McClelland (1986), the computer was first trained on ten high frequency verbs, of which nine are listed in the article: *come, feel, get, give, go, have, live, look, take*. Each of these was presented to the machine ten times and the strengths of the connections were adjusted to provide the correct output. Then 410 medium-frequency verbs were added to the list and all 420 verbs were presented to the machine 190 times, with the connection strengths being adjusted as before. At the end of this, the machine gave the expected output for all 420 verbs that it 'knew'. At this point, no further adjustments were made to the connection strengths, 86 new, low frequency verbs were presented to the machine and the outputs were noted.

Unfortunately, there has been some dispute in the literature as to what counts as a 'success' for the model, but it is really irrelevant because later experiments have done better by having longer training sessions with more verbs. Rumelhart & McClelland themselves calculated that their model got the right answer in 91% of all the cases it was presented with. According to the calculation which makes the experiment look least successful, Pinker & Prince (1988: 125) suggest that there was only a 62% success rate. Whatever the success rate and however we want to measure it, let us accept that it was an excellent result for a pioneering methodology and has been improved upon in subsequent attempts.

In the years immediately following these results, connectionism was hailed as the new revolution in linguistics which was going to make everything that linguists had done in the past obsolete and attacked as a misleading fraud. In the meantime, tempers have cooled and claims diminished on both sides, and it may be possible to see a little more light.

At first it looked as though the computer, in its learning of the past tense forms, went through just the same kinds of stage as children do when they are faced with the task of learning English past tenses. Although this looked like a boost for the connectionist side, it turned out to be based on an insufficiently detailed appreciation of what children did and the claim has now been withdrawn. At first, it looked as though, by focussing on the forms of the verbs involved, the connectionist model would not be able to cope with homophonous verbs with different past tenses like those in (2). Again, it has become clear that there is no problem here since, in any full linguistic description, verbs will have not only phonological form, but also meaning, and that the meaning can be used to distinguish the various stems.

(2) a. I'll /rɪŋ/ you tonight.   I /ræŋ/ you last night.
    b. I'll /rɪŋ/ his neck.   I /rʌŋ/ the chicken's neck.
    c. I'll /rɪŋ/ the dove.   I /rɪŋd/ the dove.

The most telling criticism of the connectionist model, it seems to me, is that it does not allow for defaults. Since every particular input is linked to its own output, there is no way for the model to know what to do if new inputs do not match existing ones. In Rumelhart & McClelland's experiment, the machine failed to find past tense forms for *glare, jump, pump, soak, trail* and *warm*. This could not happen for a real speaker of English who knows that when all else fails, you make the past tense by adding *-ed*. We have seen the value of defaults in WP morphology, but here we see the value of defaults for the real speaker and the connectionist model does not appear to allow for them.

The arguments continue. It has been suggested, for example, that some language deficits affect only irregular morphology, while others affect only regular morphology, thus supporting a dual route model with one route for regulars, one for irregulars. Attempts have been made to trace the electrical activity in the brain during the production of regular and irregular morphology, but while results from individual experiments look hopeful, there is nothing overwhelming to support either side in these. It has even been suggested (Pinker & Prince 1991) that irregular morphology works by some kind of connectionist pattern but regular morphology works by rules and defaults. While this may look as if it is trying to have the best of both worlds, it is fundamentally inimical to the connectionist programme, whose fundamental assumption is that all morphology is dealt with by the brain in the same way and that the way it is dealt with has nothing to do with morphs and morphemes. Although this is reminiscent of the WP (or a-morphous morphology) approach, the two should probably not be equated too closely: WP still uses the kind of linguistic rule that is anathema to connectionists. But this does raise another approach to the whole question, namely a consideration of morphemes. If people use morphemes, then presumably they are not using a connectionist model.

16.2 MORPHEMES

If we start with derivation, there are plenty of isolated pieces of evidence to suggest that people do not use morphemes. In one experiment in which speakers were asked to split words up into meaningful elements, many speakers failed to recognise that words such as *baker, citizenship* and *kingdom* were analysable at all (Wheeler & Schumsky, 1980). The fact that *loafward* can lose its internal structure and give us *lord* (see section 15.2) indicates that people were not using the elements *loaf* and *ward* to understand or use the word, otherwise they would have wanted to keep them (relatively) transparent. The whole phenomenon of folk etymology (see sections 9.4.4, 15.1.1) depends upon speakers trying to impose morphs where there are none, thus implying that they are not very clear about the internal structure of the words they use. Such examples might not give us much hope. Yet there is also evidence to suggest that we do use morphemes.

Some of this evidence comes from children who are learning their first language. Typically young children who learn a particular derivational pattern, over-use that pattern by adult standards, creating words which are not part of the adult norm, but which are sometimes potential words, are sometimes words which we would expect to be blocked, and sometimes ungrammatical extensions of a pattern. Whichever of these is used, they appear to indicate some awareness of a morph with a particular meaning. For example, Clark (1993: 102) lists the examples in (3) as adjectives coined by young children.

(3) | balloony | 'covered in balloons' |
nighty	'very dark, like night'
poisony	'poisonous'
walky	'able to be walked along'
windy	'blown by the wind'

This same facility remains with us as adults, and we can and do produce new words, albeit in a rather more restricted way than young children do. There is, of course, argument as to precisely what the mechanism for the production of such new words is (whether by rule or by analogy, for example) but, in any case, creating a new word on a particular pattern would seem to imply recognition of the pattern and it could be argued that this implies recognising a particular meaning attached to a particular formal element.

When we consider inflection, there is a good case to be made for irregular inflection being memorised (or perhaps produced in some kind of connectionist way in the brain), since we have seen that irregular morphology does not necessarily fit very robust generalisations at all. On the other hand, when we consider highly inflected languages (remember that Archi has over 1.5 million word-forms for every verbal lexeme) it seems uneconomical for speakers to try to recall all of the forms of a lexeme rather than producing them on-line (as it were). There is other evidence to suggest that inflectional morphemes — in the majority of cases, at any rate — are neither recalled with their bases, nor stored simply as phonological sequences. Thus the /s/ in bimorphemic *wrecks* has different phonetic properties from the /s/ in monomorphemic *Rex* (the former is longer), and natural errors such as *tell-us-ing* suggest that *-ing* is being processed on-line, not recalled (Stemberger & MacWhinney, 1986; 1988).

The classic evidence that inflected forms are produced online and not recalled comes from an experiment by Berko Gleason (1958). She presented small children with line-drawings of a small bird-like creature and said, 'Here is a wug'. She then showed a similar drawing of two of these creatures side-by-side and said, 'Now there are two of them. There are two —.' The children were left to fill in the gap, which they generally did according to adult norms even though they could not possibly have heard this plural before, because the use of an invented word precluded that option. The experimental method has been refined and reapplied more recently but the fundamental insight remains (see Prideaux, 1984 for a summary of more recent findings).

The most recent attacks on the question of whether morphemes are used in language processing comes from an experimental paradigm using priming. We can begin by explaining the paradigm (which is quite complicated) and then looking at the results. In the priming paradigm, experimental subjects are given a **lexical decision task**, that is, they are asked to decide whether a sequence of letters presented on a computer screen or a sequence of sounds presented on a tape recording do or do not represent a word of their language. If no more than this is done, subjects recognise frequent words more quickly than they recognise infrequent words, so this has to be taken into account in more complex versions of the experiment. However, what happens if each lexical decision is prefaced by the presentation of another word? If the prefaced word is totally unrelated to the word that the subject is deciding about, there is no influence. If the word is identical to the word the subject is deciding about, there is a considerable speed-up in response time. The subject's response is said to be **primed** by the prior presentation of the same word and the maximum amount of speeding up is achieved by priming with the exact word that the subject is to be asked about: this is called **repetition priming**. If we take repetition priming to be the maximum effect achievable, we then want to ask what kinds of words give this **full priming** or some degree of **partial priming** (that is, responses are faster than they would have been without any priming but not as fast as for repetition priming). Attempts at priming with words which are phonologically similar to the target word, but semantically unrelated, show no priming effect. Attempts at priming with words which are semantically similar, but phonologically unrelated (for example, with synonyms), provide a lot of priming, but the effect dissipates quickly (so *liberty* will prime *freedom* if it is the next word presented, but not if it is presented ten words further on in the experiment). Words with the same base but with different inflectional affixes will prime each other even over large numbers of intervening tests (as many as fifty, it has been suggested).

The people who undertake these experiments interpret them as follows. If all morphologically complex words were stored separately in subjects' minds, then the amount of priming for a word like *totes* given by *toting* should be no more than the amount given by *totem* (the examples are mine). But phonologically similar and semantically dissimilar words do not prime each other, so something else must be going on here. That something else is presumably semantic, but not merely semantic or the effect would dissipate quickly. Rather, we seem to have an effect like a repetition effect. But we have no repeated a word, only a morph (representing a morpheme), so the brain must have isolated the morpheme and recognised it. This implies that the brain deals with morphemes.

A close reading of all the experiments that have been carried out within this paradigm is extraordinarily confusing. Some find full priming, some partial priming, some no priming, and the differences may be independent of whether the morphology being considered is derivational or inflectional, whether prefixes or suffixes are being studied. If we try to sum up over all, we can say that the majority view is that the human brain does use morphemes in its processing of words, although this broad statement needs some refinement. First, very frequent forms may not be analysed into morphemes but recalled as wholes; second, the formatives in words like *conceive*, *deceive*, *receive* and so on. (see section 7.2) should not be taken to be morphemes for the purposes of this conclusion.

Let us step back from the set of experiments for a moment and consider what we might expect to find. We know that complex words become lexicalised with time and that speakers no longer need to use the information provided by the morphemes in the word to interpret the word (see above on *lord* and also section 15.2). This implies that speakers may know familiar words as wholes, even when they have the ability to analyse the morphs within them if necessary. Correspondingly, we would not expect to find lexicalised words being processed in terms of their morphemes as much as non-lexicalised words. Frequency would also be expected to play a role here, with more frequent words becoming established faster than less frequent words.

Unfortunately, although some of the papers in this paradigm pay lip-service to the notion of productivity, they virtually all use established words as their experimental data because only with established words can we get frequency information. We can argue that this weakens the value of the results beyond redemption.

However, there is an approach which seems to rescue all these possibilities: the **Morphological Race Model** (Anshen & Aronoff, 1988; Frauenfelder & Schreuder, 1992). According to this model, when any language user is trying to produce or understand a particular word, they have two ways of doing so. The first way is a simple look-up: does this word exist in my dictionary? As we have already seen, this will give an answer more quickly for a frequent word than for an infrequent word. The second way is to create it or analyse it morphologically. This will be a slower process than looking up a frequent word but is hypothesised not to take longer than looking up a rather rare word. The result is that, when we want a very frequent word, the look-up method will win the race and we will find the established word. However, for a very rare word, we may find the word by look-up or we may get to a word through morphological production/analysis. And, for a word which we do not know, we will have to use morphological production/analysis. This model has several benefits.

To start off with, it explains why frequent words do not need to be morphologically regular — we expect to find them by look-up. *Oxen* and *geese* have presumably survived for hundreds of years because they were common words in the language of the majority of speakers of English. *Ox* is no longer as frequent as it once was and could feasibly change. We already hear people being referred to as *silly gooses* on occasion. It also goes some way towards explaining lexicalisation: something which is used frequently is known as a unit and morphological analysis is not used to understand it, so its internal structure is free to change. But it also says that we all work with some way of producing and parsing new words and that these mechanisms are in constant use. The mechanisms need not, perhaps, involve the use of morphemes, although in many cases they will be compatible with them. Whatever the mechanisms are, the fact that they exist and are constantly used helps to explain the productivity of morphological processes.

16.3 THE SUFFIXING PREFERENCE

We have all come across people who not only complete our sentences before we have finished saying them, but even complete the words that we are in the process of saying or trying to say. This indicates that people have the ability to predict what words we are uttering before they have heard the whole word. If people can do this, it leads us to questions of how they store and access the words in their minds to allow for such rapid look-up. Various models have been suggested in recent years but the most successful of these is the **cohort model**.

Let us begin by making a simplifying assumption: you are listening to single words spoken in isolation. You hear each word presented in time and you recognise it so quickly that you cannot possibly be waiting for the end of the word to start processing the word, you must be processing it as it comes in. So assume that you hear a /p/ as the first sound. There are hundreds of words which begin with /p/ but this, nevertheless, restricts the number of words you could be listening to, because it rules out all of those which start with a vowel, with an /s/ and so on. If you next hear an /e/, the number of possible words is further restricted to things like *pest, pessary, pen, penitentiary* and so on. If that /e/ becomes nasalised, then the number of words is restricted to things like *pemmican, pen, penitentiary* and *penguin* before you even have time to hear the quality of the nasal consonant. If the nasal consonant turns out to be /ŋ/, the word cannot be anything except *penguin* because that is the only English word you know which has that introductory sequence. Thus we can say that the /ŋ/ provides the **recognition point** for the word.

Of course, in practice, it is not the sounds alone which allow us to recognise the word, because words usually occur in context. Thus, given the context *When I visited Antarctica last year a I saw a lot of* —, we are unlikely to predict *pemmican* or *penitentiaries* anyway and the recognition point in context may be even earlier. As we have already seen, we do better at recognising common words than rare ones, so that we will be more likely to predict *pest* than *pessary* until we receive conclusive evidence that we must be wrong. And even using the sounds alone, I have ignored matters such as stress or tone in this presentation, though they will also have an effect.

Nor is this all that is going on: if someone coughs loudly just as the /pe/ of *penguin* is uttered and you cannot hear it, you will still be able to use the rest of the word to work out what it must have been, but there is evidence that we do better with the beginnings of words than with the ends of word (Nooteboom, 1981).

Now consider this cohort model in the light of two kinds of word: prefixed words and suffixed words. If you are trying to identify an incoming prefixed word, the prefix will form part of the phonological material which you are trying to interpret; if you are trying to identify an incoming suffixed word, you will start by identifying the base, and much of the material which comes later (case for nouns, person for verbs, and even derivational markers whose primary function is to change the word-class of the base) will be predictable from the surroundings. Thus, it seems that, for the best exploitation of the fact that word-beginnings are perceptually salient, we should treat prefixed forms in the same way as unanalysable bases, but we can use material in suffix position to modify the meaning of the base quite easily. This means that derivational prefixes should be easier to deal with than inflectional prefixes but that prefixes should, in general, be less favoured than suffixes (at least to the extent that access to the base of the word is a useful technique for understanding the word as a whole).

We have already seen that suffixes are more usual (we can now say, more natural) than prefixes: they occur in more languages, they occur more in languages which have both (as a general rule), there are many languages which allow suffixes but not prefixes and very few which work the other way round. While it would be nice to see some of the experiments on word-recognition repeated with speakers of languages with inflectional prefixes (Swahili, for example), we can probably explain the suffixing preference across languages in terms of cognitive processes involved in word-recognition.

There may be other factors involved here as well. Hall (1992) points out, for example, that there appears to be more regressive assimilation than progressive assimilation in languages so that, while suffixes regularly have morphophonemic effects on the bases to which they are attached (consider stress shift and velar softening in English, for example), prefixes (while they may themselves have several allomorphs) tend not to distort the beginnings of their bases. If recognition of the base is important for understanding of a word, this allows the beginning of bases to remain relatively transparent and, thus, helps the comprehension process. We can also note that there seems to be a trend in English for prefixes to become more word-like: productive prefixes have word-like phonological structure and are more likely than suffixes to occur as words in their own right. This has the effect of providing more words for people to have to understand but making it easier to understand them by allowing their beginnings to be obvious.

Interestingly, recent versions of the cohort theory of word recognition have started to build in the recognition of semantic properties of words, as well as phonological properties, and have started using connectionist models to explain all the things that are going on (Gaskell & Marslen-Wilson, 1997; Marslen-Wilson, 1999). At the time of writing, these experiments are in their infancy and still leave much to be explained; nevertheless, they are likely to provide support for connectionist approaches to morphological structure and, in the longer term, this might start to throw more doubt on the notion of the morpheme.

16.4 ENVOI

For realists, the checking of theoretical constructs against actual mental behaviour is the ultimate test of any theory. It is, as this brief survey has unfortunately shown, also extremely difficult. Results are often ambiguous or contradictory, progress is made in small quanta. But only persistence will lead to clearer results.

In the meantime, the theoretical questions to which we would like answers keep changing, too. Sometimes morphological theory and psycholinguistic practice appear to be on converging courses, sometimes they appear to be diverging. The interplay between the two is nonetheless important.

At the same time, direct psycholinguistic evidence is not the only evidence we can use in discovering more about morphological systems: we have seen how patterns of diachronic change are linked to notions of naturalness and how naturalness can change our ideas about what we need to explain in morphological structure. If language is, as Meillet claimed, 'un système où tout se tient', the study of language can equally well be seen as a system where theoretical advances in one place can lead to theoretical changes in another.

Whether or not we choose to work within a strictly Lexicalist theory (or any other), the results provided by Lexicalism (and all the other theories) are relevant to the greater goal of describing morphological systems and how they function to make language a good tool for communication.

REFERENCES AND FURTHER READING

On the whole connectionist debate, see Pinker (1999). Although Pinker is not an unbiased participant in the debate, he is an entertaining and informative writer. For a summary see Bauer (2001b: 84–91).

For summaries of work in the priming paradigm, see Marslen-Wilson et al. (1994), Marslen-Wilson (1999) and Bauer (2001b).

For a textbook introduction to the cohort model, see Aitchison (1987) (or later editions). For a rather more technical, but still comprehensible, presentation, see Marslen-Wilson (1987). For cognitive interpretation of the suffixing preference, see Cutler et al. (1985) and, in particular, Hall (1992).

EXERCISES

1. Somewhere between the connectionist model and the dual route model would be a model according to which you make the past tense of verbs in terms of parallels (analogies) with rhyming verbs. Can you think of any arguments against such a position?

2. Note that in *I ringed the dove*, RING means 'put a ring on' and is derived from the noun RING (by conversion). Are there any other similar examples? Is the regular verb predictable or a fluke of this example?

3. An interpretation of priming experiments was given in section 16.2 in which it was concluded that they show that humans process words in terms of morphemes. Can you think of an alternative explanation of what is going on which would not involve morphemes?

4. The general pattern of change in English verbs over the past millennium has been a change from irregular verbs towards regular verbs. Does the Morphological Race Model help explain this change and, if so, how?

5. Find a grammar of a language which has prefixes and see whether the prefixes cause allomorphy of their bases, whether the prefixes are mainly inflectional or derivational, whether the two types differ in their causation of allomorphy and whether there are fewer prefixes than suffixes or not. What can you conclude? If you have chosen a language with which you are familiar, do you feel you have been given a fair representation of that language by the grammar?

6. Return to exercise 5 in Chapter 12. Would the notion of recognition point help in your analysis of English blends?

Appendices

APPENDIX A: MORPHOLOGICAL ANALYSIS

Morphology is largely concerned with analysis into morphs. This is frequently tested by problems from languages unknown to the student. Many such exercises can be found in, for example, Gleason (1955) and Nida (1949). Here a list of words of English is given. Some of these words are analysable into morphs, some are not. For each word, state what the morphs are and what morphemes the morphs realise. In the case of portmanteau morphs, there may be more morphemes than morphs. Remember that it is important to justify your analysis. To give you some idea about how to present a morphological analysis, some examples are given below.

Examples of Analysis

The notes do not form part of the analysis, but are included to help the student. The guide below is a slightly modified version of material written by Winifred Bauer and Janet Holmes which appeared in Holmes (1984).

When you make a morphological analysis of any word W, the following steps are necessary to support your argument.

(a) A set of other words containing the relevant morphemes in W must be provided. This set must be chosen with care. Each of the morphemes in these words should, if possible, be realised by a segmentable morph; if W contains a problem of segmentation, it is useful to include at least one word which illustrates the same problem (unless W is unique). Even if W is irregular, it is the parallel with regular forms that justifies the analysis.

(b) State the morphemes in *W*.

(c) State how each morpheme in *W* is realised in morphs. You should consider *either* the written *or* the spoken form and be consistent. In general, the spoken form is probably preferable. You should discuss your own pronunciation of the words in question if you are a native speaker of English. The pronunciations given here are widely-used ones. State whether the morphs are potentially free or obligatorily bound and discuss allomorphs if necessary.

(d) Further discussion may be necessary to highlight particular problems.

EXAMPLE A: *untruthful*.

(a) i.   Compare the following set: *unfair, unwise, unripe, unfruitful, unmindful*. These establish a pattern:

> un fair
> un wise
> un ripe
> un mindful
> un fruitful

Thus:

> un truthful

Note:

not *untie*, where *un-* has a reversative rather than a negative sense and where *tie* is a verb and not an adjective like *truthful*.

NOT *unkempt*, where *kempt* is not a potentially free form.

NOT *uncle*, which is monomorphemic.

ii.   Compare *truthful* with the following set: *careful, faithful, sorrowful*. These establish a pattern:

> care ful
>
> faith ful
>
> sorrow ful

Thus:

> truth ful

Note:

NOT *forgetful*, where *forget* is a verb not a noun.

NOT *awful*, which is not analysable in its present meaning.

NOT '*brim*'*ful*, which has a different stress pattern and is different semantically.

iii. Compare *truth* with: *warmth*, the jocular *coolth* and the somewhat irregular *depth*, *width*. These are probably sufficient to establish the pattern:

>   warm th
>
>   cool th
>
>   deep th
>
>   wide th

Thus:

>   true th

Note:

NOT *growth*, where *grow* is not an adjective, but a verb.

(b) Thus, I would conclude that the morphemes in *untruthful* are {un} {true} {th} {ful}.

(c) i.   {un} is realised by /ʌn/ (written form *un-*). Both the spoken and written forms are obligatorily bound morphs.

ii. {true} is realised by /truː/ (written form *tru-*). The spoken form is potentially free, the written form is obligatorily bound – compare the word-form /truː/ *true*.

iii. {th} is realised by /θ/ (written form *-th*). Both the spoken and written forms of the morph are obligatorily bound.

iv. {ful} is realised by /fʊl/ (written form *-ful*). Depending on your pronunciation, the spoken form may or may not be potentially free. The pronunciation given here suggests that it is. If it is potentially free, then it may be the same morpheme as is realised by the written form *full*, and the morpheme should probably be called {full}. The written form is clearly obligatorily bound.

The form is fully analysable.

(d) Two points are worth comment.

    i.   The variation in the written form between (*t*)*rue* and (*t*)*ru* occurs elsewhere in English: *truly, ruth* < *rue*.

    ii.   While there is only one regular form as a parallel for {true} + {th}, the irregular forms follow rules found elsewhere in English. For example, the /iː/ ~ /e/ alternation found in *deep/depth* is also found in pairs like *serene/serenity*.

EXAMPLE B: *children*.

(a) Consider sentences like:

    i.   The child has come home.

    ii.   The children have come home.

The difference between (i) and (ii) is that a single child is referred to in (i), while more than one is referred to in (ii). There are very few words of English where a morph with a similar form makes this difference in English. These will have to suffice to establish the relationship.

    ox en

    brethr en

Note:

NOT *flaxen, wooden* because they are not plural.

NOT *deepen, lighten* because their bases are not nouns.

Note further:

While the vowel in *ox* remains the same in *oxen*, there is a vowel change from *brother* (in the religious sense, note) to *brethren*, as there is between *child* and *children*.

The use of an {-en} morpheme for marking plurals is lexically conditioned. The particular variants of affix and base that arise probably also have to be seen as being lexically conditioned.

The solution given above depends on the definition of morpheme used in this book. There is an alternative definition of morpheme, where a wider set of facts would be relevant. Under this analysis we would want to say that other forms which could be substituted for *child* in (i) are *girl, cat, horse*. In (ii), forms which could be substituted for *children* include *girls, cats, horses*. In these cases we can segment:

{girl} + {plural} /gɜːl/ + /z/
{cat} + {plural} /kæt/ + /s/
{horse} + {plural} /hɔːs/ + /ɪz/

Note:

oxen, brethren are not chosen as parallels in this analysis because they are irregular.

In the analysis given in this book, however, the morphs found in *cats, girls* and *horses* belong to one morpheme, those found in *brethren, children* and *oxen* belong to another, although the two belong to the same morphome.

(b) Since the relationship between *ox, oxen* and *child, children* is the same, we can also say that *children* must be analysed as realising two morphemes

{child} + {plural}.

(c) Whereas *oxen* is easily analysable into morphs, *children* provides problems of analysis. There are three possible analyses:

   i.   /tʃɪld/ + /rən/ (written form *child·ren*).

   ii. /tʃɪldr/ + /ən/ (written form *childr·en*).

   iii. the form is unanalysable and is a portmanteau morph.

If you choose (i), both morphs are obligatorily bound in the spoken form. In the written form, *child* is a potentially free morph. /rən/ -*ren* is an allomorph of the morpheme {-en} and is lexically conditioned.

If you choose (ii) all the morphs are obligatorily bound in either the spoken or written forms and /ən/ -*en* is an allomorph of the morpheme {-en}.

(d) The main argument for (i) is that the morph realising {child} is very similar to the word-form *child*. The phonological alternation /aɪ/ ~ /ɪ/ illustrated in this pair of words is also found in other pairs of related words such as *divine/divinity, wide/width*.

The main argument for (ii) is that /ən/ also occurs in forms like *oxen* and this analysis reduces the number of allomorphs of {-en} that have to be recognised. *Brethren,* which might appear to have

/rən/ probably does not, since the /r/ is attributable to *brother*: /brʌðərɪnlɔː/ contains the /r/, as does the written form *brother*. Thus, *brethren* is probably best segmented as /breðr/ + /ən/ (written form *brethr·en*), as shown above.

The main argument for (iii) is that there is no other plural in English which shows precisely this combination of vowel change and affix. It is probably simpler to see this as a unique change rather than as a series of lexically conditioned phonological changes and lexically conditioned affixation process, neither of which is particularly common on its own. However, if we are going to do that, it is not clear that the parallels we set up to analyse this form in the first place are valid any longer.

EXAMPLE C: *inquire*

This example is included to illustrate how you should discuss the analysis of a more complicated word and, in particular, one where there is more than one possible morphemic analysis. There are two possible analyses of *inquire*: either it is monomorphemic or it is bimorphemic. Whichever conclusion you decide to support, it is necessary to raise all the points discussed in (a) and (d) below. In other words, deciding that *inquire* is monomorphemic does not relieve you of the necessity of discussing the arguments in favour of a bimorphemic analysis; you will need to discuss the arguments to make it clear why you find them unconvincing.

The discussion here adopts the bimorphemic analysis. This is not because it is superior to the monomorphemic analysis but because it more obviously demands discussion of all the relevant factors.

(a) i.   Compare *inquire* with *infix* (verb), *inlay, indent, inbreed, indoctrinate*. These establish a pattern:

    in fix

    in lay

    in dent

    in breed

    in doctrinate

Note:

NOT *indecent* where *in-* has a negative sense and where (*in-*)·*decent* is an adjective not a verb.

NOT *incur* where *-cur* is an obligatorily bound morph and the meaning of *in-* is not transparent: this example would not illuminate the analysis.

NOT *interest* which is undoubtedly monomorphemic.

These are sufficient to provide a basis for arguing that {in} in *inquire* is a distinct morpheme, provided that it can be shown that there is also a separate morpheme {quire}. Note that this is not necessary for *infix, inlay, indent* and *inbreed* since their roots are potentially free forms. It would be necessary in discussing the analysis of *indoctrinate,* which raises similar problems to those with *inquire.*

    ii.   Compare *inquire* with *acquire, require.* Although these share a formal element *-quire,* it is not clear that *-quire* has the same meaning in all three words and it is, therefore, not clear that it realises the same morpheme.

   iii. Compare inquire with *query, quest, question, querist.* It can be argued that all these share a morpheme with *inquire*: there appears to be a common element of meaning associated with a partially recurrent form. If we represent that morpheme as {quer}, then *-quire* in inquire realises {quer}.

(b) Accepting the above arguments, I would conclude that the morphemes in *inquire* are {in} {quer}.

    Problems with accepting these arguments are dealt with in (d) below. The alternative is to regard *inquire* as monomorphemic.

(c) i.   If *inquire* is regarded as monomorphemic the morpheme {inquire} is realised by the morph /ɪŋkwaɪə/ (written form *inquire*). According to this solution, the form is unanalysable.

    ii. If *inquire* is regarded as bimorphemic, the morpheme {in} is realised as /ɪŋ/ (written form *in-*). Both spoken and written forms are obligatorily bound morphs, unless {in} is regarded as the same morpheme as the preposition *in,* in which case the written form is a potentially free morph. The morpheme {quer} is realised by the morph /kwaɪə/ (written form *quire*). Both the spoken and written forms are obligatorily bound. According to this solution, the word is fully analysable.

(d) There are a number of problems raised by the above discussion which throw doubt on the conclusion reached.

i.   It is not clear that *in-* means 'in', 'into' in *inquire*. In *infix, inlay, inbreed*, the meaning is quite clear but, in *indict, invent*, a solution along these lines seems even less plausible.

ii. It is at least debatable whether the proposed morpheme {quer} does in fact have an identifiable and constant meaning in the words *query, quest, question, querist* and *inquire*.

iii. The morpheme {quer} postulated as underlying *query, quest, question, querist* and *inquire* involves phonological variation of a sort which is not common, that is: /iər/ ~ /e/ ~ /aɪə/ ~ /aɪr/. The written alternation of *e* with *i* is found elsewhere (for example, *stink/stench, right/rectitude*) but even this is not regular.

Here now are some English words for you to practise with. You may also use others but remember that some words raise extremely complex problems, while others are very simple.

anachronistic	ineffable
aunties	institutionalisation
beatnik	inveterate
bedraggled	jeopardised
best-seller	lexicalisation
boysenberry	lightning
bulldozer	linguistics
catholic	measles
commandant	monomorphemic
crackerjack	morphology
degenerate	pious
discombobulate	republicanism
disinclined	reserved
entreaty	sociable
ergonomics	sorority
evacuee	tablespoonful
habitation	tabloid
highlight	them

his	unfriendliness
history	Anglophilia
inconclusive	

APPENDIX B: DISCUSSION OF SELECTED EXERCISES

Chapter 1

1. In (a) grammar means 'a book containing grammatical information'; in (b) it means something like 'customary usage'; in (c) it probably means simply learning the paradigms but reference could be implied to the syntax as well; however, (c) seems to exclude information about pronunciation, which is explicitly included in (d), where it means something like 'that part of linguistic behaviour which is susceptible to generalisations' – this is the linguist's normal use of the term; in (e) reference is probably to lessons on how to write well in your native language, though notice that the form of the sentence would allow an interpretation where principles of grammatical description rather than anything to do with any particular language were being taught. Thus all five probably have different meanings and some may be ambiguous.

Chapter 2

1. *Superstition* is not a lexeme because its notation tells you it is a word-form, rather than a lexeme. Similarly, {neat} is a morpheme, even if it is the only morpheme in the lexeme NEAT. CAT is a straightforward lexeme, with word-forms *cat* and *cats*. Some authorities claim that there is no lexeme BEFORE because it is only ever realised by one word-form, *before*. I prefer to say that just as {print} is only ever realised as /print/, so BEFORE is only ever realised as *before*, but that does not prevent it from being a lexeme.

2. Sentence (a) contains 11 orthographic words, 10 different word-forms (*walked* counts only once), 10 different lexemes (this assumes the answer to question 1 above; again there is a single lexeme WALK), and 11 different grammatical words (the two *walked*-forms are different grammatical words). Sentence (b) contains 11 orthographic

words, 9 different word-forms (*banks* and *the* are repeated), 10 different lexemes (see below) and 10 different grammatical words (see also below). The point here is that *banks* 'sides of a watercourse' and *banks* 'financial institutions' are so different in meaning that they seem to belong to two different lexemes, which we can call BANK[1] and BANK[2]. Thus 'plural of BANK[1]' is a different grammatical word from 'plural of BANK[2]'. Sentence (c) contains 18 orthographic words (*wine-waiter* is one because a hyphen is not a space), 14 different word-forms (*the, stoops, them* and *refilled* recur), 14 different lexemes (THE, THEM and REFILL occur more than once each), 16 different grammatical words (*the* and *them* recur, but the two *stoops* word-forms and the two *refilled* word-forms are different grammatical words: in the first case, because there are two different lexemes STOOP, in the second, because, although there is only one lexeme, we have a past participle and a past tense).

3. This is a matter of philosophy rather than a matter of linguistics. On the one hand, we might say that given *banks* in isolation, we cannot tell which of the two it is, so the two are clearly identical, so we might as well say that the same word-form can belong to two different lexemes. On the other hand, we could argue that any word-form is a word-form of a lexeme and so, if the lexeme is different in the two cases, the word-form must also be different, even if the two we have here are homophonous. Morphologists have not answered this question, leaving the issue vague. Clearly the safest thing to say is that the two word-forms are homophonous rather than that there is just one word-form. The alternative is very tempting.

4. The ending /d/ follows a voiced phoneme, while /t/ follows a voiceless one. That is an example of phonetic conditioning. The two formal elements are allomorphs of the same morpheme. With WANT and PRETEND we find /wɒntɪd/ and /prɪtendɪd/ respectively, with a new allomorph of the same morpheme following /t/ or /d/. We can say that 'the morpheme {past tense} has three phonetically conditioned allomorphs, /ɪd/ after /t/ or /d/, /t/ after other voiceless sounds and /d/ everywhere else [alternative formulation: after other voiced sounds]'. The forms /prədjuːst/, /ɪnsʌltɪd/ and /kənteɪnd/ are consistent with this statement.

5. The allomorphs are *-ngu, -wu,* and *-ku.* The first is grammatically conditioned by the fact that the base is a pronoun, the other two are phonetically conditioned: when the base ends in a vowel we find *-wu,* when it ends in a consonant we find *-ku.* We expect the forms *purlijimanku* and *kartuwu.*

6. It would take too long to go through ever single example here, but the point is that there is not necessarily an easy answer. Either we have to take parallelism with other forms which are clearly affixes seriously or we have to distinguish between those words in which the material added to the base is a word and those where it is not, despite apparently similar behaviour. The English example is perhaps the hardest to deal with: there is no parallel for these examples, either with obligatorily bound or with potentially free morphs. They are, in many ways, marginal in the system of English (not everyone uses them or knows how to create new ones, for example), but they still confound our expectations by being so unlike everything else in the language.

7. This is a difficult question, despite its apparent simplicity, and one which is given implicitly different answers by different linguists. Arguments in favour of a positive response would have to stress that derivational affixes 'have' a meaning and a form (just like lexemes) 'have' a category – part of speech – (just like lexemes) and must be listed in the lexicon (just like lexemes). A negative response would probably favour seeing derivational affixes as functions which operate on bases rather than as 'things'. Discussion in Chapters 7 and 11 will show something of how these alternatives might work.

Chapter 3

1.–6. These do not require specific discussion.

7. The root is *do-*, the future morpheme is {gu}, with allomorphs *gu*, *ga* and *gi*, but you might not feel confident about choosing any one of those labels for the morpheme. From the data you have here, any one of them would be reasonable. The variation in the root is actually grammatically conditioned but I would be surprised if you could spot that. Haiman (1998: 547) says that the 'final vowel of the verb … is fronted when its subject is nonfirst person and nonsingular'. That is not only an unusual case, but one which involves a conjunction of features, making it harder to see what is going on, especially with so little data. The phenomenon is Ablaut/vowel mutation/modification of the base.

8. Both *feck* and *ric* are unique morphs, which can be analysed because we recognise the other morph in the word. In the case of *feckless*, we have to ask ourselves whether this is the potentially free form *less* or whether it is an affix. The potentially free form does not easily take

prefixes, while the suffix which occurs in words like *defenceless*, *hopeless*, *senseless* seems to give an appropriate semantic parallel to *feckless* (they all have to do with the quality of lacking something). Thus we probably want to see the *-less* as a suffix, which implies that *feck* is a base, not an affix. With *ric* we have parallels with words like *kingdom* (less obviously, *duchy* and *principality*) which suggest that it acts like a suffix; we do not have words like **king-land* or **priest-area* where words which are clearly compounds denote the domain of a particular ruler. This is the only thing which suggests that *ric* should be seen as a suffix rather than as a word (like *kith*).

Chapter 4

1. I would expect you to find a small number of types, including compounds (where at least in English people are very unsure as to how many words are involved) and elements derived from the fixing of some expression (like the *insofar as* case mentioned in the text). There may be overlap between those two categories. Mostly there is very little doubt about where the word-boundaries fall, though whether this is a result of literacy or not is an open question.

2. Children do not seem to spend a lot of time learning how to recognise a word, that seems to be assumed, and on the whole children have little problem with it (though there will always be a few marginal cases). It is tempting to assume that the notion of word does not presuppose literacy, but that may be too big a step to take: children learning to write can usually read first and may already have absorbed the notion of word.

4. The point of this question is to make you consider the extent to which we need the notion of word, despite the difficulty we have with it. In all probability, a language without words would be a language in which the word coincided with either the morpheme or the sentence. There are languages which approximate to these two extremes, but I suspect that all languages distinguish the three at least some of the time. Why?

Chapter 5

1. Probably none of these patterns is still productive (available). The only pattern which is still found productively is that illustrated by

bepatched, where both the *be-* and the *-ed* are present simultaneously. But you cannot tell that from the lists of words, nor even from Marchand's more extensive lists of the same patterns. Rather you have to discover, by some means, what it is still possible to use: that might involve searching texts for neologisms or asking people (preferably indirectly) what patterns are possible in their speech.

2. The point is the need to distinguish between a prefix as it appears in an analysable pattern and as it appears in a productive one. One might choose to systematise the analysable but non-productive uses of a prefix or not; one would certainly wish to comment on any productive uses.

3. Not only are all the bases monosyllabic, but they all end in an obstruent (that is, either a plosive or a fricative), with /t/, /d/ and /k/ particularly well represented. We might argue that the reason for *strengthen* with a nominal base rather than **strongen* is to fit with the constraint. The words cited are all well established but you will probably find that, if you can still use *-en*, it will sound better if you conform to these constraints, and it may be possible only if you conform to them.

4. Blocking would predict that the earliest nominalisation is always the one which persists. This does not happen (although sometimes the dates of attestation of the nominalisations are so close together that it can be hard to determine which was really in use first). Thus we have evidence that blocking does not work completely as predicted. On the other hand, it is usually the case that, unless there is a semantic distinction between two nominalisations, only one of them will persist and this is in line with the predictions made by blocking.

5. The adjectives you happen to have chosen may not reflect my expected results precisely, but I would expect you to find more adjectives that can take *-ness* than adjectives which can take *-ity* in your list. This would lead you to conclude that *-ness* is more productive than *-ity*. You may not agree with your dictionary listings (dictionaries may not always list words in *-ness* because these tend to be more semantically predictable than words in *-ity*). When you divide your adjectives into two groups, *-ity* will look rather more productive than previously because it does not usually get added to native bases. If you selected particular affixes, *-ity* might look even more productive. The suffix *-able* is a problem because it tends to allow both *-ness* and *-ity*, sometimes with no difference of meaning.

The exercise highlights the dangers of talking about 'productivity' without being clear about the domain in which the productivity operates. Blocking would predict that, if we find nouns in *-ness* and *-ity* derived from the same base, they should mean different things. Alternatively, we might argue that, if both exist at the moment, one of them is fated to vanish.

6. Just as we tend not to find *stealer* because *thief* exists, so we tend not to find *goed* because *went* exists. So *went* might be said to block *goed* in the same way that *thief* blocks *stealer*. However, while this is fine as far as it goes, it needs to be taken further: all irregular morphology might be said to block regular morphology. What was said about *went* is just as true of *strung* blocking *stringed*. In these cases, though, the places where blocking fails are not quite the same as they are in the derivational instances. Can you see differences?

Chapter 6

1. You will need to consider a number of criteria, not necessarily the ones preferred in this book, and see how each applies. Where criteria disagree, you will need to be able to argue which side of the disagreement provides the best case. I would expect the inherent/contextual distinction to help, by providing an extra intermediate category.

2. You will need to try the various criteria for each of your affixes and see whether they fall naturally into two distinct groups or not. This implies that you understand each criterion properly and can apply it, finding relevant data. My expectation is that they would not but choice of affixes is clearly crucial. Take care not to conclude more than your small-scale experiment will prove: because something works for six affixes, it does not prove it will work for all.

3. For most languages it would be seen as a case of inherent inflection (and is defined as such in the introduction of the categories of contextual and inherent inflection). There may, nevertheless, be strong arguments pulling towards the conclusion that it is derivational in some languages. Take care to apply the criteria carefully and not to conclude more than your evidence will support.

4. Many would argue that all such examples can be explained away, especially if the distinction between inherent and contextual inflection is brought to bear. The inflection which is found in the 'wrong' place is always inherent, and usually not only inherent but also irregular.

In many cases, the stem + apparent inflection cannot be understood as a regularly inflected word at all (for example, *news* is not 'the plural of NEW').

5. If the distinction between inflection and derivation has to be determined by a particular theory, it might help explain why the criteria that have been considered here do not always agree or make clear predictions. It might also explain why something like causation can be inflectional in one language and derivational in another. On the other hand, without some clear example of how this is going to work (not necessarily Anderson's fault since he is cited out of context), it could simply be a way of explaining away the problems without providing a solid alternative.

Chapter 7

1. One analysis will have a morpheme {past tense}, with all the forms illustrated being allomorphs of the same morpheme. Another will have several synonymous morphemes, all meaning 'past tense', but morphologically distinct. If you have a morphome, then that morphome will subsume various morphemes each with the meaning 'past tense'. In a theory with no morpheme, you would have to say that the meaning of past tense is realised by a number of distinct phonological operations on the stem giving rise to word-forms showing different pattern of phonemes.

2. The simplest way to answer this question might be to do it with relation to a particular set of data. In any discussion, though, the issue of notation should arise: are morphomes to be notated just like morphemes, or do they require a separate notation, and what are the arguments for each position? The other major point requiring discussion is the idea that morphomes may not have a constant meaning but, rather, a range of constant meanings, which may not be related to each other. This raises the question of how the third person singular of the present tense on verbs and the possessive on nouns are to be related in English. In nearly all verbs, the /s/, /z/ and /ɪz/ allomorphs of the third person singular morpheme coincide exactly (and under the same conditions) with the /s/, /z/ and /ɪz/ allomorphs of the possessive. But there are a few irregular verbs like *is*, *does*, *has* and *says* (at least for those who use the pronunciation /sez/) which have no comparable forms in the possessive. Is this enough to guarantee that they belong to separate morphemes or do we have to set up sub-morphemes? In general, the notion of

homophonous morphs is going to become something of a problem. If we set up two distinct lexemes EAR[1] 'organ of hearing' and EAR[2] 'structure containing cereal seeds', do the morphs realising each of these lexemes belong to the same morphome and, if so, what is the benefit to the analyst?

3. The words in the first column are chosen to be relatively neutral in meaning and not to reflect the 'light' meaning of the words in (12a). The words in the second column are chosen to provide an alternative interpretation of *gl-* as meaning something like 'slimy, sticky, unpleasant'. Were the *gl-* element to be analysed as a morph, this might give cause for concern: while homonymous morphs are to be expected, a morph which fails to have the expected meaning (or any meaning) in a particular environment would be worrying. However, we are not dealing with morphs because we are not left with recurrent meaningful units when the *gl-* is removed. In such cases, there seems to be no problem with the words in the first column of the data – words such as *glad* are simply unanalysable in these terms. Whether there is a problem with the words in the second column is a matter of opinion. We need to ask how phonaesthemes work. If we take it that they are effects associated with words (either word-forms or lexemes), we have to recognise that the meaning of the whole word is available to allow the strengthening of the 'light' or the 'unpleasant' meaning in association with the initial *gl-* (interestingly, *gloom* and *gloaming* might be argued to have both meanings). What we are seeing here is perhaps not so much a meaning, as a cross-reference to other words with similar meanings. This has been termed a **resonance**. If that is all that is involved, the apparent clash between a 'light' *gl-* and an 'unpleasant' *gl-* is no clash at all but simply a cross reference to a different set of words.

4. No. Linguistics is attempting to be scientific but it is a young science. Furthermore, while gravity works according to the same principles in every country, different languages provide different problems for analysing words into constituent parts. It might be argued to be the lack of homogeneity in the material to be analysed which causes the major problems, not the scientific method.

Chapter 8

1. There is a process of voicing agreement: the initial affricate of the affix agrees in voicing with the previous sound.

2. Following a velar nasal, the diminutive has the form /kjə/ and following a bilabial nasal it has the form /pjə/. Following a dental/alveolar nasal we, thus, expect /tjə/, although what we find is /cə/. Following an obstruent, we seem to get just /jə/. We can explain all of this if we make two assumptions. First, let us assume that /tjə/ ends up being pronounced /cə/ (this makes phonetic sense: an alveolar plosive and a palatal approximant merge as a palatal plosive). Second, let us assume that the basic form of the diminutive suffix is -[plosive]jə, with the form with no plosive derived by a sandhi rule. We can now take this further. The underlying plosive must be /t/ because this is what occurs after non-nasal sonorants (including vowels), where its form is not determined by the previous segment. Following any obstruent, the plosive is deleted. And following a nasal, the plosive assimilates to the place of articulation of the nasal. This will give us the surface forms we find attested from an underlying form /tjə/; but note how complex the sandhi rules are.

3. Since I cannot predict what your informants or research will turn up, I can only guess at the results. I would expect some degree of correlation between the various criteria but by no means a perfect correlation. In any case, I would expect variation in both stress and spelling for several of the items given. The other criteria may correlate more with degree of lexicalisation than with factors such as stress or spelling.

4. You will probably be able to find four-element compounds (such as *corporate employee relations officer* or *labour market policy regime*) without too much difficulty and may find five-element compounds. Longer ones are rare. Nevertheless, there is nothing inherently ungrammatical with a compound such as the attested *New Zealand police centennial trust lottery prize details*. However, the situations in which such detailed compounds arise are rare, so the compounds tend not to recur and, thus, cannot become established, which is unlike what happens with most lexemes. This explains the feeling but is arguably simply a matter of performance, not competence, and, thus, not something the linguist should be overly worried by.

5. See the work mentioned in the further reading section for discussion of this topic.

6. This is an open question, with no intended presuppositions as to what you will decide or why. Factors such as the relative productivity of synthetic and root compounds may provide relevant data. There is also the possibility that you would want to draw the borderline

between morphology and syntax somewhere else in the middle of what is here termed 'compounding' – this would be a solution which receives a great deal of support from grammars of English.

7. As well as adding links to the chart, you could look at adding weightings to the links already there. In either case, it seems likely that the core will remain very much where it is, while you might need to rearrange the periphery to a certain extent .

Chapter 9

1. Although not all the criteria provided in the chapter are necessarily relevant, you should look at them all and remember that any single criterion may give you misleading results, but that the weight of the criteria should allow you to decide. In this case, we have different meanings ('full of awe' and so on but not *'full of cup', and so on), different functions (*awful* is an adjective, *cupful* is a noun), the same base category (although the words in Column A have abstract nouns, while those in Column B have concrete nouns), different restrictions on the base (in the types of noun each may be added to), the same range of allomorphs, different potentiation of subsequent affixation (we can add *-ly* and *-ness* to words in Column A, but not to those in Column B) and different productivity (the form in Column B is still productive [available], that in Column A is probably not; the form in Column A is more widely generalised in established words). Together, these give a fairly clear picture of difference. Not all cases will be so clear cut.

2. This is, precisely, a less clear-cut case. It is probably easier to argue for an analysis where the two morphemes are distinct, on the basis that they mean different things (that in Column B means 'able to be VERBed' but the same analysis cannot be given for the words in Column A), they have different categories of base (noun in Column A, verb in Column B; note that some words in either column might be ambiguous, but the pattern in each column demands this analysis), they potentiate different subsequent affixation (only in Column B can we add *-ity* consistently) and they show different levels of productivity (the form in Column A is probably not available and shows very restricted generalisation; that in Column B is available and widely generalised). An argument for the same morpheme would have to build on the fact that the function of both is the same (both form adjectives), they have the same range of allomorphs (although this is dubious if those in Column B allow subsequent *-ity*

suffixation since, when -*ity* is added, the -*able* changes from /əbl/ into /ə'bɪl/) and then we would probably have to try to argue either that the meanings of the two are underlyingly the same or that there are no restrictions on the base in either case. My analysis would be that the arguments in favour of the two morpheme solution are weightier – but that is not what the question asked.

3. (a) *Dis* is a morph in *distress* only if *distress* means 'remove the tresses from'. It does not mean that so there is no analysis into morphs. There is phonological resonance only. (b) Although the form *com* can sometimes be a prefix, it does not appear to be one here. There is no meaning of 'promise' in *compromise* so there is no analysis into morphs. Note that there is not even a great deal of phonological resonance between /'kɒmprəmaɪz/ and /'prɒmɪs/ the resonance is orthographic – a type which was only briefly alluded to in the chapter. (c) Your answer here will depend upon whether you can use the word *profess* in a sentences like *She professes her subject at Oxford*. Since most young people do not know this meaning of *profess*, you would probably want to say that there is no common morph but etymological resonance. (d) *His* is not a morph in *history* (there is no meaning of *his* or of *tory* in the word *history*). Various feminist groups reanalysed this word in a kind of folk etymology and rewrote it as *herstory* in order to shock but it shocks, partly at least, because it breaks the rules of morphological analysis. The resonance is again mainly orthographic. (e) *Parson* is a morph in *parsonage*, compare *hermitage*, *orphanage* and *vicarage* (but not *blockage*, *espionage*, *plumage* or *slippage* and similar words, where -*age* has a different pronunciation or a different meaning). (f) *Tele* is a morph in *telekinesis* but you need to take care in finding parallels: *telegraph*, *telephone* and *television* are suitable parallels but not *teleconference*, *telegenic* or *telemarketing* where *tele* is a clipping of *television* or *telephone*.

4. *Preamble* is morphologically analysable into *pre·amble*, provided that the *amble* can be interpreted figuratively. Compare *preconception*, *predisposition*, *preexistence* and *amble* as a potentially free morph. *Prejudge* can also be analysed morphologically as *pre·judge*; compare *preconceive*, *predetermine*, *prepay* and *judge*, *judgement(al)*. *Prelude* can probably be analysed only etymologically, not morphologically. There is phonological resonance from the initial /pr/ with the rest of the words listed. *Pressure* can be analysed morphologically as *press·ure*, although this is no longer as semantically clear as it presumably once was. Compare *exposure*, *sculpture*, *seizure* and *press*, *impressive*, *pressing*.

5. The question was deliberately formulated to ask about your opinion because different people are likely to have different ideas of which of these pairs should be related (with proponents of seeing *germ* and *cognate* or *right* and *rectitude* as morphologically related likely to be adherents of an extreme abstract position). It is possible that individuals might reject all of these pairs, though that, too, would be a fairly extreme position. Lack of agreement is a major problem and I would not expect you to be able to provide a set of criteria to distinguish those which are included from those which are excluded. In principle, that would be possible.

6. Ideally, we would like to find reasons why particular formal elements are or are not morphs which are independent of individual speakers. We have seen how difficult that is. In realist terms, it makes sense to look at the information available to individual speakers and this might well lead us to Marchand's position. My impression is that this would not be a widely-held theoretical position today.

Chapter 10

1. *Absenteeism* presents no information. *Agnosticism* undergoes velar softening ($/k/ \rightarrow /s/$), which implies that *-ism* is on Stratum I. *Alcoholism* shows stress not affected by the affix, which implies that it is on Stratum II. *Baptism* appears to show *-ism* attached to an obligatorily bound base, which implies that it belongs to Stratum I, but it might be substituting for other affixes (*-ist, -ise*) and not be a crucial case. *Utilitarianism* appears to show *-ism* being stress neutral and so belonging to Stratum II. *Creationism* presents no information. *Reporterism* shows *-ism* outside Stratum II suffix *-er* and is, thus, evidence that it is itself on Stratum II. *Symbolism* presents no information. You might conclude that *-ism* belongs to two different strata or you might demand to know which type of behaviour is typical of this suffix overall before drawing a conclusion.

2. It is not a kind of T but a kind of model and we would thus expect *model* to be the head and to be on the right. Interestingly, Danish and Dutch – both of which work very like English in respect of headedness – appear to say *T-Model* rather than *Model-T* (but so, according to a brief search of the World Wide Web, do some speakers of English).

3. Some of the categories are open, some are not. Certainly many of the examples are easily explained away, particularly those involving

irregular morphology. Irregular morphology, more or less by definition, cannot be produced by rule but must be learned and, therefore, must be in the lexicon anyway. Thus, we can argue that irregular morphology is available before non-neutral (Stratum I) morphology applies, whether the categories involved are inflectional or derivational. The regularity of finding plurality inside compounding can be seen as an argument for not distinguishing these two strata in an English morphology – although that would not explain why it is only plural that is regularly found in this position and not other inflectional categories. To answer that, we would have to consider the types of inflection (inherent or contextual) which appear inside derivation and compounding.

4. While some of these should be soluble with a little thought, *bepatched, enlightenment* and *unhappier* contain traps. There is no verb *bepatch* from which *bepatched* could have come, so that any binary tree is going to have to be based on expectations of apparently similar constructions (on, in effect, an over-generating morphology). *Bepatched* may illustrate a rare circumfix in modern English. *Enlightenment* contains the same *en-...-en* problem that was discussed in the text. Again, we might like to consider this a circumfix but we cannot put circumfixes in our trees. *Unhappier* means 'more unhappy' and so we would expect the comparative *-er* to be added to *unhappy*. But the comparative *-er* affix can only be added to monosyllabic or disyllabic adjectives, which implies that it must be added to *happy*, with *un-* added later. This is known as a **bracketing paradox**: there is no way out in terms of such trees.

5. So what would you conclude?

Chapter 11

1. The necessity for extra rules was hinted at in the text. I hope the rules work; they are supposed to.

2. You would almost certainly have to retain some of the rule-ordering as provided for by the Elsewhere Principle. Traditional grammars attempt to give statements of rules which are otherwise not ordered. They do this by giving names to the various stages in the derivation, so that they say things like 'add <n> to the end of the plural as long as the plural does not end in <n> or <s> to form the dative plural'. We can argue as to whether there is implicit rule ordering in this or whether it is a separate convention.

3. One answer is that it is impossible but a better answer is probably that you have to do things which are counter-intuitive. For example, the empty morph -e- will almost certainly have to be fastened onto some adjacent morph and treated as a new allomorph of that morph, or it might be necessary to set up morphemes like {3rd person plural conditional} – things which, it must be said, are virtually never found in the literature!

4. The process is known as **metathesis**. Since this happens, it is to be hoped that any WP notation system can cope. Yet, at the same time, it looks as though some transformational notation is required. This would be something like '$/X/ = /C^1C^2VY/ \rightarrow /C^1VC^2Y/$'. If this is allowed, it extends the power of the notation system even further, since such a notation would allow you to move any segment to, say, the antepenultimate place in the word-form – something which never happens, as far as I know.

Chapter 12

1. You have not been given enough information to know precisely how you would copy two moras, but we must assume that each mora takes with it a (C)V slot for the skeleton, where the C may or may not be filled. The skeleton has to be copied to the right, instead of to the left, and must be associated with the melodic tier from right to left, instead of from left to right. Will this be a general principle, or will it have to be stipulated?

2. It would seem that the constraint disallows the reorganisation of material within a morph. This would mean that it disallows metathesis. But metathesis occurs as a morphological process. In order to overcome this problem, metathesis also has to be analysed as being on two tiers, as illustrated schematically in (a). If we can do this, then the constraint against crossing of association lines seems to say that metathesis cannot occur unless it has morphological value. However, historically, this is false: Modern English *bird* is from Old English *brid*, for example.

(a)

```
        u                    u
        |                    |
      CVCC                 CCVC
      |//                  \\|
      VWX                  VWX
```

3. Choosing a base in these formations is not simple. I will argue that the right-hand element is the base and that the reduplicant is on the left. There are three pieces of evidence: (a) the usual rule in English for complex words is that the right-hand element is the head (see section 10.5), so it is consistent if the right-hand element is the head here, too; (b) if the right-hand element is the base, we need only specify one vowel in the reduplicant, namely /ɪ/ (if the left-hand element were the base, we should have to specify how we knew when we were going to get /æ/ and when we were going to get /ɒ/, which does not seem to go by any general rule); (c) in most of the instances where one of the elements is a real word, it is the right-hand element (but there are counter-examples like *fiddlefaddle*). If we accept that argument, then we are going to copy that base out to the left of the base and have a phonological skeleton which is made up either of a phonological foot or of a phonological word (the evidence here is not sufficient to distinguish). However, that pattern is going to have the vowel /ɪ/ preassociated with the stressed vowel position and, thus, the vowel from the base will be unable to associate with that position. This is not necessarily unproblematic (why does the vowel not associate with the next V slot available in the skeleton?) but seems to cover what is required.

4. The -*um*- is still in the right position and the same tableau will account for it. The reduplication (which will have to occur before the attachment of -*um*- will need a constraint of left alignment, will have to have a copy of the first syllable as the reduplicant and will have to have some mechanism for ensuring that the leftmost syllable of the base is reduplicated (another form of alignment). There are no problems of ordering involved here.

5. The first part of this question is relatively straightforward and the answers are below:

acupressure	acupuncture	pressure
advertorial	advert(isement)	editorial
bikeathon	bike	telethon (*possibly* marathon)
biopreneur	biological	entrepreneur
breathalyser	breath	analyser
computeracy	computer	literacy
docudrama	documentary	drama
faction	fact	fiction
glasnostalgia	glasnost	nostalgia

glocal	global	local
instamatic	instant	automatic
Reaganomics	Reagan	economics
Sloane Ranger	Sloane Square	Lone Ranger
slurb	slum	suburb
workaholic	work	alcoholic

I am unable to find any set of rules/constraints to produce these forms but you may be cleverer. In particular, I note the following problems: *computeracy* and *glasnostalgia* are longer than either of their base words; *slurb* could equally well be *sluburb*; I can see no reason why *docudrama* is cut at the point it is. On the other hand, the structures appear far from random and, in most cases, it is possible to see why the switch-over point occurs where it does.

Chapter 13

1. *Thankful* and *fools* both show agglutination; *could* and possibly *them* (if we think of it as third person, plural and non-nominative) and *us* (on a similar analysis) show fusion; all the other words are monomorphemic and show isolation.

2. The fact that negative marking is outermost is not surprising given the notion of generality. We would expect futurity to be more relevant than subject marking and, thus, these two to be ordered the other way round. We saw in the chapter that reflexives may not have a consistent order. Given the ordering in (17), the suffixes all appear in the expected order. We have no way to discuss the interplay between prefixes and suffixes but can only discuss the affixes on each side of the root separately.

3. They actually occur in the order given in the question, though you may not have predicted that for the verbal suffixes. In particular, I do not think that you would have predicted directionality to be so close to the root, nor negation (though negation is closer to the root than we might expect on the basis of its generality in quite a number of languages).

4. The number of forms in the paradigm for the marked category (the plural) does not exceed the number of forms for the unmarked category (the singular).

5. IA: For any verb we have (illustrated) two stems and three suffixes. Stem 1 ends in *-i*, is the default stem and may occur with no suffix,

giving the future tense. When *-nyi* is suffixed to Stem 1, we have the past punctual and, when *-na* is suffixed to Stem 1, we have the past continuous. When *-n* is suffixed to Stem 2 (which ends in *-a*), we have the present. IP: Take a verb stem ending in *-i*. For the future, use the stem alone; for the past punctual, suffix *-nyi* to the stem; for the past continuous, suffix *-na* to the stem; for the present, change the final *-i* of the stem to an *-a* and then suffix *-n*. The oddity with the data is that the future, rather than the expected present, seems to be the unmarked tense.

6. Bybee's categories are meaning-based, so meaning should be important in the ordering of inflection and derivation and in determining which is which. Category-change is likely to be more relevant than many other things and is, thus, likely to be derivational. The regularity of meaning of inflectional affixes correlates with their generality (although we might want to argue that there are other important factors here, such as lexicalisation). The productiveness of inflection is also linked to the generality of the relevant morphemes. The relative ordering of derivational and inflectional is to do with relevance. The replacement, by monomorphemic forms, can be seen, in part, as being the result of the fact that derivational morphology is at the lexical end of Bybee's cline of processes (though, again, this may not be enough on its own to explain the phenomenon). I see no particular reason why inflection, rather than derivation, should have a closed set of categories, although we might try to argue that there are fewer things of sufficient generality to act as inflections than there are things of great relevance. Inflection is defined by Bybee as being at the syntactic end of the cline, so the idea that inflection is more syntactic than derivation follows from that. While other things may be important, Bybee's notions of relevance and generality can be seen as being fundamental to the distinction between inflection and derivation. Note that I have made no reference here to inherent and contextual inflection. We would expect inherent inflection to be intermediate in relevance and generality; the notions still seem to be applicable.

Chapter 14

1. No comment is given here because your results cannot be predicted. But attempting the exercise should make you think about marked and unmarked.

2. My impression is that the over-representation of diminutives in the data is not coincidence but that diminutives provide one of the few areas where the phenomenon is relatively widespread. This can probably be explained semantically. However, as far as I know, augmentatives are less prone to multiple application. If this is true, it may be because augmentatives are the marked member of the diminutive-augmentative pair: they are certainly rarer, seem to have fewer markers and, in most cases (not all), occur in languages which also have diminutives. Alternatively, there could simply be a gap in descriptions at this point.

3. If you think of nouns and verbs, your answer will almost certainly be 'no'. We could argue that the irregular *better* and *best* retain the regular *-er* and *-st* markers of comparative and superlative and this would, then, be an example of stem inflection (as would *worst* but not *worse*). If we analyse the final *-m* in *him* and *them* as a morph, we would have another case of stem inflection but we are much more likely to see these words as instances of fusion. English does arguably show some stem form derivation, in words like *amphibious, economist, phonic*, which have an obligatorily bound base.

4. In principle, we appear to be looking at the same thing and certainly the phonetically clearly related items in Table 1 are phonologically transparent in terms of (1). Again, in principle, we could use (1) to make a far more nuanced approach to phonetic relatedness in Table 1, though it might be difficult to find a similar set of criteria for semantic transparency. Also, it must be recalled that some of the examples in Table 1 are supposed to look as though they might be related in a phonologically transparent way, even though they are not really.

5. Again no comment possible in the abstract.

Chapter 15

2. Those that have changed from regular to irregular have been subject to analogical extension. Those that used to have a different past tense and past participle and now have the two the same have been subject to analogical levelling. The fact that STICK can go in both directions is confusing but probably not relevant: it has ended up with less variation than before. Note that, while a change from *swim, swam, swum* to *swim, swum, swum* is clearly analogical levelling, the same would be true of a change from *swim, swam, swum* to *swim, swam,*

swam. Yet this latter does not happen and probably could not happen. There is more to analogy than meets the eye and this has been the subject of much discussion in the literature. Moreover, given that analogical levelling would be involved in both instances, it is not necessarily clear why we would get *swim, swum, swum* rather than *swim, swimmed, swimmed*. Again, this has been the subject of discussion in the literature.

3. This is partly a matter of phonological erosion – the same loss of unstressed final vowels we have seen before. But it is also partly a matter of analogical spreading, the masculine -*s* transferring to other paradigms. To some extent, the dative plural marker was reinterpreted as just marking the plural. The numerical superiority of masculine nouns is clearly an important factor in the spread of the -*s* marking.

4. In *cafeteria*, we have to think what the base is: we would perhaps think that it is *café* but, for vernacular English speakers, it could have been *caff*. Only if it is the latter do we get a splinter -*eteria* which can go onto be used as a suffix elsewhere. Note that in *sandwicheria* we have left the /t/ behind as well, so that clearly there was no established pattern setting up a particular splinter to be reused. Either it is random or, more likely, it is affected in some way by the phonology of the output, as discussed in 12.5.

5. The question encourages you to speculate and that might be best done in a group. Generally, possible morphological changes, at least within the foreseeable future, should have some precursors in current usage: a loss of -*ing* is very unlikely; a global merger of past tense with past participle forms is more plausible given how often it occurs anyway. Morphology can be borrowed (consider the Yiddish -*nik* in *beatnik, folknik, refusenik*, etc.), so even borrowing from a language which does not usually provide loans is not ruled out. The morphological system has been completely revamped in the past (e.g. with the loss of second person singular inflections, case inflections and so on) and presumably could be again, though not in a random way (we could not drop all mention of first person plurals, for instance). But we could not just add a random first-person singular marker to verbs (say -*m*, matching the -*s* of the third person) or add a 3rd person -*s* to past tenses as well as present tenses. Although many things are possible, not all are.

Chapter 16

1. Not all verbs which rhyme take the same pattern, consider the /rɪŋ/ verbs listed in (2) and cases like *ride, rode, ridden; deride, derided, derided; slide, slid, slid;* and you might not be sure what the principal parts of ABIDE and BIDE are (or if they can be used in all these ways). In any case, you could carry out an experiment to see if it worked. If it were true, you would expect people to think of the past tense of a verb with lots of rhyming partners a lot more quickly than of the past tense of verbs with no or very few rhyming partners. You could then use a computer to measure reaction times between being asked for a past tense and providing it. It appears, for instance, that *balk* has no monosyllabic rhyming verbs in English, while *think* has at least ten (which, incidentally, do not all conjugate according to the same pattern). If you used strings which are not real words, like *menk*, you could even get cases with no real rhyming verbs and so, if the hypothesis were correct, it ought to be impossible to arrive at a past tense for these.

2. It is predictable, though it might be difficult to think of good parallel examples. Consider the following:

(a) The batter will fly out — The batter flied out (baseball: 'hit a fly ball and get out')

He'll only grandstand — He grandstanded ('behave as if showing off for the grandstand')

I'll string the beans — I stringed the beans ('remove the strings from')

The following cases are not quite parallel, since they are homophonous with irregular verbs rather than derived (indirectly) from them:

(b) I brake for horses — I braked for the horse ('applied the brake')

She'll right the boat — She righted the boat ('set it right')

I'll spit the meat. — I spitted the meat ('put on a spit')

Why *string the bow* gives *strung the bow* and not **stringed the bow* is something of a mystery in this context.

3. Whether or not you can think of an alternative explanation, it is good methodology to try: it is not often that a set of facts can be

explained in only one way! In this particular instance, we have an alternative model in the redundancy rules suggested by Jackendoff (1975). Jackendoff suggests that a word like *compete* and a word like *competition* should be linked not by rules of allomorphy as such but simply by a statement in the lexicon that there is a relationship between them. If we extend this, presumably the same could be said of *love* and *loves* (which are separate outputs of the lexicon according to the Full Entry Hypothesis – see section 10.3). Within such a model, we could have words resonating with each other in such a way as to provoke priming without any morpheme notion as such. Whether this would be significantly different from having overt morphemes is a separate point, which you might like to consider. Another alternative explanation would be that there is phonological/orthographic overlap, and that this is sufficient to cause the effects that have been noted, although the discussion in the text discounted this possibility.

4. If the verbs that have changed have been the rarest verbs, it does. You were given no information about that in the question, so you might have to speculate here or use information from other sources. Certainly, if we consider a verb like CLEAVE, the Morphological Race Model would predict that it is likely to become regular (as we have seen it has); but the same model is not obviously of great help in explaining the change of HELP from an irregular to a regular verb. An interesting assignment would be to consider the relative frequency of some verbs which have changed and some verbs which have remained irregular. What would provide a suitable data base? How do we deal with verbs which have gone from regular to irregular?

5. Whatever you find, do not conclude too much on the basis of one description of one language. If similar conclusions arise from a range of languages (and range of descriptions), you might start to feel more secure about any conclusions. The question about the fairness of the description was added to make you evaluate your data: some grammars are not very helpful with the kinds of information you happen to be looking for at any given time and you need to be able to consider the impact of that on your conclusions.

6. Part of the problem with blends is deciding how much of the first word is left in the blend: in *slanguage* is there only an *s* or is there all of *slang*? If you look at words where the two pieces abut rather than overlap as they do in *slanguage*, it seems that recognition point is not always a useful notion, although it seems a priori as though it might be a relevant consideration.

APPENDIX C: GLOSSARY

ACRONYM An acronym is a pronounceable word coined from the initial letters of the words in a name, title or phrase. An example is *TESOL* from *Teaching English as a Second or other Language* – /tiːsɒl/.

AFFIX An affix is an obligatorily bound morph which does not realise (see realisation) a lexeme. Affixes, thus, have to make reference to some other morpheme or class of morphemes in any statement of their distribution. In the French word *recherchions* 'we were looking for', the root which can realise the lexeme CHERCHER is -*cherch*- and *re*-, -*i*- and -*ons* are affixes. The commonest types of affix are prefixes, suffixes and infixes, although circumfixes, interfixes and transfixes are also mentioned by some authorities.

AGGLUTINATIVE or **AGGLUTINATING** An agglutinative language is one in which there are a number of obligatorily bound morphs, each of which realises a single morpheme. That is, there is a one-to-one correspondence between morph and morpheme in such languages. This implies that, ideally, there are no allomorphs in such languages, though the ideal is seldom met. Languages usually cited as examples of agglutinative languages are Turkish and Swahili.

ALLOMORPH An allomorph is a conditioned (see conditioning) morph. It is a conditioned realisation of a morpheme. In English the forms /t/, /d/ and /ɪd/ are phonetically conditioned allomorphs of the {-ed} past tense morpheme, determined by the final sound in the stem to which they are added. In English the use of -*ren* as the plural marker in *children* (along with a vowel change) is determined by the individual lexeme CHILD.

A-MORPHOUS MORPHOLOGY See **WORD-AND-PARADIGM.**

ANALYSABILITY A word is analysable if the linguist can perceive in it some regular correlations between meaning and form and segment the word accordingly. These correlations may or may not be perceived by the native speaker and may or may not be widely generalised or particularly productive. For example, the linguist can analyse the -*th* in *dearth* and see it as a recurrence of the same unit that occurs in *length* and *warmth*, even though most native speakers are not aware of this, although there are not many words which use this element and although it is no longer productive.

ANALYTIC See **ISOLATING.**

AVAILABILITY See under **PRODUCTIVITY.**

BACKFORMATION Backformation is the formation of words by the deletion of actual or supposed affixes in longer words. For example, the French word for 'cherry' is *cerise* which was originally borrowed into English with the final /z/ This was, however, perceived as a plural marker in English, with the result that *cherry* was created by backformation. A similar history is attached to English *pea* from an earlier *pease*.

BAHUVRIHI COMPOUND See under **COMPOUNDING**.

BASE A base is any item to which affixes may be added. Roots and stems are special types of base. A base is sometimes termed an **operand**.

BINYAN A binyan (plural, *binyanim*) is a verbal paradigm in a Semitic language, involving root-and-pattern morphology.

BLEND A blend is a new lexeme formed from parts of two or more other lexemes. There is no requirement that the blend should be made up of meaningful parts of the original lexemes, and the original lexemes are frequently unrecognisable in the blend. Examples are *stagflation* from *stagnation* and *inflation*, *smog* from *smoke* and *fog* and *tritical* from *trite* and *critical*. Blends are also called **portmanteau words**.

BLOCKING Blocking refers to the failure of a particular lexeme to become institutionalised because of the existence of a synonymous (or, occasionally, homonymous) lexeme in general use. For example, the lexeme STEALER is not in general use because of the generally used THIEF, which has the same meaning. From the verb to SUE we do not find a derivative SUER because it would be homophonous with SEWER.

For some authorities, blocking applies only to lexemes derived from the same root, so that the example with THIEF would not be a case of blocking, but the use of TYPIST rather than TYPER would be. This is not the definition that has been adopted in this book.

Some authorities refer to blocking as **pre–emption**.

BOUND MORPH See **OBLIGATORILY BOUND MORPH**.

BRACKETING PARADOX A bracketing paradox arises when different kinds of information lead the analyst to different conclusions about the structure of a word. For example, consider the term *particle physicist*. The fact that this word ends in *-ist* seems to be something determined by its base (contrast *physician* with a different meaning and **physic·er*), so that we would expect the bracketing [[*particle*] [*physic·ist*]]; however, it means 'a person who deals with particle physics', which implies the structure [[*particle physic*] *ist*]. These two cannot both be simultaneously correct, hence the paradox.

CIRCUMFIX A circumfix is a discontinuous affix which surrounds the base with which it occurs. In German the past participle is marked by the circumfix *ge···t* in a word like *ge·mach·t* 'made'.

CITATION FORM See under **LEXEME**.

CLIPPING Clipping is the process of shortening a word without changing its meaning or its part of speech, though frequently with the effect of making it stylistically less formal. Examples are *jumbo* from *jumbo jet* and *polio* from *poliomyelitis*.

CLITIC A clitic is an obligatorily bound morph which is intermediate between an affix and a word. Clitics in English include the italicised sequences in the following examples:

He'*ll* be here in a moment.

She'*s* done it already.

The President of France'*s* beliefs.

Clitics are divided into **proclitics**, which are attached before their bases, and **enclitics**, which are attached after their bases. They are also divided into **simple clitics**, which are phonetically abbreviated versions of ordinary words (as in the first two examples above), and **special clitics** which are not derived from full words (almost certainly true of the last example above).

COLLOCATION A collocation is a habitual co-occurrence of two or more items, which may be syntactic (as in *dry wine* or *turn left*) or morphological (as in *bishop·ric, road works*).

COMPLEMENTARY DISTRIBUTION See under **DISTRIBUTION**.

COMPOSITION See **COMPOUNDING**.

COMPOUNDING Compounding is the formation of new lexemes by adjoining two or more lexemes. For example, the lexeme HOUSEBOAT is a lexeme in which we can distinguish two other lexemes, HOUSE and BOAT. The lexeme HOUSEBOAT is called a 'compound lexeme' or simply a 'compound'. There are three main sub-types of compound. **Endocentric compounds** are those where the compound denotes a hyponym of the head element in the compound. A houseboat is a type of boat, so HOUSEBOAT is an endocentric compound of English. The second type are called **exocentric compounds**. These do not denote a hyponym of the head element of the compound but denote some feature of the entity which is denoted by the compound. A redskin is so called because of his red skin, but the lexeme REDSKIN does not denote a type of skin, but a type of person who has a red skin (it may, of course, also denote a potato). REDSKIN is an exocentric compound. Exocentric compounds are also called **possessive compounds** or by the Sanskrit name **bahuvrihi compound**. The third type of compound is the **dvandva compound**. A dvandva compound denotes an entity made up of the various parts listed in the form. For example, Alsace-Lorraine is made up of the former provinces of Alsace and Lorraine. The dvandva compound ALSACE-LORRAINE lists the parts of the region which it denotes. Dvandvas are also called **copulative compounds**.

Some linguists call compounding **composition**.

CONDITIONING A conditioning factor is one that determines which of a number of allomorphs will be found in a particular word-form. The allomorphs in question are said to be 'conditioned' by that factor. The three kinds of conditioning are phonetic, grammatical and lexical conditioning. Phonetic conditioning is when the choice of allomorph is determined by the phonetic environment in which it occurs; lexical conditioning is when the choice of allomorph is determined by the lexeme involved; grammatical conditioning is when the choice of allomorph is determined by some grammatical factor. In English the choice of /d/ or /t/ or /ɪd/ to mark the past tense is determined by the final sound in the stem. If that final sound is /t/ or /d/, /ɪd/ is used to mark the past tense (*wanted, moulded*). If it is not /t/ but it is still voiceless, then /t/ is used (*pushed, walked*). And if it is not /d/ but it is still voiced, /d/ is used (*hummed, loved, sagged, played*). The choice of the plural marker in the word *children* is determined by the lexeme CHILD: while other words may have -*en* plurals, no other word in English has a -*ren* plural. This type of conditioning is thus lexical conditioning. Grammatical conditioning occurs when the various allomorphs of a morpheme are determined by some grammatical (especially morphological) factor, such as gender, conjugation or declension, or the presence of a particular type of affix. For example, in Latin the ablative plural is marked by -*iːs* on first and second declension nouns, and by -(*i*)*bus* on other declension nouns. This distinction is grammatically conditioned.

Phonetic conditioning is called **phonological conditioning** by some authorities.

CONSTRUCTIONAL ICONICITY This is the principle from natural morphology that a greater amount of meaning will normally be represented by a greater amount of form. This is also referred to as **diagrammaticity**.

CONTEXTUAL INFLECTION See **INFLECTION**.

CONVERSION Conversion is the change in the part of speech of a form without any overt affix marking the change. The various types of *up* in the examples below can be seen to be related by conversion:

Robin climbed *up* the hill.
We'll have to *up* all the prices again.
Lee caught the *up* train at 2:30.
Things are on the *up* and up.
We all have our *ups* and downs.
I've only just got *up*.

Conversion is sometimes termed **functional shift** or **zero derivation** though some writers distinguish between these various terms.

COPULATIVE COMPOUND See under **COMPOUNDING**.

CRANBERRY MORPH See **UNIQUE MORPH**.

CUMULATION Cumulation is the realisation of several morphemes in a single morph. Cumulation thus refers to the type of realisation that is found in a portmanteau morph.

DEFAULT A default is the member of a morphome which applies if there are no particular circumstances which will call forth one of the alternatives. The default way of marking something need not be the most frequent method of marking it, although it will always be a productive way of marking it. For example, in German, the default marking for plural on nouns is *-s*, even though this marker is quite rare in texts; but nouns which do not obviously belong to one of the established paradigms take the *-s* plural.

DERIVATION Derivation is one of the main branches of morphology, the other being inflection. Derivation is the process of adding affixes which: (a) create new lexemes; (b) may change the part of speech of the base to which they are added; (c) may not have a regular meaning; (d) may not be fully productive and are not fully generalised. The English prefix be- can be found added to nouns in words like *bedew, beguile, benight, bewitch*, etc. This prefix creates new lexemes (BEDEW etc. from DEW etc.), it changes a noun into a verb, it does not have a regular meaning (in BEDEW be- means 'cover with', in BEGUILE 'influence by', in BENIGHT 'leave to be overtaken by' and in BEWITCH 'to affect as might a'), and it is not found added to all nouns, so that **berain, *becunning, *beday, *bewizard*, etc. are not usual, or even probable, words of English.

DIAGRAMMATICITY See **CONSTRUCTIONAL ICONICITY**.

DISCONTINUOUS MORPH A discontinuous morph is a morph which is interrupted by some other material. The most obvious discontinuous morphs are circumfixes and transfixes. It can be argued that the perfect in English is marked by the discontinuous realisation HAVE + past participle, that is, the italicised sequence in: I *have* seen it.

DISTRIBUTION The distribution of any unit is the sum of the contexts in which it can occur. For example, the suffix -*s* which marks the third person singular of the present tense in English can occur on the end of any non-modal verb in English (with a very few exceptions, such as *quoth*, which can easily be listed). This is thus the distribution of that element.

If two elements never occur in the same contexts but, instead, divide up some set of contexts between them, they are said to be in **complementary distribution**. For example, the -*s* suffix mentioned above is pronounced /s/ after voiceless obstruents, which are not sibilants, and /z/ after all other non-sibilant sounds:

Pronounced /s/	*Pronounced /z/*
ask·s	add·s
bath·s (*v*)	breathe·s
depart·s	come·s
laugh·s	call·s
stop·s	leave·s
	moo·s

These two forms are, thus, in complementary distribution and are, in fact, allomorphs of the same morpheme.

DVANDVA COMPOUND See under **COMPOUNDING**.

ELSEWHERE PRINCIPLE The Elsewhere Principle is a general principle which controls the ordering of grammatical rules. Basically, it says that, if there are two rules which could apply to the same form with the same effect, the more specific rule is applied first and the less specific is applied only if the more specific one has not applied. It is a principle which builds defaults into grammars.

EMPTY MORPH An empty morph is a recurrent form in a language that does not appear to be related to any element of meaning.

ENCLITIC See under **CLITIC**.

ENDOCENTRIC COMPOUND See under **COMPOUNDING**.

ESTABLISHED A word is said to be established to the extent that it is in general usage in the speech community. Words which are established will generally be found listed in the major dictionaries for those languages with a lexicographic tradition. A word may be established whether it is institutionalised (see institutionalisation) or lexicalised (see lexicalisation).

EXOCENTRIC COMPOUND See under **COMPOUNDING**.

EXPONENCE Exponence is the term used in word-and-paradigm morphology for realisation. It is used in particular where a single morphological property is realised by a number of separate morphs or where a number of morphological properties are realised in a single morph. The morphs are termed the **exponents** of the properties.

FEATURE PERCOLATION Feature percolation is the term given to a variety of systems designed to ensure that a feature marked on the head of a construction is also marked on the construction as a whole.

FLECTIONAL See **FUSIONAL**.

FOLK ETYMOLOGY Folk etymology is the morphological reanalysis of a word in such a way as to give it morphological structure where either there was none etymologically or where the etymological structure was different. In the first case, we have examples like *woodchuck*, possibly from Cree *otcheck*, and nothing to do with wood or throwing; in the second case, we have examples like *hamburger* which is etymologically related to *Hamburg* and has nothing to do with *ham*.

Folk etymology is also termed **popular etymology** or included as a case of reanalysis.

FORM A form is any unit which has phonological or orthographic shape.

FORMATIVE In this book, the term formative is used to refer to a recurrent element of form which correlates with derivational behaviour in some way and yet cannot be identified with a morph.

This is, however, an untraditional use and, in many works, it is used as equivalent to morph or even to morpheme. Also, what is here termed a formative is termed a morpheme by some scholars.

FREE MORPH See **POTENTIALLY FREE MORPH**.

FUNCTIONAL SHIFT See **CONVERSION**.

FUSIONAL A fusional language is one that features obligatorily bound morphs which show no one-to-one correspondence between morph and morpheme. That is, either a morpheme may have several allomorphs or there may be complex exponence relations holding between morph and morpheme, with a number of empty morphs and portmanteau morphs, as in the following example from Italian:

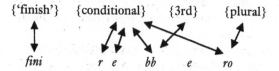

Fusional languages are also termed **flectional**, **inflective** and **inflectional** by different scholars.

GENERALISED See under **PRODUCTIVE.**

GRAMMATICAL WORD A grammatical word is a word defined by its place in a particular paradigm. For example, the word-form *is* in the last sentence represents 'the third person singular present tense indicative of BE'. The grammatical word realised by *is* is in the paradigm of the verb BE, in a position in that paradigm delimited by the various properties that have been associated with it. To name the grammatical word we have to name the lexeme and all the inflectional (see inflection) morphemes which are realised in the word-form. Note that a single word-form may represent two different grammatical words. So in

My sheep eats grass.

sheep is 'the singular of SHEEP', as can be seen by the form of the verb *eats*. (Another formulation such as 'SHEEP, singular' would be perfectly correct, as long as it covered the same information.) In

My sheep eat grass.

on the other hand, *sheep* is 'the plural of SHEEP'. Conversely, the grammatical word 'the past tense of BURN' may be either of the word-forms *burnt* or *burned*:

The books burnt quickly.

The books burned quickly.

Grammatical words are called **morphosyntactic words** by some authorities.

GRAMMATICALISATION Grammaticalisation is the process whereby linguistic material which is either lexical or pragmatic in nature becomes built in to the grammatical structure of a language. A typical instance of grammaticalisation would be the genesis of affixes indicating futurity in lexemes indicating volition or movement towards something.

Grammaticalisation is also termed **grammaticisation.**

HAPAX LEGOMENON A hapax legomenon (sometimes just called a **hapax**) is a word which occurs once only in a particular text or corpus of texts.

HEAD In a compound (see compounding) the head element is the element which: (a) determines the gender and declension/conjugation class of the whole compound; (b) carries the inflectional endings which apply to the whole compound; (c) denotes a superordinate of the whole compound. In the German *Haus·frau* 'housewife', the whole compound is feminine, like *Frau* and unlike *Haus*, and belongs to the same declension class as *Frau*. If housewives are discussed in the plural, the plural marker is added to *Frau* and not to *Haus*. And *Frau* 'woman' is a superordinate of *Hausfrau. Frau* is thus the head element.

In English the head element is almost always the right-hand element in a compound.

In derivatives the means of determining a head is currently a matter of dispute but usually it is taken that the head is the derivational suffix, following (a) and (b) above. It is less clear whether the notion extends to inflectional affixes, though it is often assumed to do so.

INCORPORATION Incorporation is usually considered to be a special kind of compounding whereby a new verb is created by forming a compound from an existing verb and a possible argument of that verb (usually its direct object). For example, in Nahuatl, a Mexican language, there is a distinction between

ni·c·qua in nacatl

I·it·eat the flesh

'I eat the meat', 'I am eating meat'

and the version with incorporation

ni·nica·qua

I·flesh·eat

'I eat meat', 'I am carnivorous'

While English does not show incorporation of this type, the flavour of it is caught in English constructions such as *house-painting, skin-diving, gun-running*.

INFIX An infix is an affix which is attached inside its base. In Latin *rumpo* 'I break' the *-m-* is an infix which does not occur in all verb forms: contrast *ruptus* 'broken'. The use of an infix always leads to the base being discontinuous. Infixes are usually inserted at some definite point in the base, such as after the first consonant or before the final syllable.

INFIXATION Infixation is the use of infixes, or the production of words using infixes.

INFLECTION Inflection is one of the main branches of morphology, the other being derivation. Inflection is the process of adding affixes which typically (a) create word-forms of an already known lexeme, not new lexemes; (b) do not change the part of speech of the base to which they are added; (c) have a regular meaning; (d) are fully productive and extremely highly generalised. The *-(e)st* ending in German which marks the 2nd person singular of verbs, for example, *machst* 'you make', *siehst* 'you see', *findest* 'you find', creates word forms of the lexemes (MACHEN, SIEHEN, FINDEN), does not change the part of speech from a verb, has a regular meaning

'2nd person singular', can be added to any verb to provide the 2nd person singular and so is fully productive.

A distinction is sometimes drawn between **inherent** and **contextual** inflection, where inherent inflection is determined by what the message is about (singular versus plural, present versus past and so on) but contextual inflection is determined by the requirements of the sentence structure (case, person agreement, gender agreement and so on).

INFLECTIONAL See **FUSIONAL**.

INFLECTIVE See **FUSIONAL**.

INHERENT INFLECTION See **INFLECTION**.

INSTITUTIONALISATION A word is said to be institutionalised if it is created by a productive morphological process and is in general use in the speech community. Institutionalisation is, thus, opposed to lexicalisation, although both create established words.

INTERFIX An interfix is an affix which occurs between two bases. The -o- that occurs in words like *anthropology*, *biology*, *biometry*, *galvanometry*, *mythology*, *typology* may be an interfix in English.

ISOLATING An isolating language is one in which most word-forms are made up of a single morph or, correspondingly, that only one morpheme is realised in the realisation of any lexeme. That is, there are no obligatorily bound morphs in the ideal isolating language. Chinese and Vietnamese are the examples of isolating languages usually cited.

Some sources use the term **analytic** with the same meaning.

LEVEL-ORDERING See **STRATAL THEORY OF MORPHOLOGY**.

LEXEME A lexeme is a dictionary word, an abstract unit of vocabulary. It is realised (see realisation) by word-forms, in such a way that the word-form represents the lexeme and any inflectional endings (see inflection) that are required. For example, *small*, *smaller*, *smallest* are all word-forms which can realise the lexeme SMALL under appropriate circumstances. While *small* only contains the lexeme SMALL, *smaller* contains the lexeme SMALL and an affix realising the morpheme {comparative}, this being an inflectional ending. Similarly, *knife*, *knives* are both word-forms which can realise the lexeme KNIFE. In writing, lexemes are generally distinguished by the use of capital letters, but this notation is not used by all linguists.

The **citation form** of a lexeme is that word-form belonging to the lexeme which is conventionally chosen to name the lexeme in dictionaries and the like. In English, the citation form of verbs is the stem (e.g. *love*), in Latin, it is the first person singular of the present tense of the indicative (e.g. *amo*) and, in French, it is the infinitive (e.g. *aimer*).

LEXICAL ITEM A lexical item is any item which is listed in the lexicon (or mental dictionary). This includes not only ordinary lexemes but also phrasal verbs (like *look up, put up with*), idioms (like *cook someone's goose*) and possibly proverbs and familiar quotations (*a stitch in time saves nine, Earth hath not anything to show more fair!*). What all of these have in common is the fact that they must be learned as wholes and their precise make-up is not predictable by rule.

Lexical items are also called **listemes**.

LEXICALISATION A word is lexicalised if it could no longer be produced according to productive rules. For example, the use of the suffix *-th* in words like *warmth* is no longer productive and, so, all such words can be said to be lexicalised. Words may be semantically lexicalised if their meaning is no longer the sum of the meanings of their parts (e.g. the meaning of *high·ness* cannot be predicted from the meanings of *high* plus *-ness*) or phonologically lexicalised if its form cannot be predicted by productive phonological processes (e.g. if *long* were used as a base in current English, it could not become *leng*, as it does in the word *length*). Words can also be lexicalised in other ways.

LISTEME See **LEXICAL ITEM**.

MENTION Language mention is the citation of linguistic forms in utterances. It contrasts with language **use**, which is the use of linguistic forms to produce utterances. In

The word 'the' contains three letters.

there is mention of *the* where it is included in inverted commas but use of the word *the* in the first word in the sentence.

METATHESIS Metathesis is the reversal of two (usually adjacent) sounds in a word. Old English *wæsp* 'wasp' comes from an earlier *wæps*. Occasionally metathesis is used as a way of modifying a word-form in order to carry morphological information.

MORPH A morph is a constituent element of a word-form. It is the realisation of a morpheme (or sometimes of more than one, see portmanteau morph). A word-form such as /ɪn·veərɪ·əbl·z/ contains the four morphs which have been separated out by decimal points.

MORPHEME The term morpheme is used in different ways by different authors and this is discussed in Chapter 7. In this book, morpheme is used for an element which represents a correlation between form and meaning at a level lower than the word. The morpheme is an abstract unit realised (see realisation) by morphs or, if by a number of conditioned items, by allomorphs. In writing, morphemes are enclosed in braces ({ }) to distinguish them from other units. For example, /t/, /d/ and /ɪd/ are phonetically conditioned (see conditioning) allomorphs of the morpheme {-ed} in English. The morph *spa* is the only morph which realises the morpheme {spa}.

Not all authorities use morpheme only in the abstract sense. For some, it is also equivalent to morph. This is particularly true in American writings.

MORPHOLOGICAL CATEGORY A morphological category is a superordinate of a number of morphological properties. That is, it is a general category to which a number of morphemes, which are in parallel distribution, can belong. For instance, the morphemes (or morphological properties) {singular} and {plural} go together to make up the morphological category of Number in most of the modern Germanic and Romance languages.

MORPHOLOGICAL PROPERTY A morphological property is one of the set of possibilities which can realise a morphological category. For instance, the morphological category Tense, in English, can be realised by either of the morphological properties present or past. Although morphological categories and properties are terms within word-and-paradigm morphology, they are nevertheless useful terms to have available in discussion. A morphological property corresponds more or less to a morpheme.

MORPHOLOGY Morphology is the study of the forms of words (etymologically from the Greek *morphe* 'form' and *-ology* 'study': compare the German translation *Formenlehre*). In other words, it is the study of the ways in which lexemes and word-forms are built up from smaller elements and the changes that are made to those smaller elements in the process of building lexemes and word-forms.

MORPHOME A morphome is a family of morphemes which share either their meaning or precisely the same set of formal representations for a different meaning. In English, {-s}, {-en}, {-im} and the morphemes realised by Ablaut, replacing *-us* with *-i*, *-a* with *-ae*, *-um* and *-on* with *-a* (as in MOUSE, ALUMNUS, FORMULA, BACTERIUM, CRITERION respectively) and other ways of marking plurality together form the morphome for plurality. Some would argue that the past participle and the passive participle in English also belong to the same morphome because, even though there are two distinguishable meanings, the form for any verb is always identical.

MORPHOSYNTACTIC WORD See **GRAMMATICAL WORD**.

NEO-CLASSICAL COMPOUNDING Neo-classical compounds are words formed in the modern European languages from elements of the classical languages, in such a way that there is no native root involved. For example, the words *geo·metry*, *pluto·crat* and *theo·sophy* are neo-classical compounds in English. Neo-classical compounding is the process of forming such neo-classical compounds.

NOMINALISATION This word has two meanings. As a countable noun, it can mean the noun derived from a base which could act as either a verb or an adjective. In this sense, we can say that *inducement* and *induction* are two different nominalisations from the verb *induce*. *Generality* is a nominalisation from the adjective *general*.

As an uncountable noun, nominalisation refers to the process of forming such nouns. In this sense, we might say that the nominalisation of *induce* with the suffix -*(t)ion* causes a change of vowel quality.

NOTATION

Braces: braces ({ }) enclose morphemes.

Capitals: capitals are used to mark lexemes.

Decimal point: a decimal point is used to separate morphs when this is useful for an exposition.

Italics: italics (or underlining) mark forms, that is morphs or word-forms. They are also used in this book to mark words.

OBLIGATORILY BOUND MORPH An obligatorily bound morph is a morph which cannot stand on its own as a word-form. An obligatorily bound morph can only form a word-form in combination with some other morph or morphs. In *absolutely*, -*ly* is an obligatorily bound morph since it must be attached to some other morph (in this case *absolute*) to make a word-form. Most sources call obligatorily bound morphs just **bound morphs**. Note that obligatorily bound morphs, like potentially free morphs, are usually identified in terms of their spoken form.

OPERAND See **BASE**.

ORTHOGRAPHIC WORD An orthographic word is a unit which, in print, is bounded by spaces on both sides. For example, the sentence

My sheepdog isn't afraid of being rammed.
1   2   3   4   5 6   7

contains seven orthographic words as indicated. An orthographic word is a word-form in the written language.

PARADIGM A set of forms, corresponding to some subset (defined in terms of a particular morphological category) of the grammatical words from a single lexeme, is termed a paradigm. Paradigms are frequently presented in tabular form, like this paradigm from Latin:

amo:	ama:mus
ama:s	ama:tis
amat	amant

A **paradigmatic relationship** is the relationship between substitutable items within a paradigm. The relationship between -o: and -a:s in the paradigm above is a paradigmatic relationship.

PHONOLOGICAL WORD The phonological word is an equivalent for the spoken language to the orthographic word for the written language. While the orthographic word is a word-form defined in terms of orthographic criteria, the phonological word is a word-form defined in terms of phonological criteria such as stress, vowel harmony and the like.

POLYSYNTHETIC A polysynthetic language is a language with a particularly high concentration of obligatorily bound morphs which bear a high semantic load. For example, in Labrador Inuttut, as well as there being obligatorily bound morphs meaning 'passive', 'intransitive', 'perfect', 'causative' and marking case relations, there are obligatorily bound morphs with meanings such as 'want', 'easy', 'often', 'be able', 'ask' and the like. The languages most often cited as examples of polysynthetic languages are the Eskimo languages.

PORTMANTEAU MORPH A portmanteau morph is a morph which realises (see realisation) more than one morpheme. The morph -a, on the end of the word-form *bella* in the Italian phrase *la mia bella cugina* 'my beautiful (female) cousin', realises both {feminine} (contrast *il mio bello cugino* 'my handsome (male) cousin') and {singular} (contrast *le mie belle cugine* 'my beautiful (female) cousins') and is, thus, a portmanteau morph.

Some scholars retain the term portmanteau morph for those instances where two distinct word-forms are reduced to a single element (e.g. French *au* from *à le*) and talk of cumulation in the instances given above.

PORTMANTEAU WORD See **BLEND**.

POSSESSIVE COMPOUND See under **COMPOUNDING**.

POTENTIALLY FREE MORPH A potentially free morph is a morph which can stand on its own as a word-form. In *absolutely, absolute* is a potentially free morph, since *absolute* is a possible word-form. Most sources call potentially free morphs just **free morphs**. Note that potentially free morphs, like obligatorily bound morphs, are usually identified in terms of their spoken form.

POTENTIATION One morphological process potentiates another if it creates a base suitable for that other process to apply to. For example, the affixation of *-ise* to an adjective such as *general* potentiates *-ing* suffixation, since *generaling* is not a possible word of English but *generalising* is.

PRE-EMPTION See **BLOCKING**.

PREFIX A prefix is an affix which is attached before its base. In *untroubled* there is just one prefix, *un-*.

PREFIXATION Prefixation is the use of prefixes or the production of words using prefixes.

PRIMARY COMPOUND See under **SYNTHETIC COMPOUND**.

PROCLITIC See under **CLITIC**.

PRODUCTIVE A process is said to be productive to the extent that it can be used in the creation of new forms in a language. In morphology, a process can be said to be **generalised** to the extent that its results can be seen in known words. Most authorities use the term 'productive' for both these meanings. For example, the 3rd person singular present tense *-s* on the end of forms like *loves*, *wanders*, *types* is productive: it can be added to any new verb to make the third person singular of the present tense. It is not completely generalised, however, since there are a very few verbs (modals such as *can, may, must, will*, etc. and *beware*) which do not have a 3rd person singular *-s* form.

We may also distinguish between **availability** (whether something can be used in the creation of new forms or not) and **profitability** (how many new words a particular process gives rise to).

An item may show **individual productivity** if a single person uses it productively but this productivity is not shared in the community at large.

PROFITABILITY See under **PRODUCTIVITY**.

PROTOTYPE The prototype of a category has all the features that are typically associated with that category across languages. Actual examples of the category in various languages will differ from the prototype, in that they may not display all the properties which are typical of the prototype and they will also display other properties which are not typical of the prototype. The prototype is, thus, a cross-linguistic ideal.

REALISATION In the sense used here, 'realise' means 'to make real'. Realisation (as an uncountable noun) is, then, the act of making real or (as a countable noun) an object which makes something else real. Abstract entities (whose technical name often ends in *-eme* in linguistics) are realised by entities which have a form (which you can see, write down, tape-record, hear, etc., etc.). So word-forms realise lexemes and any relevant inflectional affixes, morphs or allomorphs realise morphemes. Morphemes and lexemes are units of analysis constructed by the linguist to make the analysis possible; word-forms and morphs are the raw material on which the linguist has to operate to provide an analysis.

REANALYSIS Reanalysis refers to the state of affairs where speakers perceive a morphological structure which was not present historically and act on the assumption that the newly perceived structure is the correct one. In some instances this gives rise to folk etymology (*sirloin* < *sur* ['above'] *loin*), in others to linguistic change (*an apron* < *a napron*).

REDUPLICANT The reduplicant is that part of a reduplicated word (see reduplication) which is not the base; it is the bit which has been repeated to make the reduplicated word.

REDUPLICATION Reduplication has two meanings. The first is the formation of new affixes by repeating some part of the base (possibly the whole base). The second is the formation of new words using affixes created in this manner.

With the first meaning, we can say that the prefix showing future in the following Tagalog examples is created by reduplication of the first consonant and vowel of the base:

su·sulat	'will write'
ba·basa	'will read'
ʔa·ʔaral	'will teach'
ʔi·ʔibig	'will love'

In the second meaning, we can say that forms like *susulat* are created by reduplication.

REPLACIVE MORPH A replacive morph is the replacement of a phoneme or sequence of phonemes in one word-form with a different phoneme or sequence of phonemes to make a related word-form. For example, the vowel changes in the examples below could be analysed as replacive morphs:

sing	sang	sung	song
shoot	shot		

come   came

The replacive morph in the last example is /ʌ/ → /eɪ/ (orthographically *o* → *a*). For such replacement of (strings of) phonemes to be analysable as replacive morphs, it should ideally be shown that there is a parallel affixed form elsewhere in the language.

It should be noted that any analysis which includes replacive morphs is controversial and there is always an alternative way of viewing the data.

RESONANCE Resonance, as it is used in this book, refers to points of similarity between words which have the possibility of allowing speakers to draw connections between words. Resonance may be phonological, semantic or etymological and, when it is both phonological and semantic in a restricted way, we talk about words being made up of morphs.

ROOT A root is that part of a word-form which remains when all inflectional (see inflection) and derivational (see derivation) affixes have been removed. It is the basic part of a lexeme which is always realised and it cannot be further analysed into smaller morphs. In the English word *wordiness* the root is *word*. In the Latin word *amaːbunt* 'they will love' the root is *am-*. Notice that, in this latter case, the root is an obligatorily bound morph. In a word such as *typewriter*, there are two roots, *type* and *write*, even though there is only one lexeme.

ROOT-AND-PATTERN MORPHOLOGY Root-and-pattern morphology is another name for the type of morphological structure that arises through the use of transfixes. Talking about transfixes focuses on the individual elements which make up the word; talking in terms of root-and-pattern morphology focuses on the overall structure type.

ROOT COMPOUND See under **SYNTHETIC COMPOUND**.

SEMI-PRODUCTIVITY A process is said to be semi-productive if it is not fully productive in the sense that it does not apply to all possible bases defined solely in terms of the part of speech to which they belong. For example, suffixation of *-age* to a verb to produce a noun is semi-productive because, although it can be added to *carry*, *marry* and *wreck* to give *carriage*, *marriage* and *wreckage* respectively, it is not added to *bear*, *espouse* and *smash* to give **bearage*, **espousage* and **smashage*. Semi-productivity is sometimes seen as a defining feature of derivational as opposed to inflectional morphology (see derivation and inflection).

It should be noted that the validity of the notion of semi-productivity is strongly questioned in this book.

SIMPLE CLITIC See under **CLITIC**.

SIMULFIX See **SUPERFIX**.

SPECIAL CLITIC See under **CLITIC**.

STEM A stem is a base to which inflectional (see inflection) affixes can be added. In *stupidities* the stem is *stupidity* although the root is *stupid*.

Some scholars use the term 'stem' with a different meaning so care should be taken when the term is met in the literature.

STRATAL THEORY OF MORPHOLOGY The stratal theory of morphology is a theory whereby different classes of affixes are added to bases in such a way that all the affixes from one class or stratum have to be added before affixes from the next class or stratum can be added. This is also sometimes referred to as **level-ordering** since each stratum or level is ordered with respect to all others.

SUBJECT NOMINALISATION A subject nominalisation is a nominalisation which denotes the entity which would be the subject of the verb which has been nominalised. For example, a *beater* is a machine which beats. The beater is what does the beating and, so is the subject of the verb *beat* from which *beater* is derived. *Beater* is a subject nominalisation.

SUBTRACTIVE MORPH A subtractive morph is a morph which is removed by some morphological process. Consider the following sets of active and passive forms from Maori:

active	passive	gloss
huri	huri·hia	'turn'
inu	inu·mia	'drink'
karanga	karanga·tia	'call'
mau	mau·ria	'seize'
noho	noho·ia	'sit'
paa	paa·ngia	'touch'
tomo	tomo·kia	'enter'

The passive, in such cases, is not predictable from the active because the presence or absence of an initial consonant in the morph realising {passive} and the nature of the consonant is not predictable. It is, thus, frequently proposed as a more economical description for the fact that the base form for deriving all the forms listed above should contain a final consonant, which should be subtracted to provide the active form.

It should be noted that analyses which depend on subtractive morphs are frequently controversial and that it appears that speakers of Maori memorise a number of lexically conditioned (see under conditioning) passive allomorphs, rather than using a subtractive morph.

SUFFIX A suffix is an affix which is attached after its base. In *prematurely* there is just one suffix, *-ly*.

SUFFIXATION Suffixation is the use of suffixes, or the production of words using suffixes.

SUPERFIX The term 'superfix' refers to suprasegmental internal modification of a base – that is, change of tone or stress in a base, when this has the same effect as adding an affix. The stress difference between pairs such as

ˈabsent	absˈtract
ˈabsent	abˈsent
ˈfrequent	freˈquent

can be seen as a superfix. Superfixes have also been termed **suprafixes** and **simulfixes**.

SUPPLETION When two forms in a paradigm are not related to each other regularly but have idiosyncratic forms for a particular lexeme, we speak of suppletion and the forms concerned as being suppletive forms. For example, if we compare the verbs GO and WALK in English, we can see that GO has a suppletive past tense form:

go	walk
goes	walks
going	walking
went	walked

SUPRAFIX See **SUPERFIX**.

SYNCRETISM Syncretism is the neutralisation of two forms in a paradigm so that two different grammatical words are realised by homonymous word-forms. For example, in Latin there is consistent syncretism between the Dative and Ablative plural so that *reːgibus* could be either the Dative or the Ablative plural of REX 'king'.

SYNTHETIC A synthetic language is one which is not analytic. Agglutinative, fusional and polysynthetic languages are all synthetic.

SYNTHETIC COMPOUND A synthetic compound is a compound whose head element (in English the right-hand element) contains a verbal base and where the modifying element in the compound is an element which could occur in a sentence as an argument of that verb. For example, if we compare the synthetic compound *book* *launching* with the sentence *Somebody launched the book*, we see that the same verbal element {launch} is present in both and that the direct object of the verb is used as the modifying element in the compound. Other synthetic compounds are *street cleaner, language description, time-sharing* and so on.

Synthetic compounds are also termed **verbal compounds** or **verbal-nexus compounds.** They are contrasted with **root compounds** (also called **primary compounds**) which do not have such a structure. Root compounds include *textbook, computer graphics, town hall* and the like.

TRANSFIX Transfixes are discontinuous morphs which are interspersed throughout the bases with which they occur. They are mostly found in the Semitic languages. For example, the following data from Egyptian Arabic illustrates a transfix of the form 'CaaCiC (where 'C' indicates a consonant of the root) which produces subject nominalisations:

'katab	'write'
'kaatib	'clerk'
'rikib	'ride'
'raakib	'rider'
'sikin	'inhabit'
'saakin	'inhabitant'
'naʃar	'publish'
'naaʃir	'publisher'

UNIQUE MORPH A unique morph is one which only occurs in a single collocation in a language. In English, *-ric* in *bishop·ric* is a unique morph because there are no other words which have the same suffix. Unique morphs are sometimes called **cranberry morphs** because the first element in *cranberry* is supposed to be a unique morph.

USE See under **MENTION.**

VERBAL COMPOUND or **VERBAL-NEXUS COMPOUND** See **SYNTHETIC COMPOUND.**

WORD Word is a superordinate term for grammatical word, lexeme and word-form. That is, it is a term which can be used without specifying which of the more specific kinds of 'word' one means.

Note that this is not the way in which all linguists use the term. For some it means word-form, for others lexeme and for others grammatical word. Only the context can make clear which is meant.

WORD-AND-PARADIGM Word-and-paradigm is an approach to morphology which gives theoretical centrality to the notion of the paradigm and which derives the word-forms representing lexemes by a complex series of ordered rules which do not assume that the word-form will be easily analysable into morphs or that each morph will realise a single morpheme. It is also known as **a-morphous morphology**.

WORD-FORM A word-form is a form which can stand in isolation and which represents the particular shape (orthographic or phonological) in which a lexeme occurs. Thus, *am, are, be, been, being, is, was, were* are all different word-forms which, in the appropriate circumstances, can realise (see realisation) the lexeme BE. In the various possible sentences *Help me!, I help old ladies across streets. She wanted to help us. He was no help whatsoever.*, we find indistinguishable word-forms *help*. Word-forms in the spoken language can be transcribed. Word-forms in the written language can be termed orthographic words. In print, word-forms are distinguished by italics (underlining in typescript or manuscript).

ZERO DERIVATION See **CONVERSION**.

ZERO MORPH A zero morph is analysed where there is no overt marker of a particular morpheme, even though one would be expected on the basis of parallel examples in the language. For example, in Latin there is no overt marker of nominative singular on the lexeme PUER 'boy', even though there is one on a parallel lexeme DOMINUS 'lord'.

nominative	puer	domin·us
accusative	puer·um	domin·um
genitive	puer·i:	domin·i:
dative	puer·o:	domin·o:

The nominative singular of PUER might thus be analysed as *puer·Ø*, with the zero morph holding the place usually taken by overt affixes.

It should be noted that analyses with zero morphs are always controversial and that alternative analyses are always possible. Even if zero morphs are permitted in an analysis, care should be taken to avoid their proliferation.

References

Aitchison, J. (1987). *Words in the Mind*. Oxford: Blackwell.

Allen, M. (1978). *Morphological Investigations*. PhD thesis, University of Connecticut.

Anderson, G. D. & Harrison, K. D. (1999). *Tyvan*. München: Lincom Europa.

Anderson, J. (1980). 'Towards dependency morphology, the structure of the Basque verb', in J. Anderson & C. J. Ewen (eds), *Studies in Dependency Phonology*, Ludwigsburg, 227–71.

Anderson, S. R. (1977). 'On the formal description of inflection', *Papers from the Thirteenth Regional Meeting of the Chicago Linguistic Society*, 15–44.

Anderson, S. R (1982). 'Where's morphology?', *Linguistic Inquiry*, 13, 571–612.

Anderson, S. R. (1985a). 'Typological distinctions in word formation', in T. Shopen (ed.), *Language Typology and Syntactic Description III*, Cambridge: Cambridge University Press, 3–56.

Anderson, S. R. (1985b). 'Inflectional morphology', in T. Shopen (ed.), *Language Typology and Syntactic Description III*, Cambridge: Cambridge University Press, 150–201.

Anderson, S. R. (1988). 'Morphological change', in F. J. Newmeyer (ed.), *Linguistics: The Cambridge Survey, I, Linguistic Theory: foundations*, Cambridge: Cambridge University Press, 324-62.

Anderson, S. R. (1992). *A-Morphous Morphology*. Cambridge: Cambridge University Press.

Anshen, F. & Aronoff, M. (1981). 'Morphological productivity and phonological transparency', *Canadian Journal of Linguistics* 26, 63–72.

Anshen, F. & Aronoff, M. (1988). 'Producing morphologically complex words', *Linguistics* 26, 641–55.

Anttila, R. (1977). *Analogy*. The Hague: Mouton.

Archangeli, D. & Langendoen, D. T. (eds) (1997). *Optimality Theory*. Malden, MA and Oxford: Blackwell.

Aronoff, M. (1976). *Word Formation in Generative Grammar*. Cambridge, MA: MIT Press.

Aronoff, M. (1980). 'The relevance of productivity in a synchronic description of word-formation', in J. Fisiak (ed.), *Historical Morphology*, The Hague: Mouton, 71–82.

Aronoff, M. (1983). 'A decade of morphology and word formation', *Annual Review of Anthropology* 12, 355–75.

Aronoff, M. (1994a). 'Blocking', in R. E. Asher (ed.), *The Encyclopedia of Language and Linguistics*, Oxford: Pergamon, 373–4.

Aronoff, M. (1994b). *Morphology by Itself*. Cambridge, MA: MIT Press.

Asher, R. E. (1982). *Tamil*. Amsterdam: North Holland.

Ashton, E. O. (1944). *Swahili Grammar*. London: Longman.

Austin, P. (1981). *A Grammar of Diyari, South Australia*. Cambridge: Cambridge University Press.

Baayen, H. (1992). 'Quantitative aspects of morphological productivity', *Yearbook of Morphology 1991*, 109–49.

Baayen, H. & Lieber, R. (1991). 'Productivity and English derivation: a corpus-based study', *Linguistics* 29, 801–44.

Baldi, P. (1983). 'On some recent claims in morphological theory', *General Linguistics* 23, 171–90.

Barnhart, C. L., Steinmetz, S. & Barnhart, R. K. (1973). *A Dictionary of New English*. London: Longman.

Barnhart, C. L., Steinmetz, S. & Barnhart, R. K. (1980). *The Second Barnhart Dictionary of New English*. New York: Harper & Row.

Bat-El, O. (1996). 'Selecting the best of the worst: the grammar of Hebrew blends', *Phonology* 13, 283–328.

Bat-El, O. (2000). 'The grammaticality of "extragrammatical" morphology', in U. Doleschal & A. M. Thornton (eds), *Extragrammatical and Marginal Morphology*, München: Lincom, 61–81.

Bauer, L. (1978a). *The Grammar of Nominal Compounding with special reference to Danish, English and French*. Odense: Odense University Press.

Bauer, L. (1978b). 'On lexicalization', *Archivum Linguisticum* 9, 3–14.

Bauer, L. (1980). 'In the beginning was the word', *Te Reo* 23, 73–80.

Bauer, L. (1983). *English Word-formation*. Cambridge: Cambridge University Press.

Bauer, L. (1990a). 'Be-heading the word', *Journal of Linguistics* 26, 1–31.

Bauer, L. (1990b). 'Level disorder: the case of -er and -or', *Transactions of the Philological Society* 88, 97–110.

Bauer, L. (1992). 'Lexicalization and level ordering', *Linguistics* 30, 561–68.

Bauer, L. (1997). 'Derivational paradigms', *Yearbook of Morphology 1996*, 243–56

Bauer, L. (1998). 'When is a sequence of noun + noun a compound in English?' *English Language and Linguistics* 2, 65–86.

Bauer, L. (1999). 'Is the morpheme dead?' *Acta Linguistica Hafniensia* 31, 7–25.

Bauer, L. (2001a). 'Compounding', in M. Haspelmath, E. König, W. Oesterreicher & W. Raible (eds), *Language Universals and Language Typology*, Berlin and New York: de Gruyter, 695–707.

Bauer, L. (2001b). *Morphological Productivity*. Cambridge: Cambridge University Press.

Bauer, L. & Renouf, A. (2001). 'A corpus-based study of compounding in English', *Journal of English Linguistics* 29, 101–23.

Bauer, W. (1981a). 'Hae.re vs ha.e.re a note', *Te Reo* 24, 31–6.

Bauer, W. (1981b). *Aspects of the Grammar of Maori*. PhD thesis, University of Edinburgh.

Bauer, W. (1982). 'Relativization in Maori', *Studies in Language* 6, 305–42.

Bauer, W. (1997). *The Reed Reference Grammar of Māori*. Auckland: Reed.

Bazell, C. E. (1966). 'Linguistic typology', in P. Strevens (ed.), *Five Inaugural Lectures*, London: Oxford University Press, 27–49.

Beard, R. (1982). 'The plural as a lexical derivation', *Glossa* 16, 133–48.

Bentley, N. & Esar, E. (eds) (1951). *The Treasury of Humorous Quotations*. London: Dent.

Bergenholtz, H. & Mugdan, J. (1979). *Einführung in die Morphologie*. Stuttgart, etc.: Kohlhammer.

Berko Gleason, J. (1958). 'The child's learning of English morphology', *Word* 14, 150–77. Reprinted in A. Bar-Adon & W. F. Leopold (eds) *Child Language*, Englewood Cliffs, NJ: Prentice-Hall, 1971, 153-67.

Blake, F. R. (1925). *A Grammar of the Tagalog Language*. New Haven: American Oriental Society.

Bloomfield, L. (1935). *Language*. London: Allen & Unwin.

Bochner, H. (1984). 'Inflection within derivation', *The Linguistic Review* 3, 411–21.

Bolozky, S. (1999). *Measuring Productivity in Word Formation*. Leiden: Brill.

Booij, G. (1977). *Dutch Morphology: A study of word formation in generative grammar*. Dordrecht: Foris.

Booij, G. E. (1985). 'Coordination reduction in complex words: a case for prosodic phonology', in H. van der Hulst & N. Smith (eds), *Advances in Nonlinear Phonology*, Dordrecht: Foris, 143–60.

Booij, G. (1993). 'Against split morphology', in G. Booij and J. van Marle (eds), *Yearbook of Morphology 1993*, Dordrecht: Kluwer, 27–49.

Booij, G. (1996). 'Inherent versus contextual inflection and the split morphology hypothesis', *Yearbook of Morphology 1995*, 1–16.

Botha, R. P. (1981). 'A base rule theory of Afrikaans synthetic compounding', in M. Moortgat, H. v.d. Hulst & T. Hoekstra (eds), *The Scope of Lexical Rules*, Dordrecht: Foris, 1–77.

Botha, R. P. (1984a). '*A Galilean Analysis of Afrikaans Reduplication*'. *Stellenbosch Papers in Linguistics* 13.

Botha, R. P. (1984b). *Morphological Mechanisms*. Oxford, etc.: Pergamon.

Brandt, S. (1984). 'Does "cranberry" contain a cranberry morpheme?', *Nordic Linguistic Bulletin* 8/3, 6–7.

Brown, E. K. & Miller, J. E. (1980). *Syntax: A linguistic introduction to sentence structure*. London: Hutchinson.

Brown, G. (1977). *Listening to Spoken English*. London: Longman.

Butler, S. (ed.) (1990). *The Macquarie Dictionary of New Words*. Macquarie University, NSW: Macquarie Library.

Bybee, J. L. (1985). *Morphology, a study of the relation between meaning and form*. Amsterdam: Benjamins.

Bybee, J. L., Pagliuca, W. & Perkins, R. D. (1991). 'Back to the future', in E. C. Traugott & B. Heine (eds), *Approaches to Grammaticalization*, Amsterdam and Philadelphia: Benjamins, vol. II, 17–58.

Bynon, T. (1977). *Historical Linguistics*. Cambridge: Cambridge University Press.

Campbell, L. (1998). *Historical Linguistics*. Edinburgh: Edinburgh University Press.

Carroll, J. M. (1979). 'Complex compounds, phrasal embedding in lexical structures', *Linguistics* 17, 863–77.

Carstairs, A. (1983). 'Paradigm economy', *Journal of Linguistics* 19, 115–25.

Carstairs, A. (1984a). 'Outlines of a constraint on syncretism', *Folia Linguistica* 18, 73–85.

Carstairs, A. (1984b). *Constraints on Allomorphy in Inflexion*. Indiana University Linguistics Club. A revised version is now more readily available under the title *Allomorphy in Inflexion*, London: Croom Helm, 1987.

Carstairs, A. (1984c). 'Paradigm economy in the Latin third declension', *Transactions of the Philological Society*, 117–37.

Carstairs-McCarthy, A. (1998). 'Paradigmatic structure: inflectional paradigms and morphological classes', in A. Spencer & A. M. Zwicky (eds), *The Handbook of Morphology*, Oxford and Malden, MA: Blackwell, 322–34.

Chapman, C. (1996). 'Perceptual salience and affix order: noun plurals as input to word formation', *Yearbook of Morphology 1995*, 175–84.

Chelliah, S. L. (1997). *A Grammar of Meithei*. Berlin and New York: Mouton de Gruyter.

Chomsky, N. (1970). 'Remarks on nominalization', in R. Jacobs & P. Rosenbaum (eds), *Readings in English Transformational Grammar*, Waltham, MA: Ginn, 184–221.

Chomsky, N. & Halle, M. (1968). *The Sound Pattern of English*. New York: Harper & Row.

Clahsen, H., Rothweiler, M., Woest, A. & Marcus, G. F. (1992). 'Regular and irregular inflection in the acquisition of German noun plurals', *Cognition* 45, 225–55.

Clark, E. V. (1993). *The Lexicon in Acquisition*. Cambridge: Cambridge University Press.

Clark, E. V. & Clark, H. H. (1979). 'When nouns surface as verbs', *Language* 55, 767–811.

Cohen, M. (1973). *Histoire d'une langue: le français*. Paris: Éditions sociales, 4th edn.

Comrie, B. (1981). *Language Universals and Linguistic Typology*. Oxford: Blackwell.

Croft, W. (1990). *Typology and Universals*. Cambridge: Cambridge University Press.

Crystal, D. (1980). *A First Dictionary of Linguistics and Phonetics*. London: Andre Deutsch.

Cutler, A., Hawkins, J. & Gilligan, G. (1985). 'The suffixing preference: a processing explanation', *Linguistics* 23, 723–58.

Dardjowidjojo, S. (1979). 'Acronymic patterns in Indonesian', *Pacific Linguistics* Series C, 45, 143–60.

Dench, A. (1998). *Yingkarta*. München: Lincom Europa.

Derbyshire, D. C. (1979). *Hixkaryana*. Amsterdam: North Holland.

Derwing, B. L. (1973). *Transformational Grammar as a Theory of Language Acquisition*. Cambridge: Cambridge University Press.

Derwing, B. L. (1976). 'Morpheme recognition and the learning of rules for derivational morphology', *Canadian Journal of Linguistics* 21, 38–66.

Derwing, B. L. & Baker, W. J. (1979). 'Recent research on the acquisition of English morphology', in P. Fletcher & M. Garman (eds), *Language Acquisition*, Cambridge: Cambridge University Press, 209–23.

Dik, S. C. (1980). *Studies in Functional Grammar*. London, etc.: Academic Press.

Dimmendaal, G. J. (1983). *The Turkana Language*. Dordrecht: Foris.

Di Sciullo, A. & Williams, E. (1987). *On the Definition of Word*. Cambridge, MA.: MIT Press.

Doke, C. M. & Mofokeng, S. M. (1957). *Textbook of Southern Sotho Grammar*. Capetown: Maskew Miller Longman.

Dressler, W. (1977). 'Wortbildung bei Sprachverfall', in H. E. Brekle & D. Kastovsky (eds), *Perspektiven der Wortbildungsforschung*, Bonn: Bouvier, 62–9.

Dressler, W. (1981). 'General principles of poetic license in word formation', in H. Weydt (ed.), *Logos Semantikos in Honorem E. Coseriu* II, Berlin: de Gruyter, 423–31.

Dressler, W. (1982). 'Zur semiotischen Begrundung einer natürlichen Wortbildungslehre', *Klagenfurter Beitrage zur Sprachwissenschaft* 8, 72–87.

Dressler, W. (1985). 'On the predictiveness of natural morphology', *Journal of Linguistics* 21, 321–37.

Dressler, W. (1986). 'Explanation in natural morphology, illustrated with comparative and agent-noun formation', *Linguistics* 24, 519–48.

Dressler, W. (1989). 'Prototypical differences between inflection and derivation', *Zeitschrift für Phonetik, Sprachwissenschaft und Kommunikationsforschungen* 42, 3–10.

Dressler, W. (2000). 'Naturalness', in G. Booij, C. Lehmann & J. Mugdan (eds), *Morphologie/Morphology Vol I*, Berlin and New York: de Gruyter, 288–96.

Dressler, W., Mayerthaler, W., Panagl, O. & Wurzel, W. (1987). *Leitmotifs in Natural Morphology*. Amsterdam and Philadelphia, PA: Benjamins.

Durand, J. (1990). *Generative and Non-Linear Phonology*. London and New York: Longman.

Ehrman, M. E. (1972). *Contemporary Cambodian*. Washington, DC: Foreign Service Institute.

Einarsson, S. (1945). *Icelandic*. Baltimore, MD: John Hopkins Press.

England, N. C. (1983). *A Grammar of Mam, a Mayan Language*. Austin, TX: University of Texas Press.

Fabb, N. (1988). 'English suffixation is constrained only by selectional restrictions', *Natural Language and Linguistic Theory* 6, 527–39.

Fleischer, W. (1975). *Wortbildung der deutschen Gegenwartssprache*. Tübingen: Niemeyer.

Fortescue, M. (1984). *West Greenlandic*. London: Croom Helm.

Fortescue, M. (1994). 'Morphology, polysynthetic', in R. E. Asher (ed.), *The Encyclopedia of Language and Linguistics*, Oxford: Pergamon, 2600–2.

Frauenfelder, U. & Schreuder, R. (1992). 'Constraining psycholinguistic models of morphological processing and representation: the role of productivity', *Yearbook of Morphology 1991*, 165–83.

Fudge, E. (1984). *English Word-Stress*. London: George Allen & Unwin.

Gaskell, M. G. & Marslen-Wilson, W. D. (1997). 'Integrating form and meaning: a distributed model of speech perception', *Language and Cognitive Processes* 12, 613–56.

Gerdts, D. B. (1998). 'Incorporation', in A. Spencer & A. M. Zwicky (eds), *The Handbook of Morphology*, Oxford and Malden, MA: Blackwell, 84–100.

Giegerich, H. J. (1999). *Lexical Strata in English*. Cambridge: Cambridge University Press.

Givon, T. (1971). 'Historical syntax and synchronic morphology: an archeologist's fieldtrip', *Papers from the Seventh Regional Meeting of the Chicago Linguistic Society*, 394-415.

Gleason, H. A. (1955). *Workbook in Descriptive Linguistics*. New York, etc.: Holt, Rinehart and Winston.

Goldsmith, J. A. (1990). *Autosegmental and Metrical Phonology*. Oxford and Cambridge, MA: Blackwell.

Golston, C. & Wiese, R. (1996). 'Zero morphology and constraint interaction: subtraction and epenthesis in German dialects', *Yearbook of Morphology 1995*, 143–59.

Green, J. (ed.) (1991). *Neologisms*. London: Bloomsbury.

Greenberg, J. H. (1954). 'A quantitative approach to the morphological typology of language', in R. F. Spencer (ed.), *Method and Perspective in Anthropology*, Minneapolis, MN: University of Minnesota Press, 192–220.

Greenberg, J. H. (1963). 'Some universals of grammar with particular reference to the order of meaningful elements', in J. H. Greenberg (ed.), *Universals of Language*, Cambridge, MA: MIT Press, 58–90.

Haiman, J. (1985). *Natural Syntax*. Cambridge: Cambridge University Press.

Haiman, J. (1998). 'Hua (Papuan)', in A. Spenser & A. M. Zwicky (eds), *The Handbook of Morphology*. Oxford and Malden, MA: Blackwell, 539–62.

Hall, C. J. (1992). *Morphology and Mind*. London and New York: Routledge.

Halle, M. (1973). 'Prolegomena to a theory of word formation', *Linguistic Inquiry* 4, 3–16

Hammer, A. E. (1971). *German Grammar and Usage*. London: Edward Arnold.

Harrell, R. S. (1962). *A Short Reference Grammar of Moroccan Arabic*. Washington: Georgetown University Press.

Haspelmath, M. (1996). 'Word-class-changing inflection and morphological theory', *Yearbook of Morphology 1995*, 43–66.

Hass, W. de & Trommelen, M. (1993). *Morfologisch Handboek van het Nederlands*. 's-Gravenhage: SDU.

Haugen, E. (1976). *The Scandinavian Languages*. London: Faber and Faber.

Heine, B., Claudi, U. & Hünnemeyer, F. (1991). *Grammaticalization*. Chicago, IL and London: Chicago University Press.

Hockett, C. F. (1947). 'Problems of morphemic analysis', *Language* 23, 321–43. Reprinted in M. Joos (ed.), *Readings in Linguistics I*, Chicago, IL: University of Chicago Press, 1957, 229–42.

Hockett, C. F. (1954). 'Two models of grammatical description', *Word* 10, 210–31. Reprinted in M. Joos (ed.), *Readings in Linguistics I*, Chicago, IL: University of Chicago Press, 1957, 386–99

Hockett, C. F. (1987). *Refurbishing our Foundations*. Amsterdam and Philadelphia, PA: Benjamins.

Holmes, J. (1984). *Introduction to Language Study: A workbook*. Revised edition. Wellington: Victoria University.

Hopper, P. J. & Traugott, E. C. (1993). *Grammaticalization*. Cambridge, MA: Cambridge University Press.

Householder, F. W. (1966). 'Phonological theory: a brief comment', *Journal of Linguistics* 2, 99–100.

Jacob, J. M. (1968). *Introduction to Cambodian*. London: Oxford University Press.

Jackendoff, R. (1975). 'Morphological and semantic regularities in the lexicon', *Language* 51, 639–71.

Jakobson, R. (1960). 'The gender pattern of Russian', in R. Jakobson, *Selected Writings II*, The Hague: Mouton, 1971, 184–6.

Jespersen, O. (1909). *A Modern English Grammar on Historical Principles: Part I, sounds and spellings*. London: George Allen and Unwin and Copenhagen: Munksgaard.

Jones, D. (1977). *English Pronouncing Dictionary*. London: Dent. 14th edition, revised by A. C. Gimson.

Joos, Martin (ed.) (1957). *Readings in Linguistics I*, Chicago, IL and London: University of Chicago Press.

Joseph, B. D. (1998). 'Diachronic morphology', in A. Spencer & A. M. Zwicky (eds), *The Handbook of Morphology*, Oxford and Malden, MA: Blackwell, 351–73.

Kager, R. (1999). *Optimality Theory*. Cambridge: Cambridge University Press.

Karlsson, F. (1983). *Finnish Grammar*. Porvoo, etc.: Werner Soderström Osakeyhitio.

Karlsson, F. & Koskenniemi, K. (1985). 'A process model of morphology and lexicon', *Folia Linguistica* 19, 207–31.

Kelly, M. H. (1998). 'To "brunch" or to "brench": some aspects of blend structure', *Linguistics* 36, 579–90.

Kennedy, B. H. (1962). *The Revised Latin Primer*. Revised by J. Mountford. London: Longman.

Kibrik, A. E. (1998). 'Archi (Caucasian — Daghestanian)', in A. Spencer & A. M. Zwicky (eds), *The Handbook of Morphology*, Oxford and Malden, MA: Blackwell, 455–76.

Kilani-Schoch, M. (1988). *Introduction à la Morphologie Naturelle*. Berne, etc.: Peter Lang.

Kilani-Schoch, M. & Dressler, W. U. (1984). 'Natural morphology and Classical vs. Tunisian Arabic', *Wiener Linguistische Gazette*, 33–4, 51–68.

Kiparsky, P. (1982). 'Lexical morphology and phonology', in The Linguistic Society of Korea (ed.), *Linguistics in the Morning Calm*, Seoul: Hanshin, 3–91.

Kiparsky, P. (1992). 'Analogy', in W. Bright (ed.), *International Encylopedia of Linguistics*, New York and London: Oxford University Press, 56–61.

Knowles, E. (ed.) (1997). *The Oxford Dictionary of New Words*. Oxford: Oxford University Press.

Kress, G. (1997). *Before Writing*. London and New York: Routledge.

Kroeber, A. L. (1954). 'Critical summary and commentary', in R. F. Spencer (ed.), *Method and Perspective in Anthropology*, Minneapolis, MN: University of Minnesota Press, 273–99.

Kubozono, H. (1990). 'Phonological constraints on blending in English as a case for phonology-morphology interface', *Yearbook of Morphology* 3, 1–20.

Kuryłowicz, J. (1949). 'La nature des procès dits "analogiques"', in *Acta Linguistica (Hafniensia)* 5, 121–38. Reprinted in E. P. Hamp, F. W. Householder & R. Austerlitz (eds), *Readings in Linguistics II*, Chicago, IL and London: University of Chicago Press, 1966, 158–74.

Kwee, J. B. (1965). *Indonesian*. London: The English Universities Press.

Lapointe, S. G. (1981). 'A lexical analysis of the English auxiliary system', in T. Hoekstra, H. v. d. Hulst & M. Moortgat (eds), *Lexical Grammar*, Dordrecht: Foris, 215–54

Lass, R. (1984). *Phonology: An introduction to basic concepts*. Cambridge: Cambridge University Press.

Lass, R. (1992). 'Phonology and morphology', in N. Blake (ed.), *The Cambridge History of the English Language, Volume II, 1066–1476*, Cambridge: Cambridge University Press, 23–155.

Lawler, J. M. (1977). '*A* agrees with *B* in Achenese: a problem for Relational Grammar', in P. Cole & J. M. Sadock (eds), *Grammatical Relations* (Syntax and Semantics 8), New York, etc.: Academic Press, 219–48.

Lees, R. B. (1960). *The Grammar of English Nominalizations*. Bloomington, IN: Indiana University Press and The Hague: Mouton.

Lehnert, M. (1971). *Reverse Dictionary of Present-Day English*. Leipzig: VEB.

Levi, J. N. (1978). *The Syntax and Semantics of Complex Nominals*. New York, etc.: Academic Press.

Lewis, G. L. (1967). *Turkish Grammar*. Oxford: Oxford University Press.

Lieber, R. (1981). *On the Organization of the Lexicon*. Bloominton, IN: Indiana University Linguistics Club.

Lieber, R. (1992). *Deconstructing Morphology*. Chicago, IL and London: Chicago University Press.

Lightner, T. M. (1975). 'The role of derivational morphology in generative grammar', *Language* 51, 617–38.

Lightner, T. M. (1981). 'New explorations in derivational morphology', in D. Goyvaerts (ed.), *Phonology in the 1980's*, Ghent: Story-Scientia, 93–9.

Lightner, T. M. (1983). *Introduction to English Derivational Morphology*. Amsterdam and Philadelphia, PA: John Benjamins.

Lipski, J. M. (1994). *Latin American Spanish*. London and New York: Longman.

Lockwood, D. G. (1993). *Morphological Analysis and Description*. Tokyo, etc.: International Language Sciences Publishers.

Lukas, J. (1937). *A Study of the Kanuri Language*. Oxford: Oxford University Press. Reprinted by Dawsons, 1967.

Lyons, J. (1963). *Structural Semantics*. Oxford: Blackwell.

Lyons, J. (1968). *Introduction to Theoretical Linguistics*. Cambridge: Cambridge University Press.

Lyons, J. (1977). *Semantics*. Cambridge: Cambridge University Press.

Mańczak, W. (1958). 'Tendences générales des changements analogiques', *Lingua* 7, 298–325, 387–420.

Marantz, A. (1982). 'Re reduplication', *Linguistic Inquiry* 13, 435–82.

Marantz, A. (1994). 'Reduplication', in R. E. Asher (ed.), *The Encyclopedia of Language and Linguistics*, Oxford: Pergamon, 3486–7.

Marchand, H. (1964). 'A set of criteria for the establishing of derivational relationship between words unmarked by derivational morphemes', *Indogermanische Forschungen* 69, 10–19.

Marchand, H. (1969). *The Categories and Types of Present-Day English Word-Formation*. München: C. H. Beck. Second edition.

Marcus, G. F., Brinkmann, U., Clahsen, H., Wiese, R. & Pinker, S. (1995). 'German inflection: the exception that proves the rule', *Cognitive Psychology* 29, 189–256.

Marle, J. van (1985). *On the Paradigmatic Dimension of Morphological Creativity*. Dordrecht: Foris.

Marle, J. van (1996). 'The unity of morphology: on the interwovenness of the derivational and inflectional dimension of the word', *Yearbook of Morphology 1995*, 67–82.

Marslen-Wilson, W. D. (1987). 'Functional parallelism in spoken word-recognition', in U. H. Frauenfelder & L. Komisarjevsky Tyler (eds), *Spoken Word Recognition*, Cambridge, MA and London: MIT Press, 71-102.

Marslen-Wilson, W. D. (1999). 'Abstractness and combination: the morphemic lexicon', in S. Garrod & M. Pickering (eds), *Language Processing*, Hove: Psychology Press, 101–19.

Marslen-Wilson, W., Komisarjevsky Tyler, L., Waksler, R. & Older, L. (1994).

'Morphology and meaning in the English mental lexicon', *Psychological Review* 101, 3–33.

Matisoff, J. A. (1991). 'Areal and universal dimensions of grammatization in Lahu', in E. C. Traugott & B. Heine (eds), *Approaches to Grammaticalization*, Amsterdam and Philadelphia, PA: Benjamins, vol II, 383–453.

Matthews, P. H. (1970). 'Recent developments in morphology', in J. Lyons (ed.), *New Horizons in Linguistics*, Harmondsworth: Pelican, 96–114.

Matthews, P. H. (1972). *Inflectional Morphology: A theoretical study based on aspects of Latin verb conjugation*. Cambridge: Cambridge University Press.

Matthews, P. H. (1991). *Morphology*. Second edition. Cambridge: Cambridge University Press.

Matthews, P. H. (1993). *Grammatical Theory in the United States from Bloomfield to Chomsky*. Cambridge: Cambridge University Press.

Matthews, P. H. (2001). *A Short History of Structural Linguistics*. Cambridge: Cambridge University Press.

Mayerthaler, W. (1980). 'Ikonismus in der Morphologie', *Zeitschrift fur Semiotik* 2, 19–37.

Mayerthaler, W. (1981). *Morphologische Naturlichkeit*. Wiesbaden: Athenaion.

Mayerthaler, W. (1988). *Morphological Naturalness*. Tr. J. Seidler. Ann Arbor, MI: Karoma.

McCarthy, J. J. (1994). 'Morphology, nonconcatenative', in R. E. Asher (ed.), *The Encyclopedia of Language and Linguistics*, Oxford: Pergamon, 2598–600.

McCarthy, J. J. & Prince, A. S. (1995). 'Prosodic morphology', in J. A. Goldsmith (ed.), *The Handbook of Phonological Theory*, Cambridge, MA and Oxford: Blackwell, 318–66.

McCarthy, J. J. & Prince, A. S. (1998). 'Prosodic morphology', in A. Spencer & A. M. Zwicky (eds), *The Handbook of Morphology*, Oxford and Malden, MA: Blackwell, 283–305.

McMahon, A. M. S. (1994). 'Lexical phonology and morphology', in R. E. Asher (ed.), *The Encyclopedia of Language and Linguistics*, Oxford: Pergamon, 2155–60.

McMillan, J. B. (1980). 'Infixing and interposing in English', *American Speech* 55, 163–83.

Mish, F. C. (ed.) (1983). *9,000 Words*. Springfield, MA: Merriam-Webster.

Mitchell, T. F. (1956). *An Introduction to Egyptian Colloquial Arabic*. London: Oxford University Press.

Mitchell, T. F. (1962). *Colloquial Arabic*. London: The English Universities Press.

Mithun, M. (1984). 'The evolution of noun incorporation', *Language* 60, 847–94.

Mixco, M. (1997). *Mandan*. München and Newcastle: Lincom Europa.

Mugdan, J. (1986). 'Was ist eigentlich ein Morphem?' *Zeitschrift für Phonetik, Sprachwissenschaft und Kommunikationsforschung* 39, 29–43.

Muthmann, G. (1999). *Reverse English Dictionary*. Berlin and New York: Mouton de Gruyter.

Nida, E. (1949). *Morphology: the descriptive analysis of words.* Ann Arbor, MI: University of Michigan Press.

Nooteboom, S. G. (1981). 'Lexical retrieval from fragments of spoken words: beginnings vs endings', *Journal of Phonetics* 9, 407–24.

Ohlander, S. (1976). *Phonology, Meaning, Morphology.* Göteborg: Acta Universitatis Gothoburgensis.

Okada, S. (1999). 'On the conjoinability of affixal morphemes in English', *Word* 50, 339–63.

Orr, J. (1962). *Three Studies on Homonymics.* Edinburgh: Edinburgh University Press.

Perlmutter, D. M. (1988). 'The split morphology hypothesis: evidence from Yiddish', in M. Hammond & M. Noonan (eds), *Theoretical Morphology*, San Diego, CA: Academic Press, 79–100.

Pinker, S. (1999). *Words and Rules.* London: Weidenfeld & Nicolson.

Pinker, S. & Prince, A. (1988). 'On language and connectionism: analysis of a parallel distributed processing model of language acquisition', *Cognition* 28, 73–193.

Pinker, S. & Prince, A. (1991). 'Regular and irregular morphology and the psychological status of rules of grammar', *Proceedings of the Seventeenth Annual Meeting of the Berkeley Linguistics Society*, 230–51. Also in S. D. Lima, R. L. Corrigan & G. K. Iverson (eds), *The Reality of Linguistic Rules*, Amsterdam and Philadelphia, PA: Benjamins, 1994, 321–51.

Plag, I. (1998). 'Selectional restrictions in English suffixation revisited: a reply to Fabb (1988)', *Linguistics* 34, 769–98.

Plag, I. (1999). *Morphological Productivity.* Berlin and New York: Mouton de Gruyter.

Plank, F. (1981). *Morphologische (Ir-) Regularitaten.* Tübingen: Gunter Narr.

Plank, F. (1984). 'Romance disagreements: phonology interfering with syntax', *Journal of Linguistics* 20, 329–49.

Plank, F. (1991). *Paradigms.* Berlin and New York: Mouton de Gruyter.

Plank, F. (1994). 'Inflection and derivation', in R. E. Asher (ed.), *The Encyclopedia of Language and Linguistics*, Oxford: Pergamon, 1671–8.

Prideaux, G. D. (1984). *Psycholinguistics: The Experimental Study of Language.* London and Sydney: Croom Helm.

Quirk, R., Greenbaum, S., Leech, G. & Svartvik, J. (1972). *A Grammar of Contemporary English.* London: Longman.

Radford, A. (1981). *Transformational Syntax.* Cambridge: Cambridge University Press.

Rainer, F. (1996). 'Inflection inside derivation: evidence from Spanish and Portuguese', *Yearbook of Morphology 1995*, 83–91.

Renouf, A. & Baayen, R. H. (1998). 'Aviating among the hapax legomena: morphological grammaticalisation in current British newspaper English', in A. Renouf (ed.), *Explorations in Corpus Linguistics*, Amsterdam and Atlanta, GA: Rodopi, 181–9.

Robins, R. H. (1959). 'In defence of WP', *Transactions of the Philological Society*, 116–44.

Robins, R. H. (1964). *General Linguistics: An introductory survey*. London: Longmans. Revised edition, 1967.

Rowlands, E. C. (1969). *Yoruba*. London: Hodder & Stoughton.

Rude, N. (1991). 'Verbs to promotional suffixes in Sahaptian and Klamath', in E. C. Traugott & B. Heine (eds), *Approaches to Grammaticalization*, Amsterdam and Philadelphia, PA: Benjamins, vol II, 185–99.

Rudes, B. A. (1980). 'The functional development of the verbal suffix +esc+ in Romance', in J. Fisiak (ed.), *Historical Morphology*, The Hague, etc.: Mouton, 327–48.

Rumelhart, D. E. & McClelland, J. L. (1986). 'On learning the past tenses of English verbs', in J. L. McClelland, D. E. Rumelhart & the PDP Research Group (eds), *Parallel Distributed Processing Vol 2*, Cambridge, MA and London: MIT Press, 216–71.

Samuels, M. L. (1972). *Linguistic Evolution*. Cambridge: Cambridge University Press.

Sapir, E. (1911). 'The problem of noun incorporation in American languages', *American Anthropologist* 13, 250–82.

Sapir, E. (1921). *Language*. London: Harvest.

Sasse, H.-J. (1984). 'The pragmatics of noun incorporation in Eastern Cushitic languages', in F. Plank (ed.), *Objects*, London, etc.: Academic Press, 243–68.

Scalise, S. (1984). *Generative Morphology*. Dordrecht: Foris.

Scalise, S. (1988). 'Inflection and derivation', *Linguistics* 26, 561–81.

Selkirk, E. O. (1982). *The Syntax of Words*. Cambridge, MA: MIT Press.

Siegel, D. (1974). *Topics in English Morphology*. PhD thesis, MIT. Published in 1979. New York: Garland.

Simpson, J. (1998). 'Warumungu (Australian — Pama Nyungan)', in A. Spencer & A. M. Zwicky (eds), *The Handbook of Morphology*, Oxford and Malden, MA: Blackwell, 707–36.

Smith, G. (2000). 'Word remnants and co-ordination', in R. Thieroff, M. Tamrat, N. Furhop & O. Teuber (eds), *Deutsche Grammatik in Theorie und Praxis*, Tübingen: Niemeyer, 57–68.

Smith, L. R. (1982a). 'Labrador Inuttut (Eskimo) and the theory of morphology', *Studies in Language* 6, 221–44.

Smith, L. R. (1982b). 'An analysis of affixal verbal derivation and complementation in Labrador Inuttut', *Linguistic Analysis* 10, 161–89.

Spencer, A. (1998). 'Morphophonological operations', in A. Spencer & A. M. Zwicky (eds), *The Handbook of Morphology*. Oxford and Malden, MA: Blackwell, 123–43.

Stein, G. (1970). 'Zur Typologie der Suffixentstehung', *Indogermanische Forschungen* 75, 131–63.

Stein, G. (1977). 'The place of word-formation in linguistic description', in H. E. Brekle & D. Kastovsky (eds), *Perspektiven der Wortbildungsforschung*, Bonn: Bouvier, 219–35.

Stemberger, J. P. & MacWhinney, B. (1986). 'Frequency and the lexical storage of regularly inflected forms', *Memory and Cognition* 14, 17–26.

Stemberger, J. P & MacWhinney, B. (1988). 'Are inflected forms stored in the lexicon?' In M. Hammond & M. Noonan (eds), *Theoretical Morphology*, San Diego, CA: Academic, 101–16.

Stump, G. (2001). *Inflectional Morphology*. Cambridge: Cambridge University Press.

Suomi, K. (1985). 'On detecting words and word boundaries in Finnish: a survey of potential word boundary signals', *Nordic Journal of Linguistics* 8, 211–31.

Taylor, A. J. (1970). 'Reduplication in Motu', *Pacific Linguistics* Series C, 13, 1235–43.

Thiel, G. (1973). 'Die semantische Beziehungen in den Substantivkomposita der deutschen Gegenwartssprache', *Muttersprache* 83, 377–404.

Thomas, D. D. (1971). *Chrau Grammar*. Honolulu: University of Hawaii Press.

Thompson, L. C. (1965). *A Vietnamese Grammar*. Seattle: University of Washington Press.

Tiersma, P. M. (1985). *Frisian Reference Grammar*. Dordrecht: Foris.

Townsend, C. E. (1975). *Russian Word-formation*. Columbus, OH: Slavica.

Traugott, E. C. & Heine, B. (eds) (1991). *Approaches to Grammaticalization*. Amsterdam and Philadelphia, PA: Benjamins. 2 vols.

Trudgill, P. (1974). *Sociolinguistics: an introduction*. Harmondsworth: Penguin.

Tulloch, S. (ed.) (1991). *The Oxford Dictionary of New Words*. Oxford and New York: Oxford University Press.

Vennemann, T. (1974). 'Words and syllables in natural generative grammar', in A. Bruck, R. A. Fox & M. W. LaGaly (eds), *Papers from the Parasession on Natural Phonology*, Chicago, IL: Chicago Linguistic Society, 346–74.

Vincent, N. (1980). 'Words versus morphemes in morphological change: the case of Italian -*iamo*', in J. Fisiak (ed.), *Historical Morphology*, The Hague, etc.: Mouton, 383–98.

Waugh, L. R (1976). *Roman Jakobson's Science of Language*. Lisse: Peter de Ridder.

Waugh, L. R. & Lafford, B. A. (1994). 'Markedness', in R. E. Asher (ed.), *The Encyclopedia of Language and Linguistics*, Oxford: Pergamon, 2378–83.

Wheeler, C. J. & Schumsky, D. A. (1980). 'The morpheme boundaries of some English derivational suffixes', *Glossa* 14, 3–34.

Wiese, R. (1996). *The Phonology of German*. Oxford: Oxford University Press.

Williams, E. (1981). 'On the notions "Lexically Related" and "Head of a Word"', *Linguistic Inquiry* 12, 245–74.

Williams, E. S. (1976). 'Underlying tone in Margi and Igbo', *Linguistic Inquiry* 7, 463–84.

Williams, S. J. (1980). *A Welsh Grammar*. Cardiff: University of Wales Press.

Williams, T. (1965). 'On the "-ness" peril', *American Speech* 40, 279–86.

Wiltshire, C. & Marantz, A. (2000). 'Reduplication', in G. Booij, C. Lehmann & J. Mugdan (eds), *Morphologie/Morphology Vol 1*, Berlin and New York: de Gruyter, 557–67.

Wurzel, W. U. (1980). 'Some remarks on the relations between naturalness and typology', *Travaux du cercle linguistique de Copenhague* 20, 103–13.

Wurzel, W. U. (1984a). *Flexionsmorphologie und Naturlichkeit.* Berlin: Akademie-Verlag.

Wurzel, W. U. (1984b). 'On morphological naturalness', *Nordic Journal of Linguistics* 7, 165–83 = Summary in Wurzel (1984a).

Wurzel, W. U. (1985). 'Morphologische Naturlichkeit und morphologischer Wandel zur Vorhersagbarkeit von Sprachveranderungen', in J. Fisiak (ed.), *Papers from the 6th International Conference on Historical Linguistics*, Amsterdam: Benjamins and Poznan: Adam Mickiewicz University Press, 587–99.

Wurzel, W. U. (1989). *Inflectional Morphology and Naturalness.* Dordrecht, etc.: Kluwer.

Wurzel, W. U. (1994). 'Morphology, Natural', in R. E. Asher (ed.), *The Encyclopedia of Language and Linguistics*, Oxford: Pergamon, 2590–8.

Zwicky, A. M. (1978). 'On markedness in morphology', *Die Sprache* 24, 129–43.

Zwicky, A. M. (1985a). 'Clitics and particles', *Language* 61, 283–305.

Zwicky, A. M. (1985b). 'How to describe inflection', *Proceedings of the Eleventh Annual Meeting of the Berkeley Linguistics Society*, 372–86.

Zwicky, A. M. (1985c). 'Heads', *Journal of Linguistics* 21, 1–29.

Zwicky, A. M. & Pullum, G. K. (1983). 'Cliticization vs. inflection. English n't'', *Language* 59, 502–13.

Index

CPSIA information can be obtained
at www.ICGtesting.com
Printed in the USA
FSHW020143160720
71981FS

9 780878 403431